Christopher Marlowe, Havelock Ellis, John Addington Symonds

Christopher Marlowe. Edited by Havelock Ellis, with a general introd. on the English drama during the reigns of Elizabeth and James I.

Christopher Marlowe, Havelock Ellis, John Addington Symonds

Christopher Marlowe. Edited by Havelock Ellis, with a general introd. on the English drama during the reigns of Elizabeth and James I.

ISBN/EAN: 9783337261153

Printed in Europe, USA, Canada, Australia, Japan

Cover: Foto ©Thomas Meinert / pixelio.de

More available books at **www.hansebooks.com**

THE MERMAID SERIES.

EDITED BY HAVELOCK ELLIS.

THE BEST PLAYS OF THE OLD DRAMATISTS.

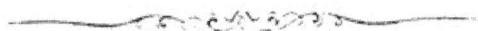

CHRISTOPHER MARLOWE.

Etched by L. Hoosner

EDWARD ALLEYN

From the picture at Dulwich College

THE BEST PLAYS OF THE OLD DRAMATISTS.

CHRISTOPHER MARLOWE

EDITED BY HAVELOCK ELLIS.

WITH A

GENERAL INTRODUCTION ON THE ENGLISH DRAMA DURING
THE REIGNS OF ELIZABETH AND JAMES I.

BY J. A. SYMONDS.

"I lie and dream of your full M[ermai]d wine.   *Beaumont.*

UNEXPURGATED EDITION.

LONDON :
VIZETELLY & CO., 42, CATHERINE ST., STRAND.
1887.

"What things have we seen
Done at the Mermaid! heard words that have been
So nimble, and so full of subtle flame,
As if that every one from whence they came
Had meant to put his whole wit in a jest,
And had resolved to live a fool the rest
Of his dull life."

Master Francis Beaumont to Ben Jonson.

"Souls of Poets dead and gone,
What Elysium have ye known,
Happy field or mossy cavern,
Choicer than the Mermaid Tavern?"

Keats.

LONDON:
BRADBURY, AGNEW, & CO., PRINTERS, WHITEFRIARS.

CONTENTS.

GENERAL INTRODUCTION.

SO much has been written about the origins of the Drama in England, that it will suffice to touch but briefly on this topic. The English, like other European nations, composed and acted Miracle Plays upon the events of sacred history and the main doctrines of the Church. Embracing the whole drama of humanity, from the Creation of the World to the Last Judgment, these Miracles, of which we possess several well-preserved specimens, might rather be regarded as immense epics scenically presented to an audience, than as plays with a plot and action. Yet certain episodes in the lengthy cycle, such for example as the Entrance of Noah into the Ark, the Sacrifice of Isaac, Nativity of our Lord, the story of the Woman taken in Adultery, and the Repentance of Magdalen, detached themselves from the main scheme, and became the subjects of free dramatic handling.

In this way the English people were familiarized at an early period with tragedy and comedy in the rough, while preparation was made for the emergence of the secular Drama as a specific form of art. Before this happened, however, a second stage had to be accomplished. Between the Miracle Play and the Drama intervened the Morality and the Interlude. The former was a peculiar species of representation, in which abstract conceptions and the personages of allegory were introduced in action under the forms of men and women. The tone of such pieces remained purely didactic, and their machinery was clumsy; yet their authors found it impossible to deal dramatically with Youth and Pleasure, Sin, Grace, and Repentance, the Devil and Death, without developing dialogue, marking character, and painting the incidents of real life. Thus the Morality led to the Interlude, which completed the disengagement of the drama from religious aims, and brought various types of human nature on the stage. The most remarkable specimen of this kind now extant may be mentioned. It is the elder Heywood's *Three P's,* in which a Pardoner, a Pedlar, and a Palmer, three characteristic figures among contemporary vagrants and impostors, are vividly delineated. From the Interlude to Farce and Comedy there was but a

short step to take ; and in England the earliest
plays, properly so-called, were of a humorous description. At the same time, tragedy began to form
itself out of serious pieces detached in detail from
the Miracle Plays. *Godly Queen Esther, King
Darius, The Conversion of St. Paul,* and so forth,
smoothed the way for secular dramas upon subjects
chosen from history and legend.

The process of dramatic evolution which I have
briefly sketched, had reached this point before the
new learning of the Italian Renaissance penetrated
English society. The people were accustomed to
scenic representations, and had traced the outlines
of what was afterwards to become the Romantic or
Shakespearian drama. At this point the attention
of cultivated people was directed to the Latin and
Italian theatre. Essayists like Sir Philip Sidney,
poets like Lord Buckhurst and Thomas Norton, tried
by their precepts and their practice to introduce
the classical style of dramatic composition into
England. They severely criticized the rhymed plays
in which the populace delighted, the involved tales
roughly versified for declamation by actors in the
yards of inns, and the incongruous blending of rude
farce with pathetic or passionate incident. It
seemed for a time as though these " courtly
makers " might divert the English Drama from its
spontaneously chosen path into the precise and
formal channels of pedantic imitation. The aris-
tocracy and learned coteries delighted in tragedies

like *Gorboduc*, or *The Misfortunes of Arthur*, which followed the model of Seneca, and competed with famous Italian masterpieces. But neither the nobility nor the universities were destined to control the theatre in England. That had already become a possession of the people ; and the people remained true to the traditions of their native though uncultivated type of art. What men like Sidney, Sackville, Norton and Hughes, effected, was in the main a certain heightening of the sense of dramatic dignity. They forced playwrights to regard principles of composition, propriety of diction, and harmony of parts, to some extent at least, in the construction of both tragedies and comedies. Furthermore, they indicated blank verse, or the unrhymed decasyllable iambic, as the proper metre for the stage.

Meanwhile our drama continued to advance upon the romantic as opposed to the classical type of art ; and since the phrase romantic is one of great importance, I must pause to explain in what sense I use it. Three personages in one of the earlier comedies preserved to us are introduced discussing the English theatre. One of these observes that though plays are represented every day in London, they are "neither right comedies nor right tragedies," but " representations of histories without any decorum." The phrase, although contemptuous, was accurate ; for the Romantic Drama observed no rules and cared for no scholastic precedents. It only aimed at presenting a tale or history in scenes; and the most accurate definition of the plays which it produced is that they were stories told in dialogue by actors on the stage. Nothing that had the shape and interest of a story came amiss to the romantic playwright; and his manner did not greatly differ in the treatment of pure farce, pathetic episode, or chronicle of past events. Thus there sprang up several species of dramatic composition in England, marked by a common artistic handling. These may be briefly enumerated as chronicle plays on English history, biographical plays on the lives of English worthies, tragedies borrowed from Roman history and Italian novels, tragedies based on domestic crimes of recent occurrence, comedies imitated from Latin and modern European literature, broad realistic farces, fanciful pieces partaking of the nature of the Masque or Ballet, pastorals of the Arcadian type, and classical mythologies. The one point, as I have already remarked, which the playwright kept steadily in view, was to sustain the interest of his audience, and to excite their curiosity by a succession of entertaining incidents. He did not mind mixing tragedy with comedy or kings with peasants, and set at naught the so-called unities of classical tradition. His paramount object was to feel and make his audience feel the reality of life exceedingly, and to evoke living men and women from the miscellaneous mass of fables which lay open to him in classical, medieval, and modern literature. Some spirited lines of the younger Heywood may here be quoted, as aptly describing the vast tracts over which the dramatists in their first ardour ranged in search of subjects :—

> " To give content to this most curious age,
> The gods themselves we have brought down to the stage,
> And figured them in planets ; made even Hell
> Deliver up the Furies, by no spell,
> (Saving the Muse's rapture); further, we
> Have trafficked by their help ; no history
> We have left unrifled, our pens have been dipped
> As well in opening each hid manuscript,
> As tracts more vulgar, whether read or sung
> In our domestic or more foreign tongue :
> Of fairy elves, nymphs of the sea and land,
> The lawns and groves, no number can be scanned
> Which we have not given feet to, nay, 'tis known
> That when our chronicles have barren grown
> Of story, we have all invention stretched,
> Dived low as to the centre, and then reached
> Unto the *primum mobile* above,
> (Nor 'scaped things intermediate) for your love ;
> These have been acted often, all have passed
> Censure, of which some live, and some are cast."

A group of cultivated men, chiefly members of the Universities, began soon after 1580 to give something like the form of high art to our romantic drama. These were Richard Edwards, George Whetstone, John Lyly, Robert Greene, George Peele, Thomas Lodge, and Thomas Nash. It is not my business to characterize their works in detail, since they will probably be made the subjects of special treatment in this series. Their chief

importance, however, may be indicated. This consists in their having contributed to the formation of
Marlowe's dramatic style. It was he who irrevo-
cably decided the destinies of the romantic drama ;
and the whole subsequent evolution of that species,
including Shakespeare's work, can be regarded as
the expansion, rectification and artistic ennoblement
of the type fixed by Marlowe's epoch-making
tragedies. In very little more than fifty years from
the publication of *Tamburlaine*, our drama had run
its course of unparalleled energy and splendour.
Expanding like a many-petalled flower of marvellous complexity and varied colours, it developed to
the utmost every form of which the romantic species
is capable, and left to Europe a mass of work
invariably vivid, though extremely unequal, over
which of course the genius of Shakespeare rules
supreme. He stands alone, and has no second ;
but without the multifarious excellences of Jonson,
Webster, Heywood, Beaumont, Fletcher, Ford,
Massinger, and a score whom it would be tedious
to enumerate, the student would have to regard
Shakespeare as an inexplicable prodigy, instead of
as the central sun of a luminous sidereal system.

In the short space of this prefatory essay, I cannot attempt to sketch the history of the drama, or
to criticize the various schools of style which were
formed in the course of its passage from maturity
to decadence. It must be enough for me to indicate in what way the genius of the English nation

expressed itself through this form of art at the
epoch when the Reformation had been accomplished,
the attacks of Spain repulsed, and the new learning
of the Renaissance assimilated.

England, alone of European nations, received the
influences of both Renaissance and Reformation
simultaneously. These two great movements of
the modern intellect, which closed the Middle Ages,
and opened a new period of mental culture for the
Western nations, have to be regarded as distinct
because their issues were different, and they were
severally accomplished by Latin and Teutonic races.
Yet both Renaissance and Reformation had a
common starting-point in humanism ; both needed
the revival of learning for their motive force ; both
effected a liberation of the spirit from authority,
superstition and decadent ideals. In the one case
this liberation of the modern spirit expressed itself
through new conceptions of social culture, new
theories of the state, new systems of education, new
arts, new sciences, and new philosophies. It was
the emancipation of the reason ; and we call it
Renaissance. In the other case it assumed a more
religious and political aspect, issuing in the revival
of pure Christianity, revolt against the Papacy as a
dominant force, and assertion of national inde-
pendence. It was the emancipation of the conscience ; and we call it Reformation. No sooner
had these two movements been defined, than they
entered on a phase of mutual hostility ; not indeed

because they were essentially antagonistic, or because they could not show a common origin, but because they expressed the tendencies of broadly differing races, and had in view divergent ideals. The Italians, to whom we owe the Renaissance, were careless about ecclesiastical reform, and sceptical as to the restoration of Christianity from its primitive sources. The Germans, who started the Reformation, were so preoccupied with things of deeper moment, that they sacrificed the culture of the Renaissance. Then Reformation generated Counter-Reformation. The Catholic reaction, led by Rome and championed by Spain, set in. Europe was involved in a series of religious wars, which impeded the tranquil evolution of the intellect on either line. So much had to be prefaced in order to explain the mental position of England.

Some time before the Catholic Powers assumed their attitude of panic-stricken and belligerent reaction, Henry VIII. committed the nation to Protestantism ; and at the same time the new learning began to penetrate society. The English people cast off obedience to Rome in doctrine, and assumed Italian humanism, simultaneously. The Reformation had been adopted by the consent of King, Lords and Commons ; and this change in the state-religion, though it was not confirmed without reaction, agitation, and bloodshed, cost the nation comparatively little disturbance. The new learning,

derived from the revival of antiquity, had already
permeated Italian and French literature. Classical
erudition had been adapted to the needs of modern
thought ; the chief Greek and Latin authors had
been translated into modern languages ; the
masterpieces of antiquity were interpreted and
made intelligible. English scholars, trained upon
the new method by private tutors or in the now
regenerated public schools, began at once to trans-
late the poets and historians of antiquity and of
Italy into the vernacular. French books were
widely read ; the best authors of Spain were assimilated ; and Germany supplied her legendary
stores and grotesque satires to the growing culture
of our race. Meanwhile the authorized version of the
Bible, which had recently been given to the public,
proved the dignity and flexibility of the mother-
tongue, and supplied the laity at once with the original sources of sacred erudition. Before the date of
Marlowe these vast collections had been made, and
we were in possession of all the materials for building up a mighty edifice of literary art. Little at
this period had been accomplished in pure poetry.
It is true that Wyat, Surrey and Sidney had accli-
matized the sonnet ; that blank verse had been
introduced ; and that Spenser was just giving his
noble epic to the world. But the people in its youthful vigour under Tudor Sovereigns, conscious of a
great deliverance from Rome, and of a bracing
struggle with reactionary powers in Europe, needed

some wider, some more comprehensive sphere for the display of its native genius ; and this it found in the romantic drama, to which, notwithstanding the efforts of students and polite persons, it adhered with the pertinacity of instinct. This drama, its own original creation, stood to the English nation in the place of all the other arts. It became for us the embodiment of that Renaissance which had given sculpture, painting, architecture and a gorgeous undergrowth of highly-coloured poetry to the Italians. England, sharing the impulse communicated to thought by southern Renaissance and northern Reformation, needed no æsthetical outlet but the drama, and had to expend her forces upon no distracting struggles of religion.

Just as the Romantic Drama was a home-product of the English people, so the method of presenting plays in London, and the material conditions of the stage, were eminently homely. It had been customary during the Middle Ages to exhibit Miracles upon wooden platforms or moveable waggons, which were set up in the market-places of towns, or on the turfed enclosures of abbatial buildings. Moralities and Interludes were shown publicly during civic entertainments, or privately at the request of companies assembled in some noble dwelling; a portion of the hall being devoted for the nonce to wandering actors. The interesting history-play of *Sir Thomas More* gives a lively picture of the way in

which the Moral Interlude was exhibited before a
select audience of the Chancellor's family. Meanwhile, when secular dramas, intended for the
delectation of the people at large, began to emerge
from the Moralities, it became customary to use the
yards of inns, bear-gardens, and such places for
their performance. This led by gradual degrees
to the establishment of regular theatres, which,
though they were violently opposed by the muni-
cipal authorities, and inveighed against from the
pulpit, contrived to root themselves in the suburbs,
along the further bank of the Thames, and in the
fields toward Shoreditch. Even the best London
theatres between the years 1580 and 1630 were
simple wooden buildings, round or hexagonal
in shape. The larger stood open to the air ; the
smaller were roofed in. The former had the name
of public, the latter of private houses. Performances took place in the afternoon, usually at
three o'clock. Scenery was almost wholly lacking :
thus if Thebes or Verona had to be imagined by
the audience, a sign-post bore the name of Thebes
or Verona upon a tower of lath and plaster. The
stage itself projected so far into the pit or yard,
as it was called, that the actors were brought close
to the spectators beneath and around them. Play-
goers who could afford this luxury, were accommo-
dated with stools upon the stage ; others might
take boxes or rooms, as they were then termed,
just above the heads of the groundlings standing

in the circular space of the yard. Prices varied
from threepence for entrance only to about two
shillings for the most expensive places in the best
theatres. No actresses appeared upon the English
boards, and all female parts were played by boys.
It was also usual for the choristers of St. Paul's
or of the Chapel Royal to perform whole dramas.
Some of Jonson's colossal Comedies were first
given to the public by these "Children;" and I
may remind students of Shakespeare's *Hamlet*
that the companies of adult actors regarded them as
formidable competitors.[1] In reading any master-
piece of the Elizabethan and Jacobean periods,
these facts should never be forgotten. To the
simplicity of the theatres, the absence of scenical
resources, and the close contact of the players with
their audience, we may ascribe many peculiarities
of our Romantic Drama—notably its disregard of
the unities of time and place, and its eloquent
appeals by descriptive passages to the imagination.
Its marvellous fecundity in second-rate artistic
work, hastily produced and readily neglected, may
also be referred to similar circumstances.

These considerations explain the extraordinary
force, variety, and imaginative splendour of the
works poured forth with such prolific energy for
the humble theatres of London during the fifty years
which followed the great date of 1587. It was a
golden time, between the perils of the Armada and

---

[1] *Hamlet*, Act 2, sc. 2.

the convulsions of the Great Rebellion, just long
enough to round and complete a monument of art
representative of our national life at its most
brilliant period.   In order to comprehend the
English Renaissance, we must not be satisfied with
studying only Shakespeare. We must learn to
know his predecessors, contemporaries, and suc-
cessors ; that multitude of men inferior to him in
stature, but of the same lineage ; each of whom in
greater or less degree was inspired with the like
genius ; each of whom possessed a clairvoyance
into human nature and a power of presenting it
vividly to the imagination which can be claimed
by no similar group of fellow-workers in the
history of any literature now known to us.   What
made the play-wrights of that epoch so great as to
deserve the phrase which Dryden found for them
—"Theirs was the giant race before the flood"—
was that they lived and wrote in fullest sympathy
with the whole people. The public to which they
appealed was the English nation, from Elizabeth
upon the throne down to the lowest ragamuffin of
the streets. In the same wooden theatres met
lords and ladies, citizens and prentices, sailors
and working-men, pickpockets, country-folk, and
captains from the wars. The men who wrote for
this mixed audience were hampered by no cum-
brous stage-properties, by no crushing gorgeous-
ness of scenery, by no academical propriety, by no
courtly etiquette, by no interference from agents

of police or spies of a jealous hierarchy. So long
as they preserved decorum in the elementary
decencies of morals and religion, their hands were
free; and they had the whole spirit of a vividly
alive and warmly interested race to stimulate their
genius. It is not to be wondered in these circumstances that men of minor talents rose above their
mediocrity; that sturdy giants like Jonson grew
to Titans; or that a Webster and a Fletcher
climbed the clouds at times and took their seat
among the gods.

If we now ask what is the distinctive mark of
this Drama, we may answer in two words: spontaneity and freedom. It has the spontaneity of
an art-product indigenous and native to our soil,
though all the culture of the Classics and the
Renaissance contributed to make it wealthy. It
has the freedom of a great race conscious of their
adolescent vigour, the freedom of combatants
victorious in a struggle only less momentous than
that of Hellas against Persia, the freedom of a land
bounded upon all sides by the ocean, the freedom
of high-spirited men devoted to a mistress who per-
sonified for them the power and majesty of Britain.
Its freedom is freedom from pedantry, from servility
to scholastic rules, from observance of foreign
or antiquated models; freedom from the dread of
political or ecclesiastical oppression; freedom from
courtly obsequiousness and class-prejudices. In
use of language, moulding of character, copying

of manners, and treatment of dramatic themes, no less than in the minor technicalities of versification, each writer stamps a recognizable mint-mark on his own work, without regard to precedent or what the lettered world will think of him. Critics who appreciate the niceties and proprieties which can to some extent be secured by Academical super-vision, may complain that the English Drama suffered from this spontaneity and freedom—that it would have attained to fairer proportions if the playwrights had aimed more at correctness, and that posterity could have foregone seven-tenths of their performances if the remaining three-tenths had exhibited maturer art and more patient execution. To deny an underlying truth in this criticism, would be idle. We are bound to acknowledge that the fine qualities of spontaneity and freedom, here displayed so liberally, have their corresponding faults of carelessness, incomplete-ness, and indifference to form. The masterpieces of our Romantic Drama, when the majority of Shakespeare's plays have been excepted, are few in number, so few indeed that they will be adequately represented in the "Mermaid Series." Yet it remains true that even the rank jungle of mediocre work surviving from that epoch is permeated with the same life and freshness, the same juvenile audacity, the same frank touch on nature, the same keen insight into human motives and emotions, as those rarer pieces of accomplished art which deserve to be classed with the monuments of Attic tragedy.   It is this stupendous mass of plays, evolved upon the same lines and vivified by one national spirit, which makes our Drama unique. The spontaneity and freedom, again, of which I have been speaking, form so conspicuous a note of Elizabethan literature that when the genius of our race and language takes a new direction under conditions favourable to liberty, as may be seen at large in the history of the present century, poets turn their eyes instinctively to the old dramatists, assimilate their audacities, and do not shun their imperfections.

We must, therefore, accept the whole crop of the fifty years from 1587 onwards, *en masse*, and must study each type of it attentively—not demanding too many masterpieces from the total aggregate, nor over-valuing each special product, but recognizing the fact that here we possess a quite exceptional set of specimens for the scientific investigation of a vigorous artistic epoch.   In spite of time and neglect, in spite of the fire of London, in spite of Warburton's too-celebrated cook, in spite of maimed editions and atrocious printers' errors, in spite lastly of Puritanical animosity, we have still at our disposal documents for building up the English Drama as a whole, which fail us in the records of any other national Drama of equal magnitude. What would not the scholar give if he could interpret the superiority of Æschylus, Sophocles,

Euripides, and Aristophanes, in the same way as
he can interpret the superiority of Shakespeare and
Jonson, by the light of a long series of supple-
mentary tragedies and comedies, expressive of one
patriotic impulse, from which the greater no less than
the minor dramatists of the age in question derived
their productive energy?

Regarding then this total mass of plays as the
subject-matter of a single critical enquiry, we find
first a stage of preparation leading up from the
Moralities, through Lyly, Peele, Greene, Nash, and
Lodge, to Marlowe. Marlowe fixes the specific
type of the Romantic Drama for England. And
here the first chapter in our history of the period
may be said to close. Dramatic style is created
and defined. A second chapter opens with a new
set of playwrights, who represent the prime and
accomplishment of English theatrical art. Shakespeare reigns supreme here, employing the highest
human genius to give the most perfect form to
Marlowe's type. Next him towers the saturnine
and humorous Titan, Ben Jonson, who broke a
path for himself, and ranged only lesser than the
greatest, because he separated his spirit from the
dominant spirit of the age. What a crowd of
worthy coadjutors gather round them! The un-
named authors of *Arden of Feversham*, and *A
Yorkshire Tragedy*, those grim examples of the
poignant realistic manner. Honest Dekker, with
his easy-going sensibilities and facile touch on

human feeling. Ponderous Chapman, smouldering into flame by flashes. Heywood, the master of homely English life, the gentlest of all poets who have swept the chords of passion. Marston, that biting satirist and tense sententious builder of blank verse. As we advance, the crowd thickens; and a third stage in the evolution of the Drama discloses for us writers who have learned from all their predecessors. Here we meet with Beaumont and Fletcher, inventors of heroical romance, gifted with inexhaustible resources in the rhetoric of tragical and comical situations, abounding in exquisite lyrical outpourings of unpremeditated song. Webster rises to Shakespeare's shoulder by his sincerity, nobility, and unerring truth to life in its most thrilling moments. Tourneur, infected by some rankling plague-spot of the soul, approaches him in sombre force; while Ford, behind them, delves with style of steel on plates of bronze his monumental scenes of spiritual anguish. Massinger, equable student of all literary manners, brings these to a focus in his work of lucid but less pungent craftsmanship. Middleton plays with searching lambent light of talent over the broad dramatic field. Cartwright, Brome, Randolph, Marmion proclaim themselves followers of Jonson in a special kind of comedy. Day invents his own delicate domain of allegorical fancy. Shirley, with more of genial inspiration and a richer vein, follows the same track as Massinger. Sturdy

journeymen, like the Rowleys, can be counted
almost by the score.   And thus we are led onward
to a fourth stage—this time, one of decadence—in
which the Crownes and Davenants and Wilsons
warn us by their incoherent and exaggerated workmanship, illuminated with occasional sparkles of
genuine talent, that every growth of art has
its declining no less than its ascending and
flourishing periods.   Lastly, when we remember
that these mutations were accomplished in some
fifty years, that every chord in human nature had
been touched, that all the resources of our language
had been tried, and that the English heroic metre
of blank verse had been adapted to the expression
of a myriad varying thoughts and feelings, we shall
pause astonished by the prodigality of mental
vigour in that fruitful epoch.

The object of the series to which this inadequate
essay forms an introduction, will have been accomplished, if the English of the Victorian age be
induced to study the best pieces of Shakespeare's
fellow-workers, and to comprehend how full and
how superb a picture they present of the large and
noble life of our Elizabethan ancestors.   Only in
this way can the reading public understand the
truth of what I have attempted to establish, namely,
that the Drama is the chief artistic utterance of the
Renaissance in England, and that in England the
Renaissance was permeated with the free pure
honest stalwart spirit of the Reformation.   Only in

this way too will they be able to appreciate the panegyric written of our drama by one of England's greatest rhetoricians, whose words shall form an apt conclusion to this essay. It is De Quincey who says : " No literature, not excepting even that of Athens, has ever presented such a multiform theatre, such a carnival display, mask and anti-mask, of impassioned life—breathing, moving, acting, suffering, laughing :

> Quicquid agunt homines : votum, timor. ira, voluptas,
> Gaudia, discursus ——

all this, but far more truly and more adequately than was or could be effected in that field of composition which the gloomy satirist contem-plated—whatsoever in fact our medieval ancestors exhibited in the ' Dance of Death,' drunk with tears and laughter, may here be reviewed, sceni-cally draped, and gorgeously coloured. What other national Drama can pretend to any com-petition with this?"

JOHN ADDINGTON SYMONDS.

CHRISTOPHER MARLOWE.

——·•‡ᴈ✦ᴈ•·——

ARLY in the sixteenth century Erasmus, accompanied by Colet, visited Canterbury. Long afterwards he remembered the cathedral and its vast towers that rise into the sky "so as to strike awe even at a distant approach," the sweet music of the bells heard from afar, the "spacious majesty" of the newly completed nave. Here, fifty years later, was born Christopher, sometime called Kit, Marlowe.[1]

Meanwhile the spirit of Erasmus, and still more the ruder spirit of Colet, had heralded a revolutionary influx of new life. At the head of the movement was set by Providence, in a mood of Rabelaisian gaiety, the figure of Henry VIII. Like another Tamburlaine, Henry VIII. had carried off the rich treasures of Canterbury, the gold and the

---

[1] Thomas Heywood wrote in 1635 : —

    "Marlo, renowned for his rare art and wit,
    Could ne'er attain beyond the name of Kit."

jewels, in six-and-twenty carts. The stream of pilgrims no longer passed along the familiar roads ; nothing remained of the shrine of St. Thomas but the bare stones, much as we see them now, worn away by the adoration of so many ages. All that was long ago ; in those days events came fast, and Elizabethan men had a trick of speaking of the near past as remote and antique. On the 26th day of February, 1564, according to the register of the parish church of St. George the Martyr, "was christened Christofer, the sonne of John Marlowe."[1]

We cannot tell the boy's dreams among the Kentish hills and fields, or beneath the jewelled windows of the great church in the city that not only still bore about it the lustre of its former sanctity, but was also the chief halting-place of princes and ambassadors who journeyed from the continent to the court of Elizabeth. Perhaps these things touched the youth little ; his own life was too vivid to be concerned much with the antique sanctities at which Colet had laughed. Nor had he mixed largely with men ; he rarely describes the actual external world of men and women ; he had little of Ben Jonson's precise observation, and nothing of Shakespeare's gentle laughter. But every page he wrote reveals a peculiarly intense full-blooded inner life, the quintessence of youthful desires and youthful dreams. His father, it has

---

[1] Shakespeare was christened exactly two months later. Chapman, Green, Peele, and Lyly were all, probably, born some ten years earlier ; Nash and Chettle about the same time as Marlowe ; Heywood about 1570 ; Ben Jonson in 1573.

now been ascertained, besides being "Clarke of St. Maries," was a shoemaker (Christopher appears to have been the second child and eldest son), and shoemakers have sometimes possessed and left to their children a strangely powerful endowment of idealism. He was educated at the King's School, Canterbury. In March, 1581, he matriculated as Pensioner of Benet College (now Corpus Christi), Cambridge; not having been elected, it seems, to either of the scholarships recently founded at Benet College for King's School boys. In 1583 he obtained his Bachelor's degree. Six years later, in 1589, Francis Kett, a fellow of Marlowe's college, was burnt at Norwich for heresies in regard to certain articles of the Christian faith, such as the Trinity and Christ's divinity. The youthful Marlowe, with his thirst for emancipation, could not fail to fall under the influence of this audacious Francis Kett.

How were the years after 1583 spent? There is no reliable evidence. It was asserted, on the unsupported evidence of a late and often inaccurate authority, that he became an actor. It has been conjectured,[1] as of Chapman, that he trailed a pike in the Low Countries, like Ben Jonson. The Eliza-

---

[1] By Colonel Cunningham, who points out that Marlowe's "familiarity with military terms and his fondness for using them are most remarkable," and that at "his home at Canterbury he was in the very track of the bold spirits who [in 1585] followed Leicester and Sidney to the wars of the Low Countries." It may also be pointed out, however, that Marlowe displays, especially in *Tamburlaine,* a remarkably extensive (though not always accurate) knowledge of Elizabethan geography. His interest in military affairs and in the geography of the world were both manifestations of the spirit of adventure then in the air.

bethan dramatists had the full Renaissance delight
in facts and in the grasp of technical detail ; they
appear to have been nearly as careful about their
"documents" as contemporary French novelists ;
the broad and genial realism of men like Ben
Jonson and Middleton and Dekker, sprang from
actual contact with the life around them, and young
Marlowe's bold spirit may, possibly, have been
touched by the impulse of adventure which at that
time drew Englishmen into all parts of the world.

About the year 1588, *Tamburlaine* was acted.[1]
There is no hesitation in this first work. The
young "god of undaunted verse," set free

> " From jigging veins of rhyming mother wits,
> And such conceits as clownage keeps in pay,"

is at once a perfect master of his " great and thundering speech." *Gorboduc* had been written in blank
verse twenty-five years before, and there had been
other essays in the use of this new medium of
expression ; on the whole, however, it had remained
cold and artificial and ill-received. It is an immense
leap from the tame pedestrian lines of *Gorboduc* to the
organised verse, with its large swelling music, of
Tamburlaine. It was not till later, however, that
Marlowe realised the full power and variety of
which blank verse is capable. The strong melody of
his early verse is simple and little varied ; the chief
variation being a kind of blank verse couplet,
generally introduced near the end of a speech, in

---

[1] Alleyn took the part of Tamburlaine. For a. brief account of
this famous actor, whose name is so intimately associated with
Marlowe's works, see Appendix.

which a tumultuous *crescendo* is followed by a grave
and severely iambic line :—

> "And sooner shall the sun fall from his sphere,
> Than Tamburlaine be slain or overcome."

In its later more developed form, Marlowe's
"mighty line" is the chief creation of English
literary art ; Shakespeare absorbed it, and gave it
out again with its familiar cadences in *Romeo and
Juliet*, and later with many broad and lovely
modifications. It has become the life-blood of
our literature ; Marlowe's place is at the heart of
English poetry, and his pulses still thrill in our
verse.

He obtained his material for *Tamburlaine*
chiefly from Pedro Mexia's Spanish life of
Timur, which was published at Seville in 1543,
and translated into Italian, French and English.
The English translation, known as Fortescue's
Foreste, appeared in 1571. Marlowe appears to
have supplemented this source by the help of the
Vita Magni Tamerlanis of Petrus Perondinus.
There is abundant evidence to show the swift and
extraordinary popularity of the new play, the
work of the first great poet who uses our modern
English speech ; for Spenser was archaic even in
his own day. The public were intoxicated with
the high astounding terms—"the swelling bom-
bast of a bragging blank verse," as Nash called it
—of the Scythian conqueror ; not less, perhaps,
with the novelty of the play's scenical effects ; and
for many years a host of writers, including Shakespeare, laughed at those royal and pampered jades

Mar.   c

of Asia that could not draw but twenty miles a day. The new perfection, however grateful to the old, could not help treading on its heels. For us, however, the wonder of *Tamburlaine*, and of Marlowe's work generally, lies in the vivid and passionate blood, in the intensely imaginative form, with which he has clothed the dry bones of his story. He had no power of *creative* imagination; Shakespeare borrows his stories, but he freely turns them to his own ends; Marlowe nearly always clings to his story, but he makes it alive with his own soaring passion. With the exception of *Edward II.*, which stands alone, Marlowe's dramas are mostly series of scenes held together by the poetic energy of his own dominating personality. He is his own hero, and the sanguinary Scythian utters the deepest secrets of the artist's heart. "What is beauty?" he asks himself.

> " If all the pens that ever poets held
> Had fed the feeling of their masters' thoughts,
> And every sweetness that inspired their hearts,
> Their minds, and muses on admirèd themes ;
> If all the heavenly quintessence they still
> From their immortal flowers of poesy,
> Wherein, as in a mirror, we perceive
> The highest reaches of a human wit ;
> If these had made one poem's period,
> And all combined in beauty's worthiness,
> Yet should there hover in their restless heads
> One thought, one grace, one wonder, at the least,
> Which into words no virtue can digest."

Tamburlaine is a divinely strong and eager-hearted poet, and these words are the key to his career. He sees for ever an unattainable loveliness beckoning him across the world, and how can his ardent blood rest "attemptless, faint and destitute?"

> "Our souls, whose faculties can comprehend
> The wondrous architecture of the world,
> And measure every wandering planet's course,
> Still climbing after knowledge infinite,
> And always moving as the restless spheres,
> Will us to wear ourselves, and never rest,
> Until we reach the ripest fruit of all,——"

the rest is Scythian bathos. Like Shelley, in some prior state of existence he had loved an Antigone, and he cannot stay. But like Keats also he has an intense feeling for the imaginative show and colour of things, of milk-white steeds laden with the heads of slain men, and

> "Besmeared with blood that makes a dainty show,"

of naked negroes, of bassoes clothed in crimson silk, of Turkey carpets beneath the chariot wheels, and of a hundred kings or more with "so many crowns of burnished gold." He is intoxicated with the physical splendours of imagination, with the vast and mysterious charm of old-world cities, of Bagdad and Babylon and Samarcand.

> "'And ride in triumph through Persepolis!'
> Is it not brave to be a king, Techelles?
> Usumcasane and Theridamas,
> Is it not passing brave to be a king,
> 'And ride in triumph through Persepolis?'"

With this song of radiant joy in the unattainable, young Kit Marlowe, like another Christopher, sailed to discover countries yet unknown, to attain the "sweet fruition" of his crown.

Not long after *Tamburlaine*, appeared the *Tragical History of Doctor Faustus.*[1] The legend of a man who sells his soul to the Devil seems to have appeared about the sixth century, and to have floated down the Middle Ages in many forms; in one form it was used by Calderon in *El Magico Prodigioso*. In the early part of the sixteenth century it became identified with a Doctor Faustus, who practised necromancy, and was the friend of Paracelsus and Cornelius Agrippa. Conrad Muth the Humanist came across a magician at Erfurt called Georgius Faustus Hemitheus of Heidelberg. Trithemius, in 1506, found a Faustus junior who boasted that if all the works of Plato and Aristotle were burnt he could restore them from memory. Melanchthon knew a Johannes Faustus born at Knütlingen, in Wurtemberg, not far from his own home, who studied magic[2] at

---

[1] The exact date is very doubtful. Mr. Bullen, in his generally admirable edition of Marlowe, thinks that the "Ballad of the life and death of Doctor Faustus the great Cungerer," licensed to be printed in Feb. 1589 (and supposed to be identical with the Roxburghe ballad with this title), was probably founded on the play. The ballad tells us that Faustus was educated by his uncle, who left his wealth to him, and gives details of his death. These and other points are not mentioned in the play, but they occur in the original prose *History of Dr. Faustus*, on which the ballad was certainly founded. The writer of the ballad passes by the most impressive scenes in the play, and we cannot assume that he was acquainted with it, although Professor Ward (in the full and interesting notes to his valuable edition of the play) while recognising the striking discrepancies, puts them aside with the curiously inadequate argument that ballads were often founded on plays.

[2] It must be recollected that in the sixteenth century "magic" frequently included chemistry and other sciences. The services rendered to science by Paracelsus and Agrippa are scarcely yet generally recognised.

Cracow, and afterwards "roamed about, and talked of secret things." The first literary version of the story of Faust was the *Volksbuch* which, published by Spiess in 1587, at Frankfort-on-the-Main, soon after appeared in England as *The History of the Damnable Life and Deserved Death of Dr. John Faustus.* To this translation of the Faust-book Marlowe generally adhered ; that is to say, in the incidents of the drama, and their sequence, he followed his authority. The wearisome comic passages, which Marlowe may or may not have written, are copied with special fidelity. Marlowe's play was probably the first dramatisation of the Faust legend : it became immediately popular, not only in England but abroad. *Faustus,* as well as the *Jew of Malta,* was acted in German by an English company in 1608, during the Carnival, at Graetz, and remained a favourite at Vienna throughout the seventeenth and eighteenth centuries. Faustus was remodelled into a sort of Don Juan—by the Jesuits, it is said, who disliked his scepticism—and in this form he came into Goethe's hands.

Goethe's opinion of Marlowe's *Faustus* we know. He had thought of translating it ; when it was mentioned he burst out with an exclamation of praise : ' How greatly it is all planned.' The three chief versions of the old legend — the *Volksbuch* with its medieval story in a Protestant garb, Marlowe's Renaissance rendering and Goethe's modern *Faust*—are all representative. The *Volksbuch* records Faust's history from his birth to his final dismemberment by the Devil, in the calmly epical fashion of a medieval legend ; all his clownish tricks are narrated with great enjoyment, but the general atmosphere is moral and Protestant.   Marlowe changed the point of view ; Faust is no longer an unintelligible magician looked at from the outside, but a living man thirsting for the infinite ; the sinner becomes a hero, a Tamburlaine, no longer eager to " ride in triumph through Persepolis," who at the thought of vaster delights has ceased to care for the finite splendours of an earthly crown.

> " A god is not so glorious as a king.
> I think the pleasure they enjoy in Heaven
> Cannot compare with kingly joys in earth,"

once exclaimed Tamburlaine's follower, Theridamas. Faustus, in his study, realising what magic promises, thinks otherwise :

> " Emperors and kings
> Are but obey'd in their several provinces :
> Nor can they raise the wind or rend the clouds ;
> But his dominion that exceeds in this
> Stretcheth as far as doth the mind of man :
> A sound magician is a demigod."

Marlowe's Faustus is not impelled like the Faustus of the legend by the desire of " worldly pleasure," nor, like Goethe's, by the vanity of knowledge ; it is power, power without bound, that he desires, all that is in the world, the lust of the flesh and the lust of the eyes and the pride of life,

> " ——a world of profit and delight
> Of power, of honour, and omnipotence."

This gives him a passionate energy, an emotional sensibility which Goethe's more shifting, sceptical and complex Faust lacks. For Marlowe, also, magic was a possible reality.

A very remarkable characteristic of Marlowe's *Faustus,* and of his work generally, which has not been sufficiently emphasised,[1] is the absence of material horror. " His raptures were all air and fire." In nothing has he shown himself so much a child of the Renaissance as in this repugnance to touch images of physical ugliness. Perondinus insists on Tamburlaine's lameness, of which Marlowe says no word ; the *Volksbuch* is crammed with details concerning the medieval Hell ; Marlowe's conception of Hell is loftier than Dante's or Milton's. In reply to the question of Faustus : " How comes it then that thou art out of Hell ? " Mephistophilis replies :

> " Why this is Hell, nor am I out of it :
>   Think'st thou that I who saw the face of God,
>   And tasted the eternal joys of Heaven,
>   Am not tormented with ten thousand Hells,
>   In being deprived of everlasting bliss ? "

Such reticence as this was entirely out of the line of dramatic tradition, and even the able revisers of the edition of *Faustus* published in 1616, contrived to bring in a plentiful supply of horrors, not only in the account of the death of Faustus, but as a description of Hell— souls toasted on burning forks, broiling live quarters, sops of flaming fire.

[1] Professor Ward, however, points out the art with which, in *Edward II.,* Marlowe avoids exciting " the sense of the loathsome."

I have already mentioned how closely Marlowe
adhered to the incidents of the prose *History*
and their sequence; such slight additions as he
makes are always for the better, as the opening
scene in the study, in which Goethe follows him.
It is in the selection of the serious incidents from
the placid prose narrative that Marlowe's genius
for the tragic poetry of intense emotion is especially
revealed. Perhaps the passage of Marlowe which
most profoundly influenced Shakespeare and other
poets is, not the awful and intense scene with which
the poem closes, but the address to Helen. The
scene that contains this wonderful passage, aflame
with impassioned loveliness, corresponds in its bare
outlines exactly to that chapter of the prose *History*
in which the Doctor, after dinner one day under-
takes to brings Helen of Troy before the students.
" This lady appeared before them," according to the
narrative, " in a most rich gown of purple velvet,
costly imbroidered; her hair hanging down loose, as
fair as the beaten gold, and of such length that it
reached down to her hams, having most amorous
cole-black eyes, a sweet and pleasant round face,
with lips as red as any cherry; her cheeks of a rose-
colour, her mouth small, her neck white like a swan;
tall and slender of personage; in sum, there was no
imperfect place in her; she looked round about her
with a roling hawke's eye, a smiling and wanton
countenance, which near-hand inflamed the hearts
of all the students, but that they persuaded themselves she was a spirit, which made them lightly
pass away such fancies : and thus fair Helena and

Faustus went out again one with another." Afterwards Helena becomes his "common concubine and bed-fellow," and has a child called Justus Faustus, who, together with his mother, after the death of Faustus vanished away. That was all. It was to this material that Marlowe set his spirit. In Goethe's great and complex work the story is refined away ; Goethe was compelled to treat magic and Hell with irony. Marlowe was the first to spiritualise as well as to dramatise the story ; at the same time its substance has not become a symbol merely, as with Goethe, who soon flings himself free of the legend. Marlowe's *Faustus*, revealing the conflicting stress of new and old, remains a chief artistic embodiment of an intellectual attitude dominant at the Renaissance.

The vigorous design and rich free verse of the *Jew of Malta* show a technical advance on *Faustus*. Only Milton, as Mr. Swinburne has somewhere remarked, has surpassed the opening soliloquy of Barabas. But after the second act the play declines ; the large conception of the Jew with his immense lust of wealth only rivalled by his love for his daughter, topples over into harsh and extravagant caricature. Marlowe seems to have worked hastily here, and when Shakespeare, a few years later, took up the same subject, although he treated it in the same spirit, the *Merchant of Venice* by force of his sweetness, humanity and humour, easily rises to a much higher pitch of art.

The *Jew of Malta* shows the transition between Marlowe the youthful tragic poet, with his intense and fascinating personality, and Marlowe the mature dramatist. In *Edward II.* Marlowe reached the summit of his art.

There is little here of that *amour de l'impossible*, which is, as Mr. Symonds observes, his characteristic note ; his passionate poetry is subdued with severe self-restraint in a supreme tragic creation. It has long been a custom among critics to compare *Edward II.* with *Richard II.* This is scarcely fair to Shakespeare ; the melodramatic and careless murder of Richard cannot be mentioned in presence of the chastened tragedy and highly-wrought pathos of Edward's last days ; the whole of Shakespeare's play, with its exuberant eloquence, its facile and diffuse poetry, is distincly inferior to Marlowe's, both in organic structure and in dramatic characterisation. It was not till ten years later that Shakespeare came near to this severe reticence, these deep and solemn tragic tones.

Besides the three parts of *Henry VI.* in which Marlowe had a considerable share, two short and fragmentary plays, not included in this volume, remain to notice. The *Massacre at Paris* deals, very freely, with contemporary French history, and could not have been an early work ;[1] it has come to us in a mutilated and corrupt condition. But when all allowance has been made it remains, by general consent, the very worst of Marlowe's dramas. It contains scarcely one powerful passage. The

---

[1] Henry III., with whose assassination the play ends, died on the 2nd August, 1589. It has been suggested that the existing version of this play is one of those short-hand piracies which seem to have been common.

Tragedy of Dido, written by Marlowe and Nash, was published a year after the former's death. It is probably an early work of Marlowe's, so far as it is his at all, and it must have been elaborated and considerably enlarged by Nash in a manner that is sometimes a caricature, perhaps not quite unconsciously, of Marlowe's manner. *Dido* must be compared to *Hero and Leander* rather than to any of Marlowe's dramas. There is a certain mellifluous sweetness in the best scenes, such as that in which Dido makes love to Æneas in the cave in which they had sought shelter from the storm.

> *Dido.* Æneas!
> *Æn.* Dido!
> *Dido.* Tell me, dear love, how found you out this cave?
> *Æn.* By chance, sweet queen, as Mars and Venus met.
> *Dido.* Why that was in a net, where we are loose:
> And yet I am not free,—O, would I were!
> *Æn.* Why, what is it that Dido may desire
> And not obtain, be it in human power?
> *Dido.* The thing that I will die before I ask,
> And yet desire to have before I die.
> *Æn.* It is not aught Æneas may achieve?
> *Dido.* Æneas! no; although his eyes do pierce.
> *Æn.* What, hath Iarbus angered her in aught?
> And will she be avenged on his life?
> *Dido.* Not angered me, except in angering thee.
> *Æn.* Who, then of all so cruel may he be
> That should detain thy eyes in his defects?
> *Dido.* The man that I do eye where'er I am:
> Whose amorous face, like Pæan, sparkles fire,
> Whenas he butts his beams on Flora's bed.
> Prometheus hath put on Cupid's shape,
> And I must perish in his burning arms:
> Æneas, O Æneas, quench these flames!
> *Æn.* What ails my queen? is she faln sick of late?
> *Dido.* Not sick, my love; but sick I must conceal
> The torment that it boots me not reveal:
> And yet I'll speak,—and yet I'll hold my peace.

Do shame her worst, I will disclose my grief:
Æneas, thou art he—what did I say?
Something it was that now I have forgot.

It seems likely that the last years of Marlowe's
life grew careless and irregular; his later plays
(putting aside *Edward II.*) show signs of swift and
over-hasty workmanship, unlike the very careful
and even work of the immature *Tamburlaine.* At
the same time the thirst after the infinite and impossible dies out, and is replaced by no sane and
cheerful content with earth's limits. *Edward II.*
is a fiercely ironical response to Tamburlaine's
supreme desire—"the sweet fruition of an earthly
crown." Marlowe, like Cyril Tourneur, lacked
altogether the tender humanity, the sweet and
genial humour which saved the sensitive Shakespeare from the bitter pride of genius, and which
marked even lesser men like Dekker and
Middleton. Greene, who died just before Marlowe, reproaches him in the death-bed ravings
of his *Groat's Worth of Wit* for his life and
opinions. Marlowe was always outspoken, one
gathers, and at this time it appears that he
attracted especial atttention as a freethinker.
Only a few days before his death, one Richard
Bame sent in a note "contayninge the opinion of
one Christofer Marlye concernynge his damnable
opinions and judgment of Relygion and scorne
of God's worde." This informer was hanged at
Tyburn next year for some degrading offence, but
there seems no reason—while making judicious
reservations—to doubt the substantial accuracy of

his statements.[1] It is noteworthy that Marlowe's
heroes are usually heathens or infidels, and he takes
every opportunity of insinuating a sceptical opinion. Probably his unorthodox views had much
to do with the accusation of "vices sent from hell"
in an anonymous play written shortly after his death.
It is certain he had friends among the finest-natured
men of his time. Walsingham was his patron;
there seems a touch of tenderness in Shakespeare's
apostrophe of the "dead shepherd" in *As you Like
It*; Nash, who had sometimes been a jealous rival,
wrote an elegy "on Marlowe's untimely death"
which has not survived; an anonymous writer in
1600 speaks lovingly of "kynde Kit Marloe;"
Edward Blunt, Marlowe's friend and publisher,
writes, in words that have a genuine ring, of "the
impression of the man that hath been dear unto us,
living an after-life in our memory;" Drayton's well-
inspired lines are familiar :—

> ——"Marlowe, bathèd in the Thespian springs,
> Had in him those brave translunary things
> That our first poets had : his raptures were
> All air and fire, which made his verses clear :
> For that fine madness still he did retain,
> Which rightly should possess a poet's brain."

Chapman also wrote concerning

> ——"his free soul, whose living subject stood
> Up to the chin in the Pierian flood."

There is no alloy of blame in the words of these

---

[1] This very interesting document is given in full in the Appendix.
Mr. Bullen (following the Rev. A. Dyce) made some important
omissions.

men, Drayton and Chapman, and they were among
the gravest as well as the best-loved of their time.
One lingers over the faintest traces of this personality which must have been so fascinating, for we
have no further trustworthy indications of the
manner of man that he was in the eyes of those
who knew him.

There is, at last, one precious fragment which we
cannot afford to pass by, for it bears Marlowe's intensely personal impress. Without this fragment of
Hero and Leander [1] we should not have known the
full sweetness and range of his genius. It is the
brightest flower of the English Renaissance, apart
from that moral energy of the Reformation of which
Chapman, together with something less than usual
of his elaborate obscurity, afterwards gave it some
faint tincture. It is a free and fresh and eager song,
"drunk with gladness,"—like Hero who "stayed
not for her robes," but straight arose to open the
door to her lover—full of ideal beauty that finds its
expression in the form and colour of things, above
all in the bodies of men and women ; for the
passion of love, apart from the passion of beauty,
Marlowe failed to grasp. No Elizabethan had so
keen a sense of physical loveliness as these lines
reveal :—

> " His body was as straight as Circe's wand ;
> Jove might have sipped out nectar from his hand.
> Even as delicious meat is to the taste,
> So was his neck in touching, and surpassed

---

[1] Marlowe's poems and translations have not received further
notice here because they will, I hope, be included in a supplemen-
tary volume of the series.

> The white of Pelops' shoulder : I could tell ye,
> How smooth his breast was, and how white his belly ;
> And whose immortal fingers did imprint
> That heavenly path with many a curious dint
> That runs along his back."

Shakespeare could not have been younger than Marlowe when he wrote his *Venus and Adonis*, which has ever since been coupled with Marlowe's poem.[1] *Venus and Adonis* is oppressive with its unexpanded power; its workmanship is perhaps more searching and thorough, though so much less felicitous than that of *Hero and Leander ;* but we turn away with delight from its massive monotonous energy, its close and sensual atmosphere, to the free and open air, the colour and light, the swift and various music of Marlowe's poem. Shelley has scarcely surpassed the sweet gravity which the verse of " our elder Shelley " here reaches :—

> " It lies not in our power to love or hate,
> For will in us is over-ruled by fate.
> When two are stripped, long e'er the course begin,
> We wish that one should lose, the other win ;
> And one especially do we affect
> Of two gold ingots, like in each respect :
> The reason no man knows, let it suffice,
> What we behold is censured by our eyes.
> Where both deliberate, the love is slight :
> Who ever loved, that loved not at first sight ? "

The peculiar beauty of these lines seems to have

---

[1] They had a wide popular reputation, resting on their supposed licentiousness, as, at a later day, *Mademoiselle de Maupin.* " I have conveyed away all her wanton pamphlets," says Harebrain in Middleton's *A Mad World, my Masters,* " as *Hero and Leander, Venus and Adonis,* O two luscious marrow-bone pies for a young married wife."

dwelt in Shakespeare's memory. It is little sur-
prising that men were not easily tired of *Hero and
Leander.* Taylor the water-poet tells us how his
fellow scullers used to sing it as they plied their
occupation on the Thames. It was these " sweet-
according rimes " of Marlowe's, which, as his enthu-
siastic young admirer, Petowe, wrote,

> "—— moved such delight,
> That men would shun their sleep in still dark night
> To meditate upon his golden lines."

In the spring of 1593 the plague raged in
London. The actors went into the provinces ;
many authors sought refuge in the country. In May
we know that Marlowe was at the little village
of Deptford, not many miles from London. There
was turbulent blood there, and wine ; there were
courtesans and daggers. Here Marlowe was slain,
killed by a serving-man, a rival in a quarrel over
bought kisses—" a bawdy serving-man."[1] They
buried him in an unknown spot, beneath the grey
towers of St. Nicholas, and they wrote in the
parish-book : " Christopher Marlow, slain by ffrancis
Archer, the 1 of June 1593."

HAVELOCK ELLIS.

[1] So the brief account of Francis Meres (*Palladis Tamia,* 1598).
There are other more suspected narratives, varying considerably
from each other, and with a marked bias in favour of moral edifi-
cation.

TAMBURLAINE THE GREAT.

IN TWO PARTS.

THE play of *Tamburlaine*, which had been acted in, or before, 1588, was published in 1590. There were subsequent editions in 1592, 1593, 1597, 1605-6. Its popularity was very great. According to Thomas Heywood, the famous actor Alleyn, in this play and in *The Jew of Malta*,

> " won
> The attribute of peerless ; "

and in Henslowe's Diary we read of Tamburlaine's crimson-velvet breeches and copper-laced coat.

From an address to the reader prefixed by the printer to the edition of 1592, it appears that the play originally contained comic scenes. " I have purposely omitted and left out," he tells us, " certain fond and frivolous gestures, digressing. and, in my poor opinion, far unmeet for the matter, which I thought might seem more tedious unto the wise than any way else to be regarded, though haply they have been of some vain-conceited fondlings greatly gaped at, what time they were shewed upon the stage in their graced deformities : nevertheless now to be mixtured in print with such matter of worth, it would prove a great disgrace to so honourable and stately a history.

The sources whence the play of *Tamburlaine* was derived have been already pointed out.[1]

---

[1] See *ante*, p. xxxiii.

TAMBURLAINE THE GREAT.

PART THE FIRST.

THE PROLOGUE.

FROM jigging veins of rhyming mother wits.
And such conceits as clownage keeps in pay,
We'll lead you to the stately tent of war,
Where you shall hear the Scythian Tamburlaine
Threatening the world with high astounding terms,
And scourging kingdoms with his conquering sword.
View but his picture in this tragic glass,
And then applaud his fortune as you please.

MYCETES, King of Persia.

COSROE, his Brother.

ORTYGIUS,

CENEUS.

MEANDER,   Persian Lords and Captains.

MENAPHON,

THERIDAMAS,

TAMBURLAINE, a Scythian Shepherd.

TECHELLES.

USUMCASANE, } his Followers.

BAJAZETH, Emperor of the Turks.

KING of ARABIA.

KING of FEZ.

KING of MOROCCO.

KING of ARGIER (Algiers).

SOLDAN of EGYPT.

GOVERNOR of DAMASCUS.

AGYDAS,   } Median Lords.

MAGNETES,

CAPOLIN, an Egyptian Captain.

PHILEMUS, a Messenger.

ZENOCRATE, Daughter of the Soldan of Egypt.

ANIPPE, her Maid.

ZABINA, Wife of Bajazeth.

EBEA, her Maid.

Virgins of Damascus.

No list of the characters is given in the early editions : the
omission is frequent in plays of this period.

TAMBURLAINE THE GREAT.

PART THE FIRST.

— ·‹∶∗∶›· —

ACT THE FIRST.

SCENE I.

Enter MYCETES, COSROE, MEANDER, THERIDAMAS, ORTYGIUS, CENEUS, MENAPHON, *with others.*

MYC. Brother Cosroe, I find myself aggrieved,
Yet insufficient to express the same ;
For it requires a great and thundering speech :
Good brother, tell the cause unto my lords ;
I know you have a better wit than I.

   Cos. Unhappy Persia, that in former age
Hast been the seat of mighty conquerors,
That, in their prowess and their policies,
Have triumphed over Afric and the bounds
Of Europe, where the sun scarce dares appear
For freezing meteors and congealèd cold,

Now to be ruled and governed by a man
At whose birthday Cynthia with Saturn joined,
And Jove, the Sun, and Mercury denied
To shed their influence in his fickle brain !
Now Turks and Tartars shake their swords at thee,
Meaning to mangle all thy provinces.

     Myc. Brother, I see your meaning well enough,
And through your planets I perceive you think
I am not wise enough to be a king :
But I refer me to my noblemen
That know my wit, and can be witnesses.
I might command you to be slain for this :
Meander, might I not?

       Meand. Not for so small a fault, my sovereign
            lord.

       Myc. I mean it not, but yet I know I might :
Yet live ; yea live, Mycetes wills it so.
Meander, thou, my faithful counsellor,
Declare the cause of my conceivèd grief,
Which is, God knows, about that Tamburlaine,
That, like a fox in midst of harvest time,
Doth prey upon my flocks of passengers ;
And, as I hear, doth mean to pull my plumes :
Therefore 'tis good and meet for to be wise.

       Meand. Oft have I heard your majesty complain
Of Tamburlaine, that sturdy Scythian thief,
That robs your merchants of Persepolis
Trading by land unto the Western Isles,
And in your confines with his lawless train
Daily commits incivil[1] outrages,
Hoping (misled by dreaming prophecies)
To reign in Asia, and with barbarous arms

       [1] Brutal.

To make himself the monarch of the East :
But ere he march in Asia, or display
His vagrant ensign in the Persian fields,
Your grace hath taken order by Theridamas,
Charged with a thousand horse, to apprehend
And bring him captive to your highness' throne.

  Myc. Full true thou speak'st, and like thyself, my
      lord,
Whom I may term a Damon for thy love :
Therefore 'tis best, if so it like you all,
To send my thousand horse incontinent [1]
To apprehend that paltry Scythian.
How like you this, my honourable lords ?
Is't not a kingly resolution ?

  Cos. It cannot choose, because it comes from you.

  Myc. Then hear thy charge, valiant Theridamas,
The chiefest captain of Mycetes' host.
The hope of Persia, and the very legs
Whereon our State doth lean as on a staff,
That holds us up, and foils our neighbour foes :
Thou shalt be leader of this thousand horse,
Whose foaming gall with rage and high disdain
Have sworn the death of wicked Tamburlaine.
Go frowning forth ; but come thou smiling home,
As did Sir Paris with the Grecian dame ;
Return with speed—time passeth swift away ;
Our life is frail, and we may die to-day.

  Ther. Before the moon renew her borrowed light,
Doubt not, my lord and gracious sovereign,
But Tamburlaine and that Tartarian rout,
Shall either perish by our warlike hands,
Or plead for mercy at your highness' feet.

              [1] Forthwith.

Myc. Go, stout Theridamas, thy words are swords,
And with thy looks thou conquerest all thy foes ;
I long to see thee back return from thence,
That I may view these milk-white steeds of mine
All loaden with the heads of killèd men,
And from their knees e'en to their hoofs below
Besmeared with blood that makes a dainty show.

   Ther. Then now, my lord, I humbly take my leave.

   Myc. Theridamas. farewell ! ten thousand times.

                    [*Exit* THERIDAMAS.

Ah, Menaphon, why stay'st thou thus behind,
When other men press forward for renown ?
Go, Menaphon, go into Scythia ;
And foot by foot follow Theridamas.

   Cos. Nay, pray you let him stay ; a greater task
Fits Menaphon than warring with a thief :
Create him Prorex [1] of all Africa,
That he may win the Babylonians' hearts
Which will revolt from Persian government,
Unless they have a wiser king than you.

   Myc. " Unless they have a wiser king than you."
These are his words ; Meander, set them down.

   Cos. And add this to them—that all Asia
Laments to see the folly of their king.

   Myc. Well. here I swear by this my royal seat,—

   Cos. You may do well to kiss it then.

   Myc. Embossed with silk as best beseems my state,
To be revenged for these contemptuous words.
Oh, where is duty and allegiance now ?
Fled to the Caspian or the Ocean main ?
What shall I call thee ? brother ?—no, a foe ;
Monster of nature !—Shame unto thy stock

[1] Viceroy.

That dar'st presume thy sovereign for to mock !
Meander, come : I am abused, Meander.

           [*Exeunt all but* COSROE *and* MENAPHON.

  Men. How now, my lord? What, mated [1] and amazed
To hear the king thus threaten like himself !

  Cos. Ah, Menaphon, I pass not [2] for his threats ;
The plot is laid by Persian noblemen
And captains of the Median garrisons
To crown me Emperor of Asia :
But this it is that doth excruciate
The very substance of my vexèd soul—
To see our neighbours that were wont to quake
And tremble at the Persian monarch's name,
Now sit and laugh our regiment [3] to scorn :
And that which might resolve [4] me into tears,
Men from the farthest equinoctial line
Have swarmed in troops into the Eastern India,
Lading their ships with gold and precious stones,
And made their spoils from all our provinces.

  Men. This should entreat your highness to rejoice,
Since Fortune gives you opportunity
To gain the title of a conqueror
By curing of this maimèd empery.
Afric and Europe bordering on your land,
And continent to your dominions,
How easily may you, with a mighty host,
Pass into Græcia, as did Cyrus once,
And cause them to withdraw their forces home,
Lest you subdue the pride of Christendom.

                [*Trumpet within.*

  Cos. But, Menaphon, what means this trumpet's sound?

  Men. Behold, my lord, Ortygius and the rest
Bringing the crown to make you Emperor !

      [1] Confounded.   [2] Care not.   [3] Rule.   [4] Dissolve.

Enter ORTYGIUS *and* CENEUS, *with others, bearing
a crown.*

Orty. Magnificent and mighty Prince Cosroe,
We, in the name of other Persian States [1]
And Commons of the mighty monarchy,
Present thee with the imperial diadem.

Cen. The warlike soldiers and the gentlemen,
That heretofore have filled Persepolis
With Afric captains taken in the field,
Whose ransom made them march in coats of gold,
With costly jewels hanging at their ears,
And shining stones upon their lofty crests,
Now living idle in the wallèd towns,
Wanting both pay and martial discipline,
Begin in troops to threaten civil war,
And openly exclaim against their king :
Therefore, to stop all sudden mutinies,
We will invest your highness Emperor,
Whereat the soldiers will conceive more joy
Than did the Macedonians at the spoil
Of great Darius and his wealthy host.

Cos. Well, since I see the state of Persia droop
And languish in my brother's government,
I willingly receive the imperial crown,
And vow to wear it for my country's good,
In spite of them shall malice [2] my estate.

Orty. And in assurance of desired success,
We here do crown thee monarch of the East,
Emperor of Asia and Persia ;
Great Lord of Media and Armenia :
Duke of Africa and Albania,
Mesopotamia and of Parthia,

---

[1] *i.e.*, Persons of state.
[2] " Malice " was frequently used as a verb.

East India and the late-discovered isles :
Chief Lord of all the wide, vast Euxine sea,
And of the ever-raging Caspian lake.

   All. Long live Cosroe, mighty Emperor!

   Cos. And Jove may never let me longer live
Than I may seek to gratify your love,
And cause the soldiers that thus honour me
To triumph over many provinces!
By whose desire of discipline in arms
I doubt not shortly but to reign sole king,
And with the army of Theridamas,
(Whither we presently will fly, my lords)
To rest secure against my brother's force.

   Orty. We knew, my lord, before we brought the
      crown,
Intending your investion so near
The residence of your despisèd brother,
The lords would not be too exasperate
To injury² or suppress your worthy title ;
Or, if they would, there are in readiness
Ten thousand horse to carry you from hence,
In spite of all suspected enemies.

   Cos. I know it well, my lord, and thank you all.

   Orty. Sound up the trumpets then. [*Trumpets sound.*

   All. God save the King!   [*Exeunt.*

---

¹ Meaning "And may Jove," &c. Marlowe had very vague
ideas respecting the Persian and Mahommedan religions. Tamburlaine often invokes Jove, and seems to be well versed in the
Greek mythology.

² "Injury," like "malice," was sometimes used as a verb by our
early writers.

Enter TAMBURLAINE *leading* ZENOCRATE, TECHELLES,
  USUMCASANE, AGYDAS, MAGNETES, Lords, *and* Soldiers, *laden with treasure.*

Tamb. Come, lady, let not this appal your thoughts ;
The jewels and the treasure we have ta'en
Shall be reserved, and you in better state,
Than if you were arrived in Syria,
Even in the circle of your father's arms.
The mighty Soldan of Ægyptia.

  Zeno. Ah, shepherd ! pity my distressèd plight,
(If, as thou seem'st, thou art so mean a man,)
And seek not to enrich thy followers
By lawless rapine from a silly maid,
Who travelling with these Median lords
To Memphis, from my uncle's country of Media,
Where all my youth I have been governèd,
Have passed the army of the mighty Turk,
Bearing his privy signet and his hand
To safe conduct us thorough Africa.

  Mag. And since we have arrived in Scythia,
Besides rich presents from the puissant Cham,
We have his highness' letters to command
Aid and assistance, if we stand in need.

  Tamb. But now you see these letters and com-
      mands
Are countermanded by a greater man ;
And through my provinces you must expect
Letters of conduct from my mightiness,
If you intend to keep your treasure safe.
But, since I love to live at liberty,

As easily may you get the Soldan's crown
As any prizes out of my precinct ;
For they are friends that help to wean my state
'Till men and kingdoms help to strengthen it,
And must maintain my life exempt from servitude.—
But, tell me, madam, is your grace betrothed ?

 Zeno. I am—my lord—for so you do import.

 Tamb. I am a lord, for so my deeds shall prove :
And yet a shepherd by my parentage.
But, lady, this fair face and heavenly hue
Must grace his bed that conquers Asia,
And means to be a terror to the world,
Measuring the limits of his empery
By east and west, as Phœbus doth his course.
Lie here ye weeds that I disdain to wear !
This complete armour and this curtle-axe [1]
Are adjuncts more beseeming Tamburlaine.
And, madam, whatsoever you esteem
Of this success and loss unvalued,[2]
Both may invest you Empress of the East ;
And these that seem but silly country swains
May have the leading of so great an host,
As with their weight shall make the mountains quake,
Even as when windy exhalations
Fighting for passage, tilt within the earth.

 Tech. As princely lions, when they rouse themselves,
Stretching their paws, and threatening herds of beasts,
So in his armour looketh Tamburlaine.
Methinks I see kings kneeling at his feet,
And he with frowning brows and fiery looks.
Spurning their crowns from off their captive heads.

---

[1] The curtle-axe (Fr. *coutelasse*) was not an axe, but a short curved
sword, which survives in the modern cutlass.
[2] Invaluable.

Usum. And making thee and me, Techelles, kings,
That even to death will follow Tamburlaine.

Tamb. Nobly resolved, sweet friends and followers !
These lords, perhaps do scorn our estimates,
And think we prattle with distempered spirits ;
But since they measure our deserts so mean.
That in conceit bear empires on our spears,
Affecting thoughts coequal with the clouds,
They shall be kept our forcèd followers.
Till with their eyes they view us emperors.

Zeno. The gods, defenders of the innocent,
Will never prosper your intended drifts,
That thus oppress poor friendless passengers.
Therefore at least admit us liberty,
Even as thou hopest to be eternised,
By living Asia's mighty Emperor.

Agyd. I hope our ladies' treasure and our own,
May serve for ransom to our liberties :
Return our mules and empty camels back,
That we may travel into Syria,
Where her betrothèd lord Alcidamas,
Expects th' arrival of her highness' person.

Mag. And wheresoever we repose ourselves.
We will report but well of Tamburlaine.

Tamb. Disdains Zenocrate to live with me ?
Or you, my lords, to be my followers ?
Think you I weigh this treasure more than you
Not all the gold in India's wealthy arms
Shall buy the meanest soldier in my train.
Zenocrate, lovelier than the love of Jove,
Brighter than is the silver Rhodope,
Fairer than whitest snow on Scythian hills,—
Thy person is more worth to Tamburlaine,
Than the possession of the Persian crown,

Which gracious stars have promised at my birth.
A hundred Tartars shall attend on thee,
Mounted on steeds swifter than Pegasus ;
Thy garments shall be made of Median silk,
Enchased with precious jewels of mine own,
More rich and valurous [1] than Zenocrate's.
With milk-white harts upon an ivory sled,
Thou shalt be drawn amidst the frozen pools,
And scale the icy mountains' lofty tops,
Which with thy beauty will be soon resolved.
My martial prizes with five hundred men,
Won on the fifty-headed Volga's waves,
Shall we all offer to Zenocrate,—
And then myself to fair Zenocrate.

   Tech. What now !—in love ?
   Tamb. Techelles, women must be flattered :
But this is she with whom I am in love.

Enter a Soldier.

   Sold. News ! news !
   Tamb. How now—what's the matter ?
   Sold. A thousand Persian horsemen are at hand,
Sent from the king to overcome us all.
   Tamb. How now, my lords of Egypt, and Zenocrate !
How !—must your jewels be restored again,
And I, that triumphed so, be overcome ?
How say you, lordings,—is not this your hope ?
   Agyd. We hope yourself will willingly restore them.
   Tamb. Such hope, such fortune, have the thousand
     horse.
Soft ye, my lords, and sweet Zenocrate !
You must be forced from me ere you go.
A thousand horsemen !—We five hundred foot !—

[1] Valuable.

An odds too great for us to stand against.
But are they rich ?—and is their armour good ?

   Sold. Their plumèd helms are wrought with beaten
      gold,
Their swords enamelled, and about their necks
Hang massy chains of gold, down to the waist,
In every part exceeding brave[1] and rich.

   Tamb. Then shall we fight courageously with them ?
Or look you I should play the orator ?

   Tech. No : cowards and faint-hearted runaways
Look for orations when the foe is near :
Our swords shall play the orator for us.

   Usum. Come ! let us meet them at the mountain top,
And with a sudden and a hot alarum,
Drive all their horses headlong down the hill.

   Tech. Come, let us march !

   Tamb. Stay, Techelles ! ask a parley first.

The Soldiers *enter.*

Open the mails, yet guard the treasure sure ;
Lay out our golden wedges to the view,
That their reflections may amaze the Persians ;
And look we friendly on them when they come ;
But if they offer word or violence,
We'll fight five hundred men-at-arms to one,
Before we part with our possession.
And 'gainst the general we will lift our swords,
And either lance his greedy thirsting throat,
Or take him prisoner, and his chain shall serve
For manacles, till he be ransomed home.

   Tech. I hear them come ; shall we encounter them ?

   Tamb. Keep all your standings and not stir a foot,
Myself will bide the danger of the brunt.

<hr>

   [1] Fine.   Trunks. Fr. *malles.*

Enter THERIDAMAS *and others.*

Ther. Where is this Scythian Tamburlaine?

Tamb. Whom seek'st thou, Persian?—I am Tambur
laine.

Ther. Tamburlaine!—

A Scythian shepherd so embellishèd

With nature's pride and richest furniture!

His looks do menace Heaven and dare the gods:

His fiery eyes are fixed upon the earth,

As if he now devised some stratagem,

Or meant to pierce Avernus' darksome vaults

To pull the triple-headed dog from hell.

Tamb. Noble and mild this Persian seems to be,

If outward habit judge the inward man.

Tech. His deep affections make him passionate.

Tamb. With what a majesty he rears his looks!

In thee, thou valiant man of Persia,

I see the folly of thy emperor.

Art thou but captain of a thousand horse,

That by characters graven in thy brows,

And by thy martial face and stout aspèct,

Deserv'st to have the leading of a host!

Forsake thy king, and do but join with me,

And we will triumph over all the world;

I hold the Fates bound fast in iron chains,

And with my hand turn Fortune's wheel about:

And sooner shall the sun fall from his sphere,

Than Tamburlaine be slain or overcome.

Draw forth thy sword, thou mighty man-at-arms,

Intending but to raze my charmèd skin,

And Jove himself will stretch his hand from Heaven

To ward the blow and shield me safe from harm.

See how he rains down heaps of gold in showers,

Mar.   C

As if he meant to give my soldiers pay !
And as a sure and grounded argument,
That I shall be the monarch of the East,
He sends this Soldan's daughter rich and brave,
To be my Queen and portly Emperess.
If thou wilt stay with me, renownèd man,
And lead thy thousand horse with my conduct,
Besides thy share of this Egyptian prize,
Those thousand horse shall sweat with martial spoil
Of conquered kingdoms and of cities sacked ;
Both we will walk upon the lofty cliffs,
And Christian merchants [1] that with Russian stems
Plough up huge furrows in the Caspian sea,
Shall vail [2] to us, as lords of all the lake.
Both we will reign as consuls of the earth,
And mighty kings shall be our senators.
Jove sometimes maskèd in a shepherd's weed,
And by those steps that he hath scaled the Heavens
May we become immortal like the gods.
Join with me now in this my mean estate,
(I call it mean because being yet obscure,
The nations far removed admire me not,)
And when my name and honour shall be spread
As far as Boreas claps his brazen wings,
Or fair Böotes sends his cheerful light,
Then shalt thou be competitor [3] with me,
And sit with Tamburlaine in all his majesty.

    Ther. Not Hermes, prolocutor to the gods,
Could use persuasions more pathetical.

    Tamb. Nor are Apollo's oracles more true,
Than thou shalt find my vaunts substantial.

    Tech. We are his friends, and if the Persian king
Should offer present dukedoms to our state,

---

[1] Merchantmen.   [2] Lower their flags.   [3] Associate.

We think it loss to make exchange for that
We are assured of by our friend's success.

   Usum. And kingdoms at the least we all expect,
Besides the honour in assured conquests,
When kings shall crouch unto our conquering swords
And hosts of soldiers stand amazed at us;
When with their fearful tongues they shall confess,
These are the men that all the world admires.

   Ther. What strong enchantments tice my yielding
      soul!
These are resolvèd, noble Scythians:
But shall I prove a traitor to my king?

   Tamb. No, but the trusty friend of Tamburlaine.

   Ther. Won with thy words, and conquered with thy
      looks,
I yield myself, my men, and horse to thee,
To be partaker of thy good or ill,
As long as life maintains Theridamas.

   Tamb. Theridamas, my friend, take here my hand,
Which is as much as if I swore by Heaven,
And called the gods to witness of my vow.
Thus shall my heart be still combined with thine
Until our bodies turn to elements,
And both our souls aspire celestial thrones.
Techelles and Casane, welcome him!

   Tech. Welcome, renownèd Persian, to us all!

   Usum. Long may Theridamas remain with us!

   Tamb. These are my friends, in whom I more re-
      joice
Than doth the King of Persia in his crown,
And by the love of Pylades and Orestes,
Whose statues we adore in Scythia,
Thyself and them shall never part from me
Before I crown you kings in Asia.

Make much of them, gentle Theridamas,
And they will never leave thee till the death.

 Ther. Nor thee nor them, thrice noble Tamburlaine,
Shall want my heart to be with gladness pierced,
To do you honour and security.

 Tamb. A thousand thanks, worthy Theridamas.
And now fair madam, and my noble lords,
If you will willingly remain with me
You shall have honours as your merits be ;
Or else you shall be forced with slavery.

 Agyd. We yield unto thee, happy Tamburlaine.

 Tamb. For you then, madam, I am out of doubt.

 Zeno. I must be pleased perforce. Wretched Zenocrate !   [*Exeunt.*

ACT THE SECOND.

SCENE I.

Enter Cosroe, Menaphon, Ortygius, *and* Ceneus,
with Soldiers.

COS. Thus far are we towards Theri-
damas,
And valiant Tamburlaine, the man of
fame,
The man that in the forehead of his
fortune
Bears figures of renown and miracle.
But tell me, that hast seen him, Menaphon,
What stature wields he, and what personage?

Men. Of stature tall, and straightly fashionèd,
Like his desire lift upward and divine;
So large of limbs, his joints so strongly knit,
Such breadth of shoulders as might mainly bear
Old Atlas' burthen;—'twixt his manly pitch,[1]
A pearl, more worth than all the world, is placed,
Wherein by curious sovereignty of art
Are fixed his piercing instruments of sight,
Whose fiery circles bear encompassèd
A heaven of heavenly bodies in their spheres,

[1] Originally the height to which a falcon soared; hence for height
in general. Here it means the shoulders.

That guides his steps and actions to the throne,
Where honour sits invested royally :
Pale of complexion, wrought in him with passion,
Thirsting with sovereignty and love of arms ;
His lofty brows in folds do figure death,
And in their smoothness amity and life ;
About them hangs a knot of amber hair,
Wrappèd in curls, as fierce Achilles' was,
On which the breath of Heaven delights to play,
Making it dance with wanton majesty.—
His arms and fingers, long, and sinewy,[1]
Betokening valour and excess of strength ;—
In every part proportioned like the man
Should make the world subdued to Tamburlaine.

   Cos. Well hast thou pourtrayed in thy terms of life
The face and personage of a wondrous man ;
Nature doth strive with Fortune and his stars
To make him famous in accomplished worth ;
And well his merits show him to be made
His fortune's master and the king of men,
That could persuade at such a sudden pinch,
With reasons of his valour and his life,
A thousand sworn and overmatching foes.
Then, when our powers in points of swords are joined
And closed in compass of the killing bullet,
Though strait the passage and the port [2] be made
That leads to palace of my brother's life,
Proud is his fortune if we pierce it not.
And when the princely Persian diadem
Shall overweigh his weary witless head,
And fall like mellowed fruit with shakes of death,

---

[1] Dyce's emendation for "snowy" or "snowy-white." Marlowe
uses the word "sinewy" elsewhere.
[2] Gate.

In fair Persia, noble Tamburlaine
Shall be my regent and remain as king.

Orty. In happy hour we have set the crown
Upon your kingly head that seeks our honour,
In joining with the man ordained by Heaven,
To further every action to the best.

Cen. He that with shepherds and a little spoil ·
Durst, in disdain of wrong and tyranny,
Defend his freedom 'gainst a monarchy,
What will he do supported by a king,
Leading a troop of gentlemen and lords,
And stuffed with treasure for his highest thoughts!

Cos. And such shall wait on worthy Tamburlaine.
Our army will be forty thousand strong,
When Tamburlaine and brave Theridamas
Have met us by the river Araris;
And all conjoined to meet the witless king,
That now is marching near to Parthia,
And with unwilling soldiers faintly armed,
To seek revenge on me and Tamburlaine,
To whom, sweet Menaphon, direct me straight.

Men. I will, my lord.   [*Exeunt.*

SCENE II.

Enter MYCETES, MEANDER, *with other* Lords *and*
Soldiers.

Myc. Come, my Meander, let us to this gear.
I tell you true, my heart is swoln with wrath
On this same thievish villain, Tamburlaine,
And on that false Cosroe, my traitorous brother.
Would it not grieve a king to be so abused

And have a thousand horsemen ta'en away?
And, which is worse, to have his diadem
Sought for by such scald[1] knaves as love him not?
I think it would ; well then, by Heavens I swear,
Aurora shall not peep out of her doors,
But I will have Cosroe by the head,
And kill proud Tamburlaine with point of sword.
Tell you the rest, Meander : I have said.

    Meand. Then having passed Armenian deserts now,
And pitched our tents under the Georgian hills,
Whose tops are covered with Tartarian thieves,
That lie in ambush, waiting for a prey,
What should we do but bid them battle straight,
And rid the world of those detested troops?
Lest, if we let them linger here awhile,
They gather strength by power of fresh supplies.
This country swarms with vile outrageous men
That live by rapine and by lawless spoil,
Fit soldiers for the wicked Tamburlaine ;
And he that could with gifts and promises
Inveigle him that led a thousand horse,
And make him false his faith unto his king,
Will quickly win such as be like himself.
Therefore cheer up your minds ; prepare to fight ;
He that can take or slaughter Tamburlaine
Shall rule the province of Albania :
Who brings that traitor's head, Theridamas,
Shall have a government in Media,
Beside the spoil of him and all his train :
But if Cosroe, (as our spials[2] say,
And as we know) remains with Tamburlaine,
His highness' pleasure is that he should live,
And be reclaimed with princely lenity.

A Spy. A hundred horsemen of my company
Scouting abroad upon these champion[1] plains
Have viewed the army of the Scythians,
Which make report it far exceeds the king's.

Meand. Suppose they be in number infinite,
Yet being void of martial discipline,
All running headlong greedy after spoils,
And more regarding gain than victory,
Like to the cruel brothers of the earth.
Sprung of the teeth of dragons venomous,
Their careless swords shall lance their fellows' throats,
And make us triumph in their overthrow.

Myc. Was there such brethren, sweet Meander, say,
That sprung of teeth of dragons venomous?

Meand. So poets say, my lord.

Myc. And 'tis a pretty toy to be a poet.
Well, well, Meander, thou art deeply read,
And having thee, I have a jewel sure.
Go on, my lord, and give your charge, I say;
Thy wit will make us conquerors to-day.

Meand. Then, noble soldiers, to entrap these thieves,
That live confounded in disordered troops,
If wealth or riches may prevail with them,
We have our camels laden all with gold,
Which you that be but common soldiers
Shall fling in every corner of the field;
And while the base-born Tartars take it up,
You, fighting more for honour than for gold,
Shall massacre those greedy-minded slaves;
And when their scattered army is subdued,
And you march on their slaughtered carcases,
Share equally the gold that bought their lives,

---

[1] The old way of spelling "champaign," Fr. *champagne.*

And live like gentlemen in Persia.
Strike up the drum ! and march courageously !
Fortune herself doth sit upon our crests.

    Myc. He tells you true, my masters : so he does.
Drums, why sound ye not, when Meander speaks ?

                  [Exeunt, drums sounding.

SCENE III.

Enter COSROE, TAMBURLAINE, THERIDAMAS, TECHELLES,
    USUMCASANE, *and* ORTYGIUS, *with others.*

    Cos. Now, worthy Tamburlaine, have I reposed
In thy approvèd fortunes all my hope.
What think'st thou, man, shall come of our attempts?
For even as from assurèd oracle,
I take thy doom for satisfaction.

    Tamb. And so mistake you not a whit, my lord ;
For fates and oracles of Heaven have sworn
To royalise the deeds of Tamburlaine,
And make them blest that share in his attempts.
And doubt you not but, if you favour me,
And let my fortunes and my valour sway
To some direction in your martial deeds,
The world will strive with hosts of men-at-arms,
To swarm unto the ensign I support :
The host of Xerxes, which by fame is said
To have drank the mighty Parthian Araris,
Was but a handful to that we will have.
Our quivering lances, shaking in the air,
And bullets, like Jove's dreadful thunderbolts,
Enrolled in flames and fiery smouldering mists,
Shall threat the gods more than Cyclopian wars :

And with our sun-bright armour as we march,
We'll chase the stars from Heaven and dim their
    eyes
That stand and muse at our admirèd arms.

Ther. You see, my lord, what working words he hath;
But when you see his actions top his speech,
Your speech will stay or so extol his worth
As I shall be commended and excused
For turning my poor charge to his direction.
And these his two renownèd friends, my lord,
Would make one thirst and strive to be retained
In such a great degree of amity.

Tech. With duty and with amity we yield
Our utmost service to the fair Cosroe.

Cos. Which I esteem as portion of my crown.
Usumcasane and Techelles both,
When she that rules in Rhamnus'[1] golden gates,
And makes a passage for all prosperous arms,
Shall make me solely Emperor of Asia,
Then shall your meeds and valours be advanced
To rooms of honour and nobility.

Tamb. Then haste, Cosroe, to be king alone,
That I with these, my friends, and all my men
May triumph in our long-expected fate.—
The king, your brother, is now hard at hand;
Meet with the fool, and rid your royal shoulders
Of such a burthen as outweighs the sands
And all the craggy rocks of Caspia.

Enter a Messenger.

Mes. My lord, we have discovered the enemy
Ready to charge you with a mighty army.

---

[1] The allusion is to Nemesis, who had a temple at Rhamnus in
Attica.—*Bullen.*

Cos. Come, Tamburlaine! now whet thy winged sword,
And lift thy lofty arm into the clouds,
That it may reach the King of Persia's crown,
And set it safe on my victorious head.

Tamb. See where it is, the keenest curtle-axe
That e'er made passage thorough Persian arms.
These are the wings shall make it fly as swift
As doth the lightning or the breath of Heaven,
And kill as sure as it swiftly flies.

Cos. Thy words assure me of kind success;
Go, valiant soldier, go before and charge
The fainting army of that foolish king.

Tamb. Usumcasane and Techelles, come!
We are enow to scare the enemy,
And more than needs to make an emperor.

[*Exeunt to the battle.*

SCENE IV.

Enter MYCETES *with his crown in his hand.*

Myc. Accursed be he that first invented war!
They knew not, ah they knew not, simple men,
How those were hit by pelting cannon shot,
Stand staggering like a quivering aspen leaf
Fearing the force of Boreas' boisterous blasts.
In what a lamentable case were I
If Nature had not given me wisdom's lore,
For kings are clouts that every man shoots at,
Our crown the pin [1] that thousands seek to cleave;

---

[1] The "clout" was the white mark in the butts at which the archers aimed, and the "pin" was the peg in the centre which fastened it.

Therefore in policy I think it good
To hide it close ; a goodly stratagem,
And far from any man that is a fool :
So shall I not be known ; or if I be,
They cannot take away my crown from me.
Here will I hide it in this simple hole.

Enter TAMBURLAINE.

Tamb. What, fearful coward, straggling from the camp,
When kings themselves are present in the field ?

Myc. Thou liest.

Tamb. Base villain ! darest give me the lie ?

Myc. Away ; I am the king ; go ; touch me not.
Thou break'st the law of arms, unless thou kneel
And cry me " mercy, noble king."

Tamb. Are you the witty King of Persia ?

Myc. Ay, marry am I : have you any suit to me ?

Tamb. I would entreat you speak but three wise words.

Myc. So I can when I see my time.

Tamb. Is this your crown ?

Myc. Ay, didst thou ever see a fairer ?

Tamb. You will not sell it, will you ?

Myc. Such another word and I will have thee executed.
    Come, give it me !

Tamb. No ; I took it prisoner.

Myc. You lie ; I gave it you.

Tamb. Then 'tis mine.

Myc. No ; I mean I let you keep it.

Tamb. Well ; I mean you shall have it again.
Here ; take it for a while : I lend it thee,
'Till I may see thee hemmed with armèd men ;
Then shalt thou see me pull it from thy head :
Thou art no match for mighty Tamburlaine.

[*Exit* TAMBURLAINE.

Myc. O gods ! Is this Tamburlaine the thief ?
I marvel much he stole it not away.

[*Trumpets sound to the battle, and he runs out.*

SCENE V.

Enter Cosroe, Tamburlaine, Meander, Theridamas,
Ortygius, Menaphon, Techelles, Usumcasane,
with others.

Tamb. Hold thee, Cosroe ! wear two imperial crowns ;
Think thee invested now as royally,
Even by the mighty hand of Tamburlaine,
As if as many kings as could encompass thee
With greatest pomp, had crowned thee emperor.

Cos. So do I, thrice renownèd man-at-arms,
And none shall keep the crown but Tamburlaine.
Thee do I make my regent of Persia,
And general lieutenant of my armies.
Meander, you, that were our brother's guide,
And chiefest counsellor in all his acts,
Since he is yielded to the stroke of war,
On your submission we with thanks excuse,
And give you equal place in our affairs.

Meand. Most happy Emperor, in humblest terms,
I vow my service to your majesty,
With utmost virtue of my faith and duty.

Cos. Thanks, good Meander : then, Cosroe, reign,
And govern Persia in her former pomp !
Now send embassage to thy neighbour kings,
And let them know the Persian king is changed,
From one that knew not what a king should do,
To one that can command what 'longs thereto.

And now we will to fair Persepolis,
With twenty thousand expert soldiers.
The lords and captains of my brother's camp
With little slaughter take Meander's course,
And gladly yield them to my gracious rule.
Ortygius and Menaphon, my trusty friends,
Now will I gratify your former good,
And grace your calling with a greater sway.

   Orty. And as we ever aimed at your behoof,
And sought your state all honour it deserved,
So will we with our powers and our lives
Endeavour to preserve and prosper it.

   Cos. I will not thank thee, sweet Ortygius;
Better replies shall prove my purposes.
And now, Lord Tamburlaine, my brother's camp
I leave to thee and to Theridamas,
To follow me to fair Persepolis.
Then will we march to all those Indian mines,
My witless brother to the Christians lost,
And ransom them with fame and usury.
And till thou overtake me, Tamburlaine,
(Staying to order all the scattered troops,)
Farewell, lord regent and his happy friends !
I long to sit upon my brother's throne.

   Meand. Your majesty shall shortly have your wish,
And ride in triumph through Persepolis.

      [*Exeunt all but* TAMBURLAINE, THERIDAMAS,
        TECHELLES, *and* USUMCASANE.

   Tamb. "And ride in triumph through Persepolis !"
Is it not brave to be a king, Techelles ?
Usumcasane and Theridamas,
Is it not passing brave to be a king,
"And ride in triumph through Persepolis ?"

   Tech. O, my lord, 'tis sweet and full of pomp.

Usum. To be a king is half to be a god.

Ther. A god is not so glorious as a king.
I think the pleasure they enjoy in Heaven,
Cannot compare with kingly joys in earth.—
To wear a crown enchased with pearl and gold,
Whose virtues carry with it life and death ;
To ask and have, command and be obeyed ;
When looks breed love, with looks to gain the prize,
Such power attractive shines in princes' eyes !

Tamb. Why say, Theridamas, wilt thou be a king?

Ther. Nay, though I praise it, I can live without it.

Tamb. What say my other friends? Will you be kings?

Tech. I, if I could, with all my heart, my lord.

Tamb. Why, that's well said, Techelles; so would I,
And so would you, my masters, would you not?

Usum. What then, my lord ?

Tamb. Why then, Casane, shall we wish for aught
The world affords in greatest novelty,
And rest attemptless, faint and destitute?
Methinks we should not : I am strongly moved,
That if I should desire the Persian crown,
I could attain it with a wondrous ease.
And would not all our soldiers soon consent,
If we should aim at such a dignity?

Ther. I know they would with our persuasions.

Tamb. Why then, Theridamas, I'll first assay
To get the Persian kingdom to myself ;
Then thou for Parthia ; they for Scythia and Media ;
And, if I prosper, all shall be as sure
As if the Turk, the Pope, Afric and Greece,
Came creeping to us with their crowns apace.

Tech. Then shall we send to this triumphing king,
And bid him battle for his novel crown?

Usum. Nay, quickly then, before his room be hot.

Tamb. 'Twill prove a pretty jest, in faith, my friends.

Ther. A jest to charge on twenty thousand men !
I judge the purchase[1] more important far.

Tamb. Judge by thyself, Theridamas, not me ;
For presently Techelles here shall haste
To bid him battle ere he pass too far,
And lose more labour than the game will quite.[2]
Then shalt thou see this Scythian Tamburlaine,
Make but a jest to win the Persian crown.
Techelles, take a thousand horse with thee,
And bid him turn him back to war with us,
That only made him king to make us sport.
We will not steal upon him cowardly,
But give him warning and more warriors.
Haste thee, Techelles, we will follow thee.

                              [*Exit* TECHELLES.

What saith Theridamas ?

   Ther. Go on for me.   [*Exeunt.*

SCENE VI.

Enter COSROE, MEANDER, ORTYGIUS, MENAPHON, *with*
Soldiers.

Cos. What means this devilish shepherd to aspire
With such a giantly presumption
To cast up hills against the face of Heaven,
And dare the force of angry Jupiter ?
But as he thrust them underneath the hills,
And pressed out fire from their burning jaws,
So will I send this monstrous slave to hell,
Where flames shall ever feed upon his soul.

---

   [1] Plunder or loot.   [2] Requite.

Mar.   D

Meand. Some powers divine, or else infernal, mixed
Their angry seeds at his conception ;
For he was never sprung of human race,
Since with the spirit of his fearful pride,
He dare so doubtlessly resolve of rule,
And by profession be ambitious.

Orty. What god, or fiend, or spirit of the earth,
Or monster turnèd to a manly shape,
Or of what mould or metle he be made,
What star or fate soever govern him,
Let us put on our meet encountering minds :
And in detesting such a devilish thief,
In love of honour and defence of right,
Be armed against the hate of such a foe,
Whether from earth, or hell, or Heaven, he grow.

Cos. Nobly resolved, my good Ortygius ;
And since we all have sucked one wholesome air,
And with the same proportion of elements
Resolve, I hope we are resembled
Vowing our loves to equal death and life.
Let's cheer our soldiers to encounter him,
That grievous image of ingratitude,
That fiery thirster after sovereignty.
And burn him in the fury of that flame,
That none can quench but blood and empery.
Resolve, my lords and loving soldiers, now
To save your king and country from decay.
Then strike up, drum ; and all the stars that make
The loathsome circle of my dated life,
Direct my weapon to his barbarous heart,
That thus opposeth him against the gods,
And scorns the powers that govern Persia !

        [*Exeunt ; drums and trumpets sounding.*

SCENE VII.

Alarms of battle within.   Enter COSROE, *wounded,* TAM-
BURLAINE, THERIDAMAS, TECHELLES, USUMCASANE,
with others.

   Cos. Barbarous and bloody Tamburlaine,
Thus to deprive me of my crown and life !
Treacherous and false Theridamas,
Even at the morning of my happy state,
Scarce being seated in my royal throne,
To work my downfall and untimely end !
An uncouth pain torments my grievèd soul,
And death arrests the organ of my voice,
Who, entering at the breach thy sword hath made,
Sacks every vein and artier[1] of my heart.—
Bloody and insatiate Tamburlaine !
   Tamb. The thirst of reign and sweetness of a crown
That caused the eldest son of heavenly Ops,
To thrust his doting father from his chair,
And place himself in the empyreal Heaven,
Moved me to manage arms against thy state.
What better precedent than mighty Jove ?
Nature that framed us of four elements,
Warring within our breasts for regiment,[2]
Doth teach us all to have aspiring minds :
Our souls, whose faculties can comprehend
The wondrous architecture of the world,
And measure every wandering planet's course,
Still climbing after knowledge infinite,
And always moving as the restless spheres,
Will us to wear ourselves, and never rest,
Until we reach the ripest fruit of all,

---

[1] Artery.   [2] Rule.

That perfect bliss and sole felicity,
The sweet fruition of an earthly crown.

Ther. And that made me to join with Tamburlaine :
For he is gross and like the massy earth,
That moves not upwards, nor by princely deeds
Doth mean to soar above the highest sort.

Tech. And that made us the friends of Tamburlaine,
To lift our swords against the Persian king.

Usum. For as when Jove did thrust old Saturn
down,
Neptune and Dis gained each of them a crown,
So do we hope to reign in Asia,
If Tamburlaine be placed in Persia.

Cos. The strangest men that ever nature made !
I know not how to take their tyrannies.
My bloodless body waxeth chill and cold,
And with my blood my life slides through my wound ;
My soul begins to take her flight to hell,
And summons all my senses to depart.—
The heat and moisture, which did feed each other,
For want of nourishment to feed them both,
Are dry and cold ; and now doth ghastly death,
With greedy talons gripe my bleeding heart,
And like a harpy tires[1] on my life.
Theridamas and Tamburlaine, I die :
And fearful vengeance light upon you both !

      [COSROE *dies.*—TAMBURLAINE *takes his crown
and puts it on.*

Tamb. Not all the curses which the Furies breathe,
Shall make me leave so rich a prize as this.
Theridamas, Techelles, and the rest,
Who think you now is King of Persia?

All. Tamburlaine ! Tamburlaine !

      [1] Preys. A term in falconry.

Tamb. Though Mars himself, the angry god of arms,
And all the earthly potentates conspire
To dispossess me of this diadem,
Yet will I wear it in despite of them,
As great commander of this eastern world,
If you but say that Tamburlaine shall reign.

   All. Long live Tamburlaine and reign in Asia!

   Tamb. So now it is more surer on my head,
Than if the gods had held a parliament,
And all pronounced me King of Persia.

[Exeunt.

ACT THE THIRD.

SCENE I.

Enter BAJAZETH, *the* KINGS *of* FEZ, MOROCCO, *and*
ARGIER,[1] *with others in great pomp.*

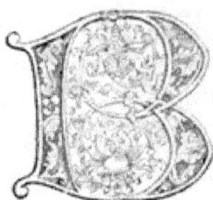

BAJ. Great Kings of Barbary and my
portly bassoes,[2]
We hear the Tartars and the eastern
thieves,
Under the conduct of one Tamburlaine,

Presume a bickering with your emperor,
And think to rouse us from our dreadful siege
Of the famous Grecian Constantinople.
You know our army is invincible ;
As many circumcisèd Turks we have,
And warlike bands of Christians renied,[3]
As hath the ocean or the Terrene sea[4]
Small drops of water when the moon begins
To join in one her semicircled horns.
Yet would we not be braved with foreign power,
Nor raise our siege before the Grecians yield,
Or breathless lie before the city walls.
    K. of Fez. Renownèd Emperor, and mighty general,

---

[1] Algiers.   [2] Bashaws or Pashas.
[3] Christians who have abjured their faith. Fr. *renier.*
[4] The Mediterranean.

What, if you sent the bassoes of your guard
To charge him to remain in Asia,
Or else to threaten death and deadly arms
As from the mouth of mighty Bajazeth.

 Baj. Hie thee, my basso, fast to Persia,
Tell him thy Lord, the Turkish Emperor,
Dread Lord of Afric, Europe, and Asia,
Great King and conqueror of Græcia,
The ocean, Terrene, and the Coal-black sea,[1]
The high and highest monarch of the world
Wills and commands (for say not I entreat),
Not once to set his foot on Africa,
Or spread his colours once in Græcia,
Lest he incur the fury of my wrath.
Tell him I am content to take a truce,
Because I hear he bears a valiant mind :
But if, presuming on his silly power,
He be so mad to manage arms with me,
Then stay thou with him ; say, I bid thee so :
And if, before the sun have measured Heaven
With triple circuit, thou regreet us not,
We mean to take his morning's next arise
For messenger he will not be reclaimed,
And mean to fetch thee in despite of him.

 Bas. Most great and puissant monarch of the earth,
Your basso will accomplish your behest,
And show your pleasure to the Persian,
As fits the legate of the stately Turk.　　　*[Exit.*

 K. of Arg. They say he is the King of Persia ;
But, if he dare attempt to stir your siege,
'Twere requisite he should be ten times more,
For all flesh quakes at your magnificence.

 Baj. True, Argier ; and trembles at my looks.

---

[1] The Black Sea.

K. of Mor. The spring is hindered by your smother-
  ing host,
For neither rain can fall upon the earth,
Nor sun reflex his virtuous beams thereon,
The ground is mantled with such multitudes.
 Baj. All this is true as holy Mahomet ;
And all the trees are blasted with our breaths.
 K. of Fez. What thinks your greatness best to be
  achieved
In pursuit of the city's overthrow ?
 Baj. I will the captive pioners of Argier
Cut off the water that by leaden pipes
Runs to the city from the mountain Carnon.
Two thousand horse shall forage up and down,
That no relief or succour come by land :
And all the sea my galleys countermand.
Then shall our footmen lie within the trench,
And with their cannons mouthed like Orcus' gulf,
Batter the walls, and we will enter in ;
And thus the Grecians shall be conquerèd. [*Exeunt.*

SCENE II.

Enter ZENOCRATE, AGYDAS, ANIPPE, *with others.*

 Agyd. Madam Zenocrate, may I presume
To know the cause of these unquiet fits,
That work such trouble to your wonted rest ?
'Tis more than pity such a heavenly face
Should by heart's sorrow wax so wan and pale,
When your offensive rape by Tamburlaine,
(Which of your whole displeasures should be most,)
Hath seemed to be digested long ago.

Zeno. Although it be digested long ago,
As his exceeding favours have deserved,
And might content the Queen of Heaven, as well
As it hath changed my first conceived disdain,
Yet since a farther passion feeds my thoughts
With ceaseless and disconsolate conceits,
Which dyes my looks so lifeless as they are,
And might, if my extremes had full events,
Make me the ghastly counterfeit of death.

Agyd. Eternal heaven sooner be dissolved,
And all that pierceth Phœbus' silver eye,
Before such hap fall to Zenocrate !

Zeno. Ah, life and soul, still hover in his breast
And leave my body senseless as the earth,
Or else unite you to his life and soul,
That I may live and die with Tamburlaine !

> *Enter, behind,* TAMBURLAINE, TECHELLES, *and others.*

Agyd. With Tamburlaine !   Ah, fair Zenocrate,
Let not a man so vile and barbarous,
That holds you from your father in despite,
And keeps you from the honours of a queen,
(Being supposed his worthless concubine,)
Be honoured with your love but for necessity.
So, now the mighty Soldan hears of you,
Your highness needs not doubt but in short time
He will with Tamburlaine's destruction
Redeem you from this deadly servitude.

Zeno. Agydas leave to wound me with these words,
And speak of Tamburlaine as he deserves.
The entertainment we have had of him
Is far from villany[1] or servitude,
And might in noble minds be counted princely.

----

[1] Subjection.

Agyd. How can you fancy one that looks so fierce,
Only disposed to martial stratagems?
Who, when he shall embrace you in his arms,
Will tell you how many thousand men he slew ;
And when you look for amorous discourse,
Will rattle forth his facts[1] of war and blood,
Too harsh a subject for your dainty ears.

Zeno. As looks the Sun through Nilus' flowing stream,
Or when the Morning holds him in her arms,
So looks my lordly love, fair Tamburlaine ;
His talk much sweeter than the Muses' song
They sung for honour 'gainst Pierides ;
Or when Minerva did with Neptune strive :
And higher would I rear my estimate
Than Juno, sister to the highest god,
If I were matched with mighty Tamburlaine.

Agyd. Yet be not so inconstant in your love ;
But let the young Arabian live in hope
After your rescue to enjoy his choice.
You see though first the King of Persia,
Being a shepherd, seemed to love you much,
Now in his majesty he leaves those looks,
Those words of favour, and those comfortings,
And gives no more than common courtesies.

Zeno. Thence rise the tears that so distain my cheeks
Fearing his love through my unworthiness.—

> [TAMBURLAINE *goes to her and takes her away*
> *lovingly by the hand, looking wrathfully on*
> AGYDAS. *Exeunt all but* AGYDAS.

Agyd. Betrayed by fortune and suspicious love,
Threatened with frowning wrath and jealousy,
Surprised with fear of hideous revenge,
I stand aghast ; but most astonièd[2]

---

[1] Deeds.   [2] Astonished. A common word with our early writers.

To see his choler shut in secret thoughts,
And wrapt in silence of his angry soul.
Upon his brows was pourtrayed ugly death ;
And in his eyes the furies of his heart
That shone as comets, menacing revenge,
And cast a pale complexion on his cheeks.
As when the seaman sees the Hyades
Gather an army of Cimmerian clouds,
(Auster and Aquilon with winged steeds,
All sweating, tilt about the watery Heavens,
With shivering spears enforcing thunder claps,
And from their shields strike flames of lightning.)
All-fearful folds his sails and sounds the main,
Lifting his prayers to the Heavens for aid
Against the terror of the winds and waves,
So fares Agydas for the late-felt frowns,
That sent a tempest to my daunted thoughts,
And make my soul divine her overthrow.

Re-enter TECHELLES *with a naked dagger, followed by*
USUMCASANE.

Tech. See you, Agydas, how the king salutes you ?
He bids you prophesy what it imports.

Agyd. I prophesied before, and now I prove
The killing frowns of jealousy and love.
He needed not with words confirm my fear,
For words are vain where working tools present
The naked action of my threatened end :
It says, Agydas, thou shalt surely die,
And of extremities elect the least ;
More honour and less pain it may procure
To die by this resolved hand of thine,
Than stay the torments he and Heaven have sworn.
Then haste, Agydas, and prevent the plagues

Which thy prolongèd fates may draw on thee.
Go, wander, free from fear of tyrant's rage,
Removèd from the torments and the hell,
Wherewith he may excruciate thy soul,
And let Agydas by Agydas die,
And with this stab slumber eternally.   [*Stabs hims lf.*

Tech. Usumcasane, see, how right the man
Hath hit the meaning of my lord, the king.

Usum. Faith, and Techelles, it was manly done ;
And since he was so wise and honourable,
Let us afford him now the bearing hence,
And crave his triple-worthy burial.

Tech. Agreed, Casane ; we will honour him.
                    [*Exeunt bearing out the body.*

SCENE III.

Enter TAMBURLAINE, TECHELLES, USUMCASANE, THERI-
DAMAS, *a* Basso, ZENOCRATE, ANIPPE, *with others.*

Tamb. Basso, by this thy lord and master knows
I mean to meet him in Bithynia :
See how he comes ! tush, Turks are full of brags,
And menace more than they can well perform.
He meet me in the field, and fetch thee hence !
Alas ! poor Turk ! his fortune is too weak
To encounter with the strength of Tamburlaine.
View well my camp, and speak indifferently ;
Do not my captains and my soldiers look
As if they meant to conquer Africa?

Bas. Your men are valiant, but their number few,
And cannot terrify his mighty host.

My lord, the great commander of the world,
Besides fifteen contributory kings,
Hath now in arms ten thousand Janissaries,
Mounted on lusty Mauritanian steeds,
Brought to the war by men of Tripoli ;
Two hundred thousand footmen that have served
In two set battles fought in Græcia ;
And for the expedition of this war,
If he think good, can from his garrisons
Withdraw as many more to follow him.

Tech. The more he brings the greater is the spoil, ✓
For when they perish by our warlike hands,
We mean to set our footmen on their steeds,
And rifle all those stately Janisars.

Tamb. But will those kings accompany your lord ?

Bas. Such as his highness please ; but some must stay
To rule the provinces he late subdued.

Tamb. [*To his* Officers.]   Then fight courageously :
     their crowns are yours ;
This hand shall set them on your conquering heads,
That made me Emperor of Asia.

Usum. Let him bring millions infinite of men,
Unpeopling Western Africa and Greece,
Yet we assure us of the victory.

Ther. Even he that in a trice vanquished two kings,
More mighty than the Turkish emperor,
Shall rouse him out of Europe, and pursue
His scattered army till they yield or die.

Tamb. Well said, Theridamas ; speak in that mood ;
For *will* and *shall* best fitteth Tamburlaine,
Whose smiling stars give him assurèd hope
.Of martial triumph ere he meet his foes.
I that am termed the scourge and wrath of God,
The only fear and terror of the world,

Will first subdue the Turk, and then enlarge
Those Christian captives, which you keep as slaves,
Burthening their bodies with your heavy chains,
And feeding them with thin and slender fare ;
That naked row about the Terrene sea,
And when they chance to rest or breathe a space,
Are punished with bastones[1] so grievously,
That they lie panting on the galley's side,
And strive for life at every stroke they give.
These are the cruel pirates of Argier,
That damnèd train, the scum of Africa,
Inhabited with straggling runagates,
That make quick havoc of the Christian blood ;
But as I live that town shall curse the time
That Tamburlaine set foot in Africa.

Enter BAJAZETH *with his* Bassoes, *the* KINGS *of* FEZ,
    MOROCCO, *and* ARGIER, ZABINA *and* EBEA.

  Baj. Bassoes and Janissaries of my guard,
Attend upon the person of your lord,
The greatest potentate of Africa.
  Tamb. Techelles, and the rest, prepare your swords ;
I mean to encounter with that Bajazeth.
  Baj. Kings of Fez, Moroccus, and Argier,
He calls me Bajazeth, whom you call lord !
Note the presumption of this Scythian slave !
I tell thee, villain, those that lead my horse,
Have to their names titles of dignity,
And dar'st thou bluntly call me Bajazeth ?
  Tamb. And know, thou Turk, that those which lead
    my horse,
Shall lead thee captive thorough Africa ;
And dar'st thou bluntly call me Tamburlaine ?

---

[1] Sticks. Ital. *bastone.*

Baj. By Mahomet my kinsman's sepulchre,
And by the holy Alcoran I swear,
He shall be made a chaste and lustless eunuch,
And in my sarell [1] tend my concubines ;
And all his captains that thus stoutly stand,
Shall draw the chariot of my emperess,
Whom I have brought to see their overthrow.

Tamb. By this my sword, that conquered Persia,
Thy fall shall make me famous through the world.
I will not tell thee how I'll handle thee,
But every common soldier of my camp
Shall smile to see thy miserable state.

K. of Fez. What means the mighty Turkish emperor,
To talk with one so base as Tamburlaine ?

K. of Mor. Ye Moors and valiant men of Barbary,
How can ye suffer these indignities ?

K. of Arg. Leave words, and let them feel your lances'
          points
Which glided through the bowels of the Greeks.

Baj. Well said, my stout contributory kings :
Your threefold army and my hugy [2] host
Shall swallow up these base-born Persians.

Tech. Puissant, renowned, and mighty Tamburlaine,
Why stay we thus prolonging of their lives ?

Ther. I long to see those crowns won by our swords,
That we may rule as kings of Africa.

Usum. What coward would not fight for such a prize ?

Tamb. Fight all courageously, and be you kings ;
I speak it, and my words are oracles.

Baj. Zabina, mother of three braver boys
Than Hercules, that in his infancy
Did pash [3] the jaws of serpents venomous ;
Whose hands are made to gripe a warlike lance,

---

[1] Seraglio. Fr. *serail*.   [2] Huge.   [3] Dash to pieces.

Their shoulders broad for complete armour fit,
Their limbs more large, and of a bigger size,
Than all the brats ysprung from Typhon's loins;
Who, when they come unto their father's age,
Will batter turrets with their manly fists ;—
Sit here upon this royal chair of state,
And on thy head wear my imperial crown,
Until I bring this sturdy Tamburlaine,
And all his captains bound in captive chains.

    Zab. Such good success happen to Bajazeth !

    Tamb. Zenocrate, the loveliest maid alive,
Fairer than rocks of pearl and precious stone,
The only paragon of Tamburlaine,
Whose eyes are brighter than the lamps of Heaven,
And speech more pleasant than sweet harmony !
That with thy looks canst clear the darkened sky,
And calm the rage of thundering Jupiter,
Sit down by her, adornèd with my crown,
As if thou wert the Empress of the world.
Stir not, Zenocrate, until thou see
Me march victoriously with all my men,
Triumphing over him and these his kings ;
Which I will bring as vassals to thy feet ;
Till then take thou my crown, vaunt of my worth,
And manage words with her, as we will arms.

    Zeno. And may my love the King of Persia,
Return with victory and free from wound !

    Baj. Now shalt thou feel the force of Turkish arms,
Which lately made all Europe quake for fear.
I have of Turks, Arabians, Moors, and Jews,
Enough to cover all Bithynia.
Let thousands die ; their slaughtered carcasses
Shall serve for walls and bulwarks to the rest
And as the heads of Hydra, so my power,

Subdued, shall stand as mighty as before.
If they should yield their necks unto the sword,
Thy soldiers' arms could not endure to strike
So many blows as I have heads for thee.
Thou know'st not, foolish, hardy Tamburlaine,
What 'tis to meet me in the open field,
That leave no ground for thee to march upon.

    Tamb. Our conquering swords shall marshal us the
       way
We use to march upon the slaughtered foe,
Trampling their bowels with our horses' hoofs ;
Brave horses bred on th' white Tartarian hills ;
My camp is like to Julius Cæsar's host,
That never fought but had the victory ;
Nor in Pharsalia was there such hot war,
As these, my followers, willingly would have.
Legions of spirits fleeting[1] in the air
Direct our bullets and our weapons' points,
And make your strokes to wound the senseless lure,[2]
And when she sees our bloody colours spread,
Then Victory begins to take her flight,
Resting herself upon my milk-white tent ?—
But come, my lords, to weapons let us fall ;
The field is ours, the Turk, his wife and all.

                   [*Exit with his followers.*

    Baj. Come, kings and bassoes, let us glut our swords,
That thirst to drink the feeble Persians' blood.

                   [*Exit with his followers.*

    Zab. Base concubine, must thou be placed by me,
That am the empress of the mighty Turk ?

---

[1] Floating.
[2] Here " lure " most probably means " light," (Fr. *lueur*) ; still
it may refer to a well-known term in falconry, signifying a decoy,
formed of leather and feathers. used to call the young hawks, and
which, when thrown into the air, had the appearance of a flying bird.

   Mar.   E

Zeno. Disdainful Turkess and unreverend boss![1]
Call'st thou me concubine, that am betrothed
Unto the great and mighty Tamburlaine?

   Zab. To Tamburlaine, the great Tartarian thief!

   Zeno. Thou wilt repent these lavish words of thine,
When thy great basso-master and thyself
Must plead for mercy at his kingly feet,
And sue to me to be your advocate.

   Zab. And sue to thee!—I tell thee, shameless girl,
Thou shalt be laundress to my waiting maid!
How lik'st thou her, Ebea?—Will she serve?

   Ebea. Madam, perhaps, she thinks she is too fine,
But I shall turn her into other weeds,
And make her dainty fingers fall to work.

   Zeno. Hear'st thou, Anippe, how thy drudge doth talk?
And how my slave, her mistress, menaceth?
Both for their sauciness shall be employed
To dress the common soldiers' meat and drink,
For we will scorn they should come near ourselves.

   Anip. Yet sometimes let your highness send for them
To do the work my chambermaid disdains.

                [_They sound to the battle within._

   Zeno. Ye gods and powers that govern Persia,
And made my lordly love her worthy king,
Now strengthen him against the Turkish Bajazeth,
And let his foes, like flocks of fearful roes
Pursued by hunters, fly his angry looks,
That I may see him issue conqueror!

   Zab. Now, Mahomet, solicit God himself,
And make him rain down murdering shot from Heaven
To dash the Scythians' brains, and strike them dead,
That dare to manage arms with him

---

[1] Cotgrave in his Dictionary has :—"A fat _bosse. Femme bien
grasse et grosse; une coche._"

That offered jewels to thy sacred shrine,
When first he warred against the Christians !

> [*They sound again to the battle within.*

Zeno. By this the Turks lie weltering in their blood,
And Tamburlaine is Lord of Africa.

Zab. Thou art deceived.—I heard the trumpets sound,
As when my emperor overthrew the Greeks,
And led them captive into Africa.
Straight will I use thee as thy pride deserves—
Prepare thyself to live and die my slave.

Zeno. If Mahomet should come from Heaven and
swear
My royal lord is slain or conquerèd,
Yet should he not persuade me otherwise
But that he lives and will be conqueror.

Re-enter BAJAZETH, *pursued by* TAMBURLAINE; *they fight,
and* BAJAZETH *is overcome.*

Tamb. Now, king of bassoes, who is conqueror?
Baj. Thou, by the fortune of this damnèd foil.[1]
Tamb. Where are your stout contributory kings?

Re-enter TECHELLES, THERIDAMAS, *and* USUMCASANE.

Tech. We have their crowns—their bodies strow the
field.
Tamb. Each man a crown!—Why kingly fought i' faith.
Deliver them into my treasury.

Zeno. Now let me offer to my gracious lord
His royal crown again so highly won.

Tamb. Nay, take the crown from her, Zenocrate,
And crown me Emperor of Africa.

Zab. No, Tamburlaine : though now thou gat the best,
Thou shalt not yet be lord of Africa.

---

[1] Defeat.

Ther. Give her the crown, Turkess: you were best.
[*He takes it from her.*

Zab. Injurious villains!—thieves!—runagates!
How dare you thus abuse my majesty?

Ther. Here, madam, you are Empress; she is none.
[*Gives it to* ZENOCRATE.

Tamb. Not now, Theridamas; her time is past.
The pillars that have bolstered up those terms,
Are fallen in clusters at my conquering feet.

Zab. Though he be prisoner, he may be ransomed.

Tamb. Not all the world shall ransom Bajazeth.

Baj. Ah, fair Zabina! we have lost the field;
And never had the Turkish emperor
So great a foil by any foreign foe.
Now will the Christian miscreants be glad,
Ringing with joy their superstitious bells,
And making bonfires for my overthrow.
But, ere I die, those foul idolaters
Shall make me bonfires with their filthy bones.
For though the glory of this day be lost,
Afric and Greece have garrisons enough
To make me sovereign of the earth again.

Tamb. Those wallèd garrisons will I subdue,
And write myself great lord of Africa.
So from the East unto the furthest West
Shall Tamburlaine extend his puissant arm.
The galleys and those pilling[1] brigandines,
That yearly sail to the Venetian gulf,
And hover in the Straits for Christians' wreck,
Shall lie at anchor in the isle Asant,[2]
Until the Persian fleet and men of war,
Sailing along the oriental sea,
Have fetched about the Indian continent,

---

[1] Plundering.   [2] Zante.—*Bullen.*

Even from Persepolis to Mexico,
And thence unto the straits of Jubalter ;[1]
Where they shall meet and join their force in one
Keeping in awe the bay of Portingale,[2]
And all the ocean by the British shore ;
And by this means I'll win the world at last.

   Baj. Yet set a ransom on me, Tamburlaine.

   Tamb. What, think'st thou Tamburlaine esteems thy
      gold?

I'll make the kings of India, ere I die,
Offer their mines to sue for peace to me,
And dig for treasure to appease my wrath.
Come, bind them both, and one lead in the Turk ;
The Turkess let my love's maid lead away.

                  [*They bind them.*

   Baj. Ah, villains !—dare you touch my sacred arms ?
O Mahomet !—O sleepy Mahomet !

   Zab. O cursèd Mahomet, that makes us thus
The slaves to Scythians rude and barbarous !

   Tamb. Come, bring them in ; and for this happy
      conquest,

Triumph and solemnise a martial feast.   [*Exeunt.*

   [1] Gibraltar.   [2] Biscay.

ACT THE FOURTH.

SCENE I.

Enter the SOLDAN *of* EGYPT, CAPOLIN, Lords, *and a*
Messenger.

OLD. Awake, ye men of Memphis !—
    hear the clang
    Of Scythian trumpets !— hear the
    basilisks.[1]
    That, roaring, shake Damascus' turrets
    down !
The rogue of Volga holds Zenocrate.
The Soldan's daughter, for his concubine,
And with a troop of thieves and vagabonds,
Hath spread his colours to our high disgrace,
While you, faint-hearted, base Egyptians.
Lie slumbering on the flowery banks of Nile,
As crocodiles that unaffrighted rest,
While thundering cannons rattle on their skins.
  Mess. Nay, mighty Soldan, did your greatness see
The frowning looks of fiery Tamburlaine,
That with his terror and imperious eyes,
Commands the hearts of his associates,
It might amaze your royal majesty.
  Sold. Villain, I tell thee, were that Tamburlaine

---

[1] Pieces of ordnance, so called from their fancied resemblance to
the fabulous serpent of that name.—*Cunningham.*

As monstrous as Gorgon [1] prince of hell.
The Soldan would not start a foot from him.
But speak, what power hath he ?

  Mess.   Mighty lord,
Three hundred thousand men in armour clad,
Upon their prancing steeds disdainfully,
With wanton paces trampling on the ground :
Five hundred thousand footmen threatening shot,
Shaking their swords, their spears, and iron bills,
Environing their standard round, that stood
As bristle-pointed as a thorny wood :
Their warlike engines and munition
Exceed the forces of their martial men.

  Sold. Nay, could their numbers countervail the stars,
Or ever-drizzling drops of April showers,
Or withered leaves that Autumn shaketh down,
Yet would the Soldan by his conquering power
So scatter and consume them in his rage,
That not a man should live to rue their fall.

  Capo. So might your highness, had you time to sort
Your fighting men, and raise your royal host ;
But Tamburlaine, by expedition,
Advantage takes of your unreadiness.

  Sold. Let him take all the advantages he can.
Were all the world conspired to fight for him,
Nay, were he devil, as he is no man,
Yet in revenge of fair Zenocrate,
Whom he detaineth in despite of us,
This arm should send him down to Erebus,
To shroud his shame in darkness of the night.

  Mess. Pleaseth your mightiness to understand,
His resolution far exceedeth all,
The first day when he pitcheth down his tents,

- - - - - - - - - -

[1] *i.e.* Demogorgon.

White is their hue, and on his silver crest,
A snowy feather spangled white he bears,
To signify the mildness of his mind,
That, satiate with spoil, refuseth blood.
But when Aurora mounts the second time
As red as scarlet is his furniture ;
Then must his kindled wrath be quenched with blood,
Not sparing any that can manage arms ;
But if these threats move not submission,
Black are his colours, black pavilion ;
His spear, his shield, his horse, his armour, plumes,
And jetty feathers, menace death and hell !
Without respect of sex, degree, or age,
He razeth all his foes with fire and sword.

   Sola. Merciless villain !—peasant, ignorant
Of lawful arms or martial discipline !
Pillage and murder are his usual trades.
The slave usurps the glorious name of war.
See, Capolin, the fair Arabian king,
That hath been disappointed by this slave
Of my fair daughter, and his princely love,
May have fresh warning to go war with us,
And be revenged for her disparagement.   [*Exeunt.*

SCENE II.

Enter TAMBURLAINE, TECHELLES, THERIDAMAS, USUM-
   CASANE, ZENOCRATE, ANIPPE, *two* Moors *drawing*
   BAJAZETH *in a cage, and* ZABINA *following him.*

   Tamb. Bring out my footstool.

               [BAJAZETH *is taken out of the cage.*
   Baj. Ye holy priests of heavenly Mahomet,

That, sacrificing, slice and cut your flesh,
Staining his altars with your purple blood;
Make Heaven to frown and every fixèd star
To suck up poison from the moorish fens,
And pour it in this glorious [1] tyrant's throat!

    Tamb. The chiefest God, first mover of that sphere,
Enchased with thousands ever-shining lamps.
Will sooner burn the glorious frame of Heaven,
Than it should so conspire my overthrow.
But, villain! thou that wishest this to me,
Fall prostrate on the low disdainful earth,
And be the footstool of great Tamburlaine,
That I may rise into my royal throne.

    Baj. First shalt thou rip my bowels with thy sword,
And sacrifice my soul to death and hell,
Before I yield to such a slavery.

    Tamb. Base villain, vassal, slave to Tamburlaine!
Unworthy to embrace or touch the ground,
That bears the honour of my royal weight:
Stoop, villain, stoop!—Stoop! for so he bids
That may command thee piecemeal to be torn,
Or scattered like the lofty cedar trees
Struck with the voice of thundering Jupiter.

    Baj. Then, as I look down to the damnèd fiends,
Fiends look on me! and thou, dread god of hell,
With ebon sceptre strike this hateful earth,
And make it swallow both of us at once!

        [TAMBURLAINE *steps upon him to mount his throne.*

    Tamb. Now clear the triple region of the air,
And let the majesty of Heaven behold
Their scourge and terror tread on emperors.
Smile stars, that reigned at my nativity,
And dim the brightness of your neighbour lamps!

---

[1] Boastful.

Disdain to borrow light of Cynthia !
For I, the chiefest lamp of all the earth,
First rising in the East with mild aspect,
But fixèd now in the meridian line,
Will send up fire to your turning spheres,
And cause the sun to borrow light of you.
My sword struck fire from his coat of steel,
Even in Bithynia, when I took this Turk ;
As when a fiery exhalation,
Wrapt in the bowels of a freezing cloud
Fighting for passage, makes the welkin crack,
And casts a flash of lightning to the earth :
But ere I march to wealthy Persia,
Or leave Damascus and the Egyptian fields,
As was the fame of Clymene's brain-sick son,
That almost brent the axle-tree of Heaven,
So shall our swords, our lances, and our shot
Fill all the air with fiery meteors :
Then when the sky shall wax as red as blood
It shall be said I made it red myself,
To make me think of nought but blood and war.

   Zab. Unworthy king, that by thy cruelty
Unlawfully usurp'st the Persian seat,
Dar'st thou that never saw an emperor,
Before thou met my husband in the field,
Being thy captive, thus abuse his state,
Keeping his kingly body in a cage,
That roofs of gold and sun-bright palaces
Should have prepared to entertain his grace ?
And treading him beneath thy loathsome feet,
Whose feet the kings of Africa have kissed.

   Tech. You must devise some torment worse, my lord,
To make these captives rein their lavish tongues.

   Tamb. Zenocrate, look better to your slave.

Zeno. She is my handmaid's slave. and she shall look
That these abuses flow not from her tongue :
Chide her, Anippe.

Anip. Let these be warnings for you then, my slave,
How you abuse the person of the king :
Or else I swear to have you whipt, stark-naked.

Baj. Great Tamburlaine, great in my overthrow,
Ambitious pride shall make thee fall as low,
For treading on the back of Bajazeth,
That should be horsèd on four mighty kings.

Tamb. Thy names, and titles, and thy dignities
Are fled from Bajazeth and remain with me,
That will maintain it 'gainst a world of kings.
Put him in again.   [*They put him back into the cage.*

Baj. Is this a place for mighty Bajazeth?
Confusion light on him that helps thee thus !

Tamb. There, whiles he lives, shall Bajazeth be kept ;
And, where I go, be thus in triumph drawn ;
And thou, his wife. shalt feed him with the scraps
My servitors shall bring thee from my board ;
For he that gives him other food than this,
Shall sit by him and starve to death himself ;
This is my mind and I will have it so.
Not all the kings and emperors of the earth,
If they would lay their crowns before my feet,
Shall ransom him, or take him from his cage.
The ages that shall talk of Tamburlaine,
Even from this day to Plato's wondrous year,[1]
Shall talk how I have handled Bajazeth ;
These Moors, that drew him from Bithynia,
To fair Damascus, where we now remain,
Shall lead him with us wheresoe'er we go.
Techelles, and my loving followers,

---

[1] See Plato's *Timæus.*

Now may we see Damascus' lofty towers,
Like to the shadows of Pyramides,
That with their beauties grace the Memphian fields :
The golden statue of their feathered bird
That spreads her wings upon the city's walls
Shall not defend it from our battering shot :
The townsmen mask in silk and cloth of gold,
And every house is as a treasury :
The men, the treasure, and the town is ours.

Ther. Your tents of white now pitched before the gates,
And gentle flags of amity displayed,
I doubt not but the governor will yield,
Offering Damascus to your majesty.

Tamb. So shall he have his life and all the rest :
But if he stay until the bloody flag
Be once advanced on my vermilion tent,
He dies, and those that kept us out so long.
And when they see us march in black array,
With mournful streamers hanging down their heads,
Were in that city all the world contained,
Not one should 'scape, but perish by our swords.

Zeno. Yet would you have some pity for my sake,
Because it is my country, and my father's.

Tamb. Not for the world, Zenocrate ; I've sworn.
Come ; bring in the Turk.   [*Exeunt.*

SCENE III.

Enter the SOLDAN, *the* KING *of* ARABIA, CAPOLIN, *and*
Soldiers *with colours flying.*

Sold. Methinks we march as Meleager did,
Environèd with brave Argolian knights,

To chase the savage Calydonian boar,
Or Cephalus with lusty Theban youths
Against the wolf that angry Themis sent
To waste and spoil the sweet Aonian fields,
A monster of five hundred thousand heads,
Compact of rapine, piracy, and spoil.
The scum of men, the hate and scourge of God,
Raves in Ægyptia and annoyeth us.
My lord, it is the bloody Tamburlaine,
A sturdy felon and a base-bred thief,
By murder raisèd to the Persian crown,
That dares control us in our territories.
To tame the pride of this presumptuous beast,
Join your Arabians with the Soldan's power,
Let us unite our royal bands in one,
And hasten to remove Damascus' siege.
It is a blemish to the majesty
And high estate of mighty emperors,
That such a base usurping vagabond
Should brave a king, or wear a princely crown.
    K. of Arab. Renownèd Soldan, have you lately heard
The overthrow of mighty Bajazeth
About the confines of Bithynia?
The slavery wherewith he persecutes
The noble Turk and his great emperess?
    Sold. I have, and sorrow for his bad success;
But noble lord of great Arabia,
Be so persuaded that the Soldan is
No more dismayed with tidings of his fall,
Than in the haven when the pilot stands,
And views a stranger's ship rent in the winds,
And shiverèd against a craggy rock;
Yet in compassion to his wretched state,
A sacred vow to Heaven and him I make,

Confirming it with Ibis' holy name.
That Tamburlaine shall rue the day, the hour,
Wherein he wrought such ignominious wrong
Unto the hallowed person of a prince,
Or kept the fair Zenocrate so long
As concubine, I fear, to feed his lust.

 K. of Arab. Let grief and fury hasten on revenge ;
Let Tamburlaine for his offences feel
Such plagues as we and Heaven can pour on him.
I long to break my spear upon his crest,
And prove the weight of his victorious arm ;
For Fame, I fear, hath been too prodigal
In sounding through the world his partial praise.

 Sold. Capolin, hast thou surveyed our powers ?

 Capol. Great Emperors of Egypt and Arabia,
The number of your hosts united is
A hundred and fifty thousand horse ;
Two hundred thousand foot, brave men-at-arms,
Courageous, and full of hardiness.
As frolic as the hunters in the chase
Of savage beasts amid the desert woods.

 K. of Arab. My mind presageth fortunate success ;
And Tamburlaine, my spirit doth foresee
The utter ruin of thy men and thee.

 Sold. Then rear your standards ; let your sounding
   drums
Direct our soldiers to Damascus' walls.
Now, Tamburlaine, the mighty Soldan comes,
And leads with him the great Arabian king,
To dim thy baseness and obscurity,
Famous for nothing but for theft and spoil ;
To raze and scatter thy inglorious crew
Of Scythians and slavish Persians.   [*Exeunt.*

SCENE IV.

A Banquet set out; to it come TAMBURLAINE, *all in scarlet*
ZENOCRATE, THERIDAMAS, TECHELLES, USUMCA-
SANE, BAJAZETH *in his cage,* ZABINA, *and others.*

Tamb. Now hang our bloody colours by Damascus,
Reflexing hues of blood upon their heads,
While they walk quivering on their city walls,
Half dead for fear before they feel my wrath,
Then let us freely banquet and carouse
Full bowls of wine unto the god of war
That means to fill your helmets full of gold,
And make Damascus spoils as rich to you,
As was to Jason Colchos' golden fleece.—
And now, Bajazeth, hast thou any stomach?

Baj. Ay, such a stomach, cruel Tamburlaine, as I
could willingly feed upon thy blood-raw heart.

Tamb. Nay thine own is easier to come by; pluck
out that: and 'twill serve thee and thy wife: Well, Zenocrate, Techelles, and the rest, fall to your victuals.

Baj. Fall to, and never may your meat digest!
Ye Furies, that can mask invisible,
Dive to the bottom of Avernus' pool,
And in your hands bring hellish poison up
And squeeze it in the cup of Tamburlaine!
Or, wingèd snakes of Lerna, cast your stings,
And leave your venoms in this tyrant's dish!

Zab. And may this banquet prove as ominous
As Progne's[1] to the adulterous Thracian king,
That fed upon the substance of his child.

Zeno. My lord, how can you tamely suffer these
Outrageous curses by these slaves of yours?

---

[1] *i.e.* Procne.

Tamb. To let them see, divine Zenocrate,
I glory in the curses of my foes,
Having the power from the imperial Heaven
To turn them all upon their proper heads.

Tech. I pray you give them leave, madam; this speech
is a goodly refreshing to them.

Ther. But if his highness would let them be fed, it
would do them more good.

Tamb. Sirrah, why fall you not to?—are you so daintily
brought up, you cannot eat your own flesh?

Baj. First, legions of devils shall tear thee in pieces.

Usum. Villain, know'st thou to whom thou speakest?

Tamb. O, let him alone. Here; eat, sir; take it from
my sword's point, or I'll thrust it to thy heart.

[BAJAZETH *takes it and stamps upon it.*

Ther. He stamps it under his feet, my lord.

Tamb. Take it up, villain, and eat it; or I will make
thee slice the brawns of thy arms into carbonadoes[1] and
eat them.

Usum. Nay, 'twere better he killed his wife, and then
she shall be sure not to be starved, and he be provided
for a month's victual beforehand.

Tamb. Here is my dagger: despatch her while she is
fat, for if she live but a while longer, she will fall into a
consumption with fretting, and then she will not be worth
the eating.

Ther. Dost thou think that Mahomet will suffer this?

Tech. 'Tis like he will when he cannot let[2] it.

Tamb. Go to; fall to your meat.—What, not a bit!
Belike he hath not been watered to day; give him some
drink. .

[*They give* BAJAZETH *water to drink, and he flings
it upon the ground.*

---

[1] Rashers.   [2] Hinder.

Tamb. Fast, and welcome, sir, while[1] hunger make
you eat.   How now, Zenocrate, do not the Turk and his
wife make a goodly show at a banquet?

Zeno. Yes, my lord.

Ther. Methinks, 'tis a great deal better than a consort[2]
of music.

Tamb. Yet music would do well to cheer up Zenocrate.
Pray thee, tell, why thou art so sad? – If thou wilt have a
song, the Turk shall strain his voice.   But why is it?

Zeno. My lord, to see my father's town besieged,
The country wasted where myself was born,
How can it but afflict my very soul?
If any love remain in you, my lord,
Or if my love unto your majesty
May merit favour at your highness' hands,
Then raise your siege from fair Damascus' walls,
And with my father take a friendly truce.

Tamb. Zenocrate, were Egypt Jove's own land,
Yet would I with my sword make Jove to stoop.
I will confute those blind geographers
That make a triple region in the world,
Excluding regions which I mean to trace,
And with this pen[3] reduce them to a map,
Calling the provinces cities and towns,
After my name and thine, Zenocrate.
Here at Damascus will I make the point
That shall begin the perpendicular;
And would'st thou have me buy thy father's love
With such a loss?—Tell me, Zenocrate.

Zeno. Honour still wait on happy Tamburlaine;
Yet give me leave to plead for him my lord.

Tamb. Content thyself: his person shall be safe

---

[1] Until.   [2] Band.   [3] Meaning his sword.

Mar.   F

And all the friends of fair Zenocrate,
If with their lives they may be pleased to yield,
Or may be forced to make me Emperor;
For Egypt and Arabia must be mine.—
Feed, you slave; thou may'st think thyself happy to be
fed from my trencher.

Baj. My empty stomach, full of idle heat,
Draws bloody humours from my feeble parts,
Preserving life by hastening cruel death.
My veins are pale; my sinews hard and dry;
My joints benumbed; unless I eat, I die.

Zab. Eat, Bajazeth: and let us live
In spite of them,—looking some happy power
Will pity and enlarge us.

Tamb. Here, Turk; wilt thou have a clean trencher?

Baj. Ay, tyrant, and more meat.

Tamb. Soft, sir; you must be dieted; too much eating will make you surfeit.

Ther. So it would, my lord, 'specially having so small a walk and so little exercise.

[*A second course of crowns is brought in.*

Tamb. Theridamas, Techelles, and Casane, here are the cates you desire to finger, are they not?

Ther. Ay, my lord: but none save kings must feed with these.

Tech. 'Tis enough for us to see them, and for Tamburlaine only to enjoy them.

Tamb. Well; here is now to the Soldan of Egypt, the King of Arabia, and the Governor of Damascus. Now take these three crowns, and pledge me, my contributory kings.—I crown you here, Theridamas, King of Argier; Techelles, King of Fez; and Usumcasane, King of Moroccus. How say you to this, Turk? These are not your contributory kings.

Baj. Nor shall they long be thine, I warrant them.

Tamb. Kings of Argier, Moroccus, and of Fez,
You that have marched with happy Tamburlaine
As far as from the frozen plage[1] of Heaven,
Unto the watery morning's ruddy bower,
And thence by land unto the torrid zone,
Deserve these titles I endow you with,
By valour and by magnanimity.
Your births shall be no blemish to your fame,
For virtue is the fount whence honour springs,
And they are worthy she investeth kings.

Ther. And since your highness hath so well vouch-
    safed ;
If we deserve them not with higher meeds
Than erst our states and actions have retained
Take them away again and make us slaves.

Tamb. Well said, Theridamas ; when holy fates
Shall 'stablish me in strong Ægyptia,
We mean to travel to the antarctic pole,
Conquering the people underneath our feet,
And be renowned as never emperors were.
Zenocrate, I will not crown thee yet,
Until with greater honours I be graced.   [*Exeunt.*

---

[1] Shore : Fr. *Plage*.

ACT THE FIFTH.

SCENE I.

Enter the GOVERNOR *of* DAMASCUS, *with several* Citizens,
and four Virgins, *having branches of laurel in their
hands.*

GOV. Still doth this man, or rather god
 of war,
 Batter our walls and beat our turrets
 down ;
 And to resist with longer stubborn-
 ness

Or hope of rescue from the Soldan's power,
Were but to bring our wilful overthrow,
And make us desperate of our threatened lives.
We see his tents have now been altered
With terrors to the last and cruellest hue.
His coal-black colours everywhere advanced,
Threaten our city with a general spoil ;
And if we should with common rites of arms
Offer our safeties to his clemency,
I fear the custom, proper to his sword,
Which he observes as parcel of his fame,
Intending so to terrify the world,
By any innovation or remorse
Will never be dispensed with till our deaths ;

Therefore, for these our harmless virgins' sakes,
Whose honours and whose lives rely on him,
Let us have hope that their unspotted prayers,
Their blubbered[1] cheeks, and hearty, humble moans,
Will melt his fury into some remorse,[2]
And use us like a loving conqueror.

 1st Virg. If humble suits or imprecations,[3]
(Uttered with tears of wretchedness and blood
Shed from the heads and hearts of all our sex,
Some made your wives and some your children)
Might have entreated your obdurate breasts
To entertain some care of our securities
Whiles only danger beat upon our walls.
These more than dangerous warrants of our death
Had never been erected as they be,
Nor you depend on such weak helps as we.

 Gov. Well, lovely virgins, think our country's care,
Our love of honour, loath to be inthralled
To foreign powers and rough imperious yokes,
Would not with too much cowardice or fear,
(Before all hope of rescue were denied)
Submit yourselves and us to servitude.
Therefore in that your safeties and our own,
Your honours, liberties, and lives were weighed
In equal care and balance with our own,
Endure as we the malice of our stars,
The wrath of Tamburlaine and power of wars ;
Or be the means the overweighing heavens
Have kept to qualify these hot extremes,
And bring us pardon in your cheerful looks.

 2nd Virg. Then here before the majesty of Heaven
And holy patrons of Ægyptia,

---

[1] The word formerly conveyed no kind of ludicrous impression.
[2] Pity.   [3] Prayers.

With knees and hearts submissive we entreat
Grace to our words and pity to our looks
That this device may prove propitious,
And through the eyes and ears of Tamburlaine
Convey events of mercy to his heart;
Grant that these signs of victory we yield
May bind the temples of his conquering head,
To hide the folded furrows of his brows,
And shadow his displeasèd countenance
With happy looks of ruth and lenity.
Leave us, my lord, and loving countrymen;
What simple virgins may persuade, we will.

    Gov. Farewell, sweet virgins, on whose safe return
Depends our city, liberty, and lives.

     [*Exeunt* GOVERNOR *and* Citizens; *the* Virgins *remain.*

Enter TAMBURLAINE, *all in black and very melancholy,*
  TECHELLES, THERIDAMAS, USUMCASANE, *with others.*

    Tamb. What, are the turtles frayed out of their nests?
Alas, poor fools! must you be first shall feel
The sworn destruction of Damascus?
They knew my custom; could they not as well
Have sent ye out, when first my milk-white flags,
Through which sweet Mercy threw her gentle beams,
Reflexing them on your disdainful eyes,
As now, when fury and incensèd hate
Flings slaughtering terror from my coal-black tents,
And tells for truth submission comes too late?

    1st Virg. Most happy King and Emperor of the
       earth,
Image of honour and nobility,
For whom the powers divine have made the world,
And on whose throne the holy Graces sit;
In whose sweet person is comprised the sum

Of Nature's skill and heavenly majesty ;
Pity our plights !　O pity poor Damascus !
Pity old age, within whose silver hairs
Honour and reverence evermore have reigned !
Pity the marriage bed, where many a lord,
In prime and glory of his loving joy,
Embraceth now with tears of ruth and blood
The jealous body of his fearful wife,
Whose cheeks and hearts so punished with conceit,
To think thy puissant, never-stayèd arm,
Will part their bodies, and prevent their souls
From heavens of comfort yet their age might bear,
Now wax all pale and withered to the death,
As well for grief our ruthless governor
Hath thus refused the mercy of thy hand,
(Whose sceptre angels kiss and furies dread,)
As for their liberties, their loves, or lives !
O then for these, and such as we ourselves,
For us, our infants, and for all our bloods,
That never nourished thought against thy rule,
Pity, O pity, sacred Emperor,
The prostrate service of this wretched town,
And take in sign thereof this gilded wreath ;
Whereto each man of rule hath given his hand,
And wished, as worthy subjects, happy means
To be investers of thy royal brows
Even with the true Egyptian diadem !

 Tamb. Virgins, in vain you labour to prevent
That which mine honour swears shall be performed.
Behold my sword ! what see you at the point ?

  1st Virg. Nothing but fear, and fatal steel, my lord.

  Tamb. Your fearful minds are thick and misty then ;
For there sits Death ; there sits imperious Death
Keeping his circuit by the slicing edge.

But I am pleased you shall not see him there ;
He now is seated on my horsemen's spears,
And on their points his fleshless body feeds.
Techelles, straight go charge a few of them
To charge these dames, and show my servant, Death,
Sitting in scarlet on their armèd spears.

    Virgins. O pity us !

    Tamb. Away with them, I say, and show them Death.

             [*The* Virgins *are taken out.*

I will not spare these proud Egyptians,
Nor change my martial observations
For all the wealth of Gihon's golden waves,
Or for the love of Venus, would she leave
The angry god of arms and lie with me.
They have refused the offer of their lives,
And know my customs are as peremptory
As wrathful planets, death, or destiny.

          Re-enter TECHELLES.

What, have your horsemen shown the virgins Death ?

    Tech. They have, my lord, and on Damascus' walls
Have hoisted up their slaughtered carcases.

    Tamb. A sight as baneful to their souls, I think,
As are Thessalian drugs or mithridate : [1]
But go, my lords, put the rest to the sword.

        [*Exeunt all except* TAMBURLAINE.

Ah, fair Zenocrate !—divine Zenocrate !—
Fair is too foul an epithet for thee,
That in thy passion[2] for thy country's love,
And fear to see thy kingly father's harm,
With hair dishevelled wip'st thy watery cheeks ;
And, like to Flora in her morning pride,

---

[1] An antidote distilled from poisons.—*Bullen.*   [2] Sorrow.

Shaking her silver tresses in the air,
Rain'st on the earth resolvèd pearl in showers,
And sprinklest sapphires on thy shining face,
Where Beauty, mother to the Muses, sits
And comments volumes with her ivory pen,
Taking instructions from thy flowing eyes;
Eyes that, when Ebena steps to Heaven,
In silence of thy solemn evening's walk,
Make, in the mantle of the richest night,
The moon, the planets, and the meteors, light;
There angels in their crystal armours fight
A doubtful battle with my tempted thoughts
For Egypt's freedom, and the Soldan's life :
His life that so consumes Zenocrate,
Whose sorrows lay more siege unto my soul,
Than all my army to Damascus' walls :
And neither Persia's sovereign, nor the Turk
Troubled my senses with conceit of foil
So much by much as doth Zenocrate.
What is beauty, saith my sufferings, then ?
If all the pens that ever poets held
Had fed the feeling of their masters' thoughts,
And every sweetness that inspired their hearts,
Their minds, and muses on admirèd themes ;
If all the heavenly quintessence they still²
From their immortal flowers of poesy,
Wherein, as in a mirror, we perceive
The highest reaches of a human wit ;

---

¹ Swinburne has written of the lines which follow the above : " In the most glorious verses ever fashioned by a poet to express with subtle and final truth the supreme aim and the supreme limit of his art, Marlowe has summed up all that can be said or thought on the office and the object, the means and the end, of this highest form of spiritual ambition."

² *i.e.*, Distil.

If these had made one poem's period,
And all combined in beauty's worthiness,
Yet should there hover in their restless heads
One thought, one grace, one wonder, at the least,
Which into words no virtue can digest.
But how unseemly is it for my sex,
My discipline of arms and chivalry,
My nature, and the terror of my name,
To harbour thoughts effeminate and faint !
Save only that in beauty's just applause,
With whose instinct the soul of man is touched ;
And every warrior that is wrapt with love
Of fame, of valour, and of victory,
Must needs have beauty beat on his conceits :
I thus conceiving and subduing both
That which hath stooped the chiefest of the gods,
Even from the fiery-spangled veil of Heaven,
To feel the lowly warmth of shepherds' flames,
And mask in cottages of strowèd reeds,
Shall give the world to note for all my birth,
That virtue solely is the sum of glory,
And fashions men with true nobility.—
Who's within there ?

Enter Attendants.

Hath Bajazeth been fed to-day ?
    Atten. Ay, my lord.
    Tamb. Bring him forth ; and let us know if the town
be ransacked.   [*Exeunt* Attendants.

Enter TECHELLES, THERIDAMAS, USUMCASANE, *and others*

    Tech. The town is ours, my lord, and fresh supply
Of conquest and of spoil is offered us.
    Tamb. That's well, Techelles ; what's the news ?

Tech. The Soldan and the Arabian king together,
March on us with such eager violence,
As if there were no way but one with us.[1]

    Tamb. No more there is not, I warrant thee, Techelles.

    Attendants *bring in* BAJAZETH *in his cage, followed
by* ZABINA; *then exeunt.*

    Ther. We know the victory is ours, my lord;
But let us save the reverend Soldan's life,
For fair Zenocrate that so laments his state.

    Tamb. That will we chiefly see unto, Theridamas,
For sweet Zenocrate, whose worthiness
Deserves a conquest over every heart.
And now, my footstool, if I lose the field,
You hope of liberty and restitution?
Here let him stay, my masters, from the tents,
Till we have made us ready for the field.
Pray for us, Bajazeth; we are going.

        [*Exeunt* TAMBURLAINE, TECHELLES, USUM-
           CASANE, *and* Persians.

    Baj. Go, never to return with victory.
Millions of men encompass thee about,
And gore thy body with as many wounds!
Sharp, forkèd arrows light upon thy horse!
Furies from the black Cocytus lake,
Break up the earth, and with their firebrands
Enforce thee run upon the baneful pikes!
Volleys of shot pierce through thy charmèd skin,
And every bullet dipt in poisoned drugs!
Or, roaring cannons sever all thy joints,
Making thee mount as high as eagles soar!

    Zab. Let all the swords and lances in the field
Stick in his breast as in their proper rooms!

---

[1] *i.e.* As if we must lose our lives.

At every pore let blood come dropping forth,
That lingering pains may massacre his heart,
And madness send his damnèd soul to hell !

Baj. Ah, fair Zabina ! we may curse his power ;
The heavens may frown, the earth for anger quake :
But such a star hath influence on his sword,
As rules the skies and countermands the gods
More than Cimmerian Styx or destiny ;
And then shall we in this detested guise,
With shame, with hunger, and with horror stay,
Griping our bowels with retorquèd[1] thoughts,
And have no hope to end our ecstasies.

Zab. Then is there left no Mahomet, no God,
No fiend, no fortune, nor no hope of end
To our infamous monstrous slaveries.
Gape earth, and let the fiends infernal view
A hell as hopeless and as full of fear
As are the blasted banks of Erebus,
Where shaking ghosts with ever-howling groans
Hover about the ugly ferryman,
To get a passage to Elysium !
Why should we live ? O, wretches, beggars, slaves !
Why live we, Bajazeth, and build up nests
So high within the region of the air
By living long in this oppression,
That all the world will see and laugh to scorn
The former triumphs of our mightiness
In this obscure infernal servitude ?

Baj. O life, more loathsome to my vexèd thoughts
Than noisome parbreak[2] of the Stygian snakes,
Which fills the nooks of hell with standing air,
Infecting all the ghosts with cureless griefs !
O dreary engines of my loathèd sight,

----

[1] Bent back.   [2] Vomit.

That see my crown, my honour, and my name
Thrust under yoke and thraldom of a thief,
Why feed ye still on day's accursèd beams
And sink not quite into my tortured soul?
You see my wife, my queen, and emperess,
Brought up and proppèd by the hand of fame,
Queen of fifteen contributory queens,
Now thrown to rooms of black abjection,
Smearèd with blots of basest drudgery,
And villainess[1] to shame, disdain, and misery.
Accursèd Bajazeth, whose words of ruth,
(That would with pity cheer Zabina's heart,
And make our souls resolve[2] in ceaseless tears ;)
Sharp hunger bites upon. and gripes the root,
From whence the issues of my thoughts do break ;
O poor Zabina !   O my queen ! my queen !
Fetch me some water for my burning breast,
To cool and comfort me with longer date,
That in the shortened sequel of my life
I may pour forth my soul into thine arms
With words of love, whose moaning intercourse
Hath hitherto been stayed with wrath and hate
Of our expressless banned inflictions.

   Zab. Sweet Bajazeth, I will prolong thy life,
As long as any blood or spark of breath
Can quench or cool the torments of my grief.   [*Exit.*

   Baj. Now, Bajazeth. abridge thy baneful days,
And beat thy brains out of thy conquered head,
Since other means are all forbidden me,
That may be ministers of my decay.
O, highest lamp of ever-living Jove,
Accursèd day ! infected with my griefs,
Hide now thy stainèd face in endless night,

---

   [1] Slave.   [2] Dissolve,

And shut the windows of the lightsome heavens!
Let ugly Darkness with her rusty coach,
Engirt with tempests, wrapt in pitchy clouds,
Smother the earth with never-fading mists!
And let her horses from their nostrils breathe
Rebellious winds and dreadful thunder-claps!
That in this terror Tamburlaine may live,
And my pined soul, resolved in liquid air,
May still excruciate his tormented thoughts!
Then let the stony dart of senseless cold
Pierce through the centre of my withered heart,
And make a passage for my loathèd life!

[He brains himself against the cage.

Re-enter ZABINA.

Zab. What do mine eyes behold? my husband dead!
His skull all riven in twain! his brains dashed out,—
The brains of Bajazeth, my lord and sovereign:
O Bajazeth, my husband and my lord!
O Bajazeth! O Turk! O Emperor!
Give him his liquor? not I. Bring milk and fire, and
my blood I bring him again.—Tear me in pieces—give
me the sword with a ball of wild-fire upon it.—Down
with him! Down with him!—Go to my child! Away!
Away! Away!—Ah, save that infant! save him, save
him!—I, even I, speak to her.—The sun was down—
streamers white, red, black—here, here, here!—Fling
the meat in his face—Tamburlaine.—Tamburlaine!—
Let the soldiers be buried.—Hell! Death, Tamburlaine,
Hell! Make ready my coach,[1] my chair, my jewels.—I
come! I come! I come!

[She runs against the cage and brains herself.

---

[1] Shakespeare apparently had this passage in his mind when he
made Ophelia exclaim, "Come, my coach," &c.

Enter ZENOCRATE *with* ANIPPE.

Zeno. Wretched Zenocrate! that liv'st to see
Damascus' walls dyed with Egyptians' blood,
Thy father's subjects and thy countrymen;
The streets strowed with dissevered joints of men
And wounded bodies gasping yet for life:
But most accurst, to see the sun-bright troop
Of heavenly virgins and unspotted maids,
(Whose looks might make the angry god of arms
To break his sword and mildly treat of love)
On horsemen's lances to be hoisted up
And guiltlessly endure a cruel death:
For every fell and stout Tartarian steed,
That stampt on others with their thundering hoofs,
When all their riders charged their quivering spears,
Began to check the ground and rein themselves,
Gazing upon the beauty of their looks.—
Ah Tamburlaine! wert thou the cause of this
That term'st Zenocrate thy dearest love?
Whose lives were dearer to Zenocrate
Than her own life, or aught save thine own love.
But see another bloody spectacle!
Ah, wretched eyes, the enemies of my heart,
How are ye glutted with these grievous objects,
And tell my soul more tales of bleeding ruth!
See, see, Anippe, if they breathe or no.
    Anippe. No breath, nor sense, nor motion in them
      both;
Ah, madam! this their slavery hath enforced,
And ruthless cruelty of Tamburlaine.
    Zeno. Earth, cast up fountains from thy entrails,
And wet thy cheeks for their untimely deaths!
Shake with their weight in sign of fear and grief!
Blush, Heaven, that gave them honour at their birth

And let them die a death so barbarous!
Those that are proud of fickle empery
And place their chiefest good in earthly pomp,
Behold the Turk and his great Emperess!
Ah, Tamburlaine! my love! sweet Tamburlaine!
That fight'st for sceptres and for slippery crowns,
Behold the Turk and his great Emperess!
Thou, that in conduct of thy happy stars
Sleep'st every night with conquests on thy brows,
And yet would'st shun the wavering turns of war,
In fear and feeling of the like distress
Behold the Turk and his great Emperess!
Ah, mighty Jove and holy Mahomet,
Pardon my love!—O, pardon his contempt
Of earthly fortune and respect of pity,
And let not conquest, ruthlessly pursued,
Be equally against his life incensed
In this great Turk and hapless Emperess!
And pardon me that was not moved with ruth
To see them live so long in misery!
Ah, what may chance to thee, Zenocrate?

Anippe. Madam, content yourself, and be resolved
Your love hath Fortune so at his command,
That she shall stay and turn her wheel no more,
As long as life maintains his mighty arm
That fights for honour to adorn your head.

Enter PHILEMUS, *a* Messenger.

Zeno. What other heavy news now brings Philemus?

Phil. Madam, your father, and the Arabian king,
The first affecter of your excellence,
Comes now, as Turnus 'gainst Æneas did,
Arm'd with lance into the Egyptian fields,
Ready for battle 'gainst my lord, the king.

Zeno. Now shame and duty, love and fear present
A thousand sorrows to my martyred soul.
Whom should I wish the fatal victory
When my poor pleasures are divided thus
And racked by duty from my cursèd heart?
My father and my first-betrothèd love
Must fight against my life and present love;
Wherein the change I use condemns my faith,
And makes my deeds infamous through the world:
But as the gods, to end the Trojans' toil
Prevented Turnus of Lavinia
And fatally enriched Æneas' love,
So for a final issue to my griefs,
To pacify my country and my love
Must Tamburlaine by their resistless pow'rs
With virtue of a gentle victory
Conclude a league of honour to my hope;
Then, as the Powers divine have pre-ordained,
With happy safety of my father's life
Send like defence of fair Arabia.

       [*Trumpets sound to the battle within: afterwards,
         the* KING *of* ARABIA *enters wounded.*

  K. of Arab. What cursèd power guides the murdering
    hands
Of this infamous tyrant's soldiers.
That no escape may save their enemies,
Nor fortune keep themselves from victory?
Lie down, Arabia, wounded to the death,
And let Zenocrate's fair eyes behold
That, as for her thou bear'st these wretched arms,
Even so for her thou diest in these arms,
Leaving thy blood for witness of thy love.

  Zeno. Too dear a witness for such love, my lord.
Behold Zenocrate! the cursèd object,

Mar.   G

Whose fortunes never mastered her griefs ;
Behold her wounded, in conceit, for thee,
As much as thy fair body is for me.

   K. of Arab. Then shall I die with full, contented heart,
Having beheld divine Zenocrate,
Whose sight with joy would take away my life
As now it bringeth sweetness to my wound,
If I had not been wounded as I am.
Ah ! that the deadly pangs I suffer now,
Would lend an hour's licence to my tongue,
To make discourse of some sweet accidents
Have chanced thy merits in this worthless bondage ;
And that I might be privy to the state
Of thy deserved contentment, and thy love ;
But, making now a virtue of thy sight,
To drive all sorrow from my fainting soul,
Since death denies me farther cause of joy,
Deprived of care, my heart with comfort dies,
Since thy desirèd hand shall close mine eyes.   [*He dies.*

  Re-enter TAMBURLAINE, *leading the* SOLDAN, TECHELLES,
    THERIDAMAS, USUMCASANE, *with others.*

   Tamb. Come, happy father of Zenocrate,
A title higher than thy Soldan's name.
Though my right hand have thus enthrallèd thee,
Thy princely daughter here shall set thee free ;
She that hath calmed the fury of my sword,
Which had ere this been bathed in streams of blood
As vast and deep as Euphrates or Nile.

   Zeno. O sight thrice welcome to my joyful soul,
To see the king, my father, issue safe
From dangerous battle of my conquering love !

   Sold. Well met, my only dear Zenocrate,
Though with the loss of Egypt and my crown.

Tamb. 'Twas I, my lord, that got the victory,
And therefore grieve not at your overthrow,
Since I shall render all into your hands,
And add more strength to your dominions
Than ever yet confirmed the Egyptian crown.
The god of war resigns his room to me,
Meaning to make me general of the world :
Jove, viewing me in arms, looks pale and wan,
Fearing my power should pull him from his throne.
Where'er I come the Fatal Sisters sweat,
And grisly Death, by running to and fro,
To do their ceaseless homage to my sword :
And here in Afric, where it seldom rains,
Since I arrived with my triumphant host,
Have swelling clouds, drawn from wide-gasping wounds,
Been oft resolved in bloody purple showers,
A meteor that might terrify the earth,
And make it quake at every drop it drinks.
Millions of souls sit on the banks of Styx
Waiting the back return of Charon's boat ;
Hell and Elysium swarm with ghosts of men,
That I have sent from sundry foughten fields,
To spread my fame through hell and up to Heaven.
And see, my lord, a sight of strange import,
Emperors and kings lie breathless at my feet :
The Turk and his great Empress, as it seems,
Left to themselves while we were at the fight,
Have desperately despatched their slavish lives :
With them Arabia, too, hath left his life :
All sights of power to grace my victory ;
And such are objects fit for Tamburlaine :
Wherein, as in a mirror, may be seen
His honour, that consists in shedding blood,
When men presume to manage arms with him.

Sold. Mighty hath God and Mahomet made thy hand,
Renownèd Tamburlaine : to whom all kings
Of force must yield their crowns and emperies ;
And I am pleased with this my overthrow.
If, as beseems a person of thy state,
Thou hast with honour used Zenocrate.

   Tamb. Her state and person want no pomp, you see :
And for all blot of foul inchastity
I record Heaven her heavenly self is clear :
Then let me find no farther time to grace
Her princely temples with the Persian crown.
But here these kings that on my fortunes wait,
And have been crowned for provèd worthiness,
Even by this hand that shall establish them,
Shall now, adjoining all their hands with mine,
Invest her here the Queen of Persia.
What saith the noble Soldan and Zenocrate !

   Sold. I yield with thanks and protestations
Of endless honour to thee for her love.

   Tamb. Then doubt I not but fair Zenocrate
Will soon consent to satisfy us both.

   Zeno. Else should I much forget myself, my lord.

   Ther. Then let us set the crown upon her head,
That long hath lingered for so high a seat.

   Tech. My hand is ready to perform the deed ;
For now her marriage-time shall work us rest.

   Usum. And here's the crown, my lord ; help set it on.

   Tamb. Then sit thou down, divine Zenocrate ;
And here we crown thee Queen of Persia,
And all the kingdoms and dominions
That late the power of Tamburlaine subdued.
As Juno, when the giants were suppressed,
That darted mountains at her brother Jove.
So looks my love, shadowing in her brows

Triumphs and trophies for my victories :
Or, as Latona's daughters, bent to arms,
Adding more courage to my conquering mind.
To gratify the sweet Zenocrate,
Egyptians, Moors, and men of Asia,
From Barbary unto the western India,
Shall pay a yearly tribute to thy sire :
And from the bounds of Afric to the banks
Of Ganges shall his mighty arm extend.
And now, my lords and loving followers,
That purchased kingdoms by your martial deeds,
Cast off your armour, put on scarlet robes,
Mount up your royal places of estate,
Environèd with troops of noblemen,
And there make laws to rule your provinces.
Hang up your weapons on Alcides' post,
For Tamburlaine takes truce with all the world.
Thy first-betrothèd love, Arabia,
Shall we with honour, as beseems, entomb
With this great Turk and his fair Emperess.
Then, after all these solemn exequies,
We will our rites of marriage solemnise.

TAMBURLAINE THE GREAT.

PART THE SECOND.

THE PROLOGUE.

THE general welcomes Tamburlaine received,
When he arrivèd last upon the stage,
Hath made our poet pen his Second Part,
Where death cuts off the progress of his pomp,
And murderous fates throw all his triumphs down.
But what became of fair Zenocrate,
And with how many cities' sacrifice
He celebrated her sad funeral,
Himself in presence shall unfold at large.

TAMBURLAINE, King of Persia.

CALYPHAS, ⎫
AMYRAS, ⎬ His sons.
CELEBINUS, ⎭

TECHELLES, King of Fez.

THERIDAMAS, King of Argier.

USUMCASANE, King of Morocco.

ORCANES, King of Natolia.

KING of JERUSALEM.

KING of TREBIZOND.

KING of SORIA.[1]

KING of AMASIA.

GAZELLUS, Viceroy of Byron.

URIBASSA.

SIGISMUND, King of Hungary.

FREDERICK, ⎫
BALDWIN, ⎬ Lords of Buda and Bohemia.

CALLAPINE, Son of BAJAZETH.

ALMEDA, his Keeper.

PERDICAS, Servant to CALYPHAS.

GOVERNOR of BABYLON.

MAXIMUS.

CAPTAIN of BALSERA.

His Son.

Physicians.

Another Captain.

Lords, Citizens, Soldiers, &c.

ZENOCRATE, Wife of TAMBURLAINE.

OLYMPIA, Wife of the Captain of Balsera.

Turkish Concubines.

---

[1] Cunningham and Bullen have Syria, and Dyce, Soria. The latter points out that Tyre, since the Arab dominion in the East, has been known as Sor; hence Soria, which is several times referred to in the play.

TAMBURLAINE THE GREAT.

PART THE SECOND.

—··:✦✧✦:·—

ACT THE FIRST.

SCENE I.

Enter ORCANES, *King of Natolia,* GAZELLUS, *Viceroy of Byron,* URIBASSA, *and their* Train, *with drums and trumpets.*

ORC. Egregious viceroys of these eastern parts,
Placed by the issue of great Bajazeth,
And sacred lord, the mighty Callapine,
Who lives in Egypt, prisoner to that slave
Which kept his father in an iron cage :—
Now have we marched from fair Natolia
Two hundred leagues, and on Danubius' banks
Our warlike host, in complete armour, rest,
Where Sigismund, the king of Hungary,
Should meet our person to conclude a truce.
What ! shall we parley with the Christian ?
Or cross the stream, and meet him in the field ?

Gaz. King of Natolia, let us treat of peace ;
We are all glutted with the Christians' blood,
And have a greater foe to fight against,—
Proud Tamburlaine, that, now in Asia,
Near Guyron's head doth set his conq'ring feet,
And means to fire Turkey as he goes.
'Gainst him, my lord, you must address your power.

    Uri. Besides, King Sigismund hath brought from
        Christendom,
More than his camp of stout Hungarians,—
Sclavonians, Almain rutters,[1] Muffes, and Danes.
That with the halbert, lance, and murdering axe,
Will hazard that we might with surety hold.

    Orc. Though from the shortest northern parallel,
Vast Grantland[2] compassed with the Frozen Sea,
(Inhabited with tall and sturdy men,
Giants as big as hugy Polypheme,)
Millions of soldiers cut the arctic line,
Bringing the strength of Europe to these arms,
Our Turkey blades shall glide through all their throats,
And make this champion[3] mead a bloody fen.
Danubius' stream, that runs to Trebizon,
Shall carry, wrapt within his scarlet waves,
As martial presents to our friends at home,
The slaughtered bodies of these Christians.
The Terrene Main, wherein Danubius falls,[4]
Shall, by this battle, be the Bloody Sea.
The wandering sailors of proud Italy
Shall meet those Christians, fleeting with the tide,
Beating in heaps against their argosies,
And make fair Europe, mounted on her bull,

---

[1] Troopers: Germ. *Reiter*.   [2] Greenland.   [3] Champaign.
[4] It is hardly necessary to remark that the Danube falls into the
Black Sea, and not into the Mediterranean.

Trapped with the wealth and riches of the world,
Alight, and wear a woful mourning weed.

Gaz. Yet, stout Orcanes, Prorex of the world,
Since Tamburlaine hath mustered all his men,
Marching from Cairo northward with his camp,
To Alexandria, and the frontier towns,
Meaning to make a conquest of our land,
'Tis requisite to parley for a peace
With Sigismund the King of Hungary,
And save our forces for the hot assaults
Proud Tamburlaine intends Natolia.

Orc. Viceroy of Byron, wisely hast thou said.
My realm, the centre of our empery,
Once lost, all Turkey would be overthrown,
And for that cause the Christians shall have peace.
Sclavonians, Almain rutters, Muffes, and Danes,
Fear[1] not Orcanes, but great Tamburlaine ;
Nor he, but fortune, that hath made him great.
We have revolted Grecians, Albanese,
Sicilians, Jews, Arabians, Turks, and Moors,
Natolians, Syrians, black Egyptians,
Illyrians, Thracians, and Bithynians,
Enough to swallow forceless Sigismund,
Yet scarce enough to encounter Tamburlaine.
He brings a world of people to the field,
From Scythia to the oriental plage
Of India, where raging Lantchidol[2]
Beats on the regions with his boisterous blows,
That never seaman yet discoveréd.
All Asia is in arms with Tamburlaine,
Even from the midst of fiery Cancer's tropic,

[1] *i.e.*, Frighten.
[2] Lantchidol is that part of the Indian Ocean which lies between Java and New Holland.—*Broughton.*

To Amazonia under Capricorn ;
And thence as far as Archipelago,
All Afric is in arms with Tamburlaine ;
Therefore, viceroy, the Christians must have peace.

Enter SIGISMUND, FREDERICK, BALDWIN, *and their*
Train, *with drums and trumpets.*

Sig. Orcanes, (as our legates promised thee,)
We, with our peers, have crossed Danubius' stream,
To treat of friendly peace or deadly war.
Take which thou wilt, for as the Romans used,
I here present thee, with a naked sword ;
Wilt thou have war, then shake this blade at me ;
If peace, restore it to my hands again,
And I will sheath it, to confirm the same.

Orc. Stay, Sigismund ! forget'st thou I am he
That with the cannon shook Vienna walls,
And made it dance upon the continent,
As when the massy substance of the earth
Quivers about the axle-tree of Heaven ?
Forget'st thou that I sent a shower of darts,
Mingled with powdered shot and feathered steel,
So thick upon the blink-eyed burghers' heads,
That thou thyself, then county palatine,
The King of Boheme, and the Austric Duke,
Sent heralds out, which basely on their knees
In all your names desired a truce of me ?
Forget'st thou, that to have me raise my siege,
Waggons of gold were set before my tents,
Stampt with the princely fowl, that in her wings,
Carries the fearful thunderbolts of Jove ?
How canst thou think of this, and offer war ?

Sig. Vienna was besieged, and I was there,
Then county palatine, but now a king,

And what we did was in extremity.
But now, Orcanes, view my royal host.
That hides these plains, and seems as vast and wide,
As doth the desert of Arabia
To those that stand on Bagdet's lofty tower ;
Or as the ocean, to the traveller
That rests upon the snowy Apennines ;
And tell me whether I should stoop so low.
Or treat of peace with the Natolian king

   Gaz. Kings of Natolia and of Hungary,
We came from Turkey to confirm a league,
And not to dare each other to the field.
A friendly parley might become you both.

   Fred. And we from Europe, to the same intent,
Which if your general refuse or scorn,
Our tents are pitched, our men stand in array,
Ready to charge you ere you stir your feet.

   Orc. So prest[1] are we ; but yet, if Sigismund
Speak as a friend, and stand not upon terms,
Here is his sword,—let peace be ratified
On these conditions, specified before,
Drawn with advice of our ambassadors.

   Sig. Then here I sheathe it, and give thee my hand,
Never to draw it out, or manage arms
Against thyself or thy confederates,
But whilst I live will be a truce with thee.

   Orc. But, Sigismund, confirm it with an oath,
And swear in sight of Heaven and by thy Christ.

   Sig. By him that made the world and saved my
     soul,
The Son of God and issue of a Maid,
Sweet Jesus Christ, I solemnly protest
And vow to keep this peace inviolable.

       [1] Ready. Fr. *prêt.*

Orc. By sacred Mahomet, the friend of God,
Whose holy Alcoran remains with us,
Whose glorious body, when he left the world,
Closed in a coffin mounted up the air,
And hung on stately Mecca's temple-roof,
I swear to keep this truce inviolable ;
Of whose conditions and our solemn oaths,
Signed with our hands, each shall retain a scroll
As memorable witness of our league.
Now, Sigismund, if any Christian king
Encroach upon the confines of thy realm,
Send word, Orcanes of Natolia
Confirmed this league beyond Danubius' stream,
And they will, trembling, sound a quick retreat ;
So am I feared among all nations.

Sig. If any heathen potentate or king
Invade Natolia, Sigismund will send
A hundred thousand horse trained to the war,
And backed by stout lanciers of Germany,
The strength and sinews of the Imperial seat.

Orc. I thank thee, Sigismund ; but, when I war,
All Asia Minor, Africa, and Greece,
Follow my standard and my thundering drums.
Come, let us go and banquet in our tents ;
I will despatch chief of my army hence
To fair Natolia and to Trebizon,
To stay my coming 'gainst proud Tamburlaine.
Friend Sigismund, and peers of Hungary,
Come, banquet and carouse with us a while,
And then depart we to our territories.   [*Exeunt*

SCENE II.

Enter CALLAPINE *with* ALMEDA, *his Keeper.*

Call. Sweet Almeda, pity the ruthful plight
Of Callapine, the son of Bajazeth,
Born to be monarch of the western world,
Yet here detained by cruel Tamburlaine.

   Alm. My lord, I pity it, and with all my heart
Wish you release ; but he whose wrath is death,
My sovereign lord, renownèd Tamburlaine,
Forbids you farther liberty than this.

   Call. Ah, were I now but half so eloquent
To paint in words what I'll perform in deeds.
I know thou would'st depart from hence with me.

   Alm. Not for all Afric : therefore move me not.

   Call. Yet hear me speak, my gentle Almeda.

   Alm. No speech to that end, by your favour, sir.

   Call. By Cairo runs——

   Alm. No talk of running, I tell you, sir.

   Call. A little farther, gentle Almeda.

   Alm. Well, sir, what of this ?

   Call. By Cairo runs to Alexandria bay
Darote's streams, wherein at anchor lies
A Turkish galley of my royal fleet,
Waiting my coming to the river side,
Hoping by some means I shall be released,
Which, when I come aboard, will hoist up sail,
And soon put forth into the Terrene sea,
Where, 'twixt the isles of Cyprus and of Crete,
We quickly may in Turkish seas arrive.
Then shalt thou see a hundred kings and more,
Upon their knees, all bid me welcome home,
Amongst so many crowns of burnished gold.

Choose which thou wilt, all are at thy command ;
A thousand galleys, manned with Christian slaves,
I freely give thee, which shall cut the Straits,
And bring armados from the coasts of Spain
Fraughted with gold of rich America ;
The Grecian virgins shall attend on thee,
Skilful in music and in amorous lays,
As fair as was Pygmalion's ivory girl
Or lovely Iö metamorphosèd.
With naked negroes shall thy coach be drawn,
And as thou rid'st in triumph through the streets
The pavement underneath thy chariot wheels
With Turkey carpets shall be coverèd,
And cloth of Arras hung about the walls,
Fit objects for thy princely eye to pierce.
A hundred bassoes, clothed in crimson silk,
Shall ride before thee on Barbarian steeds ;
And when thou goest, a golden canopy
Enchased with precious stones, which shine as bright
As that fair veil that covers all the world,
When Phœbus, leaping from the hemisphere,
Descendeth downward to the Antipodes.
And more than this—for all I cannot tell.

 Alm. How far hence lies the galley, say you ?
 Call. Sweet Almeda, scarce half a league from hence.
 Alm. But need[1] we not be spied going aboard?
 Call. Betwixt the hollow hanging of a hill,
And crookèd bending of a craggy rock,
The sails wrapt up, the mast and tacklings down,
She lies so close that none can find her out.
 Alm. I like that well : but tell me, my lord, if I should
let you go, would you be as good as your word? shall I
be made a king for my labour ?

      [1] Must.

Call. As I am Callapine the Emperor,
And by the hand of Mahomet I swear
Thou shalt be crowned a king, and be my mate.

Alm. Then here I swear, as I am Almeda
Your keeper under Tamburlaine the Great,
(For that's the style and title I have yet.)
Although he sent a thousand armèd men
To intercept this haughty enterprise,
Yet would I venture to conduct your grace,
And die before I brought you back again.

Call. Thanks, gentle Almeda : then let us haste,
Lest time be past, and lingering let[1] us both.

Alm. When you will, my lord ; I am ready.

Call. Even straight ; and farewell, cursèd Tamburlaine.
Now go I to revenge my father's death.   [*Exeunt.*

SCENE III.

Enter TAMBURLAINE, ZENOCRATE, *and their three* Sons,
CALYPHAS, AMYRAS, *and* CELEBINUS, *with drums
and trumpets.*

Tamb. Now, bright Zenocrate, the world's fair eye,
Whose beams illuminate the lamps of Heaven,
Whose cheerful looks do clear the cloudy air,
And clothe it in a crystal livery :
Now rest thee here on fair Larissa plains,
Where Egypt and the Turkish empire part
Between thy sons, that shall be emperors,
And every one commander of a world.

Zeno. Sweet Tamburlaine, when wilt thou leave these
    arms,

[1] Hinder.

Mar.   II

And save thy sacred person free from scathe,
And dangerous chances of the wrathful war?
    Tamb. When Heaven shall cease to move on both the
        poles,
And when the ground, whereon my soldiers march,
Shall rise aloft and touch the hornèd moon,
And not before, my sweet Zenocrate.
Sit up, and rest thee like a lovely queen;
So, now she sits in pomp and majesty,
When these, my sons, more precious in mine eyes,
Than all the wealthy kingdoms I subdued,
Placed by her side, look on their mother's face:
But yet methinks their looks are amorous,
Not martial as the sons of Tamburlaine:
Water and air, being symbolised in one,
Argue their want of courage and of wit;
Their hair as white as milk and soft as down,
(Which should be like the quills of porcupines
As black as jet and hard as iron or steel)
Bewrays they are too dainty for the wars;
Their fingers made to quaver on a lute,
Their arms to hang about a lady's neck,
Their legs to dance and caper in the air,[1]
Would make me think them bastards not my sons,
But that I know they issued from thy womb
That never looked on man but Tamburlaine.
    Zeno. My gracious lord, they have their mother's
        looks,
But when they list their conquering father's heart.
This lovely boy, the youngest of the three,
Not long ago bestrid a Scythian steed,
Trotting the ring, and tilting at a glove,
Which when he tainted[2] with his slender rod,

---

[1] Bullen (following Cunningham) omitted this line.   [2] Touched.

He reined him straight and made him so curvet,
As I cried out for fear he should have fallen.

Tamb. Well done, my boy, thou shalt have shield and
    lance,
Armour of proof, horse, helm, and curtle-axe,
And I will teach thee how to charge thy foe,
And harmless run among the deadly pikes.
If thou wilt love the wars and follow me,
Thou shalt be made a king and reign with me,
Keeping in iron cages emperors.
If thou exceed thy elder brothers' worth
And shine in complete virtue more than they,
Thou shalt be king before them, and thy seed
Shall issue crownèd from their mother's womb.

Cel. Yes, father : you shall see me, if I live,
Have under me as many kings as you,
And march with such a multitude of men,
As all the world shall tremble at their view.

Tamb. These words assure me, boy, thou art my son.
When I am old and cannot manage arms,
Be thou the scourge and terror of the world.

Amy. Why may not I, my lord, as well as he,
Be termed the scourge and terror of the world ?

Tamb. Be all a scourge and terror to the world,
Or else you are not sons of Tamburlaine.

Cal. But while my brothers follow arms, my lord,
Let me accompany my gracious mother ;
They are enough to conquer all the world,
And you have won enough for me to keep.

Tamb. Bastardly boy, sprung from some coward's loins,
And not the issue of great Tamburlaine ;
Of all the provinces I have subdued,
Thou shalt not have a foot unless thou bear
A mind courageous and invincible :

For he shall wear the crown of Persia
Whose head hath deepest scars, whose breast most wounds,
Which being wroth sends lightning from his eyes,
And in the furrows of his frowning brows
Harbours revenge, war, death, and cruelty;
For in a field, whose superficies
Is covered with a liquid purple veil
And sprinkled with the brains of slaughtered men,
My royal chair of state shall be advanced;
And he that means to place himself therein,
Must armèd wade up to the chin in blood.

Zeno. My lord, such speeches to our princely sons
Dismay their minds before they come to prove
The wounding troubles angry war affords.

Cel. No, madam, these are speeches fit for us,
For if his chair were in a sea of blood
I would prepare a ship and sail to it,
Ere I would lose the title of a king.

Amy. And I would strive to swim through pools of blood,
Or make a bridge of murdered carcases,
Whose arches should be framed with bones of Turks,
Ere I would lose the title of a king.

Tamb. Well, lovely boys, ye shall be emperors both,
Stretching your conquering arms from East to West;
And, sirrah, if you mean to wear a crown,
When we shall meet the Turkish deputy
And all his viceroys, snatch it from his head,
And cleave his pericranium with thy sword.

Cal. If any man will hold him, I will strike
And cleave him to the channel[1] with my sword.

Tamb. Hold him, and cleave him too, or I'll cleave thee,
For we will march against them presently.
Theridamas, Techelles, and Casane

---

[1] Collar-bone.

Promised to meet me on Larissa plains
With hosts apiece against this Turkish crew ;
For I have sworn by sacred Mahomet
To make it parcel of my empery ;
The trumpets sound, Zenocrate ; they come.

Enter THERIDAMAS *and his* Train, *with drums and trumpets.*

Tamb. Welcome, Theridamas, King of Argier.
Ther. My lord, the great and mighty Tamburlaine,—
Arch monarch of the world, I offer here
My crown, myself, and all the power I have,
In all affection at thy kingly feet.
Tamb. Thanks, good Theridamas.
Ther. Under my colours march ten thousand Greeks :
And of Argier's and Afric's frontier towns
Twice twenty thousand valiant men-at-arms,
All which have sworn to sack Natolia.
Five hundred brigandines are under sail,
Meet for your service on the sea, my lord,
That launching from Argier to Tripoli,
Will quickly ride before Natolia,
And batter down the castles on the shore.
Tamb. Well said, Argier ; receive thy crown again.

Enter TECHELLES *and* USUMCASANE *together.*

Tamb. Kings of Moroccus and of Fez, welcome.
Usum. Magnificent and peerless Tamburlaine !
I and my neighbour King of Fez have brought
To aid thee in this Turkish expedition,
A hundred thousand expert soldiers :
From Azamor [1] to Tunis near the sea
Is Barbary unpeopled for thy sake,

---

[1] A maritime town of Morocco.

And all the men in armour under me,
Which with my crown I gladly offer thee.
 Tamb. Thanks, King of Moroccus, take your crown again.
 Tech. And, mighty Tamburlaine, our earthly god,
Whose looks make this inferior world to quake,
I here present thee with the crown of Fez,
And with an host of Moors trained to the war,
Whose coal-black faces make their foes retire,
And quake for fear, as if infernal Jove
Meaning to aid thee in these Turkish arms,
Should pierce the black circumference of hell
With ugly Furies bearing fiery flags,
And millions of his strong tormenting spirits.
From strong Teselh unto Biledull [1]
All Barbary is unpeopled for thy sake.
 Tamb. Thanks, King of Fez; take here thy crown again.
Your presence, loving friends, and fellow kings.
Makes me to surfeit in conceiving joy.
If all the crystal gates of Jove's high court
Were opened wide, and I might enter in
To see the state and majesty of Heaven,
It could not more delight me than your sight.
Now will we banquet on these plains awhile,
And after march to Turkey with our camp,
In number more than are the drops that fall,
When Boreas rents a thousand swelling clouds ;
And proud Orcanes of Natolia
With all his viceroys shall be so afraid,
That though the stones, as at Deucalion's flood,
Were turned to men, he should be overcome.
Such lavish will I make of Turkish blood,

---

[1] Tesella, now Tesegdelt, an impregnable village of Morocco, lies
to the south of Mogador, and Biledull, *i.e.* Biledulgerid (the land of
dates), is situated southward of the Barbary States.

That Jove shall send his wingèd messenger
To bid me sheath my sword and leave the field ;
The sun unable to sustain the sight,
Shall hide his head in Thetis' watery lap,
And leave his steeds to fair Böotes' charge ;
For half the world shall perish in this fight.
But now, my friends, let me examine ye ;
How have ye spent your absent time from me ?

 Usum. My lord, our men of Barbary have marched
Four hundred miles with armour on their backs,
And lain in leaguer [1] fifteen months and more ;
For, since we left you at the Soldan's court,
We have subdued the southern Guallatia,
And all the land unto the coast of Spain ;
We kept the narrow Strait of Jubaltèr,
And made Canaria call us kings and lords ;
Yet never did they recreate themselves,
Or cease one day from war and hot alarms,
And therefore let them rest awhile, my lord.

 Tamb. They shall, Casane, and 'tis time i' faith.

 Tech. And I have marched along the river Nile
To Machda, where the mighty Christian priest,
Called John the Great,[2] sits in a milk-white robe,
Whose triple mitre I did take by force,
And made him swear obedience to my crown,
From thence unto Cazates did I march,
Where Amazonians met me in the field,
With whom, being women, I vouchsafed a league,
And with my power did march to Zanzibar,
The eastern part of Afric, where I viewed
The Ethiopian sea, rivers and lakes,
But neither man nor child in all the land ;
Therefore I took my course to Manico,

---

[1] The camp of a besieging force. [2] Prester John.

Where unresisted, I removed my camp;
And by the coast of Byather, at last
I came to Cubar, where the negroes dwell,
And conquering that, made haste to Nubia.
There, having sacked Borno[1] the kingly seat.
I took the king and led him bound in chains
Unto Damasco, where I stayed before.

    Tamb. Well done, Techelles. What saith Theridamas

    Ther. I left the confines and the bounds of Afric,
And thence I made a voyage into Europe,
Where by the river Tyras I subdued
Stoka, Podolia, and Codemia;
Thence crossed the sea and came to Oblia[2]
And Nigra Sylva, where the devils dance,
Which in despite of them, I set on fire.
From thence I crossed the gulf called by the name
Mare Majore[3] of the inhabitants.
Yet shall my soldiers make no period,
Until Natolia kneel before your feet.

    Tamb. Then will we triumph, banquet and carouse;
Cooks shall have pensions to provide us cates,
And glut us with the dainties of the world;
Lachryma Christi and Calabrian wines
Shall common soldiers drink in quaffing bowls,
Ay, liquid gold (when we have conquered him)
Mingled with coral and with orient pearl.
Come, let us banquet and carouse the whiles. [*Exeunt.*

---

[1] With regard to the above places on Techelles' line of march, Manico, *i.e.* Manica, is in the Mozambique territory: by Byather Biafra is supposed to have been meant, while Borno, *i.e.* Bornu, is an extensive kingdom in the eastern part of Central Africa.

[2] Tyras is now the Dniester, Stoka is a confluent of the Danube, Podolia is a Russian province, and Codemia, now Kodyma, is a confluent of the Bug. Oblia, *i.e.* Olbia, a Greek colony in Scythia, is now Stomogil on the Bug.

[3] The old name of the Black Sea. So called by Marco Polo.

ACT THE SECOND.

SCENE I.

Enter SIGISMUND, FREDERICK, BALDWIN, *and their*
Train.

SIG. Now say, my lords of Buda and
    Bohemia,
What motion is it that inflames your
    thoughts,
And stirs your valours to such sudden
    arms?

Fred. Your majesty remembers, I am sure,
What cruel slaughter of our Christian bloods
These heathenish Turks and Pagans lately made,
Betwixt the city Zula and Danubius;
How through the midst of Varna and Bulgaria,
And almost to the very walls of Rome,
They have, not long since, massacred our camp.
It resteth now, then, that your majesty
Take all advantages of time and power,
And work revenge upon these infidels.
Your highness knows, for Tamburlaine's repair.
That strikes a terror to all Turkish hearts,
Natolia hath dismissed the greatest part
Of all his army, pitched against our power.
Betwixt Cutheia and Orminius' mount,[1]
And sent them marching up to Belgasar.

---

[1] Probably Armenyes, in Transylvania.

Acantha,[1] Antioch, and Cæsarea,
To aid the Kings of Soria, and Jerusalem.
Now then, my lord, advantage take thereof,
And issue suddenly upon the rest ;
That in the fortune of their overthrow,
We may discourage all the pagan troop,
That dare attempt to war with Christians.

   Sig. But calls not then your grace to memory
The league we lately made with King Orcanes,
Confirmed by oath and articles of peace,
And calling Christ for record of our truths ?
This should be treachery and violence
Against the grace of our profession.

   Bald. No whit, my lord, for with such infidels,
In whom no faith nor true religion rests,
We are not bound to those accomplishments
The holy laws of Christendom enjoin ;
But as the faith, which they profanely plight,
Is not by necessary policy
To be esteemed assurance for ourselves,
So that we vow to them should not infringe
Our liberty of arms or victory.

   Sig. Though I confess the oaths they undertake
Breed little strength to our security.
Yet those infirmities that thus defame
Their faiths, their honours, and their religion,
Should not give us presumption to the like.
Our faiths are sound, and must be consummate,
Religious, righteous, and inviolate.

   Fred. Assure your grace 'tis superstition
To stand so strictly on dispensive faith ;
And should we lose the opportunity
That God hath given to venge our Christians' death

---

[1] *Query* Acanthus, near Mount Athos.

And scourge their foul blasphèmous Paganism,
As fell to Saul, to Balaam, and the rest,
That would not kill and curse at God's command,
So surely will the vengeance of the Highest,
And jealous anger of His fearful arm,
Be poured with rigour on our sinful heads,
If we neglect this offered victory.

   Sig. Then arm, my lords, and issue suddenly,
Giving commandment to our general host,
With expedition to assail the Pagan,
And take the victory our God hath given.   [*Exeunt.*

SCENE II.

Enter ORCANES, GAZELLUS, *and* URIBASSA, *with their*
Trains.

   Orc. Gazellus, Uribassa, and the rest,
Now will we march from proud Orminius' mount,
To fair Natolia, where our neighbour kings
Expect our power and our royal presence,
To encounter with the cruel Tamburlaine,
That nigh Larissa sways a mighty host,
And with the thunder of his martial tools
Makes earthquakes in the hearts of men and Heaven.

   Gaz. And now come we to make his sinews shake,
With greater power than erst his pride hath felt.
An hundred kings, by scores, will bid him arms,
And hundred thousands subjects to each score,
Which, if a shower of wounding thunderbolts
Should break out of the bowels of the clouds,
And fall as thick as hail upon our heads,
In partial aid of that proud Scythian,
Yet should our courages and steelèd crests,

And numbers, more than infinite, of men,
Be able to withstand and conquer him.[1]

 Uri. Methinks I see how glad the Christian king
Is made, for joy of your admitted truce,
That could not but before be terrified
With unacquainted power of our host.

    Enter a Messenger.

 Mess. Arm, dread sovereign, and my noble lords !
The treacherous army of the Christians,
Taking advantage of your slender power,
Comes marching on us, and determines straight
To bid us battle for our dearest lives.

 Orc. Traitors ! villains ! damnèd Christians !
Have I not here the articles of peace,
And solemn covenants we have both confirmed,
He by his Christ, and I by Mahomet?

 Gaz. Hell and confusion light upon their heads,
That with such treason seek our overthrow,
And care so little for their prophet, Christ !

 Orc. Can there be such deceit in Christians,
Or treason in the fleshly heart of man,
Whose shape is figure of the highest God ! .
Then, if there be a Christ, as Christians say,
But in their deeds deny him for their Christ,
If he be son to everliving Jove,
And hath the power of his outstretchèd arm :
If he be jealous of his name and honour,
As is our holy prophet, Mahomet ;—
Take here these papers as our sacrifice
And witness of thy servant's perjury.

     [*He tears to pieces the articles of peace.*

---

[1] "If the sky fall, we'll uphold it on our lances," was the boast of the French at the battle of Nicopolis, at which Sigismund was defeated by Bajazet.

Open, thou shining veil of Cynthia,
And make a passage from the empyreal Heaven,
That he that sits on high and never sleeps,
Nor in one place is circumscriptible,
But everywhere fills every continent
With strange infusion of his sacred vigour,
May in his endless power and purity,
Behold and venge this traitor's perjury!
Thou Christ, that art esteemed omnipotent,
If thou wilt prove thyself a perfect God,
Worthy the worship of all faithful hearts,
Be now revenged upon this traitor's soul,
And make the power I have left behind,
(Too little to defend our guiltless lives,)
Sufficient to discomfort and confound
The trustless force of those false Christians.
To arms, my lords!   On Christ still let us cry!
If there be Christ, we shall have victory.

SCENE III.

Alarms of battle within.—Enter SIGISMUND, *wounded.*

Sig. Discomfited is all the Christian host,
And God hath thundered vengeance from on high,
For my accursed and hateful perjury.
O, just and dreadful punisher of sin,
Let the dishonour of the pains I feel,
In this my mortal well-deserved wound,
End all my penance in my sudden death!
And let this death, wherein to sin I die,
Conceive a second life in endless mercy!   [*He dies.*

Enter ORCANES, GAZELLUS, URIBASSA, *and others.*

Orc. Now lie the Christians bathing in their bloods,
And Christ or Mahomet hath been my friend.

Gaz. See here the perjured traitor Hungary,
Bloody and breathless for his villany.

Orc. Now shall his barbarous body be a prey
To beasts and fowls, and all the winds shall breathe
Through shady leaves of every senseless tree
Murmurs and hisses for his heinous sin.
Now scalds his soul in the Tartarian streams,
And feeds upon the baneful tree of hell,
That Zoacum,[1] that fruit of bitterness,
That in the midst of fire is ingraffed,
Yet flourishes as Flora in her pride,
With apples like the heads of damnèd fiends.
The devils there, in chains of quenchless flame,
Shall lead his soul through Orcus' burning gulf,
From pain to pain, whose change shall never end.
What say'st thou yet, Gazellus, to his foil
Which we referred to justice of his Christ,
And to his power, which here appears as full
As rays of Cynthia to the clearest sight?

Gaz. 'Tis but the fortune of the wars, my lord,
Whose power is often proved a miracle.

Orc. Yet in my thoughts shall Christ be honourèd,
Not doing Mahomet an injury,
Whose power had share in this our victory;
And since this miscreant hath disgraced his faith,
And died a traitor both to Heaven and earth,
We will both watch and ward shall keep his trunk
Amidst these plains for fowls to prey upon.
Go, Uribassa, give it straight in charge.

---

[1] The description of this tree is taken from the Koran, chap. 37.

Uri. I will, my lord.   [*Exit.*

Orc. And now, Gazellus, let us haste and meet
Our army, and our brothers of Jerusalem,
Of Soria, Trebizond, and Amasia,
And happily, with full Natolian bowls
Of Greekish wine, now let us celebrate
Our happy conquest and his angry fate.   [*Exeunt.*

SCENE IV.

ZENOCRATE *is discovered lying in her bed of state, with*
TAMBURLAINE *sitting by her. About her bed are three*
PHYSICIANS *tempering potions. Around are* THERI-
DAMAS, TECHELLES, USUMCASANE, *and her three Sons.*

Tamb. Black is the beauty of the brightest day;
The golden ball of Heaven's eternal fire,
That danced with glory on the silver waves,
Now wants the fuel that inflamed his beams;
And all with faintness, and for foul disgrace,
He binds his temples with a frowning cloud,
Ready to darken earth with endless night.
Zenocrate, that gave him light and life,
Whose eyes shot fire from their ivory bowers
And tempered every soul with lively heat,
Now by the malice of the angry skies,
Whose jealousy admits no second mate,
Draws in the comfort of her latest breath,
All dazzled with the hellish mists of death.
Now walk the angels on the walls of Heaven,
As sentinels to warn the immortal souls
To entertain divine Zenocrate.
Apollo, Cynthia, and the ceaseless lamps
That gently looked upon this loathsome earth,

Shine downward now no more, but deck the Heavens,
To entertain divine Zenocrate.
The crystal springs, whose taste illuminates
Refinèd eyes with an eternal sight,
Like trièd silver, run through Paradise,
To entertain divine Zenocrate.
The cherubins and holy seraphins,
That sing and play before the King of kings,
Use all their voices and their instruments
To entertain divine Zenocrate.
And in this sweet and curious harmony,
The God that tunes this music to our souls,
Holds out his hand in highest majesty
To entertain divine Zenocrate.
Then let some holy trance convey my thoughts
Up to the palace of th' empyreal Heaven,
That this my life may be as short to me
As are the days of sweet Zenocrate.—
Physicians, will no physic do her good?

Phys. My lord, your majesty shall soon perceive :
And if she pass this fit, the worst is past.

Tamb. Tell me, how fares my fair Zenocrate?

Zeno. I fare, my lord, as other empresses,
That, when this frail and transitory flesh
Hath suckèd the measure of that vital air
That feeds the body with his dated health,
Wade with enforced and necessary change.

Tamb. May never such a change transform my love,
In whose sweet being I repose my life,
Whose heavenly presence, beautified with health,
Gives light to Phœbus and the fixèd stars !
Whose absence makes the sun and moon as dark
As when, opposed in one diameter,
Their spheres are mounted on the serpent's head,

Or else descended to his winding train.
Live still, my love, and so conserve my life,
Or, dying, be the author of my death!

Zeno. Live still, my lord! O, let my sovereign live
And sooner let the fiery element
Dissolve and make your kingdom in the sky,
Than this base earth should shroud your majesty:
For should I but suspect your death by mine,
The comfort of my future happiness,
And hope to meet your highness in the Heavens,
Turned to despair, would break my wretched breast,
And fury would confound my present rest.
But let me die, my love: yet let me die;
With love and patience let your true love die!
Your grief and fury hurts my second life.—
Yet let me kiss my lord before I die,
And let me die with kissing of my lord.
But since my life is lengthened yet a while,
Let me take leave of these my loving sons,
And of my lords, whose true nobility
Have merited my latest memory.
Sweet sons, farewell! In death resemble me,
And in your lives your father's excellence.
Some music, and my fit will cease, my lord.

                                    [*They call for music.*

  Tamb. Proud fury, and intolerable fit,
That dares torment the body of my love,
And scourge the scourge of the immortal God:
Now are those spheres, where Cupid used to sit,
Wounding the world with wonder and with love,
Sadly supplied with pale and ghastly death,
Whose darts do pierce the centre of my soul.
Her sacred beauty hath enchanted Heaven;
And had she lived before the siege of Troy,

Helen (whose beauty summoned Greece to arms,
And drew a thousand ships to Tenedos)[1]
Had not been named in Homer's Iliad ;
Her name had been in every line he wrote.
Or had those wanton poets, for whose birth
Old Rome was proud, but gazed a while on her,
Nor Lesbia nor Corinna had been named :
Zenocrate had been the argument
Of every epigram or elegy.

                        *[The music sounds.—*ZENOCRATE *dies.*

What ! is she dead ?   Techelles, draw thy sword
And wound the earth, that it may cleave in twain,
And we descend into the infernal vaults,
To hale the Fatal Sisters by the hair,
And throw them in the triple moat of hell,
For taking hence my fair Zenocrate.
Casane and Theridamas, to arms !
Raise cavalieros [2] higher than the clouds,
And with the cannon break the frame of Heaven :
Batter the shining palace of the sun,
And shiver all the starry firmament,
For amorous Jove hath snatched my love from hence,
Meaning to make her stately queen of Heaven.
What God soever holds thee in his arms,
Giving thee nectar and ambrosia,
Behold me here, divine Zenocrate,
Raving, impatient, desperate, and mad,
Breaking my steelèd lance, with which I burst
The rusty beams of Janus' temple-doors,
Letting out Death and tyrannising War,

---

    [1] " Was this the face that launched a thousand ships?"   See
" *Doctor Faustus,*" scene xiv., p. 223.
    [2] *Cavalier* is the word still used for a mound for cannons elevated
above the rest of the works of a fortress, as a horseman is raised
above a foot-soldier.—*Cunningham.*

To march with me under this bloody flag !
And if thou pitiest Tamburlaine the Great,
Come down from Heaven, and live with me again !
   Ther. Ah, good my lord, be patient ; she is dead,
And all this raging cannot make her live.
If words might serve, our voice hath rent the air ;
If tears, our eyes have watered all the earth ;
If grief, our murdered hearts have strained forth blood ;
Nothing prevails, for she is dead, my lord.
   Tamb. " For she is dead !"   Thy words do pierce my
       soul !
Ah, sweet Theridamas ! say so no more ;
Though she be dead, yet let me think she lives,
And feed my mind that dies for want of her.
Where'er her soul be, thou [*To the body*] shalt stay with
       me,
Embalmed with cassia, ambergris, and myrrh,
Not lapt in lead, but in a sheet of gold,
And till I die thou shalt not be interred.
Then in as rich a tomb as Mausolus'
We both will rest and have one epitaph
Writ in as many several languages
As I have conquered kingdoms with my sword.
This cursèd town will I consume with fire,
Because this place bereaved me of my love :
The houses, burnt, will look as if they mourned ;
And here will I set up her statua,
And march about it with my mourning camp
Drooping and pining for Zenocrate.
                     [*The scene closes.*

I 2

ACT THE THIRD.

SCENE I.

Enter the KINGS *of* TREBIZOND *and* SORIA, *one bearing a sword, and the other a sceptre ; next* ORCANES *King of* NATOLIA *and the* KING *of* JERUSALEM *with the imperial crown ; after them enters* CALLAPINE, *and after him other* Lords *and* ALMEDA. ORCANES *and the* KING *of* JERUSALEM *crown* CALLAPINE, *and the others give him the sceptre.*

RC. Callapinus Cyriclibes, otherwise Cybelius, son and successive heir to the late mighty emperor, Bajazeth, by the aid of God and his friend Mahomet, Emperor of Natolia, Jerusalem, Trebizond, Soria, Amasia, Thracia, Illyria, Carmania, and all the hundred and thirty kingdoms late contributory to his mighty father. Long live Callapinus, Emperor of Turkey !

Call. Thrice worthy kings of Natolia, and the rest,
I will requite your royal gratitudes
With all the benefits my empire yields ;
And were the sinews of the imperial seat
So knit and strengthened as when Bajazeth
My royal lord and father filled the throne,
Whose cursèd fate hath so dismembered it,

Then should you see this thief of Scythia,
This proud, usurping King of Persia,
Do us such honour and supremacy,
Bearing the vengeance of our father's wrongs.
As all the world should blot his dignities
Out of the book of base-born infamies.
And now I doubt not but your royal cares
Have so provided for this cursèd foe,
That, since the heir of mighty Bajazeth,
(An emperor so honoured for his virtues,)
Revives the spirits of all true Turkish hearts,
In grievous memory of his father's shame,
We shall not need to nourish any doubt,
But that proud fortune, who hath followed long
The martial sword of mighty Tamburlaine,
Will now retain her old inconstancy,
And raise our honours to as high a pitch,
In this our strong and fortunate encounter :
For so hath heaven provided my escape,
From all the cruelty my soul sustained,
By this my friendly keeper's happy means,
That Jove, surcharged with pity of our wrongs,
Will pour it down in showers on our heads,
Scourging the pride of cursèd Tamburlaine.

   Orc. I have a hundred thousand men in arms ;
Some, that in conquest of the perjured Christian,
Being a handful to a mighty host,
Think them in number yet sufficient
To drink the river Nile or Euphrates,
And for their power enow to win the world.

   K. of Jer. And I as many from Jerusalem,
Judæa, Gaza, and Scalonia's[1] bounds,
That on Mount Sinai with their ensigns spread,

---

[1] Scalonia, *i.e.* Ascalon.

Look like the parti-coloured clouds of Heaven
That show fair weather to the neighbour morn.

   K. of Treb. And I as many bring from Trebizond,
Chio, Famastro, and Amasia,
All bordering on the Mare Major sea,
Riso,[2] Sancina, and the bordering towns
That touch the end of famous Euphrates,
Whose courages are kindled with the flames,
The cursed Scythian sets on all their towns,
And vow to burn the villain's cruel heart.

   K. of Sor. From Soria with seventy thousand strong
Ta'en from Aleppo, Soldino, Tripoli,
And so on to my city of Damasco,
I march to meet and aid my neighbour kings ;
All which will join against this Tamburlaine,
And bring him captive to your highness' feet.

   Orc. Our battle then in martial manner pitched,
According to our ancient use, shall bear
The figure of the semicircled moon,
Whose horns shall sprinkle through the tainted air
The poisoned brains of this proud Scythian.

   Call. Well then, my noble lords, for this my friend
That freed me from the bondage of my foe,
I think it requisite and honourable,
To keep my promise and to make him king,
That is a gentleman, I know, at least.

   Alm. That's no matter, sir, for being a king ; for
Tamburlaine came up of nothing.

   K. of Jer. Your majesty may choose some 'pointed time,
Performing all your promise to the full ;
'Tis nought for your majesty to give a kingdom.

   Call. Then will I shortly keep my promise, Almeda.

   Alm. Why, I thank your majesty.   [*Exeunt.*

---

[1] The Black Sea.   [2] Evidently Rizeli, a town near Trebizond.

SCENE II.

Enter TAMBURLAINE, *with his three* Sons *and* USUMCA-
    SANE; *four* Attendants *bearing the hearse of* ZENO-
    CRATE ; *the drums sounding a doleful march ; the town
    burning.*

Tamb. So burn the turrets of this cursèd town,
Flame to the highest region of the air,
And kindle heaps of exhalations,
That being fiery meteors may presage
Death and destruction to the inhabitants !
Over my zenith hang a blazing star,
That may endure till Heaven be dissolved,
Fed with the fresh supply of earthly dregs,
Threatening a dearth and famine to this land :
Flying dragons, lightning, fearful thunderclaps,
Singe these fair plains and make them seem as black
As is the island where the Furies mask,
Compassed with Lethe, Styx, and Phlegethon,
Because my dear'st Zenocrate is dead.

Cal. This pillar, placed in memory of her,
Where in Arabian, Hebrew, Greek, is writ :—
This town, being burnt by Tamburlaine the Great,   }
Forbids the world to build it up again.   }

Amy. And here this mournful streamer shall be placed,
Wrought with the Persian and th' Egyptian arms,
To signify she was a princess born,
And wife unto the monarch of the East.

Cel. And here this table as a register
Of all her virtues and perfections.

Tamb. And here the picture of Zenocrate,
To show her beauty which the world admired ;
Sweet picture of divine Zenocrate,}

That, hanging here, will draw the gods from Heaven,
And cause the stars fixed in the southern arc,
(Whose lovely faces never any viewed
That have not passed the centre's latitude.)
As pilgrims, travel to our hemisphere,
Only to gaze upon Zenocrate.
Thou shalt not beautify Larissa plains,
But keep within the circle of mine arms.
At every town and castle I besiege,
Thou shalt be set upon my royal tent ;
And when I meet an army in the field,
Those looks will shed such influence in my camp
As if Bellona, goddess of the war,
Threw naked swords and sulphur-balls of fire
Upon the heads of all our enemies.
And now, my lords, advance your spears again :
Sorrow no more, my sweet Casane, now ;
Boys, leave to mourn ! this town shall ever mourn,
Being burnt to cinders for your mother's death.

Cal. If I had wept a sea of tears for her,
It would not ease the sorrows I sustain.

Amy. As is that town, so is my heart consumed
With grief and sorrow for my mother's death.

Cel. My mother's death hath mortified my mind,
And sorrow stops the passage of my speech.

Tamb. But now, my boys, leave off and list to me.
That mean to teach you rudiments of war ;
I'll have you learn to sleep upon the ground,
March in your armour thorough watery fens,
Sustain the scorching heat and freezing cold,
Hunger and thirst, right adjuncts of the war,
And after this to scale a castle wall,
Besiege a fort, to undermine a town,
And make whole cities caper in the air.

Then next the way to fortify your men :
In champion grounds, what figure serves you best,
For which the quinque-angle form is meet.
Because the corners there may fall more flat
Whereas the fort may fittest be assailed,
And sharpest where the assault is desperate.
The ditches must be deep ; the counterscarps [1]
Narrow and steep ; the walls made high and broad ;
The bulwarks and the rampires large and strong,
With cavalieros and thick counterforts.
And room within to lodge six thousand men.
It must have privy ditches, countermines,
And secret issuings to defend the ditch ;
It must have high argins [2] and covered ways,
To keep the bulwark fronts from battery,
And parapets to hide the musketers ;
Casemates to place the great artillery ;
And store of ordnance, that from every flank
May scour the outward curtains of the fort,
Dismount the cannon of the adverse part,
Murder the foe, and save the walls from breach.
When this is learned for service on the land,
By plain and easy demonstration
I'll teach you how to make the water mount,
That you may dry-foot march through lakes and pools,
Deep rivers, havens, creeks, and little seas,
And make a fortress in the raging waves,
Fenced with the concave of monstrous rock,
Invincible by nature of the place.
When this is done then are ye soldiers.
And worthy sons of Tamburlaine the Great.

---

[1] That side of the ditch nearest the besiegers.

[2] *Argine* (Ital.) is an earthwork, and here means the *glacis*.   The *covered way* is the protected road between the *argin* and the *counter-scarp.—Cunningham.*

Cal. My lord, but this is dangerous to be done;
We may be slain or wounded ere we learn.

Tamb. Villain ! Art thou the son of Tamburlaine,
And fear'st to die, or with a curtle-axe
To hew thy flesh, and make a gaping wound?
Hast thou beheld a peal of ordnance strike
A ring of pikes, mingled with shot [1] and horse,
Whose shattered limbs, being tossed as high as Heaven,
Hang in the air as thick as sunny motes,
And canst thou, coward, stand in fear of death?
Hast thou not seen my horsemen charge the foe,
Shot through the arms, cut overthwart the hands,
Dyeing their lances with their streaming blood,
And yet at night carouse within my tent,
Filling their empty veins with airy wine,
That, being concocted, turns to crimson blood,
And wilt thou shun the field for fear of wounds?
View me, thy father, that hath conquered kings,
And, with his horse, marched round about the earth,
Quite void of scars, and clear from any wound,
That by the wars lost not a drop of blood,
And see him lance his flesh to teach you all.

                              [*He cuts his arm.*

A wound is nothing, be it ne'er so deep;
Blood is the god of war's rich livery.
Now look I like a soldier, and this wound
As great a grace and majesty to me,
As if a chain of gold, enamellèd,
Enchased with diamonds, sapphires, rubies,

---

[1] "Mingled with *shot*" means with musketeers. Bullen proposed
to read "foot" instead of "shot," but the alteration is unnecessary.
In *A New Way to Pay Old Debts* (near the end) Massinger uses the
word "shot" in a similar sense :—

                 " Say there were a squadron
Of pikes, lined through with shot, when I am mounted
Upon my injuries, shall I fear to charge them?"

And fairest pearl of wealthy India,
Were mounted here under a canopy,
And I sate down clothed with a massy robe,
That late adorned the Afric potentate,
Whom I brought bound unto Damascus' walls.
Come, boys, and with your fingers search my wound,
And in my blood wash all your hands at once,
While I sit smiling to behold the sight.
Now, my boys, what think ye of a wound?

   Cal. I know not what I should think of it; methinks
     it is a pitiful sight.

   Cel. 'Tis nothing : give me a wound, father.

   Amy. And me another, my lord.

   Tamb. Come, sirrah, give me your arm.

   Cel. Here, father, cut it bravely, as you did your own.

   Tamb. It shall suffice thou darest abide a wound ;
My boy, thou shalt not lose a drop of blood
Before we meet the army of the Turk :
But then run desperate through the thickest throngs,
Dreadless of blows, of bloody wounds, and death ;
And let the burning of Larissa-walls,
My speech of war, and this my wound you see,
Teach you, my boys, to bear courageous minds,
Fit for the followers of great Tamburlaine !
Usumcasane, now come let us march
Towards Techelles and Theridamas,
That we have sent before to fire the towns
The towers and cities of these hateful Turks,
And hunt that coward, faint-heart runaway,
With that accursèd traitor Almeda,
Till fire and sword have found them at a bay.

   Usum. I long to pierce his bowels with my sword,
That hath betrayed my gracious sovereign,—
That cursed and damnèd traitor Almeda.

Tamb. Then let us see if coward Callapine
Dare levy arms against our puissance,
That we may tread upon his captive neck.
And treble all his father's slaveries.   [*Exeunt.*

SCENE III.

Enter TECHELLES, THERIDAMAS. *and their* Train.

Ther. Thus have we marched northward from Tam-
     burlaine,
Unto the frontier point of Soria ;
And this is Balsera, their chiefest hold,[1]
Wherein is all the treasure of the land.

Tech. Then let us bring our light artillery,
Minions. falc'nets, and sakers[2] to the trench,
Filling the ditches with the walls' wide breach,
And enter in to seize upon the hold.
How say you, soldiers ? shall we or not ?

Sold. Yes, my lord, yes ; come, let's about it.

Ther. But stay awhile ; summon a parley, drum.
It may be they will yield it quietly,
Knowing two kings, the friends to Tamburlaine,
Stand at the walls with such a mighty power.

A parley sounded.—The CAPTAIN *appears on the walls,
     with* OLYMPIA *his* Wife, *and his* Son.

Capt. What require you, my masters ?

Ther. Captain, that thou yield up thy hold to us.

Capt. To you ! Why, do you think me weary of it ?

Tech. Nay, captain, thou art weary of thy life,
If thou withstand the friends of Tamburlaine !

---

[1] Fortress.   [2] These were all small pieces of ordnance.

Ther. These pioners of Argier in Africa,
Even in the cannon's face, shall raise a hill
Of earth and faggots higher than the fort,
And over thy argins and covered ways
Shall play upon the bulwarks of thy hold
Volleys of ordnance, till the breach be made
That with his ruin fills up all the trench,
And when we enter in, not Heaven itself
Shall ransom thee, thy wife, and family.

    Tech. Captain, these Moors shall cut the leaden pipes,
That bring fresh water to thy men and thee,
And lie in trench before thy castle walls,
That no supply of victual shall come in,
Nor any issue forth but they shall die ;
And, therefore, captain, yield it quietly.

    Capt. Were you, that are the friends of Tamburlaine,
Brothers of holy Mahomet himself,
I would not yield it : therefore do your worst :
Raise mounts, batter, intrench, and undermine,
Cut off the water, all convoys that come,[1]
Yet I am resolute, and so farewell.

        [CAPTAIN, OLYMPIA, *and their* Son *retire from
          the walls.*

    Ther. Pioners, away ! and where I stuck the stake,
Intrench with those dimensions I prescribed,
Cast up the earth towards the castle wall,
Which, till it may defend you, labour low,
And few or none shall perish by their shot.

    Pio. We will, my lord.   [*Exeunt* Pioners.

    Tech. A hundred horse shall scout about the plains
To spy what force comes to relieve the hold.
Both we, Theridamas, will entrench our men,
And with the Jacob's staff[2] measure the height

---

[1] "Can" in the old editions.   [2] A mathematical instrument.

And distance of the castle from the trench,
That we may know if our artillery
Will carry full point-blank unto their walls.

   Ther. Then see the bringing of our ordnance
Along the trench into the battery,
Where we will have gabions of six feet broad
To save our cannoniers from musket shot.
Betwixt which shall our ordnance thunder forth,
And with the breach's fall, smoke, fire, and dust,
The crack, the echo, and the soldier's cry,
Make deaf the ear and dim the crystal sky.

   Tech. Trumpets and drums, alarum presently :
And, soldiers, play the men ; the hold is yours. [*Exeunt.*

SCENE IV.

Alarm within.— Enter the CAPTAIN, *with* OLYMPIA,
and his Son.

   Olymp. Come, good my lord, and let us haste from
      hence
Along the cave that leads beyond the foe ;
No hope is left to save this conquered hold.

   Capt. A deadly bullet, gliding through my side,
Lies heavy on my heart ; I cannot live.
I feel my liver pierced, and all my veins,
That there begin and nourish every part,
Mangled and torn, and all my entrails bathed
In blood that straineth from their orifex.
Farewell, sweet wife ! sweet son, farewell ! I die. [*He dies.*

   Olymp. Death, whither art thou gone, that both we live ?
Come back again, sweet Death, and strike us both !
One minute end our days ! and one sepulchre

Contain our bodies !   Death, why com'st thou not?
Well, this must be the messenger for thee :

> [*Drawing a dagger.*

Now, ugly Death, stretch out thy sable wings,
And carry both our souls where his remains.
Tell me, sweet boy, art thou content to die?
These barbarous Scythians, full of cruelty,
And Moors, in whom was never pity found,
Will hew us piecemeal, put us to the wheel,
Or else invent some torture worse than that :
Therefore die by thy loving mother's hand,
Who gently now will lance thy ivory throat,
And quickly rid thee both of pain and life.

   Son. Mother, despatch me, or I'll kill myself :
For think you I can live and see him dead?
Give me your knife, good mother, or strike home :
The Scythians shall not tyrannise on me :
Sweet mother, strike, that I may meet my father.

> [*She stabs him and he dies.*

   Olymp. Ah, sacred Mahomet, if this be sin,
Entreat a pardon of the God of Heaven,
And purge my soul before it come to thee.

> [*She burns the bodies of her* Husband *and* Son
> *and then attempts to kill herself.*

Enter THERIDAMAS, TECHELLES, *and all their* Train.

   Ther. How now, madam, what are you doing?
   Olymp. Killing myself, as I have done my son,
Whose body, with his father's, I have burnt,
Lest cruel Scythians should dismember him.
   Tech. 'Twas bravely done, and, like a soldier's wife.
Thou shalt with us to Tamburlaine the Great,
Who, when he hears how resolute thou art,
Will match thee with a viceroy or a king.

Olymp. My lord deceased was dearer unto me
Than any viceroy, king, or emperor ;
And for his sake here will I end my days.
    Ther. But, lady, go with us to Tamburlaine,
And thou shalt see a man, greater than Mahomet,
In whose high looks is much more majesty
Than from the concave superficies
Of Jove's vast palace, the empyreal orb,
Unto the shining bower where Cynthia sits,
Like lovely Thetis, in a crystal robe ;
That treadeth fortune underneath his feet,
And makes the mighty god of arms his slave ;
On whom Death and the Fatal Sisters wait
With naked swords and scarlet liveries :
Before whom, mounted on a lion's back,
Rhamnusia bears a helmet full of blood,
And strews the way with brains of slaughtered men ;
By whose proud side the ugly Furies run,
Hearkening when he shall bid them plague the world ;
Over whose zenith, clothed in windy air,
And eagle's wings joined to her feathered breast,
Fame hovereth, sounding of her golden trump,
That to the adverse poles of that straight line.
Which measureth the glorious frame of Heaven,
The name of mighty Tamburlaine is spread,
And him, fair lady, shall thy eyes behold.
Come !
    Olymp. Take pity of a lady's ruthful tears,
That humbly craves upon her knees to stay
And cast her body in the burning flame,
That feeds upon her son's and husband's flesh.
    Tech. Madam, sooner shall fire consume us both,
Than scorch a face so beautiful as this,
In frame of which Nature hath showed more skill

Than when she gave eternal chaos form,
Drawing from it the shining lamps of Heaven.

Ther. Madam, I am so far in love with you,
That you must go with us—no remedy.

Olymp. Then carry me, I care not, where you will,
And let the end of this my fatal journey
Be likewise end to my accursèd life.

Tech. No, madam, but the beginning of your joy:
Come willingly therefore.

Ther. Soldiers, now let us meet the general,
Who by this time is at Natolia,
Ready to charge the army of the Turk.
The gold and silver, and the pearl, we got,
Rifling this fort, divide in equal shares:
This lady shall have twice as much again
Out of the coffers of our treasury.   [*Exeunt.*

SCENE V.

Enter CALLAPINE, ORCANES, ALMEDA, *and the* KINGS
of JERUSALEM, TREBIZOND, *and* SORIA, *with their*
Trains.—*To them enters a* Messenger.

Mes. Renownèd emperor, mighty Callapine,
God's great lieutenant over all the world!
Here at Aleppo, with a host of men,
Lies Tamburlaine, this King of Persia,
(In numbers more than are the quivering leaves
Of Ida's forest, where your highness' hounds,
With open cry, pursue the wounded stag.)
Who means to girt Natolia's walls with siege,
Fire the town, and overrun the land.

Call. My royal army is as great as his,

Mar.   K

That, from the bounds of Phrygia to the sea
Which washeth Cyprus with his brinish waves,
Covers the hills, the valleys, and the plains.
Viceroys and peers of Turkey, play the men !
Whet all your swords, to mangle Tamburlaine,
His sons, his captains, and his followers ;
By Mahomet ! not one of them shall live ;
The field wherein this battle shall be fought .
For ever term the Persian's sepulchre,
In memory of this our victory !

    Orc. Now, he that calls himself the scourge of
        Jove,
The emperor of the world, and earthly god,
Shall end the warlike progress he intends,
And travel headlong to the lake of hell,
Where legions of devils, (knowing he must die
Here, in Natolia, by your highness' hands,)
All brandishing their brands of quenchless fire.
Stretching their monstrous paws, grin with their teeth
And guard the gates to entertain his soul.

    Call. Tell me, viceroys, the number of your men,
And what our army royal is esteemed.

    K. of Jer. From Palestina and Jerusalem,
Of Hebrews threescore thousand fighting men
Are come since last we showed your majesty.

    Orc. So from Arabia Desert, and the bounds
Of that sweet land, whose brave metropolis
Re-edified the fair Semiramis,
Came forty thousand warlike foot and horse,
Since last we numbered to your majesty.

    K. of Treb. From Trebizond, in Asia the Less,
Naturalised Turks and stout Bithynians
Came to my bands, full fifty thousand more
('That, fighting, know not what retreat doth mean,

Nor e'er return but with the victory,)
Since last we numbered to your majesty.

K. of Sor. Of Sorians from Halla is repaired,
And neighbour cities of your highness' land.
Ten thousand horse, and thirty thousand foot,
Since last we numbered to your majesty ;
So that the royal army is esteemed
Six hundred thousand valiant fighting men.

Call. Then welcome, Tamburlaine, unto thy death.
Come, puissant viceroys, let us to the field,
(The Persians' sepulchre,) and sacrifice
Mountains of breathless men to Mahomet,
Who now, with Jove, opens the firmament
To see the slaughter of our enemies.

Enter TAMBURLAINE *with his three* Sons,
USUMCASANE, *and others.*

Tamb. How now, Casane ? See a knot of kings,
Sitting as if they were a-telling riddles.

Usum. My lord, your presence makes them pale and wan :
Poor souls ! they look as if their death were near.

Tamb. And so he is, Casane ; I am here :
But yet I'll save their lives, and make them slaves.
Ye petty kings of Turkey, I am come,
As Hector did into the Grecian camp,
To overdare the pride of Graecia,
And set his warlike person to the view
Of fierce Achilles, rival of his fame :
I do you honour in the simile ;
For if I should, as Hector did Achilles,
(The worthiest knight that ever brandished sword),
Challenge in combat any of you all,
I see how fearfully ye would refuse,
And fly my glove as from a scorpion.

K 2

Orc. Now thou art fearful of thy army's strength,
Thou would'st with overmatch of person fight;
But, shepherd's issue, base-born Tamburlaine,
Think of thy end! this sword shall lance thy throat.

Tamb. Villain! the shepherd's issue (at whose birth
Heaven did afford a gracious aspèct,
And joined those stars that shall be opposite
Even till the dissolution of the world,
And never meant to make a conqueror
So famous as is mighty Tamburlaine,)
Shall so torment thee and that Callapine,
That, like a roguish runaway, suborned
That villain there, that slave, that Turkish dog,
To false his service to his sovereign,
As ye shall curse the birth of Tamburlaine.

Call. Rail not, proud Scythian! I shall now revenge
My father's vile abuses, and mine own.

K. of Jer. By Mahomet! he shall be tied in chains,
Rowing with Christians in a brigandine
About the Grecian isles to rob and spoil,
And turn him to his ancient trade again:
Methinks the slave should make a lusty thief.

Call. Nay, when the battle ends, all we will meet,
And sit in council to invent some pain
That most may vex his body and his soul.

Tamb. Sirrah, Callapine! I'll hang a clog about your
neck for running away again; you shall not trouble me
thus to come and fetch you;
But as for you, viceroys, you shall have bits,
And, harnessed like my horses, draw my coach;
And when ye stay, be lashed with whips of wire.
I'll have you learn to feed on provender
And in a stable lie upon the planks.

Orc. But, Tamburlaine, first thou shalt kneel to us,
And humbly crave a pardon for thy life.

K. of Treb. The common soldiers of our mighty host
Shall bring thee bound unto the general's tent.

K. of Sor. And all have jointly sworn thy cruel death,
Or bind thee in eternal torments' wrath.

Tamb. Well, sirs, diet yourselves : you know I shall
have occasion shortly to journey you.

Cel. See, father,
How Almeda the jailor looks upon us.

Tamb. Villain ! traitor ! damnèd fugitive !
I'll make thee wish the earth had swallowed thee,
See'st thou not death within my wrathful looks ?
Go, villain, cast thee headlong from a rock,
Or rip thy bowels, and rend out thy heart
To appease my wrath ! or else I'll torture thee,
Searing thy hateful flesh with burning irons
And drops of scalding lead, while all thy joints
Be racked and beat asunder with the wheel :
For, if thou liv'st, not any element
Shall shroud thee from the wrath of Tamburlaine.

Call. Well, in despite of thee he shall be king.
Come, Almeda ; receive this crown of me,
I here invest thee king of Ariadan
Bordering on Mare Roso,[1] near to Mecca.

Orc. What ! Take it, man.

Alm. Good my lord, let me take it. [*To Tamburlaine.*

Call. Dost thou ask him leave ? Here ; take it.

Tamb. Go to, sirrah, take your crown, and make up
the half dozen. So, sirrah, now you are a king, you
must give arms.

Orc. So he shall, and wear thy head in his scutcheon.

Tamb. No ; let him hang a bunch of keys on his
standard to put him in remembrance he was a jailor,
that when I take him, I may knock out his brains with

---

[1] The Red Sea.

them, and lock you in the stable, when you shall come
sweating from my chariot.

K. of Treb. Away: let us to the field, that the villain
may be slain.

Tamb. Sirrah, prepare whips and bring my chariot to
my tent, for as soon as the battle is done, I'll ride in
triumph through the camp.

Enter THERIDAMAS, TECHELLES, *and their* Train.

How now, ye petty kings?   Lo, here are bugs [1]
Will make the hair stand upright on your heads,
And cast your crowns in slavery at their feet.
Welcome, Theridamas and Techelles, both!
See ye this rout, and know ye this same king?

Ther. Ay, my lord ; he was Callapine's keeper.

Tamb. Well, now ye see he is a king ; look to him.
Theridamas, when we are fighting, lest he hide his crown
as the foolish King of Persia did.

K. of Sor. No, Tamburlaine : he shall not be put to
that exigent, I warrant thee.

Tamb. You know not. sir——
But now. my followers and my loving friends,
Fight as you ever did, like conquerors,
The glory of this happy day is yours.
My stern aspèct shall make fair victory.
Hovering betwixt our armies, light on me
Loaden with laurel wreaths to crown us all.

Tech. I smile to think how, when this field is fought
And rich Natolia ours, our men shall sweat
With carrying pearl and treasure on their backs.

Tamb. You shall be princes all, immediately :
Come, fight ye Turks, or yield us victory.

Orc. No ; we will meet thee, slavish Tamburlaine.

[*Exeunt.*

Bugbears.

ACT THE FOURTH.

SCENE I.

Alarums within.—AMYRAS *and* CELEBINUS *issue from
the tent where* CALYPHAS *sits asleep.*

MY. Now in their glories shine the
golden crowns
Of these proud Turks, much like so
many suns
That half dismay the majesty of
Heaven.

Now, brother, follow we our father's sword.
That flies with fury swifter than our thoughts.
And cuts down armies with his conquering wings.

Cel. Call forth our lazy brother from the tent,
For if my father miss him in the field,
Wrath, kindled in the furnace of his breast.
Will send a deadly lightning to his heart.

Amy. Brother, ho ! what given so much to sleep !
You cannot leave it, when our enemies' drums
And rattling cannons thunder in our ears
Our proper ruin and our father's foil ?

Cal. Away, ye fools ! my father needs not me,
Nor you in faith, but that you will be thought
More childish-valorous than manly-wise.
If half our camp should sit and sleep with me,
My father were enough to scare the foe.

You do dishonour to his majesty,
To think our helps will do him any good.

 Amy. What, dar'st thou then be absent from the field,
Knowing my father hates thy cowardice,
And oft hath warned thee to be still in field,
When he himself amidst the thickest troops
Beats down our foes, to flesh our taintless swords?

 Cal. I know, sir, what it is to kill a man;
It works remorse of conscience in me;
I take no pleasure to be murderous,
Nor care for blood when wine will quench my thirst.

 Cel. O cowardly boy! Fie! for shame come forth!
Thou dost dishonour manhood and thy house.

 Cal. Go, go, tall¹ stripling, fight you for us both,
And take my other toward brother here,
For person like to prove a second Mars.
'Twill please my mind as well to hear you both
Have won a heap of honour in the field
And left your slender carcases behind,
As if I lay with you for company.

 Amy. You will not go then?

 Cal. You say true.

 Amy. Were all the lofty mounts of Zona Mundi
That fill the midst of farthest Tartary
Turned into pearl and proffered for my stay,
I would not bide the fury of my father,
When, made a victor in these haughty arms,
He comes and finds his sons have had no shares
In all the honours he proposed for us.

 Cal. Take you the honour, I will take my ease;
My wisdom shall excuse my cowardice.
I go into the field before I need!

    [*Alarums.*—AMYRAS *and* CELEBINUS *run out.*

     ¹ Brave, bold

The bullets fly at random where they list ;
And should I go and kill a thousand men,
I were as soon rewarded with a shot,
And sooner far than he that never fights :
And should I go and do no harm nor good,
I might have harm which all the good I have,
Joined with my father's crown, would never cure.
I'll to cards.   Perdicas !

Enter PERDICAS.

Perd. Here, my lord.

Cal. Come, thou and I will go to cards to drive away the time.

Perd. Content, my lord ; but what shall we play for?

Cal. Who shall kiss the fairest of the Turk's concubines first, when my father hath conquered them.

Perd. Agreed, i' faith.   [*They play.*

Cal. They say I am a coward, Perdicas, and I fear as little their taratantaras, their swords or their cannons, as I do a naked lady in a net of gold, and, for fear I should be afraid, would put it off and come to bed with me.

Perd. Such a fear, my lord, would never make ye retire.

Cal. I would my father would let me be put in the front of such a battle once to try my valour. [*Alarms within.*] What a coil they keep ! I believe there will be some hurt done anon amongst them.   [*Exeunt.*

SCENE II.

Enter TAMBURLAINE, THERIDAMAS, TECHELLES, USUMCA-
SANE, AMYRAS, *and* CELEBINUS, *leading in* ORCANES
and the KINGS *of* JERUSALEM, TREBIZOND, *and* SORIA.

Tamb. See now, ye slaves, my children stoop[1] your pride,

---

[1] Bends.

And lead your bodies sheeplike to the sword.
Bring them, my boys, and tell me if the wars
Be not a life that may illustrate gods,
And tickle not your spirits with desire
Still to be trained in arms and chivalry?

Amy. Shall we let go these kings again, my lord,
To gather greater numbers 'gainst our power,
That they may say it is not chance doth this,
But matchless strength and magnanimity?

Tamb. No, no, Amyras; tempt not fortune so:
Cherish thy valour still with fresh supplies,
And glut it not with stale and daunted foes.
But where's this coward villain, not my son,
But traitor to my name and majesty?

　　　　　　[*He goes in and brings* CALYPHAS *out.*

Image of sloth and picture of a slave,
The obloquy and scorn of my renown!
How may my heart, thus fired with mine eyes,
Wounded with shame and killed with discontent,
Shroud any thought may hold my striving hands
From martial justice on thy wretched soul?

Ther. Yet pardon him, I pray your majesty.
Tech. and Usum. Let all of us entreat your highness'
　　　pardon.

Tamb. Stand up, ye base, unworthy soldiers!
Know ye not yet the argument of arms?

Amy. Good my lord, let him be forgiven for once,
And we will force him to the field hereafter.

Tamb. Stand up, my boys, and I will teach ye arms,
And what the jealousy of wars must do.
O Samarcanda (where I breathèd first
And joyed the fire of this martial flesh),
Blush, blush, fair city, at thine honour's foil,[1]

　　　　　　[1] Soil.

And shame of nature, which Jaertis'[1] stream,
Embracing thee with deepest of his love,
Can never wash from thy distainèd brows !
Here, Jove, receive his fainting soul again ;
A form not meet to give that subject essence
Whose matter is the flesh of Tamburlaine :
Wherein an incorporeal spirit moves,
Made of the mould whereof thyself consists.
Which makes me valiant, proud, ambitious,
Ready to levy power against thy throne,
That I might move the turning spheres of Heaven !
For earth and all this airy region
Cannot contain the state of Tamburlaine.
By Mahomet ! thy mighty friend, I swear,
   n sending to my issue such a soul,
    'reated of the massy dregs of earth,
    he scum and tartar of the elements.
Wherein was neither courage, strength, or wit,
But folly, sloth, and damnèd idleness.
Thou hast procured a greater enemy
Than he that darted mountains at thy head,
Shaking the burthen mighty Atlas bears :   ,
Whereat thou trembling hid'st thee in the air,
Clothed with a pitchy cloud for being seen :
And now, ye cankered curs of Asia,
That will not see the strength of Tamburlaine,
Although it shine as brightly as the sun ;
Now you shall feel the strength of Tamburlaine,
And, by the state of his supremacy,   [*Stabs* CALYPHAS.
Approve the difference 'twixt himself and you.

    Orc. Thou show'st the difference 'twixt ourselves and
        thee,
In this thy barbarous damnèd tyranny.

---

[1] Jaertis, *i.e.* Jaxartes, now the Ser-Daria in Bokhara.

K. of Jer. Thy victories are grown so violent,
That shortly Heaven, filled with the meteors
Of blood and fire thy tyrannies have made,
Will pour down blood and fire on thy head,
Whose scalding drops will pierce thy seething brains,
And, with our bloods, revenge our bloods on thee.

Tamb. Villains ! these terrors and these tyrannies
(If tyrannies war's justice ye repute,)
I execute, enjoined me from above,
To scourge the pride of such as Heaven abhors ;
Nor am I made arch-monarch of the world,
Crowned and invested by the hand of Jove
For deeds of bounty or nobility ;
But since I exercise a greater name,
The scourge of God, and terror of the world,
I must apply myself to fit those terms,
In war, in blood, in death, in cruelty,
And plague such peasants as resist in me,
The power of Heaven's eternal majesty.
Theridamas, Techelles, and Casane,
Ransack the tents and the pavilions
Of these proud Turks, and take their concubines,
Making them bury this effeminate brat,
For not a common soldier shall defile
His manly fingers with so faint a boy,
Then bring those Turkish harlots to my tent,
And I'll dispose them as it likes me best ;
Meanwhile, take him in.

Sold. We will, my lord.

[*Exeunt with the body of* CALYPHAS.

K. of Jer. O damnèd monster ! Nay, a fiend of hell,
Whose cruelties are not so harsh as thine,
Nor yet imposed with such a bitter hate !

Orc. Revenge it, Rhadamanth and Æacus,

And let your hates, extended in his pains,
Excel the hate wherewith he pains our souls.

  K. of Treb. May never day give virtue to his eyes,
Whose sight, composed of fury and of fire,
Doth send such stern affections to his heart.

  K. of Sor. May never spirit, vein, or artier, feed
The cursèd substance of that cruel heart !
But, wanting moisture and remorseful [1] blood,
Dry up with anger, and consume with heat.

  Tamb. Well, bark, ye dogs ; I'll bridle all your tongues,
And bind them close with bits of burnished steel,
Down to the channels of your hateful throats ;
And, with the pains my rigour shall inflict,
I'll make ye roar, that earth may echo forth
The far-resounding torments ye sustain :
As when an herd of lusty Cymbrian bulls
Run mourning round about the females' miss, [2]
And, stung with fury of their following,
Fill all the air with troublous bellowing :
I will, with engines never exercised,
Conquer, sack, and utterly consume
Your cities and your golden palaces ;
And, with the flames that beat against the clouds,
Incense the Heavens, and make the stars to melt,
As if they were the tears of Mahomet,
For hot consumption of his country's pride ;
And, till by vision or by speech I hear
Immortal Jove say " Cease, my Tamburlaine,"
I will persist, a terror to the world,
Making the meteors (that, like armèd men,
Are seen to march upon the towers of Heaven),
Run tilting round about the firmament,
And break their burning lances in the air,

-----

[1] Compassionate.   [2] Loss.

For honour of my wondrous victories.
Come, bring them in to our pavilion.   [*Exeunt.*

SCENE III.

OLYMPIA *discovered alone.*

Olym. Distressed Olympia, whose weeping eyes
Since thy arrival here behold no sun,
But closed within the compass of a tent
Hath stained thy cheeks, and made thee look like death,
Devise some means to rid thee of thy life,
Rather than yield to his detested suit,
Whose drift is only to dishonour thee ;
And since this earth, dewèd with thy brinish tears,
Affords no herbs whose taste may poison thee,
Nor yet this air, beat often with thy sighs,
Contagious smells and vapours to infect thee,
Nor thy close cave a sword to murder thee :
Let this invention be the instrument.

Enter THERIDAMAS.

Ther. Well met, Olympia ; I sought thee in my tent,
But when I saw the place obscure and dark,
Which with thy beauty thou was't wont to light,
Enraged, I ran about the fields for thee,
Supposing amorous Jove had sent his son,
The wingèd Hermes, to convey thee hence ;
But now I find thee, and that fear is past.
Tell me, Olympia, wilt thou grant my suit ?

Olym. My lord and husband's death, with my sweet son's
(With whom I buried all affections
Save grief and sorrow, which torment my heart,)
Forbids my mind to entertain a thought

That tends to love, but meditate on death,
A fitter subject for a pensive soul.

Ther. Olympia, pity him, in whom thy looks
Have greater operation and more force
Than Cynthia's in the watery wilderness,
For with thy view my joys are at the full.
And ebb again as thou departest from me.

Olym. Ah, pity me, my lord! and draw your sword,
Making a passage for my troubled soul,
Which beats against this prison to get out,
And meet my husband and my loving son.

Ther. Nothing but still thy husband and thy son!
Leave this, my love, and listen more to me.
Thou shalt be stately queen of fair Argier;
And clothed in costly cloth of massy gold,
Upon the marble turrets of my court
Sit like to Venus in her chair of state,
Commanding all thy princely eye desires;
And I will cast off arms to sit with thee,
Spending my life in sweet discourse of love.

Olym. No such discourse is pleasant in mine ears,
But that where every period ends with death,
And every line begins with death again.
I cannot love, to be an emperess.

Ther. Nay, lady, then, if nothing will prevail,
I'll use some other means to make you yield:
Such is the sudden fury of my love,
I must and will be pleased, and you shall yield:
Come to the tent again.

Olym. Stay now, my lord; and, will you save my honour,
I'll give your grace a present of such price,
As all the world cannot afford the like.

Ther. What is it?

Olym. An ointment which a cunning alchymist,

Distilléd from the purest balsamum
And simplest extracts of all minerals,
In which the essential form of marble stone,
Tempered by science metaphysical,
And spells of magic from the mouths of spirits,
With which if you but 'noint your tender skin,
Nor pistols, sword, nor lance, can pierce your flesh.

 Ther. Why, madam, think you to mock me thus pal-
  pably ?

 Olym. To prove it, I will 'noint my naked throat,
Which, when you stab, look on your weapon's point,
And you shall see't rebated [1] with the blow.

 Ther. Why gave you not your husband some of it,
If you loved him, and it so precious ?

 Olym. My purpose was, my lord, to spend it so,
But was prevented by his sudden end ;
And for a present, easy proof thereof,
That I dissemble not, try it on me.

 Ther. I will, Olympia, and will keep it for
The richest present of this eastern world.

       [*She anoints her throat.* [2]

 Olym. Now stab, my lord, and mark your weapon's point,
That will be blunted if the blow be great.

 Ther. Here then, Olympia.   [*Stabs her.*
What, have I slain her ! Villain, stab thyself ;
Cut off this arm that murderèd thy love,
In whom the learnèd rabbis of this age
Might find as many wondrous miracles
As in the theoria of the world.

---

 [1] Blunted.

 [2] Collier showed that this incident is borrowed from Ariosto's *Or-
lando Furioso,* Book xxix., " where Isabella, to save herself from the
lawless passion of Rodomont, anoints her neck with a decoction of
herbs which she pretends will render it invulnerable : she then presents her throat to the Pagan, who, believing her assertion aims a
blow and strikes off her head."

Now hell is fairer than Elysium ;
A greater lamp than that bright eye of Heaven,
From whence the stars do borrow all their light,
Wanders about the black circumference ;
And now the damnèd souls are free from pain,
For every Fury gazeth on her looks ;
Infernal Dis is courting of my love,
Inventing masks and stately shows for her,
Opening the doors of his rich treasury
To entertain this queen of chastity ;
Whose body shall be tombed with all the pomp
The treasure of my kingdom may afford.

                    [*Exit, with the body.*

SCENE IV.

Enter TAMBURLAINE *drawn in his chariot by the* KINGS
   of TREBIZOND *and* SORIA, *with bits in their mouths :
   in his right hand he has a whip with which he
   scourgeth them, while his left hand holds the reins ;
   then come* TECHELLES, THERIDAMAS, USUMCASANE,
   AMYRAS, *and* CELEBINUS *with the* KINGS *of* NATOLIA
   and* JERUSALEM, *led by five or six common* Soldiers.

  Tamb. Holla, ye pampered jades of Asia !
What ! can ye draw but twenty miles a day,
And have so proud a chariot at your heels,
And such a coachman as great Tamburlaine,
But from Asphaltis, where I conquered you,
To Byron here, where thus I honour you !
The horse that guide the golden eye of Heaven,
And blow the morning from their nosterils,
Making their fiery gait above the clouds,

    Mar.   L

Are not so honoured in their governor,
As you, ye slaves, in mighty Tamburlaine.
The headstrong jades of Thrace Alcides tamed,
That King Egeus fed with human flesh,
And made so wanton that they knew their strengths,
Were not subdued with valour more divine
Than you by this unconquered arm of mine.
To make you fierce, and fit my appetite,
You shall be fed with flesh as raw as blood,
And drink in pails the strongest muscadel ;
If you can live with it, then live, and draw
My chariot swifter than the racking [1] clouds ;
If not, then die like beasts, and fit for naught
But perches for the black and fatal ravens.
Thus am I right the scourge of highest Jove ;
And see the figure of my dignity
By which I hold my name and majesty !

   Amy. Let me have coach, my lord, that I may ride,
And thus be drawn by these two idle kings.

   Tamb. Thy youth forbids such ease, my kingly boy ;
They shall to-morrow draw my chariot,
While these their fellow-kings may be refreshed.

   Orc. O thou that sway'st the region under earth,
And art a king as absolute as Jove,
Come as thou didst in fruitful Sicily,
Surveying all the glories of the land,
And as thou took'st the fair Proserpina,
Joying the fruit of Ceres' garden-plot,
For love, for honour, and to make her queen,
So for just hate, for shame, and to subdue
This proud contemner of thy dreadful power,
Come once in fury and survey his pride,
Haling him headlong to the lowest hell.

----

[1] Scudding.

Ther. Your majesty must get some bits for these,
To bridle their contemptuous, cursing tongues,
That, like unruly, never-broken jades,
Break through the hedges of their hateful mouths.
And pass their fixed bounds exceedingly.

Tech. Nay, we will break the hedges of their mouths,
And pull their kicking colts[1] out of their pastures.

Usum. Your majesty already hath devised
A mean, as fit as may be, to restrain
These coltish coach-horse tongues from blasphemy.

Cel. How like you that, sir king? why speak you not?

K. of Jer. Ah, cruel brat, sprung from a tyrant's loins!
How like his cursèd father he begins
To practise taunts and bitter tyrannies!

Tamb. Ay, Turk, I tell thee, this same boy is he
That must (advanced in higher pomp than this)
Rifle the kingdoms I shall leave unsacked,
If Jove, esteeming me too good for earth,
Raise me to match the fair Aldeboran,
Above the threefold astracism of Heaven,
Before I conquer all the triple world.
Now, fetch me out the Turkish concubines;
I will prefer them for the funeral
They have bestowed on my abortive son.

      [*The* Concubines *are brought in.*

Where are my common soldiers now, that fought
So lion-like upon Asphaltis' plains?

Sold. Here, my lord.

Tamb. Hold ye, tall[2] soldiers, take ye queens apiece—
I mean such queens as were kings' concubines—

---

[1] Dyce, Cunningham and Bullen consider that "kicking colts" applies to colt's teeth, *i.e.* first teeth; but "hedges" evidently refers to teeth, and "kicking colts" to tongues, already compared to "jades," and shortly afterwards spoken of as "coltish coach-horse tongues." [2] Brave.

Take them ; divide them, and their jewels too,
And let them equally serve all your turns.

   Sold. We thank you.

   Tamb. Brawl not. I warn you, for your lechery :
For every man that so offends shall die.

   Orc. Injurious tyrant, wilt thou so defame
The hateful fortunes of thy victory,
To exercise upon such guiltless dames
The violence of thy common soldiers' lust ?

   Tamb. Live continent then, ye slaves, and meet not me
With troops of harlots at your slothful heels.

   Con. O pity us, my lord, and save our honours.

   Tamb. Are ye not gone, ye villains, with your spoils ?

                 [*They run away with the* Concubines.

   K. of Jer. O merciless, infernal cruelty !

   Tamb. Save your honours !   'Twere but time indeed,
Lost long before ye knew what honour meant.

   Ther. It seems they meant to conquer us, my lord,
And make us jesting pageants for their trulls.

   Tamb. And now themselves shall make our pageants,
And common soldiers jest with all their trulls.
Let them take pleasure soundly in their spoils,
Till we prepare our march to Babylon,
Whither we next make expedition.

   Tech. Let us not be idle then, my lord,
But presently be prest[1] to conquer it.

   Tamb. We will, Techelles.   Forward then, ye jades.
Now crouch, ye kings of greatest Asia,
And tremble when ye hear this scourge will come
That whips down cities and controlleth crowns,
Adding their wealth and treasure to my store.
The Euxine sea, north to Natolia ;
The Terrene, west ; the Caspian, north-north-east ;

                 [1] Ready.

And on the south, Sinus Arabicus ;
Shall all be loaden with the martial spoils
We will convey with us to Persia.
Then shall my native city, Samarcanda,
And crystal waves of fresh Jaertis' stream,
The pride and beauty of her princely seat,
Be famous through the furthest continents,
For there my palace-royal shall be placed,
Whose shining turrets shall dismay the Heavens,
And cast the fame of Ilion's tower to hell.
Thorough the streets with troops of conquered kings,
I'll ride in golden armour like the sun ;
And in my helm a triple plume shall spring,
Spangled with diamonds, dancing in the air,
To note me emperor of the threefold world,
Like [1] to an almond tree y-mounted high
Upon the lofty and celestial mount
Of ever-green Selinus quaintly decked
With blooms more white than Erycina's brows,
Whose tender blossoms tremble every one,
At every little breath through Heaven is blown.
Then in my coach, like Saturn's royal son
Mounted, his shining chariot gilt with fire,
And drawn with princely eagles through the path
Paved with bright crystal and enchased with stars,
When all the gods stand gazing at his pomp,
So will I ride through Samarcanda streets,
Until my soul, dissevered from this flesh,
Shall mount the milk-white way, and meet him there.
To Babylon, my lords ; to Babylon !   [*Exeunt.*

---

[1] This and the five following lines are borrowed with slight variations from the *Faerie Queene*, i. 7 (stanza 32). Bullen suggests that
Marlowe must have seen the passage in MS. The *Faerie Queene*
was published in 1590.

ACT THE FIFTH.

SCENE I.

Enter the GOVERNOR *of* BABYLON, MAXIMUS, *and others
upon the walls.*

GOV. What saith Maximus?

 Max. My lord, the breach the
   enemy hath made
 Gives such assurance of our overthrow
 That little hope is left to save our
   lives,
Or hold our city from the conqueror's hands.
Then hang out flags, my lord, of humble truce,
And satisfy the people's general prayers,
That Tamburlaine's intolerable wrath
May be suppressed by our submission.

 Gov. Villain, respects thou more thy slavish life
Than honour of thy country or thy name?
Are not my life and state as dear to me,
The city, and my native country's weal,
As anything of price with thy conceit?
Have we not hope, for all our battered walls,
To live secure and keep his forces out,
When this our famous lake of Limnasphaltis
Makes walls afresh with everything that falls
Into the liquid substance of his stream,
More strong than are the gates of death or hell?

What faintness should dismay our courages
When we are thus defenced against our foes,
And have no terror but his threatening looks.

Enter above a Citizen. *who kneels to the* GOVERNOR.

Cit. My lord, if ever you did deed of ruth,
And now will work a refuge for our lives,
Offer submission, hang up flags of truce,
That Tamburlaine may pity our distress,
And use us like a loving conqueror.
Though this be held his last day's dreadful siege,
Wherein he spareth neither man nor child,
Yet are there Christians of Georgia here,
Whose state was ever pitied and relieved,
Would get his pardon if your grace would send.

Gov. How is my soul environèd with cares !
And this eternized city, Babylon,
Filled with a pack of faint-heart fugitives
That thus entreat their shame and servitude !

Enter another Citizen.

2nd Cit. My lord, if ever you will win our hearts,
Yield up the town and save our wives and children :
For I will cast myself from off these walls
Or die some death of quickest violence
Before I bide the wrath of Tamburlaine.

Gov. Villains, cowards, traitors to our state !
Fall to the earth and pierce the pit of hell,
That legions of tormenting spirits may vex
Your slavish bosoms with continual pains !
I care not, nor the town will ever yield,
As long as any life is in my breast.

Enter THERIDAMAS, TECHELLES, *with* Soldiers.

Ther. Thou desperate governor of Babylon,

To save thy life, and us a little labour,
Yield speedily the city to our hands,
Or else be sure thou shalt be forced with pains,
More exquisite than ever traitor felt.

   Gov. Tyrant! I turn the traitor in thy throat,
And will defend it in despite of thee.—
Call up the soldiers to defend these walls!

   Tech. Yield, foolish governor; we offer more
Than ever yet we did to such proud slaves
As durst resist us till our third day's siege.
Thou seest us prest to give the last assault,
And that shall bide no more regard of parley.

   Gov. Assault and spare not; we will never yield.
             [Alarms: and they scale the walls.

Enter TAMBURLAINE *drawn in his chariot by the* KINGS
    of TREBIZOND *and* SORIA; AMYRAS, CELEBINUS, *and*
    USUMCASANE; *with the two spare* KINGS *of* NATOLIA
    and JERUSALEM *led by* Soldiers; *and others.*

   Tamb. The stately buildings of fair Babylon,
Whose lofty pillars, higher than the clouds,
Were wont to guide the seaman in the deep,
Being carried thither by the cannon's force,
Now fill the mouth of Limnasphaltis' lake
And make a bridge unto the battered walls.
Where Belus, Ninus, and great Alexander
Have rode in triumph, triumphs Tamburlaine,
Whose chariot wheels have burst the Assyrians' bones,
Drawn with these kings on heaps of carcases.
Now in the place where fair Semiramis,
Courted by kings and peers of Asia,
Hath trod the measures,[1] do my soldiers march;
And in the streets, where brave Assyrian dames

        [1] A slow stately dance.

Have rid in pomp like rich Saturnia,
With furious words and frowning visages
My horsemen brandish their unruly blades.

Re-enter THERIDAMAS *and* TECHELLES, *bringing in the*
GOVERNOR *of* BABYLON.

Who have ye there, my lords?
    Ther. The sturdy governor of Babylon,
That made us all the labour for the town,
And used such slender reckoning of your majesty.
    Tamb. Go, bind the villain; he shall hang in chains
Upon the ruins of this conquered town.
Sirrah, the view of our vermilion tents,
(Which threatened more than if the region'
Next underneath the element of fire
Were full of comets and of blazing stars,
Whose flaming trains should reach down to the earth,)
Could not affright you; no, nor I myself,
The wrathful messenger of mighty Jove,
That with his sword hath quailed all earthly kings,
Could not persuade you to submission,
But still the ports [1] were shut; villain! I say,
Should I but touch the rusty gates of hell,
The triple-headed Cerberus would howl
And make black Jove to crouch and kneel to me;
But I have sent volleys of shot to you,
Yet could not enter till the breach was made.
    Gov. Nor, if my body could have stopt the breach,
Should'st thou have entered, cruel Tamburlaine.
'Tis not thy bloody tents can make me yield,
Nor yet thyself, the anger of the Highest,
For though thy cannon shook the city walls,
My heart did never quake, or courage faint.

             [1] Gates.

Tamb. Well, now I'll make it quake ; go draw him up,
Hang him in chains upon the city walls,
And let my soldiers shoot the slave to death.

Gov. Vile monster ! born of some infernal hag,
And sent from hell to tyrannise on earth,
Do all thy worst ; nor death, nor Tamburlaine,
Torture, nor pain, can daunt my dreadless mind.

Tamb. Up with him, then ; his body shall be scared.

Gov. But, Tamburlaine, in Limnasphaltis' lake
There lies more gold than Babylon is worth,
Which when the city was besieged, I hid.
Save but my life and I will give it thee.

Tamb. Then for all your valour you would save your
        life ?
Whereabout lies it ?

Gov. Under a hollow bank, right opposite
Against the western gate of Babylon.

Tamb. Go thither, some of you, and take his gold ;—
                    [*Exeunt some of the* Attendants.
The rest—forward with execution !
Away with him hence, let him speak no more.
I think I make your courage something quail.
                [*Exeunt other* Attendants *with the* GOVERNOR
                    of BABYLON.
When this is done, we'll march from Babylon,
And make our greatest haste to Persia.
These jades are broken-winded and half tired,
Unharness them, and let me have fresh horse.
            [Attendants *unharness the* KINGS *of* TREBI-
                ZOND *and* SORIA.
So, now their best is done to honour me,
Take them and hang them both up presently.

K. of Treb. Vile tyrant ! barbarous bloody Tambur-
        laine !

Tamb. Take them away, Theridamas; see them despatched.

Ther. I will, my lord.

      [*Exit with the* KINGS *of* TREBIZOND *and* SORIA.

Tamb. Come, Asian viceroys; to your tasks awhile,
And take such fortune as your fellows felt.

Orc. First let thy Scythian horse tear both our limbs.
Rather than we should draw thy chariot,
And like base slaves abject our princely minds
To vile and ignominious servitude.

K. of Jer. Rather lend me thy weapon, Tamburlaine,
That I may sheathe it in this breast of mine.
A thousand deaths could not torment our hearts
More than the thought of this doth vex our souls.

Amy. They will talk still, my lord, if you don't bridle
them.

Tamb. Bridle them, and let me to my coach.

      [*They bridle the* KINGS *of* NATOLIA *and* JERU-
SALEM *and harness them to the chariot. The*
GOVERNOR *is seen hanging in chains on the walls.*

      Re-enter THERIDAMAS.

Amy. See now, my lord, how brave the captain hangs.

Tamb. 'Tis brave indeed, my boy; well done.
Shoot first, my lord, and then the rest shall follow.

Ther. Then have at him to begin withal.

      [THERIDAMAS *shoots at the* GOVERNOR.

Gov. Yet save my life, and let this wound appease
The mortal fury of great Tamburlaine.

Tamb. No, though Asphaltis' lake were liquid gold,
And offered me as ransom for thy life,
Yet should'st thou die.   Shoot at him all at once.

      [*They shoot.*

So now he hangs like Bagdet's governor,

Having as many bullets in his flesh
As there be breaches in her battered wall.
Go now, and bind the burghers hand and foot,
And cast them headlong in the city's lake.
Tartars and Persians shall inhabit there,
And to command the city, I will build
A lofty citadel that all Africa,
Which hath been subject to the Persian king,
Shall pay me tribute for in Babylon.

    Tech. What shall be done with their wives and children,
      my lord?

    Tamb. Techelles, drown them all, man, woman, and
      child.
Leave not a Babylonian in the town.

    Tech. I will about it straight. Come, soldiers.

                      [Exit with Soldiers.

    Tamb. Now, Casane, where's the Turkish Alcoran,
And all the heaps of superstitious books
Found in the temples of that Mahomet,
Whom I have thought a god? They shall be burnt.

    Usum. Here they are, my lord.

    Tamb. Well said; let there be a fire presently.

                      [They light a fire.

In vain, I see, men worship Mahomet:
My sword hath sent millions of Turks to hell,
Slain all his priests, his kinsmen, and his friends,
And yet I live untouched by Mahomet.
There is a God, full of revenging wrath,
From whom the thunder and the lightning breaks,
Whose scourge I am, and him will I obey:
So, Casane, fling them in the fire.   *[They burn the books.*
Now, Mahomet, if thou have any power,
Come down thyself and work a miracle:
Thou art not worthy to be worshippèd,

That suffers flame of fire to burn the writ
Wherein the sum of thy religion rests.
Why send'st thou not a furious whirlwind down
To blow thy Alcoran up to thy throne.
Where men report thou sit'st by God himself?
Or vengeance on the head of Tamburlaine
That shakes his sword against thy majesty.
And spurns the abstracts of thy foolish laws?
Well, soldiers. Mahomet remains in hell:
He cannot hear the voice of Tamburlaine;
Seek out another Godhead to adore,
The God that sits in Heaven, if any God;
For he is God alone. and none but he.

Re-enter TECHELLES.

Tech. I have fulfilled your highness' will, my lord.
Thousands of men. drowned in Asphaltis' lake,
Have make the waters swell above the banks.
And fishes, fed by human carcases.
Amazed, swim up and down upon the waves.
As when they swallow assafœtida.
Which makes them fleet[1] aloft and gape for air.
    Tamb. Well then, my friendly lords, what now remains.
But that we leave sufficient garrison.
And presently depart to Persia
To triumph after all our victories?
    Ther. Ay, good my lord; let us in haste to Persia.
And let this captain be removed the walls
To some high hill about the city here.
    Tamb. Let it be so; about it, soldiers;
But stay; I feel myself distempered suddenly.
    Tech. What is it dares distemper Tamburlaine?
    Tamb. Something, Techelles; but I know not what—

---

[1] Float.

But forth, ye vassals ! whatsoe'er it be,
Sickness or death can never conquer me.   [*Exeunt.*

SCENE II.

Enter CALLAPINE, *the* KING *of* AMASIA, *a* Captain *and*
Soldiers, *with drums and trumpets.*

Call. King of Amasia, now our mighty host
Marcheth in Asia Major where the streams
Of Euphrates and Tigris swiftly run,
And here may we behold great Babylon
Circled about with Limnasphaltis' lake
Where Tamburlaine with all his army lies,
Which being faint and weary with the siege,
We may lie ready to encounter him
Before his host be full from Babylon,
And so revenge our latest grievous loss,
If God or Mahomet send any aid.

 K. of Ama. Doubt not, my lord, but we shall conquer
  him.
The monster that hath drunk a sea of blood,
And yet gapes still for more to quench his thirst,
Our Turkish swords shall headlong send to hell,
And that vile carcase drawn by warlike kings
The fowls shall eat ; for never sepulchre
Shall grace this base-born tyrant Tamburlaine.

 Call. When I record[1] my parents' slavish life,
Their cruel death, mine own captivity,
My viceroy's bondage under Tamburlaine,
Methinks I could sustain a thousand deaths
To be revenged of all his villany.

[1] Recall.

Ah, sacred Mahomet ! thou that hast seen
Millions of Turks perish by Tamburlaine,
Kingdoms made waste, brave cities sacked and burnt,
And but one host is left to honour thee.
Aid thy obedient servant, Callapine,
And make him after all these overthrows
To triumph over cursèd Tamburlaine.

    K. of Ama. Fear not, my lord ; I see great Mahomet
Clothèd in purple clouds, and on his head
A chaplet brighter than Apollo's crown,
Marching about the air with armèd men
To join with you against this Tamburlaine.

    Capt. Renownèd general, mighty Callapine,
Though God himself and holy Mahomet
Should come in person to resist your power,
Yet might your mighty host encounter all,
And pull proud Tamburlaine upon his knees
To sue for mercy at your highness' feet.

    Call. Captain, the force of Tamburlaine is great,
His fortune greater, and the victories
Wherewith he hath so sore dismayed the world
Are greatest to discourage all our drifts ;
Yet when the pride of Cynthia is at full,
She wanes again, and so shall his, I hope ;
For we have here the chief selected men
Of twenty several kingdoms at the least :
Nor ploughman, priest, nor merchant, stays at home ;
All Turkey is in arms with Callapine ;
And never will we sunder camps and arms
Before himself or his be conquerèd.
This is the time that must eternise me
For conquering the tyrant of the world.
Come, soldiers, let us lie in wait for him,
And if we find him absent from his camp,

Or that it be rejoined again at full,
Assail it and be sure of victory.   [*Exeunt.*

SCENE III.

Enter THERIDAMAS, TECHELLES, *and* USUMCASANE.

Ther. Weep, heavens, and vanish into liquid tears !
Fall, stars that govern his nativity,
And summon all the shining lamps of Heaven
To cast their bootless fires to the earth,   •
And shed their feeble influence in the air ;
Muffle your beauties with eternal clouds,
For Hell and Darkness pitch their pitchy tents,
And Death with armies of Cimmerian spirits
Gives battle 'gainst the heart of Tamburlaine !
Now in defiance of that wonted love
Your sacred virtues poured upon his throne
And made his state an honour to the Heavens,
These cowards invisible assail his soul,
And threaten conquest on our sovereign ;
But if he die your glories are disgraced ;
Earth droops and says that hell in Heaven is placed.
    Tech. O then, ye powers that sway eternal seats
And guide this massy substance of the earth,
If you retain desert of holiness
As your supreme estates instruct our thoughts,
Be not inconstant, careless of your fame,—
Bear not the burthen of your enemies' joys
Triumphing in his fall whom you advanced,
But as his birth, life, health, and majesty
Were strangely blest and governèd by Heaven,
So honour, Heaven, (till Heaven dissolvèd be)
His birth, his life, his health, and majesty !

Usum. Blush, Heaven, to lose the honour of thy name !
To see thy footstool set upon thy head !
And let no baseness in thy haughty breast
Sustain a shame of such inexcellence,
To see the devils mount in angels' thrones,
And angels dive into the pools of hell !
And though they think their painful date is out,
And that their power is puissant as Jove's,
Which makes them manage arms against thy state,
Yet make them feel the strength of Tamburlaine,
(Thy instrument and note of majesty,)
Is greater far than they can thus subdue :
For if he die thy glory is disgraced ;
Earth droops and says that hell in Heaven is placed.

Enter TAMBURLAINE *drawn in his chariot by the captive*
Kings *as before*; AMYRAS, CELEBINUS, *and* Physicians.

Tamb. What daring god torments my body thus,
And seeks to conquer mighty Tamburlaine ?
Shall sickness prove me now to be a man,
That have been termed the terror of the world ?
Techelles and the rest, come, take your swords,
And threaten him whose hand afflicts my soul.
Come, let us march against the powers of Heaven,
And set black streamers in the firmament,
To signify the slaughter of the gods.
Ah, friends, what shall I do ?   I cannot stand.
Come carry me to war against the gods
That thus envy the health of Tamburlaine.

Ther. Ah, good my lord, leave these impatient words,
Which add much danger to your malady.

Tamb. Why, shall I sit and languish in this pain ?
No, strike the drums, and in revenge of this,
Come, let us charge our spears and pierce his breast.
Mar.   M

Whose shoulders bear the axis of the world,
That, if I perish, Heaven and earth may fade.
Theridamas, haste to the court of Jove,
Will him to send Apollo hither straight,
To cure me, or I'll fetch him down myself.

Tech. Sit still, my gracious lord ; this grief will cease,
And cannot last, it is so violent.

Tamb. Not last, Techelles ?—No ! for I shall die.
See, where my slave, the ugly monster, Death,
Shaking and quivering, pale and wan for fear,
Stands aiming at me with his murdering dart,
Who flies away at every glance I give,
And, when I look away, comes stealing on.
Villain, away, and hie thee to the field !
I and mine army come to load thy back
With souls of thousand mangled carcases.
Look, where he goes ; but see, he comes again,
Because I stay : Techelles, let us march
And weary Death with bearing souls to hell.

1st Phy. Pleaseth your majesty to drink this potion,
Which will abate the fury of your fit,
And cause some milder spirits govern you.

Tamb. Tell me what think you of my sickness now ?

1st Phy. I viewed your urine, and the hypostasis
Thick and obscure, doth make your danger great ;
Your veins are full of accidental heat,
Whereby the moisture of your blood is dried.
The humidum and calor, which some hold
Is not a parcel of the elements,
But of a substance more divine and pure,
Is almost clean extinguishèd and spent ;
Which, being the cause of life, imports your death.
Besides, my lord, this day is critical,
Dangerous to those whose crisis is as yours

Your artiers, which alongst the veins convey
The lively spirits which the heart engenders,
Are parched and void of spirits, that the soul,
Wanting those organons by which it moves,
Cannot endure, by argument of art.
Yet, if your majesty may escape this day,
No doubt but you shall soon recover all.

   Tamb. Then will I comfort all my vital parts,
And live, in spite of death, above a day. [*Alarms within.*

              Enter Messenger.

   Mes. My lord, young Callapine, that lately fled from
your majesty, hath now gathered a fresh army, and hearing your absence in the field, offers to set upon us
presently.

   Tamb. See, my physicians now, how Jove hath sent
A present medicine to recure my pain.
My looks shall make them fly, and might I follow,
There should not one of all the villain's power
Live to give offer of another fight.

   Usum. I joy, my lord, your highness is so strong,
That can endure so well your royal presence,
Which only will dismay the enemy.

   Tamb. I know it will, Casane. Draw, you slaves;
In spite of death, I will go show my face.

        [*Alarums.—Exit* TAMBURLAINE *and the rest,
            with the exception of the* Physicians. *They
            all presently re-enter.*

   Tamb. Thus are the villain cowards fled for fear,
Like summer's vapours vanished by the sun;
And could I but awhile pursue the field,
That Callapine should be my slave again.
But I perceive my martial strength is spent.
In vain I strive and rail against those powers,

That mean to invest me in a higher throne,
As much too high for this disdainful earth.
Give me a map; then let me see how much
Is left for me to conquer all the world,
That these, my boys, may finish all my wants.

[One brings a map.

Here I began to march towards Persia,
Along Armenia and the Caspian Sea,
And thence unto Bithynia, where I took
The Turk and his great Empress prisoners.
Thence marched I into Egypt and Arabia,
And here, not far from Alexandria,
Whereas the Terrene and the Red Sea meet,
Being distant less than full a hundred leagues,
I meant to cut a channel to them both,
That men might quickly sail to India.[1]
From thence to Nubia near Borno lake,

[1] Bullen (following Cunningham) points to this as an anticipation of the present Suez Canal, but a canal extending from the most eastern branch of the Nile in the neighbourhood of Bubastis to Arsinoe (Suez) on the Red Sea was commenced by Sesostris, who reigned 1394—1328 B.C., and was completed by Ptolemy Philadelphus II. about 277 B.C. It had become partly silted up when Amrou, the Arab conqueror of Egypt, restored and extended it in the direction of Old Cairo. He wanted to bring the end of it directly into the Mediterranean instead of into the Nile, but Omar the Caliph, fearing that the Mediterranean corsairs would then be able to sail direct into the Red Sea, forbade this. It was filled up by Ali Mansour in 775. to hinder the passage of the rebel troops from Arabia : but traces of it remain, and its course is partly followed by the existing Suez Canal.

Marlowe's lines, however, were evidently inspired by the following fact. Vasco de Gama's discovery of the sea-route to India by the Cape of Good Hope in 1497 having dealt a terrible blow to the commercial prosperity of Venice—it may be said, indeed, to have led to its ruin—the Venetian Republic at the beginning of the sixteenth century wished, if possible, to pierce the Isthmus of Suez according to a plan laid before them by Niccolo da Conti. The project was started, but the Mameluke Sultans of Egypt opposed it, and the Republic not being strong enough to carry it out by force, it had to be given up.

And so along the Æthiopian sea,
Cutting the Tropic line of Capricorn,
I conquered all as far as Zanzibar.
Then, by the northern part of Africa,
I came at last to Græcia, and from thence
To Asia, where I stay against my will;
Which is from Scythia, where I first began,
Backwards and forwards near five thousand leagues.
Look here, my boys; see what a world of ground
Lies westward from the midst of Cancer's line,
Unto the rising of this earthly globe;
Whereas the sun, declining from our sight,
Begins the day with our Antipodes!
And shall I die, and this unconquerèd?
Lo, here, my sons, are all the golden mines,
Inestimable drugs and precious stones,
More worth than Asia and the world beside;
And from the Antarctic Pole eastward behold
As much more land, which never was descried,
Wherein are rocks of pearl that shine as bright
As all the lamps that beautify the sky!
And shall I die, and this unconquerèd?
Here, lovely boys; what death forbids my life,
That let your lives command in spite of death.

Amy. Alas, my lord, how should our bleeding hearts,
Wounded and broken with your highness' grief,
Retain a thought of joy or spark of life?
Your soul gives essence to our wretched subjects,
Whose matter is incorporate in your flesh.

Cel. Your pains do pierce our souls; no hope survives,
For by your life we entertain our lives.

Tamb. But, sons, this subject, not of force enough
To hold the fiery spirit it contains,
Must part, imparting his impressions

By equal portions into both your breasts;
My flesh, divided in your precious shapes,
Shall still retain my spirit, though I die,
And live in all your seeds immortally.
Then now remove me, that I may resign
My place and proper title to my son.
First, take my scourge and my imperial crown,
And mount my royal chariot of estate,
That I may see thee crowned before I die.
Help me, my lords, to make my last remove.

       [They lift him from the chariot.

 Ther. A woful change, my lord, that daunts our thoughts,
More than the ruin of our proper souls!

 Tamb. Sit up, my son, and let me see how well
Thou wilt become thy father's majesty.

 Amy. With what a flinty bosom should I joy
The breath of life and burthen of my soul,
If not resolved into resolved pains,
My body's mortified lineaments
Should exercise the motions of my heart,
Pierced with the joy of any dignity!
O father! if the unrelenting ears
Of death and hell be shut against my prayers,
And that the spiteful influence of Heaven,
Deny my soul fruition of her joy;
How should I step, or stir my hateful feet
Against the inward powers of my heart,
Leading a life that only strives to die,
And plead in vain unpleasing sovereignty?

 Tamb. Let not thy love exceed thine honour, son,
Nor bar thy mind that magnanimity
That nobly must admit necessity.
Sit up, my boy, and with those silken reins
Bridle the steelèd stomachs of those jades.

Ther. My lord, you must obey his majesty,
Since fate commands and proud necessity.

Amy. Heavens witness me with what a broken heart
And damnèd spirit I ascend this seat,
And send my soul, before my father die,
His anguish and his burning agony !

[*They crown* AMYRAS.

Tamb. Now fetch the hearse of fair Zenocrate ;
Let it be placed by this my fatal chair,
And serve as parcel of my funeral.

Usum. Then feels your majesty no sovereign ease,
Nor may our hearts, all drowned in tears of blood,
Joy any hope of your recovery ?

Tamb. Casane, no ; the monarch of the earth,
And eyeless monster that torments my soul,
Cannot behold the tears ye shed for me,
And therefore still augments his cruelty.

Tech. Then let some God oppose his holy power
Against the wrath and tyranny of Death,
That his tear-thirsty and unquenchèd hate
May be upon himself reverberate !

[*They bring in the hearse of* ZENOCRATE.

Tamb. Now eyes enjoy your latest benefit,
And when my soul hath virtue of your sight,
Pierce through the coffin and the sheet of gold,
And glut your longings with a heaven of joy.
So reign, my son ; scourge and control those slaves,
Guiding thy chariot with thy father's hand.
As precious is the charge thou undertakest
As that which Clymene's brain-sick son did guide,
When wandering Phœbe's ivory cheeks were scorched,
And all the earth, like Ætna, breathing fire ;
Be warned by him, then ; learn with awful eye
To sway a throne as dangerous as his ;

For if thy body thrive not full of thoughts
As pure and fiery as Phyteus'[1] beams,
The nature of these proud rebelling jades
Will take occasion by the slenderest hair,
And draw thee piecemeal like Hippolitus,
Through rocks more steep and sharp than Caspian clifts.
The nature of thy chariot will not bear
A guide of baser temper than myself,
More than Heaven's coach the pride of Phaeton.
Farewell, my boys; my dearest friends farewell!
My body feels, my soul doth weep to see
Your sweet desires deprived my company,
For Tamburlaine, the scourge of God, must die.

             [*He dies.*

  Amy. Meet Heaven and Earth, and here let all things
    end,
For Earth hath spent the pride of all her fruit,
And Heaven consumed his choicest living fire.
Let Earth and Heaven his timeless[2] death deplore,
For both their worths will equal him no more.

   [1] Probably a form of "Pythius."   [2] Untimely.

THE TRAGICAL HISTORY OF

DR. FAUSTUS.

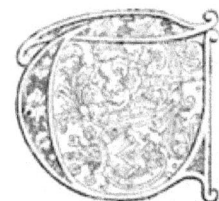

THE earliest known edition of *The Tragical History of Doctor Faustus* is that of 1604; there is a second edition with date of 1609, agreeing in almost every particular with the first; a third edition with new scenes and many alterations, was published in 1616. The text here given is that of 1604, with some readings adopted from the edition of 1616, in general agreement with the texts of Dyce and Bullen. It is very doubtful if any of the additions in the edition of 1616 are by Marlowe; Mr. Bullen thinks that some of them are. They are often ingenious, and sometimes they are improvements. They appear to be written by a clever and facile imitator of Marlowe's style. The comic additions are taken from the prose *History of the damnable Life and deserved Death of Dr. John Faustus;* the serious additions are closely moulded on Marlowe's early work. We know that in 1602 William Bride and Samuel Rowley received four pounds for making "adicyones" to *Faustus.* I have retained the excellent plan, introduced by Professor Ward and adopted by Mr. Bullen, of dividing the play into scenes only: it is a dramatic poem rather than a regular drama.

THE POPE.
CARDINAL of LORRAIN.
EMPEROR of GERMANY.
DUKE of VANHOLT.
FAUSTUS.
VALDES, } Friends to FAUSTUS.
CORNELIUS, }
WAGNER, Servant to FAUSTUS.
Clown.
ROBIN.
RALPH.
Vintner, Horse-Courser, Knight, Old Man, Scholars,
    Friars, and Attendants.

DUCHESS of VANHOLT.

LUCIFER.
BELZEBUB.
MEPHISTOPHILIS.
Good Angel.
Evil Angel.
The Seven Deadly Sins.
Devils.
Spirits in the shape of ALEXANDER THE GREAT, of
    his Paramour, and of HELEN of TROY.

Chorus.

THE TRAGICAL HISTORY OF
DOCTOR FAUSTUS.

—··❧︎⁜❧︎··—

Enter CHORUS.

HORUS. Not marching now in fields
    of Trasymene,
    Where Mars did mate[1] the Carthagi-
      nians ;
    Nor sporting in the dalliance of
    love.
In courts of kings where state is overturned ;
Nor in the pomp of proud audacious deeds,
Intends our Muse to vaunt his heavenly verse :
Only this, gentlemen,—we must perform
The form of Faustus' fortunes, good or bad ;
To patient judgments we appeal our plaud,
And speak for Faustus in his infancy.
Now is he born, his parents base of stock,
In Germany, within a town called Rhodes ;[2]
Of riper years to Wertenberg he went,

---

[1] Confound. The Carthaginians were, however, victorious at Lake
Trasimenus.
[2] Roda, in the Duchy of Saxe-Altenburg.—*Bullen.*

Whereas his kinsmen[1] chiefly brought him up.
So soon he profits in divinity,
The fruitful plot of scholarism graced,
That shortly he was graced with doctor's name,
Excelling all whose sweet delight disputes
In heavenly matters of theology ;
Till swollen with cunning[2] of a self-conceit,
His waxen wings did mount above his reach,
And, melting, Heavens conspired his overthrow ;
For, falling to a devilish exercise,
And glutted now with learning's golden gifts,
He surfeits upon cursèd necromancy.
Nothing so sweet as magic is to him,
Which he prefers before his chiefest bliss.
And this the man that in his study sits !   *[Exit.*

SCENE I.

FAUSTUS *discovered in his Study.*[3]

AUST. Settle thy studies, Faustus, and
          begin
      To sound the depth of that thou wilt
          profess ;
      Having commenced, be a divine in
          show,
Yet level at the end of every art,
And live and die in Aristotle's works.

[1] Whereas, *i.e.* where. Perhaps "kinsmen" should be "kinsman ;" it is "uncle" in the prose *History.*
[2] *i.e.* Knowledge. The word occurs throughout the play in the sense of knowledge or skill.
[3] Dyce suggests that probably the Chorus, before going out, drew a curtain, and disclosed Faustus sitting in his study.

Sweet Analytics, 'tis thou hast ravished me, *[Reads.*
Bene disserere est finis logices.
Is to dispute well logic's chiefest end?
Affords this art no greater miracle?
Then read no more, thou hast attained the end;
A greater subject fitteth Faustus' wit:
Bid *on cai me on*[1] farewell; Galen come,
Seeing *Ubi desinit Philosophus ibi incipit Medicus;*
Be a physician, Faustus, heap up gold,
And be eternised for some wondrous cure. *[Reads.*
Summum bonum medicinæ sanitas,
The end of physic is our body's health.
Why, Faustus, hast thou not attained that end?
Is not thy common talk found Aphorisms?[2]
Are not thy bills[3] hung up as monuments,
Whereby whole cities have escaped the plague,
And thousand desperate maladies been eased?
Yet art thou still but Faustus and a man.
Couldst thou make men to live eternally,
Or, being dead, raise them to life again,
Then this profession were to be esteemed.
Physic, farewell.—Where is Justinian? *[Reads.*
Si una eademque res legatur duobus, alter rem, alter
valorem rei, &c.
A pretty case of paltry legacies! *[Reads.*
Ex hæreditare filium non potest pater nisi, &c.

---

[1] This is Mr. Bullen's emendation. Ed. 1604 reads "Oneay-maeon," by which Marlowe meant the Aristotelian ὂν καὶ μὴ ὂν ("being and not being"). The later 4tos. give (with various spelling) "Œconomy," which is nonsense.

[2] Maxims of medical practice.

[3] Prescriptions by which he had worked his cures. Professor Ward thinks the reference is rather to "the advertisements by which, as a migratory physician, he had been in the habit of announcing his advent, and perhaps his system of cures, and which were now 'hung up as monuments' *in perpetuum*."—*Bullen.*

Such is the subject of the Institute
And universal Body of the Law.
This study fits a mercenary drudge,
Who aims at nothing but external trash;
Too servile and illiberal for me.
When all is done divinity is best;
Jerome's Bible, Faustus, view it well.   [*Reads.*
Stipendium peccati mors est. Ha! *Stipendium, &c.*
The reward of sin is death. That's hard.   [*Reads.*
Si peccasse negamus fallimur et nulla est in nobis veritas.
If we say that we have no sin we deceive ourselves, and
there's no truth in us. Why then, belike we must sin,
and so consequently die.
Ay, we must die an everlasting death.
What doctrine call you this, *Che sera sera,*
What will be shall be?   Divinity, adieu!
These metaphysics of magicians
And necromantic books are heavenly:
Lines, circles, scenes, letters, and characters:
Ay, these are those that Faustus most desires.
O what a world of profit and delight,
Of power, of honour, of omnipotence
Is promised to the studious artisan!
All things that move between the quiet poles
Shall be at my command: emperors and kings
Are but obeyèd in their several provinces,
Nor can they raise the wind or rend the clouds;
But his dominion that exceeds in this
Stretcheth as far as doth the mind of man,
A sound magician is a mighty god:
Here, Faustus, tire thy brains to gain a deity.
Wagner!

---

[1] The old form of spelling for "sarà."

Enter WAGNER.

　　　Commend me to my dearest friends,
The German Valdes and Cornelius ;
Request them earnestly to visit me.

　　Wag. I will, sir.　　　　　　　　　　　　[*Exit.*

　　Faust. Their conference will be a greater help to me
Than all my labours, plod I ne'er so fast.

Enter Good Angel *and* Evil Angel.

　　G. Ang. O Faustus ! lay that damnèd book aside,
And gaze not on it lest it tempt thy soul,
And heap God's heavy wrath upon thy head.
Read, read the Scriptures : that is blasphemy.

　　E. Ang. Go forward, Faustus, in that famous art,
Wherein all Nature's treasure is contained :
Be thou on earth as Jove is in the sky,
Lord and commander of these elements. \
　　　　　　　　　　　　　　　[*Exeunt* Angels.

　　Faust. How am I glutted with conceit of this !
Shall I make spirits fetch me what I please,
Resolve me of all ambiguities,
Perform what desperate enterprise I will?
I'll have them fly to India for gold,
Ransack the ocean for orient pearl,
And search all corners of the new-found world
For pleasant fruits and princely delicates;
I'll have them read me strange philosophy
And tell the secrets of all foreign kings ;
I'll have them wall all Germany with brass,
And make swift Rhine circle fair Wertenberg,
I'll have them fill the public schools with silk,
Wherewith the students shall be bravely clad ;
I'll levy soldiers with the coin they bring,

Mar.　　　　　　　　　　　　　　　　　　　N

And chase the Prince of Parma from our land,
And reign sole king of all the provinces ;
Yea, stranger engines for the brunt of war
Than was the fiery keel at Antwerp's bridge,[1]
I'll make my servile spirits to invent.

Enter VALDES *and* CORNELIUS.[2]

Come, German Valdes and Cornelius,
And make me blest with your sage conference.
Valdes, sweet Valdes, and Cornelius,
Know that your words have won me at the last
To practise magic and concealèd arts :
Yet not your words only, but mine own fantasy
That will receive no object, for my head

---

[1] This refers to an incident at the blockade of Antwerp by the Prince of Parma in 1585, which is thus described in Grimestone's *Generall Historie of the Netherlands*, p. 875, ed. 1609 :—" They of Antuerpe knowing that the bridge and the Stocadoes were finished, made a great shippe, to be a meanes to breake all this work of the prince of Parmaes ; this great shippe was made of mason's worke within, in the manner of a vaulted caue : vpon the hatches there were layed myll-stones, graue-stones, and others of great weight ; and within the vault were many barrels of powder, ouer the which there were holes ; and in them they had put matches, hanging at a thred, the which burning vntill they came vnto the thred, would fall into the powder, and so blow vp all. And for that they could not haue any one in this shippe to conduct it, Lanckhaer, a sea captaine of the Hollanders, being then in Antuerpe, gaue them counsell to tye a great beame at the end of it, to make it to keepe a straight course in the middest of the streame. In this sort floated this shippe the fourth of Aprill, vntill that it came vnto the bridge ; where (within a while after) the powder wrought his effect, with such violence, as the vessell, and all that was within it, and vpon it, flew in pieces, carrying away a part of the Stocado and of the bridge. The marquesse of Roubay Vicont of Gant, Gaspar of Robles lord of Billy, and the Seignior of Torchies, brother vnto the Seignior of Bours, with many others, were presently slaine : which were torne in pieces, and dispersed abroad, both vpon the land and vpon the water."

[2] This is the famous Cornelius Agrippa. German (possibly meant for " Hermann ") Valdes is not known. Various improbable persons have been brought forward. In Scene II. it is said " they two are infamous through the world." I can only suggest that Marlowe may have meant Paracelsus.

But ruminates on necromantic skill.
Philosophy is odious and obscure,
Both law and physic are for petty wits;
Divinity is basest of the three,
Unpleasant, harsh, contemptible, and vile:
'Tis magic, magic that hath ravished me.
Then, gentle friends, aid me in this attempt;
And I that have with concise syllogisms
Gravelled the pastors of the German church,
And made the flowering pride of Wertenberg
Swarm to my problems, as the infernal spirits
On sweet Musæus,[1] when he came to hell,
Will be as cunning as Agrippa[2] was,
Whose shadow made all Europe honour him.

 Vald. Faustus, these books, thy wit, and our experience
Shall make all nations to canonise us.
As Indian Moors obey their Spanish lords,
So shall the spirits of every element
Be always serviceable to us three;
Like lions shall they guard us when we please;
Like Almain rutters[3] with their horsemen's staves
Or Lapland giants,[4] trotting by our sides;
Sometimes like women or unwedded maids,
Shadowing more beauty in their airy brows
Than have the white breasts of the queen of love:
From Venice shall they drag huge argosies,
And from America the golden fleece
That yearly stuffs old Philip's treasury;
If learnèd Faustus will be resolute.

---

[1] Cf. Virgil. *Æn.* vi. 667.

[2] *i. e.* Cornelius Agrippa whom he is addressing, here spoken of as another person. "In Book i. of his work *De Occulta Philosophia*, Agrippa gives directions for the operations of sciomancy."—*Ward.*

[3] Troopers. Germ. *Reiters.*

[4] On the contrary, Laplanders are almost dwarfs. Marlowe falls into a similar error in *Tamburlaine.* See *ante*, p. 90.

N 2

Faust. Valdes, as resolute am I in this
As thou to live ; therefore object it not.

Corn. The miracles that magic will perform
Will make thee vow to study nothing else.
He that is grounded in astrology,
Enriched with tongues, well seen in minerals,
Hath all the principles magic doth require.
Then doubt not, Faustus, but to be renowned,
And more frequented for this mystery
Than heretofore the Delphian Oracle.
The spirits tell me they can dry the sea,
And fetch the treasure of all foreign wrecks,
Ay, all the wealth that our forefathers hid
Within the massy entrails of the earth ;
Then tell me, Faustus, what shall we three want ?

Faust. Nothing, Cornelius ! O this cheers my soul !
Come show me some demonstrations magical,
That I may conjure in some bushy grove,
And have these joys in full possession.

Vald. Then haste thee to some solitary grove,
And bear wise Bacon's and Albanus'[1] works,
The Hebrew Psalter and New Testament;
And whatsoever else is requisite
We will inform thee ere our conference cease.

Corn. Valdes, first let him know the words of art ;
And then, all other ceremonies learned,
Faustus may try his cunning by himself.

Vald. First I'll instruct thee in the rudiments,
And then wilt thou be perfecter than I.

---

[1] Düntzer suggests that Marlowe refers to Pietro d'Abano, an
Italian physician and alchemist who narrowly escaped burning by
the Inquisition. He was born about 1250 and died about 1316,
and wrote a work called *Conciliator Differentiarum Philosophorum
et Medicorum.* "Albanus" was changed by Mitford into "Alber-
tus," the schoolman, whose works were considered to possess magical
properties.

Faust. Then come and dine with me. and after meat,
We'll canvas every quiddity thereof ;
For ere I sleep I'll try what I can do :
This night I'll conjure tho' I die therefore.   [*Exeunt.*

SCENE II.

Enter two Scholars.[1]

1st Schol. I wonder what's become of Faustus that was
wont to make our schools ring with *sic probo ?*

2nd Schol. That shall we know, for see here comes his
boy.

Enter WAGNER.

1st Schol. How now, sirrah !   Where's thy master?

Wag. God in heaven knows !

2nd Schol. Why, dost not thou know ?

Wag. Yes, I know.   But that follows not.

1st Schol. Go to, sirrah ! leave your jesting, and tell us
where he is.

Wag. That follows not necessary by force of argument,
that you, being licentiates, should stand upon : therefore
acknowledge your error and be attentive.

2nd Schol. Why, didst thou not say thou knewest ?

Wag. Have you any witness on't ?

1st Schol. Yes, sirrah, I heard you.

Wag. Ask my fellows if I be a thief.

2nd Schol. Well, you will not tell us?

Wag. Yes, sir, I will tell you ; yet if you were not
dunces, you would never ask me such a question ; for is
not he *corpus naturale ?* and is not that *mobile ?* then
wherefore should you ask me such a question ? But that

[1] It has been suggested that the scene is before Faustus's house.
as Wagner presently speaks of his master being within at dinner.

I am by nature phlegmatic, slow to wrath, and prone to lechery (to love, I would say), it were not for you to come within forty feet of the place of execution, although I do not doubt to see you both hanged the next sessions. Thus having triumphed over you, I will set my countenance like a precisian, and begin to speak thus :—Truly, my dear brethren, my master is within at dinner, with Valdes and Cornelius, as this wine, if it could speak, would inform your worships ; and so the Lord bless you, preserve you, and keep you, my dear brethren, my dear brethren.   [*Exit.*

1st Schol. Nay, then, I fear he has fallen into that damned Art, for which they two are infamous through the world.

2nd Schol. Were he a stranger, and not allied to me, yet should I grieve for him. But come, let us go and inform the Rector, and see if he by his grave counsel can reclaim him.

1st Schol. O, but I fear me nothing can reclaim him.

2nd Schol. Yet let us try what we can do.   [*Exeunt.*

SCENE III.

Enter FAUSTUS *to conjure.*[1]

Faust. Now that the gloomy shadow of the earth
Longing to view Orion's drizzling look,
Leaps from the antarctic world unto the sky,
And dims the welkin with her pitchy breath,[2]
Faustus, begin thine incantations,

---

[1] The scene is supposed to be a grove. See the conversation between Faustus and Valdes towards the end of Scene I.

[2] Bullen points out that the above four lines are repeated verbatim in the first scene of *Taming of a Shrew,* 1594.

And try if devils will obey thy hest,
Seeing thou hast prayed and sacrificed to them.
Within this circle is Jehovah's name,
Forward and backward anagrammatised,
The breviated names of holy saints,
Figures of every adjunct to the Heavens,
And characters of signs and erring [1] stars,
By which the spirits are enforced to rise :
Then fear not, Faustus, but be resolute,
And try the uttermost magic can perform.

*Sint mihi Dei Acherontis propitii ! Valeat numen triplex
Jehovæ ! Ignei, aerii, aquatani spiritus, salvete ! Orientis
princeps Belzebub, inferni ardentis monarcha, et Demogorgon, propitiamus vos, ut appareat et surgat Mephistophilis. Quid tu moraris ? [2] per Jehovam, Gehennam, et con-
secratam aquam quam nunc spargo, signumque crucis quod
nunc facio, et per vota nostra, ipse nunc surgat nobis dicatus
Mephistophilis !*

Enter MEPHISTOPHILIS.

I charge thee to return and change thy shape ;
Thou art too ugly to attend on me.
Go, and return an old Franciscan friar ;
That holy shape becomes a devil best.   [*Exit* MEPHIS.
I see there's virtue in my heavenly words ;
Who would not be proficient in this art ?
How pliant is this Mephistophilis,
Full of obedience and humility !
Such is the force of magic and my spells :
Now Faustus, thou art conjuror laureat,
That canst command great Mephistophilis :
Quin regis Mephistophilis fratris imagine.

---

[1] *i.e.* Wandering.
[2] "Quid tu moraris?" preparatory to a weightier invocation,
suggested by Mr. Fleay and Mr. Bullen, in place of "quod tumeraris."

Re-enter MEPHISTOPHILIS *like a Franciscan* Friar.[1]

Meph. Now, Faustus, what would'st thou have me
    to do?

Faust. I charge thee wait upon me whilst I live,
To do whatever Faustus shall command,
Be it to make the moon drop from her sphere,
Or the ocean to overwhelm the world.

Meph. I am a servant to great Lucifer,
And may not follow thee without his leave :
No more than he commands must we perform.

Faust. Did not he charge thee to appear to me?

Meph. No, I came hither of mine own accord.

Faust. Did not my conjuring speeches raise thee?
    Speak.

Meph. That was the cause, but yet *per accidens ;*
For when we hear one rack the name of God,
Abjure the Scriptures and his Saviour Christ,
We fly in hope to get his glorious soul ;
Nor will we come, unless he use such means
Whereby he is in danger to be damned :
Therefore the shortest cut for conjuring
Is stoutly to abjure the Trinity,
And pray devoutly to the Prince of Hell.

Faust. So Faustus hath
Already done ; and holds this principle,
There is no chief but only Belzebub,
To whom Faustus doth dedicate himself.
This word "damnation" terrifies not him,

---

[1] In the prose *History* we read : — " After Dr. Faustus had made
his promise to the devill, in the morning betimes he called the spirit
before him, and commanded him that he should alwayes come to
him like a fryer after the order of Saint Francis, with a bell in his
hand like Saint Anthony, and to ring it once or twice before he
appeared, that he might know of his certaine coming."

For he confounds hell in Elysium ;
His ghost be with the old philosophers !
But, leaving these vain trifles of men's souls,
Tell me what is that Lucifer thy lord ?

   Meph. Arch-regent and commander of all spirits.

   Faust. Was not that Lucifer an angel once?

   Meph. Yes, Faustus, and most dearly loved of God.

   Faust. How comes it then that he is Prince of devils?

   Meph. O, by aspiring pride and insolence ;
For which God threw him from the face of Heaven.

   Faust. And what are you that live with Lucifer?

   Meph. Unhappy spirits that fell with Lucifer,
Conspired against our God with Lucifer,
And are for ever damned with Lucifer.

   Faust. Where are you damned ?

   Meph. In hell.

   Faust. How comes it then that thou art out of hell?

   Meph. Why this is hell, nor am I out of it :
Think'st thou that I who saw the face of God,
And tasted the eternal joys of Heaven,
Am not tormented with ten thousand hells,
In being deprived of everlasting bliss?
O Faustus ! leave these frivolous demands,
Which strike a terror to my fainting soul.

   Faust. What, is great Mephistophilis so passionate
For being deprivèd of the joys of Heaven?
Learn thou of Faustus manly fortitude,
And scorn those joys thou never shalt possess.
Go bear these tidings to great Lucifer :
Seeing Faustus hath incurred eternal death
By desperate thoughts against Jove's deity,
Say he surrenders up to him his soul,
So he will spare him four and twenty years,
Letting him live in all voluptuousness ;

Having thee ever to attend on me ;
To give me whatsoever I shall ask,
To tell me whatsoever I demand,
To slay mine enemies, and aid my friends,
And always be obedient to my will.
Go and return to mighty Lucifer,
And meet me in my study at midnight,
And then resolve[1] me of thy master's mind.

    Meph. I will, Faustus.   [*Exit.*

    Faust. Had I as many souls as there be stars,
I'd give them all for Mephistophilis.
By him I'll be great Emperor of the world,
And make a bridge thorough the moving air,
To pass the ocean with a band of men :
I'll join the hills that bind the Afric shore,
And make that country continent to Spain,
And both contributory to my crown.
The Emperor shall not live but by my leave,
Nor any potentate of Germany.
Now that I have obtained what I desire,
I'll live in speculation of this art
Till Mephistophilis return again.   [*Exit.*

SCENE IV.

Enter WAGNER *and* Clown.[2]

    Wag. Sirrah, boy, come hither.

    Clown. How, boy! Swowns, boy! I hope you have seen many boys with such pickadevaunts[3] as I have; boy, quotha !

---

[1] *i.e.* Inform me.
[2] It is suggested by Dyce that the scene is probably a street.
[3] Beards cut to a sharp point (Fr. *pic-à-devant*).

Wag. Tell me. sirrah, hast thou any comings in ?

Clown. Ay, and goings out too. You may see else.

Wag. Alas, poor slave ! see how poverty jesteth in his nakedness ! the villain is bare and out of service, and so hungry that I know he would give his soul to the devil for a shoulder of mutton, though 'twere blood-raw.

Clown. How? My soul to the Devil for a shoulder of mutton, though 'twere blood-raw ! Not so, good friend. By'r Lady, I had need have it well roasted and good sauce to it, if I pay so dear.

Wag. Well, wilt thou serve us, and I'll make thee go like *Qui mihi discipulus ?* [1]

Clown. How, in verse ?

Wag. No, sirrah ; in beaten silk and stavesacre. [2]

Clown. How, how, Knave's acre ! [3] I, I thought that was all the land his father left him. Do you hear? I would be sorry to rob you of your living.

Wag. Sirrah, I say in stavesacre.

Clown. Oho ! Oho ! Stavesacre ! Why then belike if I were your man I should be full of vermin.

Wag. So thou shalt, whether thou beest with me or no. But, sirrah, leave your jesting, and bind yourself presently unto me for seven years, or I'll turn all the lice about thee into familiars, and they shall tear thee in pieces.

Clown. Do you hear, sir ? You may save that labour : they are too familiar with me already : swowns ! they are as bold ᵛ flesh as if they had paid for their meat and

---

[1] Dyce points out that these are the first words of W. Lily's "*Ad discipulos carmen de moribus.*"

[2] A ranunculaceous plant (Delphinium staphisagria), still used for destroying lice.

[3] Knave's Acre (Poultney Street) described by Strype as narrow, and chiefly inhabited by dealers in old goods and glass bottles.

Wag. Well, do you hear, sirrah? Hold, take these
guilders.   [*Gives money.*

Clown. Gridirons! what be they?

Wag. Why, French crowns.

Clown. Mass, but in the name of French crowns, a
man were as good have as many English counters. And
what should I do with these?

Wag. Why, now, sirrah, thou art at an hour's warning,
whensoever and wheresoever the Devil shall fetch thee.

Clown. No, no. Here, take your gridirons again.

Wag. Truly I'll none of them.

Clown. Truly but you shall.

Wag. Bear witness I gave them him.

Clown. Bear witness I give them you again.

Wag. Well, I will cause two devils presently to fetch
thee away—Baliol and Belcher.

Clown. Let your Baliol and your Belcher come here,
and I'll knock them, they were never so knocked since
they were devils! Say I should kill one of them, what
would folks say? " Do you see yonder tall fellow in the
round slop[1]—he has killed the devil." So I should be
called Kill-devil all the parish over.

Enter two Devils : *the* Clown *runs up and down crying.*

Wag. Baliol and Belcher! Spirits, away! [*Exeunt* Devils.

Clown. What, are they gone? A vengeance on them,
they have vile long nails! There was a he-devil, and a
she-devil! I'll tell you how you shall know them; all
he-devils has horns, and all she-devils has clifts and
cloven feet.

Wag. Well, sirrah, follow me.

Clown. But, do you hear—if I should serve you, would
you teach me to raise up Banios and Belcheos?

---

[1] Wide breeches, trunk hose.

Wag. I will teach thee to turn thyself to anything; to
a dog, or a cat, or a mouse, or a rat, or anything.

Clown. How! a Christian fellow to a dog or a cat, a
mouse or a rat! No, no, sir. If you turn me into anything, let it be in the likeness of a little pretty frisking
flea, that I may be here and there and everywhere. Oh,
I'll tickle the pretty wenches' plackets; I'll be amongst
them, i' faith.

Wag. Well, sirrah, come.

Clown. But, do you hear, Wagner?

Wag. How! Baliol and Belcher!

Clown. O Lord! I pray, sir, let Banio and Belcher go
sleep.

Wag. Villain—call me Master Wagner, and let thy left
eye be diametarily fixed upon my right heel, with *quasi
vestigiis nostris insistere.*   [*Exit.*

Clown. God forgive me, he speaks Dutch fustian.
Well, I'll follow him: I'll serve him, that's flat.   [*Exit.*

SCENE V.

FAUSTUS *discovered in his Study.*

Faust. Now, Faustus, must
Thou needs be damned, and canst thou not be saved:
What boots it then to think of God or Heaven?
Away with such vain fancies, and despair:
Despair in God, and trust in Belzebub;
Now go not backward: no, Faustus, be resolute:
Why waver'st thou? O, something soundeth in mine ears
"Abjure this magic, turn to God again!"
Ay, and Faustus will turn to God again.
To God?——He loves thee not—

The God thou serv'st is thine own appetite,
Wherein is fixed the love of Belzebub ;
To him I'll build an altar and a church,
And offer lukewarm blood of new-born babes.

Enter Good Angel *and* Evil Angel.

G. Ang. Sweet Faustus, leave that execrable art.

Faust. Contrition, prayer, repentance ! What of them ?

G. Ang. O, they are means to bring thee unto Heaven.

E. Ang. Rather, illusions—fruits of lunacy,
That makes men foolish that do trust them most.

G. Ang. Sweet Faustus, think of Heaven, and heavenly
things.

E. Ang. No, Faustus, think of honour and of wealth.
                              [*Exeunt* Angels.

Faust. Of wealth !
Why the signiory of Embden shall be mine.
When Mephistophilis shall stand by me,
What God can hurt thee?   Faustus, thou art safe :
Cast no more doubts.   Come, Mephistophilis,
And bring glad tidings from great Lucifer ;—
Is't not midnight?   Come, Mephistophilis ;
Veni, veni, Mephistophile !

Enter MEPHISTOPHILIS.

Now tell me, what says Lucifer thy lord ?

Meph. That I shall wait on Faustus whilst he lives,
So he will buy my service with his soul.

Faust. Already Faustus hath hazarded that for thee.

Meph. But, Faustus, thou must bequeath it solemnly,
And write a deed of gift with thine own blood,
For that security craves great Lucifer.
If thou deny it, I will back to hell.

Faust. Stay, Mephistophilis ! and tell me what good
Will my soul do thy lord.

Meph. Enlarge his kingdom.

Faust. Is that the reason why he tempts us thus?

Meph. Solamen miseris socios habuisse doloris.

Faust. Why, have you any pain that tortures[1] others?

Meph. As great as have the human souls of men.
But tell me, Faustus, shall I have thy soul?
And I will be thy slave, and wait on thee,
And give thee more than thou hast wit to ask.

　Faust. Ay, Mephistophilis, I give it thee.

　Meph. Then, Faustus, stab thine arm courageously,
And bind thy soul that at some certain day
Great Lucifer may claim it as his own;
And then be thou as great as Lucifer.

　Faust. [stabbing his arm.] Lo, Mephistophilis, for love
　　of thee,
I cut mine arm, and with my proper blood
Assure my soul to be great Lucifer's,
Chief lord and regent of perpetual night!
View here the blood that trickles from mine arm,
And let it be propitious for my wish.

　Meph. But, Faustus, thou must
Write it in manner of a deed of gift

　Faust. Ay, so I will. [*Writes.*] But, Mephistophilis,
My blood congeals, and I can write no more.

　Meph. I'll fetch thee fire to dissolve it straight.
　　　　　　　　　　　　　　　　　　　[*Exit.*

　Faust. What might the staying of my blood portend?
Is it unwilling I should write this bill?
Why streams it not that I may write afresh?
Faustus gives to thee his soul. Ah, there it stayed.
Why should'st thou not? Is not thy soul thine own?
Then write again, *Faustus gives to thee his soul.*

---

[1] "You" is of course the antecedent of "that."—*Bullen.*

Re-enter MEPHISTOPHILIS *with a chafer of coals.*

Meph. Here's fire.   Come, Faustus, set it on.[1]
Faust. So now the blood begins to clear again ;
Now will I make an end immediately.   [*Writes.*
Meph. O what will not I do to obtain his soul. [*Aside.*
Faust. Consummatum est : this bill is ended,
And Faustus hath bequeathed his soul to Lucifer.
But what is this inscription on mine arm ?
Homo, fuge ! Whither should I fly ?
If unto God, he'll throw me down to hell.
My senses are deceived ; here's nothing writ :—
I see it plain ; here in this place is writ
Homo, fuge ! Yet shall not Faustus fly.
Meph. I'll fetch him somewhat to delight his mind.
                                                     [*Exit.*

Re-enter MEPHISTOPHILIS *with* Devils, *who give crowns
and rich apparel to* FAUSTUS, *dance, and depart.*

Faust. Speak, Mephistophilis. what means this show ?
Meph. Nothing, Faustus, but to delight thy mind withal,
And to show thee what magic can perform.
Faust. But may I raise up spirits when I please ?
Meph. Ay, Faustus, and do greater things than these.
Faust. Then there's enough for a thousand souls.
Here, Mephistophilis, receive this scroll,
A deed of gift of body and of soul :
But yet conditionally that thou perform
All articles prescribed between us both.
Meph. Faustus, I swear by hell and Lucifer
To effect all promises between us made.

---

[1] The sixth chapter of the prose *History* is headed—"How Dr.
Faustus set his blood in a saucer on warme ashes and writ as 'ol-
loweth."

Faust. Then hear me read them : *On these conditions following. First, that Faustus may be a spirit in form and substance. Secondly, that Mephistophilis shall be his servant, and at his command. Thirdly, shall do for him and bring him whatsoever he desires.*[1] *Fourthly, that he shall be in his chamber or house invisible. Lastly, that he shall appear to the said John Faustus, at all times, and in what form or shape soever he pleases. I, John Faustus, of Wertenberg, Doctor, by these presents do give both body and soul to Lucifer, Prince of the East, and his minister, Mephistophilis : and furthermore grant unto them, that twenty-four years being expired, the articles above written inviolate, full power to fetch or carry the said John Faustus, body and soul, flesh, blood, or goods, into their habitation wheresoever. By me,*   *John Faustus.*

Meph. Speak, Faustus, do you deliver this as your
    deed ?
Faust. Ay, take it, and the Devil give thee good on't !
Meph. Now, Faustus, ask what thou wilt.
Faust. First will I question with thee about hell.
Tell me where is the place that men call hell ?
Meph. Under the Heavens.
Faust. Ay, but whereabout ?
Meph. Within the bowels of these elements,
Where we are tortured and remain for ever ;
Hell hath no limits, nor is circumscribed
In one self place ; for where we are is hell,
And where hell is there must we ever be :
And, to conclude, when all the world dissolves,

---

[1] The words "he desires" are not in the old quartos. Dyce first pointed out that in the prose *History of Dr. Faustus*, the third article runs thus :—That Mephistophilis should bring him anything and do for him whatsoever "—a later edition adding " he desired," and another " he requireth."

And every creature shall be purified,
All places shall be hell that is not Heaven.

 Faust. Come, I think hell's a fable.

 Meph. Ay, think so still, till experience change thy
  mind.

 Faust. Why, think'st thou then that Faustus shall be
  damned?

 Meph. Ay, of necessity, for here's the scroll
Wherein thou hast given thy soul to Lucifer.

 Faust. Ay, and body too; but what of that?
Think'st thou that Faustus is so fond [1] to imagine
That, after this life, there is any pain?
Tush; these are trifles, and mere old wives' tales.

 Meph. But, Faustus, I am an instance to prove the
  contrary,
For I am damnèd, and am now in hell.

 Faust. How! now in hell?
Nay, an this be hell, I'll willingly be damned here;
What? walking, disputing, &c.?
But, leaving off this, let me have a wife,
The fairest maid in Germany;
For I am wanton and lascivious,
And cannot live without a wife.

 Meph. How—a wife?
I prithee, Faustus, talk not of a wife.

 Faust. Nay, sweet Mephistophilis, fetch me one, for I
will have one.

 Meph. Well—thou wilt have one. Sit there till I
come: I'll fetch thee a wife in the Devil's name. [*Exit.*

 Re-enter MEPHISTOPHILIS *with a* Devil *dressed like a*
  woman, with fireworks.

 Meph. Tell me, Faustus, how dost thou like thy wife?

---

[1] Foolish.

Faust. A plague on her for a hot whore !

Meph. Tut, Faustus,

Marriage is but a ceremonial toy ;

And if thou lovest me, think no more of it.

I'll cull thee out the fairest courtesans,

And bring them every morning to thy bed ;

She whom thine eye shall like, thy heart shall have,

Be she as chaste as was Penelope,

As wise as Saba,[1] or as beautiful

As was bright Lucifer before his fall.

Here, take this book, peruse it thoroughly : [*Gives a book.*

The iterating[2] of these lines brings gold ;

The framing of this circle on the ground

Brings whirlwinds, tempests, thunder and lightning ;

Pronounce this thrice devoutly to thyself,

And men in armour shall appear to thee,

Ready to execute what thou desir'st.

Faust. Thanks, Mephistophilis ; yet fain would I have
a book wherein I might behold all spells and incantations.
that I might raise up spirits when I please.

Meph. Here they are, in this book.   [*Turns to them.*

Faust. Now would I have a book where I might see
all characters and planets of the heavens, that I might
know their motions and dispositions.

Meph. Here they are too.   [*Turns to them.*

Faust. Nay, let me have one book more,   and then I
have done,—wherein I might see all plants, herbs, and
trees that grow upon the earth.

Meph. Here they be.

Faust. O, thou art deceived.

Meph. Tut, I warrant thee. [*Turns to them.   Exeunt.*

---

[1] *i.e.* Sabæa, the Queen of Sheba.
[2] Repeating.

SCENE VI.

Enter FAUSTUS *and* MEPHISTOPHILIS.

Faust. When I behold the heavens, then I repent,
And curse thee, wicked Mephistophilis,
Because thou hast deprived me of those joys.

Meph. Why, Faustus,
Thinkest thou Heaven is such a glorious thing?
I tell thee 'tis not half so fair as thou,
Or any man that breathes on earth.

Faust. How prov'st thou that?

Meph. 'Twas made for man, therefore is man more
excellent.

Faust. If it were made for man, 'twas made for me;
I will renounce this magic and repent.

Enter Good Angel *and* Evil Angel.

G. Ang. Faustus, repent; yet God will pity thee.

E. Ang. Thou art a spirit; God can not pity thee.

Faust. Who buzzeth in mine ears I am a spirit?
Be I a devil, yet God may pity me;
Ay, God will pity me if I repent.

E. Ang. Ay, but Faustus never shall repent.

[*Exeunt* Angels.

Faust. My heart's so hardened I cannot repent.
Scarce can I name salvation, faith, or heaven,
But fearful echoes thunder in mine ears
" Faustus, thou art damned!"   Then swords and knives,
Poison, gun, halters, and envenomed steel
Are laid before me to despatch myself.
And long ere this I should have slain myself,
Had not sweet pleasure conquered deep despair.

---

¹ The scene is supposed to be a room in Faustus's house.

Have not I made blind Homer sing to me
Of Alexander's love and Œnon's death?
And hath not he that built the walls of Thebes
With ravishing sound of his melodious harp,
Made music with my Mephistophilis?
Why should I die then, or basely despair?
I am resolved: Faustus shall ne'er repent—
Come, Mephistophilis, let us dispute again,
And argue of divine astrology.
Tell me, are there many heavens above the moon?
Are all celestial bodies but one globe,
As is the substance of this centric earth?

Meph. As are the elements, such are the spheres
Mutually folded in each other's orb,
And, Faustus,
All jointly move upon one axletree
Whose terminine is termed the world's wide pole;
Nor are the names of Saturn, Mars, or Jupiter
Feigned, but are erring stars.

Faust. But tell me, have they all one motion both,
situ et tempore.

Meph. All jointly move from east to west in twenty-four hours upon the poles of the world; but differ in their motion upon the poles of the zodiac.

Faust. Tush!
These slender trifles Wagner can decide;
Hath Mephistophilis no greater skill?
Who knows not the double motion of the planets?
The first is finished in a natural day:
The second thus: as Saturn in thirty years; Jupiter in twelve; Mars in four; the Sun, Venus, and Mercury in a year; the moon in twenty eight days. Tush, these are freshmen's suppositions. But tell me, hath every sphere a dominion or *intelligentia*?

Meph. Ay.

Faust. How many heavens. or spheres, are there?

Meph. Nine : the seven planets. the firmament, and the empyreal heaven.

Faust. Well, resolve me in this question : Why have we not conjunctions, oppositions, aspects, eclipses, all at one time, but in some years we have more, in some less?

Meph. Per inæqualem motum respectu totius.

Faust. Well, I am answered.   Tell me who made the world.

Meph. I will not.

Faust. Sweet Mephistophilis, tell me.

Meph. Move me not, for I will not tell thee.

Faust. Villain, have I not bound thee to tell me any-thing?

Meph. Ay, that is not against our kingdom ; but this is. Think thou on hell, Faustus, for thou art damned.

Faust. Think, Faustus, upon God that made the world.

Meph. Remember this.   [*Exit.*

Faust. Ay, go, accursèd spirit, to ugly hell.
'Tis thou hast damned distressèd Faustus' soul.
Is't not too late?

Re-enter Good Angel *and* Evil Angel.

E. Ang. Too late.

G. Ang. Never too late, if Faustus can repent.

E. Ang. If thou repent, devils shall tear thee in pieces.

G. Ang. Repent, and they shall never raze thy skin.
                                                      [*Exeunt* Angels.

Faust. Ah, Christ my Saviour,
Seek to save distressèd Faustus' soul !

Enter LUCIFER, BELZEBUB, *and* MEPHISTOPHILIS.

Luc. Christ cannot save thy soul, for he is just;
There's none but I have interest in the same.

Faust. O, who art thou that look'st so terrible?

Luc. I am Lucifer,
And this is my companion-prince in hell.

Faust. O Faustus! they are come to fetch away thy soul!

Luc. We come to tell thee thou dost injure us;
Thou talk'st of Christ contrary to thy promise;
Thou should'st not think of God: think of the Devil.[1]

Faust. Nor will I henceforth: pardon me in this,
And Faustus vows never to look to Heaven,
Never to name God, or to pray to him,
To burn his Scriptures, slay his ministers,
And make my spirits pull his churches down.

Luc. Do so, and we will highly gratify thee. Faustus,
we are come from hell to show thee some pastime: sit
down, and thou shalt see all the Seven Deadly Sins
appear in their proper shapes.

Faust. That sight will be as pleasing unto me,
As Paradise was to Adam the first day
Of his creation.

Luc. Talk not of Paradise nor creation, but mark this
show: talk of the Devil, and nothing else: come away!

Enter the Seven Deadly Sins.

Now, Faustus, examine them of their several names and
dispositions.

Faust. What art thou—the first?

Pride. I am Pride. I disdain to have any parents.

---

[1] I venture to relegate the meaningless line which follows: ' And
of his dam too," for which no editor considers Marlowe responsible,
to a foot-note.

I am like to Ovid's flea :[1] I can creep into every corner
of a wench ; sometimes, like a periwig, I sit upon her
brow ; or like a fan of feathers, I kiss her lips ; indeed I
do—what do I not ? But, fie, what a scent is here ! I'll
not speak another word, except the ground were per-
fumed, and covered with cloth of arras.

Faust. What art thou—the second ?

Cov't. I am Covetousness, begotten of an old churl in
an old leathern bag ; and might I have my wish I would
desire that this house and all the people in it were turned
to gold, that I might lock you up in m·· good chest. O,
my sweet gold !

Faust. What art thou—the third ?

Wrath. I am Wrath. I had neither father nor mother :
I leapt out of a lion's mouth when I was scarce half an
hour old ; and ever since I have run up and down the
world with this case[2] of rapiers, wounding myself when
I had nobody to fight withal. I was born in hell ; and
look to it, for some of you shall be my father.

Faust. What art thou—the fourth ?

Envy. I am Envy, begotten of a chimney sweeper and
an oyster-wife. I cannot read, and therefore wish all
books were burnt. I am lean with seeing others eat. O
that there would come a famine through all the world,
that all might die, and I live alone ! then thou should'st
see how fat I would be. But must thou sit and I stand !
Come down with a vengeance !

Faust. Away, envious rascal ! What art thou—the fifth ?

Glut. Who, I, sir ? I am Gluttony. My parents are
all dead, and the devil a penny they have left me, but a

---

[1] An allusion to the mediæval *Carmen de Pulice,* formerly ascribed
to Ovid.—*Bullen.*

[2] A pair of rapiers worn in a single sheath, and used one in each
hand.

bare pension, and that is thirty meals a day and ten bevers [1]—a small trifle to suffice nature. O, I come of a royal parentage ! My grandfather was a Gammon of Bacon, my grandmother was a Hogshead of Claret-wine ; my godfathers were these, Peter Pickleherring, and Martin Martlemas-beef ; [2] O, but my godmother, she was a jolly gentlewoman, and well beloved in every good town and city ; her name was Mistress Margery March-beer. [3] Now, Faustus, thou hast heard all my progeny, wilt thou bid me to supper ?

Faust. No, I'll see thee hanged : thou wilt eat up all my victuals.

Glut. Then the Devil choke thee !

Faust. Choke thyself, glutton ! Who art thou - the sixth?

Sloth. I am Sloth.   I was begotten on a sunny bank, where I have lain ever since ; and you have done me great injury to bring me from thence : let me be carried thither again by Gluttony and Lechery. I'll not speak another word for a king's ransom.

Faust. What are you, Mistress Minx, the seventh and last?

Lech. Who, I, sir ?   I am one that loves an inch of raw mutton better than an ell of fried stockfish ; and the first letter of my name begins with L. [4]

Luc. Away to hell, to hell ! Now, Faustus, how dost thou like this ?   [*Exeunt the* Sins.

Faust. O, this feeds my soul !

---

[1] Refreshments taken between meals.

[2] Martlemas or Martinmas was the customary time for hanging up provisions, which had been previously salted, to dry. Our ancestors lived chiefly upon salted meat in the spring, owing to the winter-fed cattle not being fit for use.   St. Martin's day is November 11th.

[3] The March brewing was much esteemed in those days, as it is in Germany at the present time.

[4] All the quartos have " Lechery."   The change which was first proposed by Collier has been adopted by Dyce and other editors.

Luc. Tut, Faustus, in hell is all manner of delight.

Faust. O might I see hell, and return again,
How happy were I then!

Luc. Thou shalt; I will send for thee at midnight.
In meantime take this book; peruse it throughly,
And thou shalt turn thyself into what shape thou wilt.

Faust. Great thanks, mighty Lucifer!
This will I keep as chary as my life.

Luc. Farewell, Faustus, and think on the Devil.

Faust. Farewell, great Lucifer!

> [*Exeunt* LUCIFER *and* BELZEBUB.
> Come, Mephistophilis.
> [*Exeunt.*

Enter CHORUS.

HORUS. Learned Faustus,
To know the secrets of astronomy,
Graven in the book of Jove's high
    firmament,
Did mount himself to scale Olympus'
    top,
Being seated in a chariot burning bright,
Drawn by the strength of yoky dragons' necks.
He now is gone to prove cosmography,
And, as I guess, will first arrive at Rome,
To see the Pope and manner of his court,
And take some part of holy Peter's feast,
That to this day is highly solemnised.[1]   [*Exit.*

---

[1] In the edition of 1616 the speech of the Chorus is ingeniously
expanded as follows:—

> *Chor.* Learned Faustus,
> To find the secrets of Astronomy
> Graven in the book of Jove's high firmament,

SCENE VII.

Enter FAUSTUS *and* MEPHISTOPHILIS.[1]

Faust. Having now, my good Mephistophilis,
Passed with delight the stately town of Trier,[2]
Environed round with airy mountain-tops,
With walls of flint, and deep entrenchèd lakes,
Not to be won by any conquering prince;
From Paris next, coasting the realm of France,
We saw the river Maine fall into Rhine,
Whose banks are set with groves of fruitful vines;
Then up to Naples, rich Campania,
Whose buildings fair and gorgeous to the eye,
The streets straight forth, and paved with finest brick,
Quarter the town in four equivalents :
There saw we learnèd Maro's golden tomb,

> Did mount him up to scale Olympus' top ;
> Where, sitting in a chariot burning bright,
> Drawn by the strength of yoked dragons' necks,
> He views the clouds, the planets, and the stars,
> The tropic zones, and quarters of the sky,
> From the bright circle of the hornèd moon
> Even to the height of *Primum Mobile* ;
> And, whirling round with this circumference,
> Within the concave compass of the pole,
> From east to west his dragons swiftly glide,
> And in eight days did bring him home again.
> Not long he stayed within his quiet house,
> To rest his bones after his weary toil ;
> But new exploits do hale him out again :
> And, mounted then upon a dragon's back,
> That with his wings did part the subtle air,
> He now is gone to prove cosmography,
> That measures coasts and kingdoms of the earth ;
> And, as I guess, will first arrive at Rome,
> To see the Pope and manner of his court,
> And take some part of holy Peter's feast,
> The which this day is highly solemnised.   [*Exit.*

This represents the revisers of the play at their best.

[1] The scene is the Pope's Privy Chamber.   [2] Treves.

The way he cut, an English mile in length,
Thorough a rock of stone in one night's space ;[1]
From thence to Venice, Padua, and the rest,
In one[2] of which a sumptuous temple stands,
That threats the stars with her aspiring top.[3]
Thus hitherto has Faustus spent his time :
But tell me, now, what resting-place is this ?
Hast thou, as erst I did command,
Conducted me within the walls of Rome ?

Meph. Faustus, I have; and, because we will not be
unprovided, I have taken from his Holiness' privy-chamber
for our use.

Faust. I hope his Holiness will bid us welcome.

Meph. Tut, 'tis no matter, man, we'll be bold with his
good cheer.
And now, my Faustus, that thou may'st perceive
What Rome containeth to delight thee with,
Know that this city stands upon seven hills
That underprop the groundwork of the same :
Just through the midst runs flowing Tiber's stream,
With winding banks that cut it in two parts :
Over the which four stately bridges lean,
That make safe passage to each part of Rome :
Upon the bridge called Ponte Angelo
Erected is a castle passing strong,
Within whose walls such store of ordnance are,

[1] Virgil was regarded as a magician in the Middle Ages.
[2] The prose *History* shows the "sumptuous temple" to be St. Mark's at Venice.
[3] In the edition of 1616 the two following lines are added :—

"Whose frame is paved with sundry coloured stones,
 And roofed aloft with curious work in gold."

The addition is an interesting example of the close fashion in which the revisers clung to the prose *History*, wherein we read "how all the pavement was set with coloured stones, and all the roof or loft of the church double gilded over."

And double [1] cannons formed of carvèd brass,
As match the days within one complete year :
Besides the gates and high pyramides,[2]
Which Julius Cæsar brought from Africa.

Faust. Now by the kingdoms of infernal rule,
Of Styx, of Acheron, and the fiery lake
Of ever-burning Phlegethon, I swear
That I do long to see the monuments
And situation of bright-splendent Rome :
Come therefore, let's away.

Meph. Nay, Faustus, stay; I know you'd see the Pope,
And take some part of holy Peter's feast,
Where thou shalt see a troop of bald-pate friars,
Whose *summum bonum* is in belly-cheer.

Faust. Well, I'm content to compass them some sport,
And by their folly make us merriment.
Then charm me, Mephistophilis, that I
May be invisible, to do what I please
Unseen of any whilst I stay in Rome.

                    [MEPHISTOPHILIS *charms him.*

Meph. So, Faustus, now
Do what thou wilt, thou shalt not be discerned.

Sound a sonnet.[3]   Enter the POPE *and the* CARDINAL *of*
LORRAIN *to the banquet, with* Friars *attending.*

Pope. My Lord of Lorrain, wilt please you draw near?
Faust. Fall to, and the devil choke you an you spare!

---

[1] This may mean simply large cannons, or as Ward points out, cannon with double bores. Two cannons with *triple* bores were taken from the French at Malplaquet, and are now in the Woolwich Museum.

[2] Evidently obelisks are here meant, although the word "pyramides" was formerly applied to church spires.

[3] Written in half a dozen other forms—Sennet, Senet, Synnet, Cynet, Signet and Signate. Nares defines it as "a particular set of notes on the trumpet or cornet, different from a flourish."

Pope. How now ! Who's that which spake?—Friars,
    look about.

1*st Friar.* Here's nobody, if it like your Holiness.

Pope. My lord, here is a dainty dish was sent me from
the Bishop of Milan.

Faust. I thank you, sir.   [*Snatches the dish.*

Pope. How now ! Who's that which snatched the meat
from me ? Will no man look ? My Lord, this dish was
sent me from the Cardinal of Florence.

Faust. You say true ; I'll ha't.   [*Snatches the dish.*

Pope. What, again ! My lord, I'll drink to your grace.

Faust. I'll pledge your grace.   [*Snatches the cup.*

C. of Lor. My lord, it may be some ghost newly
crept out of purgatory, come to beg a pardon of your
Holiness.   .

Pope. It may be so.   Friars, prepare a dirge to lay the
fury of this ghost.   Once again, my lord, fall to.

        [*The* POPE *crosses himself.*

Faust. What, are you crossing of yourself?
Well, use that trick no more I would advise you.

        [*The* POPE *crosses himself again.*

Well, there's the second time.   Aware the third,
I give you fair warning.

        [*The* POPE *crosses himself again, and* FAUSTUS
            *hits him a box of the ear; and they all run
            away.*

Come on, Mephistophilis, what shall we do ?

Meph. Nay, I know not   We shall be cursed with
bell, book, and candle.

Faust. How ! bell, book, and candle,—candle, book,
    and bell,
Forward and backward to curse Faustus to hell !
Anon you shall hear a hog grunt, a calf bleat, an ass bray,
Because it is Saint Peter's holiday.

Re-enter the Friars *to sing the Dirge.*

1st Friar. Come, brethren, let's about our business
with good devotion.

They sing:

Cursed be he that stole away his Holiness' meat from
　　　the table ! *Maledicat Dominus !*
Cursed be he that struck his Holiness a blow on the face !
　　　Maledicat Dominus !
Cursed be he that took Friar Sandelo a blow on the
　　　pate ! *Maledicat Dominus !*
Cursed be he that disturbeth our holy dirge ! *Maledicat
　　　Dominus !*
Cursed be he that took away his Holiness' wine !
　　　Maledicat Dominus ! Et omnes sancti ! Amen !
　　　[MEPHISTOPHILIS *and* FAUSTUS *beat the* Friars, *and
　　　fling fireworks among them : and so exeunt.*

Enter CHORUS.

CHORUS. When Faustus had with plea-
　　　　　sure ta'en the view
　　　　Of rarest things, and royal courts of kings,
　　　　He stayed his course, and so returnèd
　　　　　home ;　　　　　　　　　　[grief,
　　　　Where such as bear his absence but with
I mean his friends, and near'st companions,
Did gratulate his safety with kind words,
And in their conference of what befell,
Touching his journey through the world and air,
They put forth questions of Astrology,
Which Faustus answered with such learnèd skill,
As they admired and wondered at his wit.

Now is his fame spread forth in every land;
Amongst the rest the Emperor is one,
Carolus the Fifth, at whose palace now
Faustus is feasted 'mongst his noblemen.
What there he did in trial of his art,
I leave untold—your eyes shall see performed.   [*Exit.*

SCENE VIII.

Enter ROBIN *the Ostler with a book in his hand.*[1]

Robin. O, this is admirable! here I ha' stolen one of
Dr. Faustus's conjuring books, and i' faith I mean to
search some circles for my own use. Now will I make
all the maidens in our parish dance at my pleasure, stark
naked before me; and so by that means I shall see more
than e'er I felt or saw yet.

Enter RALPH *calling* ROBIN.

Ralph. Robin, prithee come away; there's a gentleman tarries to have his horse, and he would have his
things rubbed and made clean: he keeps such a chafing
with my mistress about it; and she has sent me to look
thee out; prithee come away.

Robin. Keep out, keep out, or else you are blown up;
you are dismembered, Ralph: keep out, for I am about
a roaring piece of work.

Ralph. Come, what dost thou with that same book?
Thou can'st not read.

Robin. Yes, my master and mistress shall find that I
can read, he for his forehead, she for her private study;
she's born to bear with me, or else my art fails.

---

[1] The scene is supposed to be an inn-yard.

Ralph. Why, Robin, what book is that?

Robin. What book ! why the most intolerable book for conjuring that e'er was invented by any brimstone devil.

Ralph. Can'st thou conjure with it ?

Robin. I can do all these things easily with it : first, I can make thee drunk with ippocras[1] at any tabern[2] in Europe for nothing ; that's one of my conjuring works.

Ralph. Our Master Parson says that's nothing.

Robin. True, Ralph ; and more, Ralph, if thou hast any mind to Nan Spit, our kitchenmaid, then turn her and wind her to thy own use as often as thou wilt, and at midnight.

Ralph. O brave Robin, shall I have Nan Spit, and to mine own use ? On that condition I'd feed thy devil with horsebread[3] as long as he lives, of free cost.

Robin. No more, sweet Ralph : let's go and make clean our boots, which lie foul upon our hands, and then to our conjuring in the Devil's name.   [*Exeunt.*

SCENE IX.

Enter ROBIN *and* RALPH *with a silver goblet.*

Robin. Come, Ralph, did not I tell thee we were for ever made by this Doctor Faustus' book ? *ecce signum,* here's a simple purchase[4] for horsekeepers ; our horses shall eat no hay as long as this lasts.

Ralph. But, Robin, here come the vintner.

Robin. Hush ! I'll gull him supernaturally.

---

[1] " Hippocrates, a medicated drink composed usually of red wine, but sometimes white, with the addition of sugar and spices."—*Nares.*

[2] Tavern.

[3] It was a common practice among our ancestors to feed horses on bread. Nares quotes from Gervase Markham a recipe for making horse-loaves.—*Bullen.*   [4] Booty.

Enter Vintner.

Drawer, I hope all is paid: God be with you; come,
   Ralph.

Vint. Soft, sir; a word with you. I must yet have a
goblet paid from you, ere you go.

Robin. I, a goblet, Ralph; I, a goblet! I scorn you,
and you are but a[1] &c. I, a goblet! search me.

Vint. I mean so, sir, with your favour. [*Searches him.*

Robin. How say you now?

Vint. I must say somewhat to your fellow. You, sir!

Ralph. Me, sir! me, sir! search your fill. [Vintner
searches him.] Now, sir, you may be ashamed to burden
honest men with a matter of truth.

Vint. Well, t'one of you hath this goblet about you.

Robin. You lie, drawer, 'tis afore me. [*Aside.*] Sirrah
you, I'll teach you to impeach honest men;—stand by;
—I'll scour you for a goblet!—stand aside you had best,
I charge you in the name of Belzebub. Look to the
goblet, Ralph.   [*Aside to* RALPH.

Vint. What mean you, sirrah?

Robin. I'll tell you what I mean. [*Reads from a book.*]
Sanctobulorum Periphrasticon — Nay, I'll tickle you,
vintner. Look to the goblet, Ralph.   [*Aside to* RALPH.

[*Reads.*] *Polypragmos Belseborams framanto pacostiphos
tostu, Mephistophilis, &c.*

Enter MEPHISTOPHILIS, *sets squibs at their backs, and
then exit. They run about.*

Vint. O nomine Domini! what meanest thou, Robin?
thou hast no goblet.

---

[1] The actor was at liberty to supply the abuse. Mr. Bullen mentions
that in an old play, the *Tryall of Chevalry* (1605), the stage direction occurs, " Exit Clown, speaking *anything.*"

Ralph. *Peccatum peccatorum!* Here's thy goblet, good
vintner.   [*Gives the goblet to* Vintner, *who exit.*

Robin. *Misericordia pro nobis!* What shall I do?
Good Devil, forgive me now, and I'll never rob thy library
more.

Re-enter MEPHISTOPHILIS.

Meph. Monarch of hell, under whose black survey
Great potentates do kneel with awful fear,
Upon whose altars thousand souls do lie,
How am I vexèd with these villains' charms?
From Constantinople am I hither come
Only for pleasure of these damnèd slaves.

Robin. How from Constantinople? You have had a
great journey: will you take sixpence in your purse to
pay for your supper, and begone?

Meph. Well, villains, for your presumption, I transform
thee into an ape, and thee into a dog; and so begone.

[*Exit.*

Robin. How, into an ape; that's brave! I'll have fine
sport with the boys. I'll get nuts and apples enow.

Ralph. And I must be a dog.

Robin. I'faith thy head will never be out of the
pottage pot.   [*Exeunt.*

SCENE X.

Enter EMPEROR, FAUSTUS, *and a* Knight *with*
Attendants.[1]

Emp. Master Doctor Faustus, I have heard strange
report of thy knowledge in the black art, how that none

[1] The scene is an apartment in the Emperor's palace. Much of
the text of this scene is closely borrowed from the prose *History.*

in my empire nor in the whole world can compare with thee for the rare effects of magic : they say thou hast a familiar spirit, by whom thou canst accomplish what thou list. This therefore is my request, that thou let me see some proof of thy skill, that mine eyes may be witnesses to confirm what mine ears have heard reported: and here I swear to thee by the honour of mine imperial crown, that, whatever thou doest, thou shalt be no ways prejudiced or endamaged.

Knight. I'faith he looks much like a conjuror. [*Aside.*.

Faust. My gracious sovereign, though I must confess myself far inferior to the report men have published, and nothing answerable to the honour of your imperial majesty, yet for that love and duty binds me thereunto, I am content to do whatsoever your majesty shall command me.

Emp. Then, Doctor Faustus, mark what I shall say.
As I was sometime solitary set
Within my closet, sundry thoughts arose
About the honour of mine ancestors,
How they had won by prowess such exploits,
Got such riches, subdued so many kingdoms
As we that do succeed, or they that shall
Hereafter possess our throne, shall
(I fear me) ne'er attain to that degree
Of high renown and great authority ;
Amongst which kings is Alexander the Great,
Chief spectacle of the world's pre-eminence,
The bright shining of whose glorious acts
Lightens the world with his reflecting beams,
As when I hear but motion made of him
It grieves my soul I never saw the man.
If therefore thou by cunning of thine art
Canst raise this man from hollow vaults below,.

Where lies entombed this famous conqueror,
And bring with him his beauteous paramour,
Both in their right shapes, gesture, and attire
They used to wear during their time of life,
Thou shalt both satisfy my just desire,
And give me cause to praise thee whilst I live.

Faust. My gracious lord, I am ready to accomplish your request so far forth as by art, and power of my Spirit, I am able to perform.

Knight. I'faith that's just nothing at all.   [*Aside.*

Faust. But, if it like your grace, it is not in my ability to present before your eyes the true substantial bodies of those two deceased princes, which long since are consumed to dust.

Knight. Ay, marry, Master Doctor, now there's a sign of grace in you, when you will confess the truth. [*Aside.*

Faust. But such spirits as can lively resemble Alexander and his paramour shall appear before your grace in that manner that they both lived in, in their most flourishing estate ; which I doubt not shall sufficiently content your imperial majesty.

Emp. Go to, Master Doctor, let me see them presently.

Knight. Do you hear, Master Doctor?   You bring Alexander and his paramour before the Emperor !

Faust. How then, sir ?

Knight. I'faith that's as true as Diana turned me to a stag !

Faust. No, sir, but when Actæon died, he left the horns for you.   Mephistophilis, begone.   [*Exit* MEPHISTO.

Knight. Nay, an you go to conjuring, I'll begone.
                                    [*Exit.*

Faust. I'll meet with you anon for interrupting me so.
Here they are, my gracious lord.

Re-enter MEPHISTOPHILIS *with* Spirits *in the shape of*
ALEXANDER *and his* Paramour.

Emp. Master Doctor, I heard this lady while she
lived had a wart or mole in her neck : how shall I know
whether it be so or no?

Faust. Your highness may boldly go and see.

Emp. Sure these are no spirits, but the true substantial bodies of those two deceased princes.

[*Exeunt* Spirits.

Faust. Will't please your highness now to send for the
knight that was so pleasant with me here of late ?

Emp. One of you call him forth !   [*Exit* Attendant.

Re-enter the Knight *with a pair of horns on his head.*

How now, sir knight ! why I had thought thou had'st
been a bachelor, but now I see thou hast a wife, that
not only gives thee horns, but makes thee wear them.
Feel on thy head.

Knight. Thou damnèd wretch and execrable dog,
Bred in the concave of some monstrous rock,
How darest thou thus abuse a gentleman?
Villain, I say, undo what thou hast done !

Faust. O, not so fast, sir ; there's no haste ; but,
good, are you remembered how you crossed me in my
conference with the Emperor ?   I think I have met with
you for it.

Emp. Good Master Doctor, at my entreaty release
him : he hath done penance sufficient.

Faust. My gracious lord, not so much for the injury
he offered me here in your presence, as to delight you
with some mirth, hath Faustus worthily requited this
injurious knight : which, being all I desire, I am content
to release him of his horns : and, sir knight, hereafter

speak well of scholars. Mephistophilis, transform him
straight. [MEPHISTOPHILIS *removes the horns.*] Now, my
good lord, having done my duty I humbly take my leave.

Emp. Farewell, Master Doctor; yet, ere you go,
Expect from me a bounteous reward.   [*Exeunt.*

SCENE XI.

Enter FAUSTUS *and* MEPHISTOPHILIS.[1]

Faust. Now, Mephistophilis, the restless course
That Time doth run with calm and silent foot,
Shortening my days and thread of vital life,
Calls for the payment of my latest years :
Therefore, sweet Mephistophilis, let us
Make haste to Wertenberg.

Meph. What, will you go on horseback or on foot?

Faust. Nay, till I'm past this fair and pleasant green,
I'll walk on foot.

Enter a Horse-Courser.[2]

Horse-C. I have been all this day seeking one Master
Fustian : mass, see where he is ! God save you, Master
Doctor !

Faust. What, horse-courser ! You are well met.

Horse-C. Do you hear, sir ? I have brought you forty
dollars for your horse.

Faust. I cannot sell him so : if thou likest him for
fifty, take him.

Horse-C. Alas, sir, I have no more.—I pray you speak
for me.

---

[1] The scene is "a fair and pleasant green," presently alluded to
by Faustus, and is supposed to change to a room in Faustus's house
where the latter falls asleep in his chair.   [2] Horse-dealer.

Meph. I pray you let him have him : he is an honest fellow, and he has a great charge, neither wife nor child.

Faust. Well, come, give me your money. [*Horse-Courser gives* FAUSTUS *the money.*] My boy will deliver him to you. But I must tell you one thing before you have him ; ride him not into the water at any hand.

Horse-C. Why, sir, will he not drink of all waters ?

Faust. O yes, he will drink of all waters, but ride him not into the water : ride him over hedge or ditch, or where thou wilt, but not into the water.

Horse-C. Well, sir.—Now am I made man for ever: I'll not leave my horse for twice forty : if he had but the quality of hey-ding-ding, hey-ding-ding, I'd make a brave living on him : he has a buttock as slick[1] as an eel. [*Aside.*] Well, God b' wi' ye, sir, your boy will deliver him me : but hark you, sir ; if my horse be sick or ill at ease, if I bring his water to you, you'll tell me what it is.

Faust. Away, you villain ; what, dost think I am a horse-doctor ?   [*Exit* Horse-Courser.
What art thou, Faustus, but a man condemned to die ?
Thy fatal time doth draw to final end ;
Despair doth drive distrust unto my thoughts :
Confound these passions with a quiet sleep :
Tush, Christ did call the thief upon the cross ;
Then rest thee, Faustus, quiet in conceit.

                    [*Sleeps in his chair.*

Re-enter Horse-Courser, *all wet, crying.*

Horse-C. Alas, alas ! Doctor Fustian quotha ? mass, Doctor Lopus[2] was never such a doctor : has given me a purgation has purged me of forty dollars ; I shall never

---

[1] Smooth.

[2] Dr. Lopez, physician to Queen Elizabeth. He was hanged in 1594 for having received a bribe from the court of Spain to poison the Queen ; as Marlowe was dead before the doctor came into notoriety, he could hardly have written this.

see them more. But yet, like an ass as I was, I would not be ruled by him, for he bade me I should ride him into no water: now I, thinking my horse had had some rare quality that he would not have had me known of, I, like a venturous youth, rid him into the deep pond at the town's end. I was no sooner in the middle of the pond, but my horse vanished away, and I sat upon a bottle of hay, never so near drowning in my life. But I'll seek out my Doctor, and have my forty dollars again, or I'll make it the dearest horse!—O, yonder is his snipper-snapper.—Do you hear? you hey-pass,¹ where's your master?

Meph. Why, sir, what would you? You cannot speak with him.

Horse-C. But I will speak with him.

Meph. Why, he's fast asleep. Come some other time.

Horse-C. I'll speak with him now, or I'll break his glass windows about his ears.

Meph. I tell thee he has not slept this eight nights.

Horse-C. An he have not slept this eight weeks I'll speak with him.

Meph. See where he is, fast asleep.

Horse-C. Ay, this is he. God save you, Master Doctor. Master Doctor, Master Doctor Fustian!—Forty dollars, forty dollars for a bottle of hay!

Meph. Why, thou seest he hears thee not.

Horse-C. So ho, ho!—so ho, ho! [*Hollas in his ear.*] No, will you not wake? I'll make you wake ere I go. [*Pulls* FAUSTUS *by the leg, and pulls it away.*] Alas, I am undone! What shall I do?

Faust. O my leg, my leg! Help, Mephistophilis! call the officers. My leg, my leg!

Meph. Come, villain, to the constable.

¹ A juggler's term, like "presto, fly!" Hence applied to the juggler himself.—*Bullen.*

Horse-C. O lord, sir, let me go, and I'll give you forty dollars more.

Meph. Where be they?

Horse-C. I have none about me. Come to my ostry[1] and I'll give them you.

Meph. Begone quickly.   [*Horse-Courser runs away.*

Faust. What, is he gone? Farewell he! Faustus has his leg again, and the horse-courser, I take it, a bottle of hay for his labour. Well, this trick shall cost him forty dollars more.

Enter WAGNER.

How now, Wagner, what's the news with thee?

Wag. Sir, the Duke of Vanholt[2] doth earnestly entreat your company.

Faust. The Duke of Vanholt! an honourable gentle-man, to whom I must be no niggard of my cunning. Come, Mephistophilis, let's away to him.   [*Exeunt.*

SCENE XII.

Enter the DUKE *of* VANHOLT, *the* DUCHESS, FAUSTUS, *and* MEPHISTOPHILIS.[3]

Duke. Believe me, Master Doctor, this merriment hath much pleased me.

Faust. My gracious lord, I am glad it contents you so well.—But it may be, madam, you take no delight in this. I have heard that great-bellied women do long for some dainties or other: what is it, madam? tell me, and you shall have it.

Duchess. Thanks, good Master Doctor; and for I see

---

[1] Hostelry.
[2] Anhalt in the *Volksbuch*, Anholt in the prose *History*.
[3] The scene is the Court of the Duke of Anhalt.

your courteous intent to pleasure me. I will not hide from you the thing my heart desires; and were it now summer, as it is January and the dead time of the winter, I would desire no better meat than a dish of ripe grapes.

Faust. Alas, madam, that's nothing! Mephistophilis, begone. [*Exit* MEPHISTOPHILIS.] Were it a greater thing than this, so it would content you, you should have it.

Re-enter MEPHISTOPHILIS *with grapes.*

Here they be, madam ; wilt please you taste on them ?

Duke. Believe me, Master Doctor, this makes me wonder above the rest, that being in the dead time of winter, and in the month of January, how you should come by these grapes.

Faust. If it like your grace, the year is divided into two circles over the whole world, that, when it is here winter with us, in the contrary circle it is summer with them, as in India, Saba, and farther countries in the East: and by means of a swift spirit that I have I had them brought hither, as you see.—How do you like them, madam ; be they good ?

Duchess. Believe me, Master Doctor, they be the best grapes that e'er I tasted in my life before.

Faust. I am glad they content you so, madam.

Duke. Come, madam, let us in, where you must well reward this learned man for the great kindness he hath showed to you.

Duchess. And so I will, my lord ; and, whilst I live, rest beholding[1] for this courtesy.

Faust. I humbly thank your grace.

Duke. Come, Master Doctor, follow us and receive your reward.　　　　　　　　　　　　　　[*Exeunt.*

---

[1] Beholden.

SCENE XIII.

Enter WAGNER.[1]

Wag. I think my master shortly means to die,
For he hath given to me all his goods :
And yet, methinks, if that death were so near,
He would not banquet, and carouse and swill
Amongst the students, as even now he doth,
Who are at supper with such belly-cheer
As Wagner ne'er beheld in all his life.
See where they come ! belike the feast is ended. [*Exit.*

SCENE XIV.

Enter FAUSTUS, *with two or three* Scholars *and*
MEPHISTOPHILIS.

1st Schol. Master Doctor Faustus, since our conference
about fair ladies, which was the beautifullest in all the
world, we have determined with ourselves that Helen of
Greece was the admirablest lady that ever lived : therefore, Master Doctor, if you will do us that favour, as to
let us see that peerless dame of Greece, whom all the
world admires for majesty, we should think ourselves
much beholding unto you.

Faust. Gentlemen,
For that I know your friendship is unfeigned,
And Faustus' custom is not to deny
The just requests of those that wish him well,
You shall behold that peerless dame of Greece,
No otherways for pomp and majesty,
Than when Sir Paris crossed the seas with her,

---

[1] This and the following scene are inside Faustus's house.

And brought the spoils to rich Dardania.

Be silent, then, for danger is in words.

> [*Music sounds, and* HELEN *passeth over the stage.*

2nd Schol. Too simple is my wit to tell her praise,
Whom all the world admires for majesty.

3rd Schol. No marvel though the angry Greeks pursued
With ten years' war the rape of such a queen,
Whose heavenly beauty passeth all compare.

1st Schol. Since we have seen the pride of Nature's works,
And only paragon of excellence,
Let us depart ; and for this glorious deed
Happy and blest be Faustus evermore.

Faustus. Gentlemen, farewell—the same I wish to you.

> [*Exeunt* Scholars.

Enter an Old Man.

Old Man. Ah, Doctor Faustus, that I might prevail
To guide thy steps unto the way of life,
By which sweet path thou may'st attain the goal
That shall conduct thee to celestial rest !
Break heart, drop blood, and mingle it with tears,
Tears falling from repentant heaviness
Of thy most vile and loathsome filthiness,
The stench whereof corrupts the inward soul
With such flagitious crimes of heinous sins
As no commiseration may expel,
But mercy, Faustus, of thy Saviour sweet,
Whose blood alone must wash away thy guilt.

Faust. Where art thou, Faustus ? wretch, what hast
thou done ?
Damned art thou, Faustus, damned ; despair and die !
Hell calls for right, and with a roaring voice
Says " Faustus ! come ! thine hour is almost come ! "
And Faustus now will come to do the right.

> [MEPHISTOPHILIS *gives him a dagger*

Old Man. Ah stay, good Faustus, stay thy desperate
　　steps !
I see an angel hovers o'er thy head,
And, with a vial full of precious grace,
Offers to pour the same into thy soul :
Then call for mercy, and avoid despair.

Faust. Ah, my sweet friend, I feel
Thy words do comfort my distressèd soul.
Leave me a while to ponder on my sins.

Old Man. I go, sweet Faustus, but with heavy cheer,
Fearing the ruin of thy hopeless soul.　　　　　[*Exit.*

Faust. Accursèd Faustus, where is mercy now ?
I do repent ; and yet I do despair ;
Hell strives with grace for conquest in my breast :
What shall I do to shun the snares of death ?

Meph. Thou traitor, Faustus, I arrest thy soul
For disobedience to my sovereign lord ;
Revolt, or I'll in piecemeal tear thy flesh.

Faust. Sweet Mephistophilis, entreat thy lord
To pardon my unjust presumption,
And with my blood again I will confirm
My former vow I made to Lucifer.

Meph. Do it then quickly, with unfeignèd heart,
Lest greater danger do attend thy drift.
　　　　　[FAUSTUS *stabs his arm and writes on a paper*
　　　　　　　with his blood.[1]

Faust. Torment, sweet friend, that base and crookèd age,
That durst dissuade me from thy Lucifer,
With greatest torments that our hell affords.

Meph. His faith is great : I cannot touch his soul ;
But what I may afflict his body with
I will attempt, which is but little worth.

Faust. One thing, good servant, let me crave of thee,

---

[1] This stage-direction is not in the early editions : it was suggested by Dyce.

To glut the longing of my heart's desire,—
That I might have unto my paramour
That heavenly Helen. which I saw of late.
Whose sweet embracings may extinguish clean
These thoughts that do dissuade me from my vow,
And keep mine oath I made to Lucifer.

Meph. Faustus, this or what else thou shalt desire
Shall be performed in twinkling of an eye.

Re-enter HELEN.

Faust. Was this the face that launched a thousand ships [1]
And burnt the topless towers of Ilium?
Sweet Helen, make me immortal with a kiss. [*Kisses her.*
Her lips suck forth my soul ; see where it flies !—
Come, Helen, come, give me my soul again.
Here will I dwell, for Heaven is in these lips,
And all is dross that is not Helena.
I will be Paris, and for love of thee,
Instead of Troy, shall Wertenberg be sacked :
And I will combat with weak Menelaus,
And wear thy colours on my plumèd crest :
Yea, I will wound Achilles in the heel,
And then return to Helen for a kiss.
Oh, thou art fairer than the evening air
Clad in the beauty of a thousand stars ;
Brighter art thou than flaming Jupiter
When he appeared to hapless Semele :
More lovely than the monarch of the sky
In wanton Arethusa's azured arms :
And none but thou shalt be my paramour.   [*Exeunt.*

---

[1] Shakespeare surely remembered this line when he wrote of
Helen in *Troilus and Cressida*, ii. 2 : —
　　　" Why, she is a pearl
Whose price hath launched above a thousand ships."—*Bullen.*
See *ante*, p. 114.

SCENE XV.

Enter the Old Man.[1]

Accursèd Faustus, miserable man,
That from thy soul exclud'st the grace of Heaven,
And fly'st the throne of his tribunal seat !

Enter Devils.

Satan begins to sift me with his pride :
As in this furnace God shall try my faith,
My faith, vile hell, shall triumph over thee.
Ambitious fiends ! see how the heavens smile
At your repulse, and laugh your state to scorn !
Hence, hell ! for hence I fly unto my God.

[*Exeunt on one side* Devils—*on the other*, Old Man.

SCENE XVI.

Enter FAUSTUS *with* Scholars.[2]

Faust. Ah, gentlemen !

1st Schol. What ails Faustus ?

Faust. Ah, my sweet chamber-fellow, had I lived with
thee, then had I lived still ! but now I die eternally.
Look, comes he not, comes he not ?

2nd Schol. What means Faustus ?

3rd Schol. Belike he is grown into some sickness by
being over solitary.

1st Schol. If it be so, we'll have physicians to cure him.
'Tis but a surfeit. Never fear, man.

Faust. A surfeit of deadly sin that hath damned both
body and soul.

---

[1] Dyce supposes the scene to be a room in the Old Man's house,
and Bullen "a room of Faustus's house, whither the Old Man has
come to exhort Faustus to repentance."
[2] The scene is a room in Faustus's house.

2nd Schol. Yet, Faustus, look up to Heaven : remember God's mercies are infinite.

Faust. But Faustus' offences can never be pardoned : the serpent that tempted Eve may be saved, but not Faustus. Ah, gentlemen, hear me with patience, and tremble not at my speeches! Though my heart pants and quivers to remember that I have been a student here these thirty years, oh. would I had never seen Wertenberg, never read book ! and what wonders I have done, all Germany can witness, yea, all the world : for which Faustus hath lost both Germany and the world, yea Heaven itself, Heaven, the seat of God, the throne of the blessed, the kingdom of joy ; and must remain in hell for ever, hell, ah, hell, for ever ! Sweet friends ! what shall become of Faustus being in hell for ever ?

3rd Schol. Yet, Faustus, call on God.

Faust. On God, whom Faustus hath abjured! on God, whom Faustus hath blasphemed! Ah, my God, I would weep, but the Devil draws in my tears. Gush forth blood instead of tears! Yea, life and soul! Oh, he stays my tongue ! I would lift up my hands, but see, they hold them, they hold them !

All. Who, Faustus?

Faust. Lucifer and Mephistophilis. Ah, gentlemen, I gave them my soul for my cunning !

All. God forbid !

Faust. God forbade it indeed ; but Faustus hath done it : for vain pleasure of twenty-four years hath Faustus lost eternal joy and felicity. I writ them a bill with mine own blood : the date is expired ; the time will come, and he will fetch me.

1st Schol. Why did not Faustus tell us of this before, that divines might have prayed for thee ?

Faust. Oft have I thought to have done so : but the

Devil threatened to tear me in pieces if I named God; to fetch both body and soul if I once gave ear to divinity: and now 'tis too late. Gentlemen, away! lest you perish with me.

2nd Schol. Oh, what shall we do to save Faustus?

Faust. Talk not of me, but save yourselves, and depart.

3rd Schol. God will strengthen me. I will stay with Faustus.

1st Schol. Tempt not God, sweet friend: but let us into the next room, and there pray for him.

Faust. Ay, pray for me, pray for me! and what noise soever ye hear, come not unto me, for nothing can rescue me.

2nd Schol. Pray thou, and we will pray that God may have mercy upon thee.

Faust. Gentlemen, farewell: if I live till morning I'll visit you: if not——Faustus is gone to hell.

All. Faustus, farewell.

        [*Exeunt* Scholars. *The clock strikes eleven.*

Faust. Ah, Faustus,

Now hast thou but one bare hour to live,
And then thou must be damned perpetually!
Stand still, you ever-moving spheres of Heaven,
That time may cease, and midnight never come:
Fair Nature's eye, rise, rise again and make
Perpetual day; or let this hour be but
A year, a month, a week, a natural day,
That Faustus may repent and save his soul!
O lente, lente, currite noctis equi! [1]

---

[1] "At si, quem malis, Cephalum complexa teneres,
   Clamares 'lente currite noctis equi.'"
           OVID's *Amores*, i. 13, ll. 39-40.

"By an exquisite touch of nature—the brain involuntarily summoning words employed for other purposes in happier hours—Faust cries aloud the line which Ovid whispered in Corinna's arms."—*J. A. Symonds.*

The stars move still, time runs, the clock will strike,
The Devil will come, and Faustus must be damned.
O, I'll leap up to my God! Who pulls me down?
See, see where Christ's blood streams in the firmament!
One drop would save my soul—half a drop: ah, my Christ!
Ah, rend not my heart for naming of my Christ!
Yet will I call on him: O spare me, Lucifer!—
Where is it now? 'tis gone: and see where God
Stretcheth out his arm, and bends his ireful brows!
Mountain and hills come, come and fall on me,
And hide me from the heavy wrath of God!
No! no!
Then will I headlong run into the earth;
Earth gape! O no, it will not harbour me!
You stars that reigned at my nativity,
Whose influence hath allotted death and hell,
Now draw up Faustus like a foggy mist
Into the entrails of yon labouring clouds,
That when they vomit forth into the air,
My limbs may issue from their smoky mouths,
So that my soul may but ascend to Heaven.

      [*The clock strikes the half hour.*

Ah, half the hour is past! 'twill all be past anon!
O God!
If thou wilt not have mercy on my soul,
Yet for Christ's sake whose blood hath ransomed me,
Impose some end to my incessant pain;
Let Faustus live in hell a thousand years—
A hundred thousand, and—at last—be saved!
O, no end is limited to damnèd souls!
Why wert thou not a creature wanting soul?
Or why is this immortal that thou hast?
Ah, Pythagoras' metempsychosis! were that true,
This soul should fly from me, and I be changed

Unto some brutish beast: all beasts are happy.
For, when they die,
Their souls are soon dissolved in elements ;
But mine must live, still to be plagued in hell.
Curst be the parents that engendered me !
No, Faustus : curse thyself : curse Lucifer
That hath deprived thee of the joys of Heaven.

       [The clock strikes twelve.

O, it strikes, it strikes ! Now, body, turn to air,
Or Lucifer will bear thee quick to hell.

       [Thunder and lightning.

O soul, be changed into little water-drops,
And fall into the ocean—ne'er be found. *[Enter* Devils.
My God ! my God ! look not so fierce on me !
Adders and serpents, let me breathe awhile !
Ugly hell, gape not ! come not, Lucifer !
I'll burn my books !—Ah Mephistophilis !

      [Exeunt Devils *with* FAUSTUS.

Enter CHORUS.

CHO. Cut is the branch that might have
  grown full straight,
And burnèd is Apollo's laurel bough,
That sometime grew within this learnèd
  man.
Faustus is gone ; regard his hellish fall,
Whose fiendful fortune may exhort the wise
Only to wonder at unlawful things,
Whose deepness doth entice such forward wits
To practise more than heavenly power permits. *[Exit.*

THE JEW OF MALTA.

ALTHOUGH *The Jew of Malta* was written between 1588 and 1592, there is no earlier edition of the play than the quarto of 1633. This was furnished with a brace of Prologues and Epilogues by Thomas Heywood, the dramatist, who tells the public that

> " by the best of poets in that age "

the play was

> " writ many years agone,
> And in that age thought second unto none."

The source of the story is unknown ; Mr. Symonds, arguing chiefly from its unrelieved cruelty, thinks it may be taken from some Spanish novel.

THE PROLOGUE.

Enter MACHIAVEL.

Machiavel. Albeit the world thinks Machiavel is dead,
Yet was his soul but flown beyond the Alps,
And now the Guise[1] is dead, is come from France,
To view this land, and frolic with his friends.
To some perhaps my name is odious,
But such as love me guard me from their tongues ;
And let them know that I am Machiavel,
And weigh not men, and therefore not men's words.
Admired I am of those that hate me most.
Though some speak openly against my books,
Yet they will read me, and thereby attain
To Peter's chair : and when they cast me off,
Are poisoned by my climbing followers.
I count religion but a childish toy,
And hold there is no sin but ignorance.
Birds of the air will tell of murders past !
I am ashamed to hear such fooleries.
Many will talk of title to a crown :
What right had Cæsar to the empery?
Might first made kings, and laws were then most sure
When like the Draco's they were writ in blood.
Hence comes it that a strong-built citadel
Commands much more than letters can import ;
Which maxim had but Phalaris observed,
He had never bellowed, in a brazen bull,
Of great ones' envy. Of the poor petty wights
Let me be envied and not pitied !
But whither am I bound?   I come not, I,
To read a lecture here in Britain,
But to present the tragedy of a Jew,
Who smiles to see how full his bags are crammed,
Which money was not got without my means.
I crave but this—grace him as he deserves,
And let him not be entertained the worse
Because he favours me.   [*Exit.*

[1] The Duc de Guise, who had organised the Massacre of St. Bar-
tholomew in 1572, and was assassinated in 1588.

FERNEZE, Governor of Malta.

LODOWICK, his Son.

SELIM CALYMATH, Son of the Grand Seignior.

MARTIN DEL BOSCO, Vice-Admiral of Spain.

MATHIAS, a Gentleman.

BARABAS, a wealthy Jew.

ITHAMORE, BARABAS' slave.

JACOMO,
BARNARDINE. } Friars.

PILIA-BORSA, a Bully.

Two Merchants.

Three Jews.

Knights, Bassoes, Officers, Guard, Messengers, Slaves, and Carpenters.

KATHARINE, mother of MATHIAS.

ABIGAIL, Daughter of BARABAS.

BELLAMIRA, a Courtesan.

Abbess.

Two Nuns.

MACHIAVEL,[1] Speaker of the Prologue.

Scene.—Malta.

[1] This distinguished Florentine, degraded into a personification of unscrupulous policy, was frequently appealed to on the Elizabethan stage.

THE JEW OF MALTA.

ACT THE FIRST.

SCENE I.

BARABAS *discovered in his counting-house, with heaps of
gold before him.*

BAR. So that of thus much that return was
     made :
And of the third part of the Persian ships,
There was the venture summed and satis-
     fied.
As for those Sabans,[1] and the men of Uz,
That bought my Spanish oils and wines of Greece,
Here have I purst their paltry silverlings.
Fie ; what a trouble 'tis to count this trash
Well fare the Arabians, who so richly pay
The things they traffic for with wedge of gold,
Whereof a man may easily in a day

---

[1] Old ed. "Samintes ;" modern editors print "Samnites," between whom and the "men of Uz" there can be no possible connection. We have Saba for Sabæa in *Faustus* [see p. 195].—*Bullen.*

Tell[1] that which may maintain him all his life.
The needy groom that never fingered groat,
Would make a miracle of thus much coin :
But he whose steel-barred coffers are crammed full,
And all his lifetime hath been tired,
Wearying his fingers' ends with telling it,
Would in his age be loth to labour so,
And for a pound to sweat himself to death.
Give me the merchants of the Indian mines,
That trade in metal of the purest mould ;
The wealthy Moor, that in the eastern rocks
Without control can pick his riches up,
And in his house heap pearls like pebble-stones,
Receive them free, and sell them by the weight ;
Bags of fiery opals, sapphires, amethysts,
Jacinths, hard topaz, grass-green emeralds,
Beauteous rubies, sparkling diamonds,
And seld-seen[2] costly stones of so great price,
As one of them indifferently rated,
And of a carat of this quantity,
May serve in peril of calamity
To ransom great kings from captivity.
This is the ware wherein consists my wealth ;
And thus methinks should men of judgment frame
Their means of traffic from the vulgar trade,
And as their wealth increaseth, so inclose
Infinite riches in a little room.
But now how stands the wind ?
Into what corner peers my halcyon's bill ?[3]
Ha ! to the east ? yes : see, how stand the vanes ?
East and by south : why then I hope my ships

---

[1] Count.   [2] *i.e.* Seldom seen.
[3] It was an ancient belief that a suspended stuffed halcyon (*i.e.* kingfisher) would indicate the quarter from which the wind blew.

I sent for Egypt and the bordering isles,
Are gotten up by Nilus' winding banks :
Mine argosy from Alexandria,
Loaden with spice and silks, now under sail,
Are smoothly gliding down by Candy shore
To Malta, through our Mediterranean sea.
But who comes here ?

Enter a Merchant.

How now ?

Merch. Barabas, thy ships are safe,
Riding in Malta-road : and all the merchants
With other merchandise are safe arrived,
And have sent me to know whether yourself
Will come and custom ¹ them.

Bar. The ships are safe thou say'st, and richly fraught.
Merch. They are.
Bar. Why then go bid them come ashore,
And bring with them their bills of entry :
I hope our credit in the custom-house
Will serve as well as I were present there.
Go send 'em threescore camels, thirty mules,
And twenty waggons to bring up the ware.
But art thou master in a ship of mine,
And is thy credit not enough for that ?

Merch. The very custom barely comes to more
Than many merchants of the town are worth,
And therefore far exceeds my credit, sir.

Bar. Go tell 'em the Jew of Malta sent thee, man :
Tush ! who amongst 'em knows not Barabas ?

Merch. I go.

Bar. So then, there's somewhat come.
Sirrah, which of my ships art thou master of ?

¹ *i.e.* Enter them at the custom-house.

Merch. Of the Speranza, sir.

Bar. And saw'st thou not
Mine argosy at Alexandria?
Thou could'st not come from Egypt, or by Caire,
But at the entry there into the sea,
Where Nilus pays his tribute to the main,
Thou needs must sail by Alexandria.

Merch. I neither saw them, nor inquired of them:
But this we heard some of our seamen say,
They wondered how you durst with so much wealth
Trust such a crazèd vessel, and so far.

Bar. Tush, they are wise! I know her and her strength.
But go, go thou thy ways, discharge thy ship,
And bid my factor bring his loading in.   [*Exit* Merch.
And yet I wonder at this argosy.

Enter a second Merchant.

2nd Merch. Thine argosy from Alexandria,
Know, Barabas, doth ride in Malta-road,
Laden with riches, and exceeding store
Of Persian silks, of gold, and orient pearl.

Bar. How chance you came not with those other
    ships
That sailed by Egypt?

2nd Merch. Sir, we saw 'em not.

Bar. Belike they coasted round by Candy shore
About their oils, or other businesses.
But 'twas ill done of you to come so far
Without the aid or conduct of their ships.

2nd Merch. Sir, we were wafted by a Spanish fleet,
That never left us till within a league,
That had the galleys of the Turk in chase.

Bar. O!—they were going up to Sicily:—
Well, go,

And bid the merchants and my men despatch
And come ashore, and see the fraught [1] discharged.

    2nd Merch. I go.   [*Exit.*

    Bar. Thus trowls our fortune in by land and sea,
And thus are we on every side enriched :
These are the blessings promised to the Jews.
And herein was old Abram's happiness :
What more may Heaven do for earthly man
Than thus to pour out plenty in their laps,
Ripping the bowels of the earth for them.
Making the seas their servants. and the winds
To drive their substance with successful blasts ?
Who hateth me but for my happiness ?
Or who is honoured now but for his wealth ?
Rather had I a Jew be hated thus,
Than pitied in a Christian poverty :
For I can see no fruits in all their faith,
But malice. falsehood, and excessive pride.
Which methinks fits not their profession.
Haply some hapless man hath conscience,
And for his conscience lives in beggary.
They say we are a scattered nation :
I cannot tell, but we have scambled [2] up
More wealth by far than those that brag of faith.
There's Kirriah Jairim, the great Jew of Greece,
Obed in Bairseth, Nones in Portugal.
Myself in Malta, some in Italy,
Many in France, and wealthy every one :
Ay, wealthier far than any Christian.
I must confess we come not to be kings ;
That's not our fault : alas, our number's few,
And crowns come either by succession,
Or urged by force : and nothing violent

       [1] Freight.   [2] Scrambled.

Oft have I heard tell, can be permanent.
Give us a peaceful rule, make Christians kings,
That thirst so much for principality.
I have no charge, nor many children,
But one sole daughter, whom I hold as dear
As Agamemnon did his Iphigen:
And all I have is hers.   But who comes here?

         Enter three Jews.[1]

    1st Jew.   Tush, tell not me ; 'twas done of policy.
    2nd Jew.   Come, therefore, let us go to Barabas,
For he can counsel best in these affairs ;
And here he comes.
    Bar.   Why, how now, countrymen !
Why flock you thus to me in multitudes?
What accident's betided to the Jews?
    1st Jew.   A fleet of warlike galleys, Barabas,
Are come from Turkey, and lie in our road :
And they this day sit in the council-house
To entertain them and their embassy.
    Bar.   Why, let 'em come, so they come not to war ;
Or let 'em war, so we be conquerors—
Nay, let 'em combat, conquer, and kill all !
So they spare me, my daughter, and my wealth.   [*Aside.*
    1st. Jew.   Were it for confirmation of a league,
They would not come in warlike manner thus.
    2nd Jew.   I fear their coming will afflict us all.
    Bar.   Fond[2] men ! what dream you of their multitudes.
What need they treat of peace that are in league?
The Turks and those of Malta are in league.
Tut, tut, there is some other matter in't.
    1st Jew.   Why, Barabas, they come for peace or war.

---

   [1] The scene is here supposed to be shifted to a street or to the
Exchange.   [2] *i.e.* Foolish.

Bar. Haply for neither, but to pass along
Towards Venice by the Adriatic Sea ;
With whom they have attempted many times,
But never could effect their stratagem.

 3rd Jew. And very wisely said. It may be so.

 2nd Jew. But there's a meeting in the senate-house,
And all the Jews in Malta must be there.

 Bar. Hum ; all the Jews in Malta must be there ?
Ay, like enough, why then let every man
Provide him, and be there for fashion-sake.
If anything shall there concern our state,
Assure yourselves I'll look—unto myself. [*Aside.*

 1st Jew. I know you will. Well, brethren, let us go.

 2nd Jew. Let's take our leaves. Farewell, good
  Barabas.

 Bar. Farewell, Zaareth ; farewell, Temainte.

         [*Exeunt* Jews.

And, Barabas, now search this secret out :
Summon thy senses, call thy wits together :
These silly men mistake the matter clean.
Long to the Turk did Malta contribute :
Which tribute, all in policy I fear,
The Turks have let increase to such a sum
As all the wealth of Malta cannot pay ;
And now by that advantage thinks belike
To seize upon the town : ay, that he seeks.
Howe'er the world go, I'll make sure for one,
And seek in time to intercept the worst,
Warily guarding that which I ha' got.
Ego mihimet sum semper proximus.[1]
Why, let 'em enter, let 'em take the town. [*Exit.*

---

[1] Misquoted from Terence's *Andria*, iv. 1. 12. The words should
be " Proximus sum egomet mihi."

SCENE II.

Enter FERNEZE, *Governor of Malta,* Knights, *and* Officers;
met by CALYMATH *and* Bassoes *of the Turk.*[1]

Fern. Now, Bassoes,[2] what demand you at our hands?

1st Bas. Know, Knights of Malta, that we came from
Rhodes,
From Cyprus, Candy, and those other Isles
That lie betwixt the Mediterranean seas.

Fern. What's Cyprus, Candy, and those other Isles
To us, or Malta? What at our hands demand ye?

Cal. The ten years' tribute that remains unpaid.

Fern. Alas! my lord, the sum is over-great,
I hope your highness will consider us.

Cal. I wish, grave governor, 'twere in my power
To favour you, but 'tis my father's cause,
Wherein I may not, nay, I dare not dally.

Fern. Then give us leave, great Selim Calymath.
                    [*Consults apart with the* Knights.

Cal. Stand all aside, and let the knights determine.
And send to keep our galleys under sail,
For happily[3] we shall not tarry here;
Now, governor, say, how are you resolved?

Fern. Thus: since your hard conditions are such
That you will needs have ten years' tribute past,
We may have time to make collection
Amongst the inhabitants of Malta for't.

1st Bas. That's more than is in our commission.

Cal. What, Callipine! a little courtesy.
Let's know their time, perhaps it is not long;
And 'tis more kingly to obtain by peace

---

[1] The scene is supposed to be inside the council-house.
[2] Bashaws or Pashas.   [3] *i.e.* Haply.

Than to enforce conditions by constraint.
What respite ask you, governor?

 Fern. But a month.

 Cal. We grant a month, but see you keep your promise.
Now launch our galleys back again to sea,
Where we'll attend the respite you have ta'en.
And for the money send our messenger.
Farewell, great governor and brave Knights of Malta.

 Fern. And all good fortune wait on Calymath!

     [*Exeunt* CALYMATH *and* Bassoes.

Go one and call those Jews of Malta hither:
Were they not summoned to appear to-day?

 Off. They were, my lord, and here they come.

   Enter BARABAS *and three* Jews.

 1st Knight. Have you determined what to say to them?

 Fern. Yes, give me leave:—and, Hebrews, now come
   near.
From the Emperor of Turkey is arrived
Great Selim Calymath, his highness' son,
To levy of us ten years' tribute past,
Now then, here know that it concerneth us—

 Bar. Then, good my lord, to keep your quiet still,
Your lordship shall do well to let them have it.

 Fern. Soft, Barabas, there's more 'longs to 't than so.
To what this ten years' tribute will amount,
That we have cast, but cannot compass it
By reason of the wars that robbed our store;
And therefore are we to request your aid.

 Bar. Alas, my lord, we are no soldiers:
And what's our aid against so great a prince?

 1st Knight. Tut, Jew, we know thou art no soldier;
Thou art a merchant and a moneyed man,
And 'tis thy money, Barabas, we seek.

 Mar.   K

Bar. How, my lord! my money?

Fern. Thine and the rest.

For, to be short, amongst you't must be had.

   1st Jew. Alas, my lord, the most of us are poor.

   Fern. Then let the rich increase your portions.

   Bar. Are strangers with your tribute to be taxed?

   2nd Knight. Have strangers leave with us to get their
       wealth?

Then let them with us contribute.

   Bar. How! equally?

   Fern. No. Jew, like infidels.

For through our sufferance of your hateful lives,

Who stand accursèd in the sight of Heaven.

These taxes and afflictions are befallen.

And therefore thus we are determinèd.

Read there the articles of our decrees.

   Officer (*reads*) " First, the tribute-money of the Turks
shall all be levied amongst the Jews, and each of them to
pay one half of his estate."

   Bar. How, half his estate? I hope you mean not
mine.   [*Aside.*

   Fern. Read on.

   Off. (*reading*). "Secondly, he that denies[1] to pay shall
straight become a Christian."

   Bar. How! a Christian? Hum, what's here to do?
                                   [*Aside.*

   Off. (*reading*). "Lastly, he that denies this shall
absolutely lose all he has."

   The three Jews. O my lord, we will give half.

   Bar. O earth-mettled villains, and no Hebrews born!

And will you basely thus submit yourselves

To leave your goods to their arbitrament?

   Fern. Why, Barabas, wilt thou be christenèd?

---

          [1] Refuses.

Bar. No. governor. I will be no convertite.[1]

Fern. Then pay thy half.

Bar. Why. know you what you did by this device?
Half of my substance is a city's wealth.
Governor, it was not got so easily ;
Nor will I part so slightly therewithal.

Fern. Sir, half is the penalty of our decree,
Either pay that. or we will seize on all.

Bar. Corpo di Dio ! stay ! you shall have the half ;
Let me be used but as my brethren are.

Fern. No, Jew. thou hast denied the articles,
And now it cannot be recalled.

> [*Exeunt* Officers. *on a sign from* FERNEZE.

Bar. Will you then steal my goods ?
Is theft the ground of your religion ?

Fern. No, Jew, we take particularly thine
To save the ruin of a multitude :
And better one want for the common good
Than many perish for a private man :
Yet, Barabas, we will not banish thee,
But here in Malta. where thou gott'st thy wealth,
Live still ; and. if thou canst, get more.

Bar. Christians, what or how can I multiply ?
Of naught is nothing made.

1st Knight. From naught at first thou cam'st to little
 wealth,
From little unto more. from more to most :
If your first curse fall heavy on thy head,
And make thee poor and scorned of all the world,
'Tis not our fault, but thy inherent sin.

Bar. What, bring you Scripture to confirm your
 wrongs ?
Preach me not out of my possessions.

---

[1] *i.e.* Convert.

Some Jews are wicked, as all Christians are :
But say the tribe that I descended of
Were all in general cast away for sin,
Shall I be tried by their transgression ?
The man that dealeth righteously shall live :
And which of you can charge me otherwise ?

 Fern. Out, wretched Barabas !
Sham'st thou not thus to justify thyself,
As if we knew not thy profession ?
If thou rely upon thy righteousness,
Be patient and thy riches will increase.
Excess of wealth is cause of covetousness :
And covetousness, O, 'tis a monstrous sin.

 Bar. Ay, but theft is worse : tush ! take not from me
  then,
For that is theft ! and if you rob me thus,
I must be forced to steal and compass more.

 1st Knight. Grave governor, listen not to his exclaims.
Convert his mansion to a nunnery ;
His house will harbour many holy nuns.

 Fern. It shall be so.

    Re-enter Officers.

        Now, officers, have you done ?

 Off. Ay, my lord, we have seized upon the goods
And wares of Barabas, which being valued,
Amount to more than all the wealth in Malta.
And of the other we have seized half.

 Fern. Then we'll take order for the residue.

 Bar. Well then, my lord, say, are you satisfied ?
You have my goods, my money, and my wealth,
My ships, my store, and all that I enjoyed ;
And, having all, you can request no more ;
Unless your unrelenting flinty hearts

Suppress all pity in your stony breasts,
And now shall move you to bereave my life.

Fern. No, Barabas, to stain our hands with blood
Is far from us and our profession.

Bar. Why, I esteem the injury far less
To take the lives of miserable men
Than be the causers of their misery.
You have my wealth, the labour of my life,
The comfort of mine age, my children's hope,
And therefore ne'er distinguish of the wrong.

Fern. Content thee, Barabas, thou hast naught but right.

Bar. Your extreme right does me exceeding wrong:
But take it to you, i' the devil's name.

Fern. Come, let us in, and gather of these goods
The money for this tribute of the Turk.

1st Knight. 'Tis necessary that be looked unto:
For if we break our day, we break the league,
And that will prove but simple policy.

> [*Exeunt all except* BARABAS *and the* Jews.

Bar. Ay, policy! that's their profession,
And not simplicity, as they suggest.
The plagues of Egypt, and the curse of Heaven,
Earth's barrenness, and all men's hatred
Inflict upon them, thou great *Primus Motor!*
And here upon my knees, striking the earth,
I ban their souls to everlasting pains
And extreme tortures of the fiery deep,   .
That thus have dealt with me in my distress.

1st Jew. O yet be patient, gentle Barabas.

Bar. O silly brethren, born to see this day;
Why stand you thus unmoved with my laments?
Why weep you not to think upon my wrongs?
Why pine not I, and die in this distress?

1st Jew. Why, Barabas, as hardly can we brook

The cruel handling of ourselves in this :
Thou seest they have taken half our goods.

   Bar. Why did you yield to their extortion?
You were a multitude, and I but one :
And of me only have they taken all.

   1st Jew. Yet, brother Barabas, remember Job.

   Bar. What tell you me of Job?   I wot his wealth
Was written thus : he had seven thousand sheep,
Three thousand camels, and two hundred yoke
Of labouring oxen, and five hundred
She-asses : but for every one of those,
Had they been valued at indifferent rate,
I had at home, and in mine argosy,
And other ships that came from Egypt last,
As much as would have bought his beasts and him,
And yet have kept enough to live upon :
So that not he, but I may curse the day,
Thy fatal birth-day, forlorn Barabas ;
And henceforth wish for an eternal night,
That clouds of darkness may inclose my flesh,
And hide these extreme sorrows from mine eyes :
For only I have toiled to inherit here
The months of vanity and loss of time,
And painful nights, have been appointed me.

   2nd Jew. Good Barabas, be patient.

   Bar. Ay, I pray, leave me in my patience.   You,
Were ne'er possessed of wealth, are pleased with want ;
But give him liberty at least to mourn,
That in a field amidst his enemies
Doth see his soldiers slain, himself disarmed,
And knows no means of his recovery :
Ay, let me sorrow for this sudden chance ;
'Tis in the trouble of my spirit I speak ;
Great injuries are not so soon forgot.

1st Jew. Come, let us leave him ; in his ireful
    mood
Our words will but increase his ecstasy.[1]
   2nd Jew. On, then : but trust me 'tis a misery
To see a man in such affliction. —
Farewell, Barabas !   [*Exeunt the three* Jews.[2]
   Bar. Ay, fare you well.
See the simplicity of these base slaves,
Who, for the villains have no wit themselves,
Think me to be a senseless lump of clay
That will with every water wash to dirt :
No, Barabas is born to better chance,
And framed of finer mould than common men,
That measure naught but by the present time.
A reaching thought will search his deepest wits,
And cast with cunning for the time to come :
For evils are apt to happen every day.—

       Enter ABIGAIL.

But whither wends my beauteous Abigail ?
O ! what has made my lovely daughter sad ?
What, woman ! moan not for a little loss :
Thy father hath enough in store for thee.
   Abig. Not for myself, but agèd Barabas :
Father, for thee lamenteth Abigail :
But I will learn to leave these fruitless tears,
And, urgèd thereto with my afflictions,
With fierce exclaims run to the senate-house,
And in the senate reprehend them all,
And rend their hearts with tearing of my hair,
Till they reduce[3] the wrongs done to my father.

---

[1] Violent emotion.
[2] Dyce suggests that on the Jews' departure the scene is supposed
to shift to a street near Barabas's house.
[3] *i.e.* Repair.

Bar. No, Abigail, things past recovery
Are hardly cured with exclamations.
Be silent, daughter, sufferance breeds ease,
And time may yield us an occasion
Which on the sudden cannot serve the turn.
Besides, my girl, think me not all so fond [1]
As negligently to forego so much
Without provision for thyself and me,
Ten thousand portagues,[2] besides great pearls,
Rich costly jewels, and stones infinite,
Fearing the worst of this before it fell,
I closely hid.

 Abig. Where, father?

 Bar. In my house, my girl.

 Abig. Then shall they ne'er be seen of Barabas:
For they have seized upon thy house and wares.

 Bar. But they will give me leave once more, I trow,
To go into my house.

 Abig. That may they not:
For there I left the governor placing nuns,
Displacing me; and of thy house they mean
To make a nunnery, where none but their own sect [3]
Must enter in; men generally barred.

 Bar. My gold! my gold! and all my wealth is
   gone!
You partial heavens, have I deserved this plague?
What, will you thus oppose me, luckless stars,
To make me desperate in my poverty?
And knowing me impatient in distress,
Think me so mad as I will hang myself,
That I may vanish o'er the earth in air,
And leave no memory that e'er I was?
No, I will live; nor loathe I this my life:

---

[1] Foolish.　　　[2] Portuguese gold coins.　　　[3] *i.e.* Sex.

And, since you leave me in the ocean thus
To sink or swim, and put me to my shifts,
I'll rouse my senses and awake myself.
Daughter! I have it : thou perceiv'st the plight
Wherein these Christians have oppressèd me :
Be ruled by me, for in extremity
We ought to make bar of no policy.

Abig. Father, whate'er it be to injure them
That have so manifestly wrongèd us,
What will not Abigail attempt ?

Bar. Why, so ;
Then thus, thou told'st me they have turned my house
Into a nunnery, and some nuns are there ?

Abig. I did.

Bar. Then, Abigail, there must my girl
Entreat the abbess to be entertained.

Abig. How, as a nun ?

Bar. Ay, daughter, for religion
Hides many mischiefs from suspicion.

Abig. Ay, but, father, they will suspect me there.

Bar. Let 'em suspect ; but be thou so precise
As they may think it done of holiness.
Entreat 'em fair, and give them friendly speech,
And seem to them as if thy sins were great,
Till thou hast gotten to be entertained.

Abig. Thus, father, shall I much dissemble.

Bar. Tush !
As good dissemble that thou never mean'st,
As first mean truth and then dissemble it,—
A counterfeit profession is better
Than unseen hypocrisy.

Abig. Well, father, say that I be entertained,
What then shall follow ?

Bar. This shall follow then ;

There have I hid, close underneath the plank
That runs along the upper-chamber floor.
The gold and jewels which I kept for thee.
But here they come : be cunning, Abigail.

 Abig. Then, father, go with me.

 Bar. No, Abigail, in this
It is not necessary I be seen :
For I will seem offended with thee for't :
Be close, my girl, for this must fetch my gold.

         [*They retire.*

  Enter Friar JACOMO, Friar BARNARDINE, Abbess,
    and a Nun.

 F. Jac. Sisters, we now are almost at the new-made
   nunnery.

 Abb. The better ; for we love not to be seen :
'Tis thirty winters long since some of us
Did stray so far amongst the multitude.

 F. Jac. But, madam, this house
And waters of this new-made nunnery
Will much delight you.

 Abb. It may be so ; but who comes here?

       [ABIGAIL *comes forward.*

 Abig. Grave abbess, and you, happy virgins' guide,
Pity the state of a distressèd maid.

 Abb. What art thou, daughter?

 Abig. The hopeless daughter of a hapless Jew,
The Jew of Malta, wretched Barabas ;
Sometime the owner of a goodly house,
Which they have now turned to a nunnery.

 Abb. Well, daughter, say, what is thy suit with us?

 Abig. Fearing the afflictions which my father feels
Proceed from sin, or want of faith in us,
I'd pass away my life in penitence,

And be a novice in your nunnery,
To make atonement for my labouring soul.

 F. Jac. No doubt, brother, but this proceedeth of the
  spirit.

 F. Barn. Ay, and of a moving spirit too, brother : but
  come,

Let us entreat she may be entertained.

 Abb. Well, daughter, we admit you for a nun.

 Abig. First let me as a novice learn to frame
My solitary life to your strait laws,
And let me lodge where I was wont to lie.
I do not doubt, by your divine precepts
And mine own industry, but to profit much.

 Bar. As much, I hope, as all I hid is worth. [*Aside.*

 Abb. Come, daughter, follow us.

 Bar. (*coming forward*). Why, how now, Abigail,
What makest thou amongst these hateful Christians ?

 F. Jac. Hinder her not, thou man of little faith,
For she has mortified herself.

 Bar. How ! mortified ?

 F. Jac. And is admitted to the sisterhood.

 Bar. Child of perdition, and thy father's shame !
What wilt thou do among these hateful fiends ?
I charge thee on my blessing that thou leave
These devils, and their damnèd heresy.

 Abig. Father, forgive me —   [*She goes to him.*
 Bar. Nay, back, Abigail,
(And think upon the jewels and the gold;

     [*Aside to* ABIGAIL *in a whisper.*

The board is markèd thus that covers it.)
Away, accursèd, from thy father's sight.

 F. Jac. Barabas, although thou art in misbelief,
And wilt not see thine own afflictions,
Yet let thy daughter be no longer blind.

Bar. Blind friar, I reck not thy persuasions,
(The board is markèd thus [1] that covers it.)

> [*Aside to* ABIGAIL *in a whisper.*

For I had rather die than see her thus.
Wilt thou forsake me too in my distress,
Seducèd daughter? (Go, forget not,) [*Aside in a whisper.*
Becomes it Jews to be so credulous?
(To-morrow early I'll be at the door.) [*Aside in a whisper.*
No, come not at me; if thou wilt be damned,
Forget me, see me not, and so be gone.
(Farewell, remember to-morrow morning.)

> [*Aside in a whisper.*

Out, out, thou wretch!

> [*Exeunt, on one side* BARABAS, *on the other side*
> Friars, Abbess, Nun, *and* ABIGAIL; *as they*
> *are going out,*

Enter MATHIAS.

Math. Who's this? fair Abigail, the rich Jew's daughter,
Become a nun! her father's sudden fall
Has humbled her and brought her down to this:
Tut, she were fitter for a tale of love,
Than to be tirèd out with orisons:
And better would she far become a bed,
Embracèd in a friendly lover's arms,
Than rise at midnight to a solemn mass.

Enter LODOWICK.

Lod. Why, how now, Don Mathias! in a dump?
Math. Believe me, noble Lodowick, I have seen
The strangest sight, in my opinion,
That ever I beheld.

---

[1] The old edition has † inserted here, presumably to indicate the
sign that Barabas was to make with his hand.

Lod. What was't, I prithee?

Math. A fair young maid, scarce fourteen years of age,
The sweetest flower in Cytherea's field,
Cropt from the pleasures of the fruitful earth,
And strangely metamorphosèd nun.

Lod. But say, what was she?

Math. Why, the rich Jew's daughter.

Lod. What, Barabas, whose goods were lately seized?
Is she so fair?

Math. And matchless beautiful;
As, had you seen her, 'twould have moved your heart,
Though countermined with walls of brass, to love,
Or at the least to pity.

Lod. And if she be so fair as you report,
'Twere time well spent to go and visit her:
How say you, shall we?

Math. I must and will, sir; there's no remedy.

Lod. And so will I too, or it shall go hard.
Farewell, Mathias.

Math. Farewell, Lodowick.   [*Exeunt severally.*

ACT THE SECOND.

SCENE I.

Enter BARABAS *with a light.*[1]

BAR. Thus, like the sad presaging raven, that tolls
The sick man's passport in her hollow beak,
And in the shadow of the silent night
Doth shake contagion from her sable [wings ;
Vexed and tormented runs poor Barabas
With fatal curses towards these Christians.
The uncertain pleasures of swift-footed time
Have ta'en their flight, and left me in despair ;
And of my former riches rests no more
But bare remembrance, like a soldier's scar,
That has no further comfort for his maim.
O thou, that with a fiery pillar led'st
The sons of Israel through the dismal shades,
Light Abraham's offspring ; and direct the hand
Of Abigail this night ; or let the day
Turn to eternal darkness after this !
No sleep can fasten on my watchful eyes,
Nor quiet enter my distempered thoughts,
Till I have answer of my Abigail.

[1] The scene is before Barabas's house, now turned into a nunnery.

Enter ABIGAIL *above.*

Abig. Now have I happily espied a time
To search the plank my father did appoint ;
And here behold, unseen, where I have found
The gold, the pearls, and jewels, which he hid.

Bar. Now I remember those old women's words,
Who in my wealth would tell me winter's tales,
And speak of spirits and ghosts that glide by night
About the place where treasure hath been hid :
And now methinks that I am one of those :
For whilst I live, here lives my soul's sole hope,
And, when I die, here shall my spirit walk.

Abig. Now that my father's fortune were so good
As but to be about this happy place ;
'Tis not so happy : yet when we parted last,
He said he would attend me in the morn.
Then, gentle sleep, where'er his body rests,
Give charge to Morpheus that he may dream
A golden dream, and of the sudden wake,
Come and receive the treasure I have found.

Bar. Bueno para todos mi ganado no era :
As good go on as sit so sadly thus.
But stay, what star shines yonder in the east ?
The loadstar of my life, if Abigail.
Who's there ?

   Abig. Who's that ?

   Bar. Peace, Abigail, 'tis I.

   Abig. Then, father, here receive thy happiness.

   Bar. Hast thou't ?

   Abig. Here, [*Throws down the bags*] hast thou't ?
There's more, and more, and more.

   Bar. O my girl,
My gold, my fortune, my felicity !

Strength to my soul, death to mine enemy!
Welcome the first beginner of my bliss!
O Abigail, Abigail, that I had thee here too!
Then my desires were fully satisfied:
But I will practise thy enlargement thence:
O girl! O gold![1] O beauty! O my bliss!

> [*Hugs the bags.*

Abig. Father, it draweth towards midnight now,
And 'bout this time the nuns begin to wake;
To shun suspicion, therefore, let us part.

Bar. Farewell, my joy, and by my fingers take
A kiss from him that sends it from his soul.

> [*Exit* ABIGAIL *above.*

Now Phœbus ope the eyelids of the day,
And for the raven wake the morning lark,
That I may hover with her in the air:
Singing o'er these, as she does o'er her young.
Hermoso placer de los dineros.   ·   [*Exit.*

SCENE II.

Enter FERNEZE, MARTIN DEL BOSCO, *and* Knights.

Fern. Now, captain, tell us whither thou art bound?
Whence is thy ship that anchors in our road?
And why thou cam'st ashore without our leave?

Bosc. Governor of Malta, hither am I bound;
My ship, the Flying Dragon, is of Spain,
And so am I: Del Bosco is my name;
Vice-admiral unto the Catholic King.

1st Knight. 'Tis true, my lord, therefore entreat[2] him
    well.

---

[1] We have a kind of echo of this in Shylock's "My daughter, O
    " &c.   [2] *i.e.* Treat.

Bosc. Our fraught[1] is Grecians, Turks, and Afric Moors.
For late upon the coast of Corsica,
Because we vailed[2] not to the Turkish[3] fleet,
Their creeping galleys had us in the chase:
But suddenly the wind began to rise,
And then we luffed and tacked,[4] and fought at ease:
Some have we fired, and many have we sunk;
But one amongst the rest became our prize:
The captain's slain, the rest remain our slaves,
Of whom we would make sale in Malta here.

Fern. Martin del Bosco, I have heard of thee;
Welcome to Malta, and to all of us;
But to admit a sale of these thy Turks
We may not, nay, we dare not give consent
By reason of a tributary league.

1st Knight. Del Bosco, as thou lov'st and honour'st us,
Persuade our governor against the Turk;
This truce we have is but in hope of gold,
And with that sum he craves might we wage war.

Bosc. Will Knights of Malta be in league with Turks,
And buy it basely too for sums of gold?
My lord, remember that, to Europe's shame,
The Christian Isle of Rhodes, from whence you came,
Was lately lost, and you were stated[5] here
To be at deadly enmity with Turks.

Fern. Captain, we know it, but our force is small.

Bosc. What is the sum that Calymath requires?

Fern. A hundred thousand crowns.

Bosc. My lord and king hath title to this isle,
And he means quickly to expel you hence;
Therefore be ruled by me, and keep the gold:

---

[1] Freight.　[2] *i.e.* Did not lower our flags.　[3] Old ed. "Spanish."
[4] Old ed. "left and tooke." The correction was made by Dyce.
[5] Established.

Mar.　　　　　　　　　　　　　　　　　S

I'll write unto his majesty for aid,
And not depart until I see you free.

Fern. On this condition shall thy Turks be sold :
Go, officers, and set them straight in show.

                                [*Exeunt* Officers.

Bosco, thou shalt be Malta's general ;
We and our warlike Knights will follow thee
Against these barb'rous misbelieving Turks.

Bosc. So shall you imitate those you succeed :
For when their hideous force environed Rhodes,
Small though the number was that kept the town,
They fought it out. and not a man survived
To bring the hapless news to Christendom.

Fern. So will we fight it out ; come, let's away :
Proud daring Calymath, instead of gold,
We'll send thee bullets wrapt in smoke and fire :
Claim tribute where thou wilt, we are resolved,
Honour is bought with blood and not with gold.

                                       [*Exeunt.*

SCENE III.

Enter Officers *with* ITHAMORE *and other* Slaves.[1]

1*st Off.* This is the market-place, here let 'em stand :
Fear not their sale, for they'll be quickly bought.

2*nd Off.* Every one's price is written on his back,
And so much must they yield or not be sold.

1*st Off.* Here comes the Jew ; had not his goods been
       seized,
He'd given us present money for them all.

Enter BARABAS.

Bar. In spite of these swine-eating Christians,—

      [1] The scene is the market-place.

Unchosen nation, never circumcised,
Such as (poor villains!) were ne'er thought upon
Till Titus and Vespasian conquered us,—
Am I become as wealthy as I was:
They hoped my daughter would ha' been a nun;
But she's at home, and I have bought a house
As great and fair as is the governor's;
And there in spite of Malta will I dwell,
Having Ferneze's hand, whose heart I'll have;
Ay, and his son's too, or it shall go hard.
I am not of the tribe of Levi, I,
That can so soon forget an injury.
We Jews can fawn like spaniels when we please:
And when we grin we bite, yet are our looks
As innocent and harmless as a lamb's.
I learned in Florence how to kiss my hand,
Heave up my shoulders when they call me dog,[1]
And duck as low as any barefoot friar;
Hoping to see them starve upon a stall,
Or else be gathered for in our synagogue,
That, when the offering-basin comes to me,
Even for charity I may spit into't.
Here comes Don Lodowick, the governor's son,
One that I love for his good father's sake.

Enter LODOWICK.

Lod. I hear the wealthy Jew walkèd this way:
I'll seek him out, and so insinuate,
That I may have a sight of Abigail;
For Don Mathias tells me she is fair.

Bar. Now will I show myself

---

[1] This recalls Shylock's "Still have I borne it with a patient shrug."

S 2

To have more of the serpent than the dove;
That is—more knave than fool.   [*Aside.*

  Lod. Yond' walks the Jew; now for fair Abigail.

  Bar. Ay, ay, no doubt but she's at your command.
                                  [*Aside.*

  Lod. Barabas, thou know'st I am the governor's son.

  Bar. I would you were his father, too, sir;
That's all the harm I wish you.—The slave looks
Like a hog's-cheek new singed.   [*Aside.*

  Lod. Whither walk'st thou, Barabas?

  Bar. No farther: 'tis a custom held with us,
That when we speak with Gentiles like to you,
We turn into the air to purge ourselves:
For unto us the promise doth belong.

  Lod. Well, Barabas, canst help me to a diamond?

  Bar. O, sir, your father had my diamonds.
Yet I have one left that will serve your turn:—
I mean my daughter: but ere he shall have her
I'll sacrifice her on a pile of wood.
I ha' the poison of the city for him,
And the white leprosy.   [*Aside.*

  Lod. What sparkle does it give without a foil?

  Bar. The diamond that I talk of ne'er was foiled:—[1]
But when he touches it, it will be foiled:—   [*Aside.*
Lord Lodowick, it sparkles bright and fair.

  Lod. Is it square or pointed, pray let me know.

  Bar. Pointed it is, good sir—but not for you. [*Aside.*

  Lod. I like it much the better.

  Bar. So do I too.

  Lod. How shows it by night?

  Bar. Outshines Cynthia's rays:
You'll like it better far o' nights than days.   [*Aside.*

  Lod. And what's the price?

---

[1] Defiled.

Bar. Your life an if you have it. [*Aside.*] O my
    lord,
We will not jar about the price ; come to my house
And I will give't your honour—with a vengeance. [*Aside.*
    Lod. No, Barabas, I will deserve it first.
    Bar. Good sir,
Your father has deserved it at my hands,
Who, of mere charity and Christian truth,
To bring me to religious purity,
And as it were in catechising sort,
To make me mindful of my mortal sins,
Against my will, and whether I would or no,
Seized all I had, and thrust me out o' doors,
And made my house a place for nuns most chaste.
    Lod. No doubt your soul shall reap the fruit of it.
    Bar. Ay, but, my lord, the harvest is far off.
And yet I know the prayers of those nuns
And holy friars, having money for their pains,
Are wondrous ;—and indeed do no man good :   [*Aside.*
And seeing they are not idle, but still doing,
'Tis likely they in time may reap some fruit,
I mean in fulness of perfection.
    Lod. Good Barabas, glance not at our holy nuns.
    Bar. No, but I do it through a burning zeal,—
Hoping ere long to set the house afire ;
For though they do a while increase and multiply,
I'll have a saying to that nunnery.—   [*Aside.*
As for the diamond, sir, I told you of,
Come home and there's no price shall make us part,
Even for your honourable father's sake.—
It shall go hard but I will see your death.—   [*Aside.*
But now I must be gone to buy a slave.
    Lod. And, Barabas, I'll bear thee company.
    Bar. Come then—here's the market-place.

What's the price of this slave? Two hundred crowns!
Do the Turks weigh so much?

1st Off. Sir, that's his price.

Bar. What, can he steal that you demand so much?
Belike he has some new trick for a purse :
And if he has, he is worth three hundred plates,[1]
So that, being bought, the town-seal might be got
To keep him for his lifetime from the gallows :
The sessions day is critical to thieves,
And few or none 'scape but by being purged.

Lod. Rat'st thou this Moor but at two hundred plates?

1st Off. No more, my lord.

Bar. Why should this Turk be dearer than that Moor?

1st Off. Because he is young and has more qualities.

Bar. What, hast the philosopher's stone ? an thou hast,
break my head with it, I'll forgive thee.

Slave. No, sir ; I can cut and shave.

Bar. Let me see, sirrah, are you not an old shaver?

Slave. Alas, sir ! I am a very youth.

Bar. A youth ? I'll buy you, and marry you to Lady
Vanity,[2] if you do well.

Slave. I will serve you, sir.

Bar. Some wicked trick or other. It may be, under
colour of shaving, thou'lt cut my throat for my goods.
Tell me, hast thou thy health well ?

Slave. Ay, passing well.

Bar. So much the worse ; I must have one that's
sickly, an't be but for sparing victuals : 'tis not a stone of
beef a day will maintain you in these chops ; let me see
one that's somewhat leaner.

1st Off. Here's a leaner, how like you him ?

Bar. Where wast thou born ?

---

[1] Pieces of silver coin.
[2] An allegorical character in the old moralities.

Itha. In Thrace : brought up in Arabia.

Bar. So much the better, thou art for my turn.
An hundred crowns ? I'll have him ; there's the coin.

                                    [*Gives money.*

1st Off. Then mark him, sir, and take him hence.

Bar. Ay, mark him, you were best, for this is he
That by my help shall do much villainy.   [*Aside.*
My lord, farewell : Come, sirrah, you are mine.
As for the diamond, it shall be yours ;
I pray, sir, be no stranger at my house,
All that I have shall be at your command.

        Enter MATHIAS *and his* Mother KATHERINE.

Math. What makes the Jew and Lodowick so private ?
I fear me 'tis about fair Abigail.   [*Aside.*

Bar. Yonder comes Don Mathias, let us stay ;[1]

                                    [*Exit* LODOWICK.

He loves my daughter, and she holds him dear :
But I have sworn to frustrate both their hopes,
And be revenged upon the governor.

Kath. This Moor is comeliest, is he not ? speak, son.

Math. No, this is the better, mother : view this well.

Bar. Seem not to know me here before your mother,
Lest she mistrust the match that is in hand :
When you have brought her home, come to my house ;
Think of me as thy father : son, farewell.

Math. But wherefore talked Don Lodowick with you ?

Bar. Tush ! man, we talked of diamonds, not of Abigail.

Kath. Tell me, Mathias, is not that the Jew ?

Bar. As for the comment on the Maccabees,
I have it, sir, and 'tis at your command.

Math. Yes, madam, and my talk with him was but
About the borrowing of a book or two.

        [1] *i.e.* Break off our conversation.

Kath. Converse not with him, he's cast off from heaven.
Thou hast thy crowns, fellow ; come, let's away.

Math. Sirrah, Jew, remember the book.

Bar. Marry will I, sir.

[*Exeunt* MATHIAS *and his* Mother.

Off. Come, I have made reasonable market ; let's
away.   [*Exeunt* Officers *with* Slaves.

Bar. Now let me know thy name, and therewithal
Thy birth, condition, and profession.

Itha. Faith, sir, my birth is but mean : my name's
Ithamore, my profession what you please.

Bar. Hast thou no trade? then listen to my words,
And I will teach thee that shall stick by thee :
First be thou void of these affections,
Compassion, love, vain hope, and heartless fear,
Be moved at nothing, see thou pity none,
But to thyself smile when the Christians moan.

Itha. O brave! master, I worship your nose[1] for this.

Bar. As for myself, I walk abroad o' nights
And kill sick people groaning under walls :
Sometimes I go about and poison wells ;
And now and then, to cherish Christian thieves,
I am content to lose some of my crowns,
That I may, walking in my gallery,
See 'em go pinioned along by my door.
Being young, I studied physic, and began
To practise first upon the Italian ;
There I enriched the priests with burials,
And always kept the sextons' arms in ure[2]
With digging graves and ringing dead men's knells :

---

[1] Barabas was represented on the stage with a large false nose.
In Rowley's *Search for Money* (1609) allusion is made to the "arti-
ficiall Jewe of Maltaes nose."
[2] Use.

And after that was I an engineer,
And in the wars 'twixt France and Germany,
Under pretence of helping Charles the Fifth,
Slew friend and enemy with my stratagems.
Then after that was I an usurer,
And with extorting, cozening, forfeiting,
And tricks belonging unto brokery,
I filled the jails with bankrupts in a year,
And with young orphans planted hospitals,
And every moon made some or other mad,
And now and then one hang himself for grief,
Pinning upon his breast a long great scroll
How I with interest tormented him.
But mark how I am blest for plaguing them :
I have as much coin as will buy the town.
But tell me now, how hast thou spent thy time?

   Itha. 'Faith, master,
In setting Christian villages on fire,
Chaining of eunuchs, binding galley-slaves.
One time I was an ostler in an inn,
And in the night-time secretly would I steal
To travellers' chambers, and there cut their throats :
Once at Jerusalem, where the pilgrims kneeled,
I strewèd powder on the marble stones,
And therewithal their knees would rankle so,
That I have laughed a-good[1] to see the cripples
Go limping home to Christendom on stilts.

   Bar. Why this is something : make account of me
As of thy fellow ; we are villains both :
Both circumcisèd, we hate Christians both :
Be true and secret, thou shalt want no gold.
But stand aside, here comes Don Lodowick.

          [1] *i.e.* In good earnest.

Enter LODOWICK.[1]

Lod. O Barabas, well met;
Where is the diamond you told me of?
　　Bar. I have it for you, sir; please you walk in with
　　me:
What ho, Abigail! open the door, I say.

Enter ABIGAIL *with letters.*

　　Abig. In good time, father: here are letters come
From Ormus, and the post stays here within.
　　Bar. Give me the letters.—Daughter, do you hear,
Entertain Lodowick the governor's son
With all the courtesy you can afford;
Provided that you keep your maidenhead.
Use him as if he were a Philistine,
Dissemble, swear, protest, vow love to him,
He is not of the seed of Abraham.　　　　　　　*[Aside.*
I am a little busy, sir, pray pardon me.
Abigail, bid him welcome for my sake.
　　Abig. For your sake and his own he's welcome hither.
　　Bar. Daughter, a word more: kiss him; speak him fair,
And like a cunning Jew so cast about,
That ye be both made sure[2] ere you come out.　　*[Aside.*
　　Abig. O father! Don Mathias is my love.
　　Bar. I know it: yet I say, make love to him;
Do, it is requisite it should be so—　　　　　　*[Aside.*
Nay, on my life, it is my factor's hand—
But go you in, I'll think upon the account.
　　　　　[Exeunt ABIGAIL *and* LODOWICK *into the house.*
The account is made, for Lodowick he dies.
My factor sends me word a merchant's fled

---

　　[1] Dyce supposes a change of scene here to the outside of Barabas's
house.　　　　　　　　　　[2] Affianced.

That owes me for a hundred tun of wine :
I weigh it thus much [*Snapping his fingers*] : I have
    wealth enough.
For now by this has he kissed Abigail ;
And she vows love to him, and he to her.
As sure as Heaven rained manna for the Jews,
So sure shall he and Don Mathias die :
His father was my chiefest enemy.

Enter MATHIAS.

Whither goes Don Mathias ? stay awhile.
    Math. Whither, but to my fair love Abigail ?
    Bar. Thou know'st, and Heaven can witness this is
    true,
That I intend my daughter shall be thine.
    Math. Ay, Barabas, or else thou wrong'st me much.
    Bar. O, Heaven forbid I should have such a thought.
Pardon me though I weep : the governor's son
Will, whether I will or no, have Abigail :
He sends her letters, bracelets, jewels, rings.
    Math. Does she receive them ?
    Bar. She? No, Mathias, no, but sends them back,
And when he comes, she locks herself up fast ;
Yet through the keyhole will he talk to her,
While she runs to the window looking out,
When you should come and hale him from the door.
    Math. O treacherous Lodowick !
    Bar. Even now as I came home, he slipt me in,
And I am sure he is with Abigail.
    Math. I'll rouse him thence.
    Bar. Not for all Malta, therefore sheathe your sword ;
If you love me, no quarrels in my house ;
But steal you in, and seem to see him not ;
I'll give him such a warning ere he goes

As he shall have small hopes of Abigail.
Away, for here they come.

Re-enter LODOWICK *and* ABIGAIL.

Math. What, hand in hand! I cannot suffer this.
Bar. Mathias, as thou lovest me, not a word.
Math. Well, let it pass, another time shall serve.

[*Exit into the house.*

Lod. Barabas, is not that the widow's son?
Bar. Ay, and take heed, for he hath sworn your death.
Lod. My death? what, is the base-born peasant mad?
Bar. No, no, but happily he stands in fear
Of that which you, I think, ne'er dream upon,
My daughter here, a paltry silly girl.
Lod. Why, loves she Don Mathias?
Bar. Doth she not with her smiling answer you?
Abig. He has my heart; I smile against my will.

[*Aside.*

Lod. Barabas, thou know'st I've loved thy daughter
    long.
Bar. And so has she done you, even from a child.
Lod. And now I can no longer hold my mind.
Bar. Nor I the affection that I bear to you.
Lod. This is thy diamond, tell me shall I have it?
Bar. Win it, and wear it, it is yet unsoiled.
O! but I know your lordship would disdain
To marry with the daughter of a Jew;
And yet I'll give her many a golden cross [1]
With Christian posies round about the ring.
Lod. 'Tis not thy wealth, but her that I esteem.
Yet crave I thy consent.
Bar. And mine you have, yet let me talk to her.—

---

[1] A piece of money with a cross marked on one of its sides, like the Portuguese cruzado.

This offspring of Cain, this Jebusite,
That never tasted of the Passover,
Nor e'er shall see the land of Canaan,
Nor our Messias that is yet to come ;
This gentle maggot, Lodowick, I mean,
Must be deluded : let him have thy hand,
But keep thy heart till Don Mathias comes.   [*Aside.*

   Abig. What, shall I be betrothed to Lodowick ?

   Bar. It's no sin to deceive a Christian ;
For they themselves hold it a principle,
Faith is not to be held with heretics ;
But all are heretics that are not Jews ;
This follows well, and therefore, daughter, fear not.
                                      [*Aside.*

I have entreated her, and she will grant.

   Lod. Then, gentle Abigail, plight thy faith to me.

   Abig. I cannot choose, seeing my father bids.—
Nothing but death shall part my love and me.   [*Aside.*

   Lod. Now have I that for which my soul hath longed.

   Bar. So have not I, but yet I hope I shall.   [*Aside.*

   Abig. O wretched Abigail, what hast thou done ?
                                        [*Aside.*

   Lod. Why on the sudden is your colour changed ?

   Abig. I know not, but farewell, I must be gone.

   Bar. Stay her, but let her not speak one word more.

   Lod. Mute o' the sudden ! here's a sudden change.

   Bar. O, muse not at it, 'tis the Hebrews' guise,
That maidens new betrothed should weep awhile :
Trouble her not ; sweet Lodowick, depart :
She is thy wife, and thou shalt be mine heir.

   Lod. O, is't the custom ? then I am resolved :
But rather let the brightsome heavens be dim,
And nature's beauty choke with stifling clouds,

                                [1] Satisfied.

Than my fair Abigail should frown on me.—
There comes the villain, now I'll be revenged.

Re-enter MATHIAS.

Bar. Be quiet, Lodowick, it is enough
That I have made thee sure to Abigail.

Lod. Well, let him go.   [*Exit.*

Bar. Well, but for me, as you went in at doors
You had been stabbed, but not a word on't now;
Here must no speeches pass, nor swords be drawn.

Math. Suffer me, Barabas, but to follow him.

Bar. No; so shall I, if any hurt be done,
Be made an accessory of your deeds;
Revenge it on him when you meet him next.

Math. For this I'll have his heart.

Bar. Do so; lo here I give thee Abigail.

Math. What greater gift can poor Mathias have?
Shall Lodowick rob me of so fair a love?
My life is not so dear as Abigail.

Bar. My heart misgives me, that, to cross your love,
He's with your mother; therefore after him.

Math. What, is he gone unto my mother?

Bar. Nay, if you will, stay till she comes herself.

Math. I cannot stay; for if my mother come,
She'll die with grief.   [*Exit.*

Abig. I cannot take my leave of him for tears:
Father, why have you thus incensed them both?

Bar. What's that to thee?

Abig. I'll make 'em friends again.

Bar. You'll make 'em friends!
Are there not Jews enow in Malta,
But thou must doat upon a Christian?

Abig. I will have Don Mathias, he is my love.

Bar. Yes, you shall have him: go put her in.

Itha. Ay, I'll put her in.   [*Puts* ABIGAIL *in.*

Bar. Now tell me, Ithamore, how lik'st thou this?

Itha. Faith, master, I think by this
You purchase both their lives; is it not so?

Bar. True; and it shall be cunningly performed.

Itha. O master, that I might have a hand in this.

Bar. Ay, so thou shalt, 'tis thou must do the deed:
Take this, and bear it to Mathias straight,

[*Gives a letter.*

And tell him that it comes from Lodowick.

Itha. 'Tis poisoned, is it not?

Bar. No, no, and yet it might be done that way:
It is a challenge feigned from Lodowick.

Itha. Fear not; I will so set his heart afire,
That he shall verily think it comes from him.

Bar. I cannot choose but like thy readiness:
Yet be not rash, but do it cunningly.

Itha. As I behave myself in this, employ me hereafter

Bar. Away then.   [*Exit* ITHAMORE.

So, now will I go in to Lodowick,
And, like a cunning spirit, feign some lie.
Till I have set 'em both at enmity.   [*Exit.*

ACT THE THIRD.

SCENE I.

Enter BELLAMIRA, *a Courtesan.*[1]

BELL. Since this town was besieged, my
gain grows cold :
The time has been that, but for one bare
night,
A hundred ducats have been freely given :
But now against my will I must be chaste ;
And yet I know my beauty doth not fail.
From Venice merchants, and from Padua
Were wont to come rare-witted gentlemen,
Scholars I mean, learnèd and liberal ;
And now, save Pilia-Borsa, comes there none,
And he is very seldom from my house ;
And here he comes.

Enter PILIA-BORSA.

Pilia. Hold thee, wench, there's something for thee to
spend.   [*Shews a bag of silver.*

Bell. 'Tis silver. I disdain it.

Pilia. Ay, but the Jew has gold,
And I will have it, or it shall go hard.

---

[1] The scene is the outside of Bellamira's house, and it is suggested
that she makes her appearance on the verandah or on a balcony.

Court. Tell me, how cam'st thou by this?

Pilia. 'Faith, walking the back-lanes, through the gardens, I chanced to cast mine eye up to the Jew's counting-house, where I saw some bags of money, and in the night I clambered up with my hooks, and, as I was taking my choice, I heard a rumbling in the house: so I took only this, and run my way: but here's the Jew's man.

Bell. Hide the bag.

Enter ITHAMORE.

Pilia. Look not towards him, let's away; zoons, what a looking thou keep'st; thou'lt betray 's anon.

[*Exeunt* BELLAMIRA *and* PILIA-BORSA.

Itha. O the sweetest face that ever I beheld! I know she is a courtesan by her attire: now would I give a hundred of the Jew's crowns that I had such a concubine.

Well, I have delivered the challenge in such sort,
As meet they will, and fighting die: brave sport. [*Exit.*

SCENE II.

Enter MATHIAS.[1]

Math. This is the place: now Abigail shall see
Whether Mathias holds her dear or no.

Enter LODOWICK.

What, dares the villain write in such base terms?

[*Reading a letter.*

Lod. I did it; and revenge it if thou dar'st.

[*They fight.*

---

[1] The scene is a street.

Enter BARABAS, *above, on a balcony.*

Bar. O! bravely fought; and yet they thrust not home.
Now, Lodovico! now, Mathias! So——   [*Both fall.*
So now they have showed themselves to be tall [1] fellows.
   [*Cries within.*] Part 'em, part 'em.

Bar. Ay, part 'em now they are dead.   Farewell, fare-
      well.   [*Exit.*

Enter FERNEZE, KATHERINE, *and* Attendants.

Fern. What sight is this!—my Lodowick slain!
These arms of mine shall be thy sepulchre.

Kath. Who is this? my son Mathias slain!

Fern. O Lodowick! had'st thou perished by the Turk,
Wretched Ferneze might have 'venged thy death.

Kath. Thy son slew mine, and I'll revenge his death.

Fern. Look, Katherine, look!—thy son gave mine
      these wounds.

Kath. O leave to grieve me, I am grieved enough.

Fern. O! that my sighs could turn to lively breath;
And these my tears to blood, that he might live.

Kath. Who made them enemies?

Fern. I know not, and that grieves me most of all.

Kath. My son loved thine.

Fern. And so did Lodowick him.

Kath. Lend me that weapon that did kill my son,
And it shall murder me.

Fern. Nay, madam, stay; that weapon was my son's,
And on that rather should Ferneze die.

Kath. Hold, let's inquire the causers of their deaths,
That we may 'venge their blood upon their heads.

Fern. Then take them up, and let them be interred
Within one sacred monument of stone;

---

[1] Brave.

Upon which altar I will offer up
My daily sacrifice of sighs and tears,
And with my prayers pierce impartial heavens,
Till they reveal the causers of our smarts,
Which forced their hands divide united hearts :
Come, Katherine, our losses equal are,
Then of true grief let us take equal share.

> [*Exeunt with the bodies.*

SCENE III.

Enter ITHAMORE.[1]

Itha. Why, was there ever seen such villainy,
So neatly plotted, and so well performed ?
Both held in hand, and flatly both beguiled?

Enter ABIGAIL.

Abig. Why, how now, Ithamore, why laugh'st thou so ?
Itha. O mistress, ha ! ha ! ha !
Abig. Why, what ail'st thou ?
Itha. O my master !
Abig. Ha !
Itha. O mistress ! I have the bravest, gravest, secret, subtle, bottle-nosed knave to my master, that ever gentleman had.
Abig. Say, knave, why rail'st upon my father thus?
Itha. O, my master has the bravest policy.
Abig. Wherein?
Itha. Why, know you not ?
Abig. Why, no.
Itha. Know you not of Mathias' and Don Lodowick's disaster?

[1] The scene is a room in Barabas's house.

T 2

Abig. No, what was it?

Itha. Why, the devil invented a challenge, my master writ it, and I carried it, first to Lodowick, and *imprimis* to Mathias.

And then they met, and, as the story says,
In doleful wise they ended both their days.

Abig. And was my father furtherer of their deaths?

Itha. Am I Ithamore?

Abig. Yes.

Itha. So sure did your father write, and I carry the challenge.

Abig. Well, Ithamore, let me request thee this,
Go to the new-made nunnery, and inquire
For any of the friars of Saint Jaques,
And say, I pray them come and speak with me.

Itha. I pray, mistress, will you answer me but one question?

Abig. Well, sirrah, what is't?

Itha. A very feeling one; have not the nuns fine sport with the friars now and then?

Abig. Go to, sirrah sauce, is this your question? get ye gone.

Itha. I will, forsooth, mistress.   [*Exit.*

Abig. Hard-hearted father, unkind Barabas!
Was this the pursuit of thy policy!
To make me show them favour severally,
That by my favour they should both be slain?
Admit thou lov'dst not Lodowick for his sire,
Yet Don Mathias ne'er offended thee:
But thou wert set upon extreme revenge,
Because the governor[1] dispossessed thee once,

---

[1] "Prior" in the old editions, which both Dyce and Bullen follow. Cunningham substituted "governor," which is evidently correct.

And could'st not 'venge it, but upon his son
Nor on his son, but by Mathias' means ;
Nor on Mathias, but by murdering me.
But I perceive there is no love on earth,
Pity in Jews, or piety in Turks.
But here comes cursed Ithamore, with the friar.

Enter ITHAMORE *and* Friar JACOMO.

F. Jac. *Virgo, salve.*
Itha. When ! duck you !
Abig. Welcome, grave friar ; Ithamore, begone.

                            [Exit ITHAMORE.

Know, holy sir, I am bold to solicit thee.
    F. Jac. Wherein ?
    Abig. To get me be admitted for a nun.
    F. Jac. Why, Abigail, it is not yet long since
That I did labour thy admission,
And then thou did'st not like that holy life.
    Abig. Then were my thoughts so frail and uncon-
        firmed,
And I was chained to follies of the world :
But now experience, purchaséd with grief,
Has made me see the difference of things.
My sinful soul, alas, hath paced too long
The fatal labyrinth of misbelief,
Far from the sun that gives eternal life.
    F. Jac. Who taught thee this ?
    Abig. The abbess of the house,
Whose zealous admonition I embrace :
O, therefore, Jacomo, let me be one,
Although unworthy, of that sisterhood.
    F. Jac. Abigail, I will, but see thou change no more,
For that will be most heavy to thy soul.
    Abig. That was my father's fault.

F. Jac. Thy father's! how?

Abig. Nay, you shall pardon me.—O Barabas,
Though thou deservest hardly at my hands,
Yet never shall these lips bewray thy life.   [*Aside.*

F. Jac. Come, shall we go?

Abig. My duty waits on you.   [*Exeunt.*

SCENE IV.

Enter BARABAS, *reading a letter.*[1]

Bar. What, Abigail become a nun again!
False and unkind; what, hast thou lost thy father?
And all unknown, and unconstrained of me,
Art thou again got to the nunnery?
Now here she writes, and wills me to repent.
Repentance! *Spurca!* what pretendeth[2] this?
I fear she knows—'tis so—of my device
In Don Mathias' and Lodovico's deaths:
If so, 'tis time that it be seen into:
For she that varies from me in belief
Gives great presumption that she loves me not;
Or loving, doth dislike of something done. —
But who comes here?

Enter ITHAMORE.

O Ithamore, come near;
Come near, my love; come near, thy master's life,
My trusty servant, nay, my second self:
For I have now no hope but even in thee,
And on that hope my happiness is built.
When saw'st thou Abigail?

---

[1] The scene is still within Barabas's house, but an interval of time has elapsed.   [2] *i.e.* Portendeth.

Itha. To day.

Bar. With whom?

Itha. A friar.

Bar. A friar! false villain, he hath done the deed.

Itha. How, sir?

Bar. Why, made mine Abigail a nun.

Itha. That's no lie, for she sent me for him.

Bar. O unhappy day!
False, credulous, inconstant Abigail!
But let 'em go: and, Ithamore, from hence
Ne'er shall she grieve me more with her disgrace;
Ne'er shall she live to inherit aught of mine,
Be blest of me, nor come within my gates,
But perish underneath my bitter curse.
Like Cain by Adam for his brother's death.

Itha. O master!

Bar. Ithamore, entreat not for her, I am moved,
And she is hateful to my soul and me:
And 'less thou yield to this that I entreat,
I cannot think but that thou hat'st my life.

Itha. Who, I, master? Why, I'll run to some rock,
And throw myself headlong into the sea:
Why, I'll do anything for your sweet sake.

Bar. O trusty Ithamore, no servant, but my friend:
I here adopt thee for mine only heir,
All that I have is thine when I am dead,
And whilst I live use half; spend as myself;
Here take my keys, I'll give 'em thee anon:
Go buy thee garments: but thou shalt not want:
Only know this, that thus thou art to do:
But first go fetch me in the pot of rice
That for our supper stands upon the fire.

Itha. I hold my head my master's hungry. [*Aside.*] I
  go, sir.   [*Exit.*

Bar. Thus every villain ambles after wealth,
Although he ne'er be richer than in hope :
But, husht !

Re-enter ITHAMORE *with the pot.*

Itha. Here 'tis, master,

Bar. Well said, Ithamore ; what, hast thou brought
The ladle with thee too?

Itha. Yes, sir, the proverb says he that eats with the
devil had need of a long spoon. I have brought you a
ladle.

Bar. Very well, Ithamore, then now be secret;
And for thy sake, whom I so dearly love,
Now shalt thou see the death of Abigail,
That thou may'st freely live to be my heir.

Itha. Why, master, will you poison her with a mess of
rice porridge? that will preserve life, make her round and
plump, and batten more than you are aware.

Bar. Ay, but, Ithamore, seest thou this?
It is a precious powder that I bought
Of an Italian, in Ancona, once,
Whose operation is to bind, infect,
And poison deeply, yet not appear
In forty hours after it is ta'en.

Itha. How, master?

Bar. Thus, Ithamore.
This even they use in Malta here,—'tis called
Saint Jacques' Even,—and then I say they use
To send their alms unto the nunneries :
Among the rest bear this, and set it there ;
There's a dark entry where they take it in,
Where they must neither see the messenger,
Nor make inquiry who hath sent it them.

Itha. How so?

Bar. Belike there is some ceremony in't.
There, Ithamore, must thou go place this pot !
Stay, let me spice it first.

Itha. Pray do, and let me help you, master.   Pray let
me taste first.

Bar. Prythee do [ITHAMORE *tastes*] : what say'st thou
   now ?

Itha. Troth, master, I'm loth such a pot of pottage
should be spoiled.

Bar. Peace, Ithamore, 'tis better so than spared.
Assure thyself thou shalt have broth by the eye.
My purse, my coffer, and myself is thine.

Itha. Well, master, I go.

Bar. Stay, first let me stir it, Ithamore.
As fatal be it to her as the draught
Of which great Alexander drunk and died :
And with her let it work like Borgia's wine,
Whereof his sire, the Pope, was poisonèd.
In few,[1] the blood of Hydra, Lerna's bane :
The juice of hebon,[2] and Cocytus' breath,
And all the poisons of the Stygian pool
Break from the fiery kingdom ; and in this
Vomit your venom and invenom her
That like a fiend hath left her father thus.

Itha. What a blessing has he given't ! was ever pot of
rice porridge so sauced ! [*Aside.*] What shall I do
with it?

Bar. O, my sweet Ithamore, go set it down,
And come again so soon as thou hast done,
For I have other business for thee.

Itha. Here's a drench to poison a whole stable of
Flanders mares : I'll carry 't to the nuns with a powder.

---

[1] *i.e.*, In short.
[2] The juice of ebony, formerly regarded as a deadly poison.

Bar. And the horse pestilence to boot ; away !

Itha. I am gone.

Pay me my wages, for my work is done.   [*Exit.*

Bar. I'll pay thee with a vengeance, Ithamore. [*Exit.*

SCENE V.

Enter FERNEZE, MARTIN, DEL BOSCO, Knights,
and Basso.[1]

Fern. Welcome, great basso ; how fares Calymath?
What wind drives you thus into Malta-road?

Bas. The wind that bloweth all the world besides,—
Desire of gold.

Fern. Desire of gold, great sir ?
That's to be gotten in the Western Ind :
In Malta are no golden minerals.

Bas. To you of Malta thus saith Calymath :
The time you took for respite is at hand,
For the performance of your promise passed,
And for the tribute-money I am sent.

Fern. Basso, in brief, 'shalt have no tribute here,
Nor shall the heathens live upon our spoil :
First will we raze the city walls ourselves,
Lay waste the island, hew the temples down,
And, shipping off our goods to Sicily,
Open an entrance for the wasteful sea,
Whose billows beating the resistless banks,
Shall overflow it with their refluence.

Bas. Well, Governor, since thou hast broke the league
By flat denial of the promised tribute,
Talk not of razing down your city walls,

---

[1] The scene is the interior of the council-house.

You shall not need trouble yourselves so far,
For Selim Calymath shall come himself,
And with brass bullets batter down your towers,
And turn proud Malta to a wilderness
For these intolerable wrongs of yours ;
And so farewell.

   Fern. Farewell :   *[Exit* Basso.

   Fern. And now, ye men of Malta, look about,
And let's provide to welcome Calymath :
Close your portcullis, charge your basilisks,[1]
And as you profitably take up arms,
So now courageously encounter them ;
For by this answer, broken is the league,
And naught is to be looked for now but wars,
And naught to us more welcome is than wars. *[Exeunt.*

SCENE VI.

Enter Friar Jacomo *and* Friar Barnardine.[2]

   F. Jac. O, brother, brother, all the nuns are sick,
And physic will not help them : they must die.

   F. Barn. The abbess sent for me to be confessed :
O, what a sad confession will there be !

   F. Jac. And so did fair Maria send for me :
I'll to her lodging : hereabouts she lies.   *[Exit.*

Enter Abigail.

   F. Barn. What, all dead, save only Abigail ?

   Abig. And I shall die too, for I feel death coming.
Where is the friar that conversed with me ?

---

[1] Cannon. See note, p. 54.
[2] The scene is the interior of the convent.

F. Barn. O, he is gone to see the other nuns.

Abig. I sent for him, but seeing you are come,
Be you my ghostly father : and first know,
That in this house I lived religiously,
Chaste, and devout, much sorrowing for my sins ;
But ere I came ——

F. Barn. What then?

Abig. I did offend high Heaven so grievously,
As I am almost desperate for my sins :
And one offence torments me more than all.
You knew Mathias and Don Lodowick?

F. Barn. Yes, what of them?

Abig. My father did contract me to 'em both :
First to Don Lodowick ; him I never loved ;
Mathias was the man that I held dear,
And for his sake did I become a nun.

F. Barn. So, say how was their end?

Abig. Both jealous of my love, envied[1] each other,
And by my father's practice,[2] which is there
Set down at large, the gallants were both slain.

                              [*Gives a written paper.*

F. Barn. O monstrous villainy!

Abig. To work my peace, this I confess to thee ;
Reveal it not, for then my father dies.

F. Barn. Know that confession must not be revealed,
The canon law forbids it, and the priest
That makes it known, being degraded first,
Shall be condemned, and then sent to the fire.

Abig. So I have heard ; pray, therefore keep it close.
Death seizeth on my heart : ah gentle friar,
Convert my father that he may be saved,
And witness that I die a Christian.   [*Dies.*

---

[1] *i.e.*, Hated. Formerly the word was in common use in thi
sense.   [2] Artifice.

F. Barn. Ay, and a virgin too; that grieves me
most :
But I must to the Jew and exclaim on him,
And make him stand in fear of me.

Re-enter Friar JACOMO.

F. Jac. O brother, all the nuns are dead, let's bury
them.

F. Barn. First help to bury this, then go with me
And help me to exclaim against the Jew.

F. Jac. Why, what has he done?

F. Barn. A thing that makes me tremble to unfold.

F. Jac. What, has he crucified a child? [1]

F. Barn. No, but a worse thing: 'twas told me in
shrift,
Thou know'st 'tis death an if it be revealed.
Come, let's away.   [*Exeunt.*

---

[1] This was a crime of which the Jews were often accused, especially, according to Tovey (in his *Anglia Judaica*), when the king
happened to be in want of money.

ACT THE FOURTH.

SCENE I.

Enter BARABAS *and* ITHAMORE. *Bells within.*[1]

AR. There is no music to[2] a Christian's
  knell :
How sweet the bells ring now the nuns
  are dead,
That sound at other times like tinker's
  pans !
I was afraid the poison had not wrought :
Or, though it wrought, it would have done no good,
For every year they swell, and yet they live ;
Now all are dead, not one remains alive.

  Itha. That's brave, master, but think you it will not
be known ?

  Bar. How can it, if we two be secret ?

  Itha. For my part fear you not.

  Bar. I'd cut thy throat if I did.

  Itha. And reason too.
But here's a royal monastery hard by ;
Good master, let me poison all the monks.

  Bar. Thou shalt not need, for now the nuns are dead
They'll die with grief.

  Itha. Do you not sorrow for your daughter's death ?

  Bar. No, but I grieve because she lived so long.

---

[1] The scene is a street in Malta.   [2] *i.e.,* Equal to.

An Hebrew born, and would become a Christian :
Cazzo, diabolo.

Enter Friar JACOMO *and* Friar BARNARDINE.

Itha. Look, look, master, here come two religious
caterpillars.

Bar. I smelt 'em ere they came.

Itha. God-a-mercy, nose ! come, let's begone.

F. Barn. Stay, wicked Jew, repent, I say, and stay.

F. Jac. Thou hast offended, therefore must be damned.

Bar. I fear they know we sent the poisoned broth.

Itha. And so do I, master ; therefore speak 'em fair.

F. Barn. Barabas, thou hast——

F. Jac. Ay, that thou hast——

Bar. True. I have money, what though I have ?

F. Barn. Thou art a——

F. Jac. Ay, that thou art, a——

Bar. What needs all this ? I know I am a Jew.

F. Barn. Thy daughter——

F. Jac. Ay, thy daughter——

Bar. O speak not of her ! then I die with grief.

F. Barn. Remember that——

F. Jac. Ay, remember that ——

Bar. I must needs say that I have been a great usurer.

F. Barn. Thou hast committed——

Bar. Fornication—but that was in another country ;
And besides, the wench is dead.

F. Barn. Ay, but, Barabas,
Remember Mathias and Don Lodowick.

Bar. Why, what of them ?

F. Barn. I will not say that by a forged challenge they
met.

Bar. She has confest, and we are both undone,
My bosom inmate ! but I must dissemble.—— [*Aside.*

O holy friars, the burthen of my sins
Lie heavy on my soul ; then pray you tell me,
Is't not too late now to turn Christian ?
I have been zealous in the Jewish faith,
Hard-hearted to the poor, a covetous wretch,
That would for lucre's sake have sold my soul.
A hundred for a hundred I have ta'en ;
And now for store of wealth may I compare
With all the Jews of Malta ; but what is wealth ?
I am a Jew, and therefore am I lost.
Would penance serve to atone for this my sin,
I could afford to whip myself to death——

   Itha. And so could I ; but penance will not serve.

   Bar. To fast, to pray, and wear a shirt of hair,
And on my knees creep to Jerusalem.
Cellars of wine, and sollars[1] full of wheat,
Warehouses stuft with spices and with drugs,
Whole chests of gold, in bullion, and in coin,
Besides I know not how much weight in pearl,
Orient and round, have I within my house ;
At Alexandria, merchandise unsold :
But yesterday two ships went from this town,
Their voyage will be worth ten thousand crowns.
In Florence, Venice, Antwerp, London, Seville,
Frankfort, Lubeck, Moscow, and where not,
Have I debts owing ; and in most of these,
Great sums of money lying in the banco :
All this I'll give to some religious house.
So I may be baptized, and live therein.

   F. Jac. O good Barabas, come to our house.

   F. Barn. O no, good Barabas, come to our house ;
And, Barabas, you know——

---

[1] Attics; lofts (Latin, *solarium*). The word is still in use in some
parts of England and in legal documents.

Bar. I know that I have highly sinned.
You shall convert me, you shall have all my wealth.

F. Jac. O Barabas, their laws are strict.

Bar. I know they are, and I will be with you.

F. Barn. They wear no shirts, and they go barefoot
  too.

Bar. Then 'tis not for me ; and I am resolved
You shall confess me, and have all my goods.

                                  [*To* Friar BARNARDINE.

F. Jac. Good Barabas, come to me.

Bar. You see I answer him, and yet he stays ;
Rid him away, and go you home with me.

F. Jac. I'll be with you to-night.

Bar. Come to my house at one o'clock this night.

F. Jac. You hear your answer, and you may be gone.

F. Barn. Why, go get you away.

F. Jac. I will not go for thee.

F. Barn. Not ! then I'll make thee go.

F. Jac. How, dost call me rogue ?   [*They fight.*

Itha. Part 'em. master. part 'em.

Bar. This is mere frailty, brethren ; be content.
Friar Barnardine, go you with Ithamore :
You know my mind, let me alone with him.

                                  [*Aside to* F. BARNARDINE.

F. Jac. Why does he go to thy house ? let him be
  gone.

Bar. I'll give him something and so stop his mouth.

                    [*Exit* ITHAMORE *with* Friar BARNARDINE.

I never heard of any man but he
Maligned the order of the Jacobins :
But do you think that I believe his words ?
Why, brother, you converted Abigail ;
And I am bound in charity to requite it,
And so I will.   O Jacomo, fail not, but come.

  Mar.   U

F. Jac. But, Barabas, who shall be your godfathers?
For presently you shall be shrived.

Bar. Marry, the Turk [1] shall be one of my godfathers,
But not a word to any of your covent. [2]

F. Jac. I warrant thee, Barabas.   [*Exit.*

Bar. So, now the fear is past, and I am safe,
For he that shrived her is within my house ;
What if I murdered him ere Jacomo comes?
Now I have such a plot for both their lives
As never Jew nor Christian knew the like:
One turned my daughter, therefore he shall die ;
The other knows enough to have my life,
Therefore 'tis not requisite he should live.
But are not both these wise men to suppose
That I will leave my house, my goods, and all,
To fast and be well whipt? I'll none of that.
Now Friar Barnardine I come to you,
I'll feast you, lodge you, give you fair words,
And after that, I and my trusty Turk—
No more, but so : it must and shall be done.   [*Exit.*

SCENE II.

Enter BARABAS *and* ITHAMORE. [3]

Bar. Ithamore, tell me, is the friar asleep?

Itha. Yes ; and I know not what the reason is,
Do what I can he will not strip himself,
Nor go to bed, but sleeps in his own clothes ;
I fear me he mistrusts what we intend.

Bar. No, 'tis an order which the friars use :
Yet, if he knew our meanings, could he 'scape?

---

[1] Ithamore.   [2] Convent (as in "Covent Garden").
[3] The scene is a room in the house of Barabas.

Itha. No, none can hear him, cry he ne'er so loud.

Bar. Why, true, therefore did I place him there :
The other chambers open towards the street.

Itha. You loiter, master; wherefore stay we thus?
O how I long to see him shake his heels.

Bar. Come on, sirrah.
Off with your girdle, make a handsome noose.

[ITHAMORE *takes off his girdle and ties a noose
in it.*

Friar, awake! [*They put the noose round the* Friar's *neck.*

F. Barn. What, do you mean to strangle me?

Itha. Yes, 'cause you use to confess.

Bar. Blame not us but the proverb, Confess and be
hanged; pull hard!

F. Barn. What, will you have [1] my life?

Bar. Pull hard, I say; you would have had my goods.

Itha. Ay, and our lives too, therefore pull amain.

[*They strangle him.*

'Tis neatly done, sir, here's no print at all.

Bar. Then it is as it should be; take him up.

Itha. Nay, master, be ruled by me a little. [*Stands the
body upright against the wall and puts a staff in its hand.*]
So, let him lean upon his staff; excellent! he stands as if
he were begging of bacon.[2]

Bar. Who would not think but that this friar lived?
What time o' night is't now, sweet Ithamore?

Itha. Towards one.

Bar. Then will not Jacomo be long from hence.

[*Exeunt.*

---

[1] The old edition has "save," but from Barabas's retort, "You
would have had my goods," the word is most likely a misprint.

[2] It would appear from the following scene that the body was
stood up outside of the house.

SCENE III.

Enter Friar Jacomo.[1]

F. Jac. This is the hour wherein I shall proceed;[2]
O happy hour wherein I shall convert
An infidel, and bring his gold into our treasury!
But soft, is not this Barnardine? it is;
And, understanding I should come this way,
Stands here a purpose, meaning me some wrong,
And intercept my going to the Jew.—
Barnardine!
Wilt thou not speak? thou think'st I see thee not;
Away, I'd wish thee, and let me go by:
No, wilt thou not? nay, then, I'll force my way;
And see, a staff stands ready for the purpose:
As thou lik'st that, stop me another time.

[*Takes the staff and strikes the body, which falls down.*

Enter Barabas *and* Ithamore.

Bar. Why, how now, Jacomo, what hast thou done?

F. Jac. Why, stricken him that would have struck at me.

Bar. Who is it? Barnardine! now out, alas, he's slain!

Itha. Ay, master, he's slain; look how his brains drop
out on's nose.

F. Jac. Good sirs, I have done't, but nobody knows it
but you two—I may escape.

Bar. So might my man and I hang with you for
company.

Itha. No, let us bear him to the magistrates.

F. Jac. Good Barabas, let me go.

Bar. No, pardon me; the law must have its course.
I must be forced to give in evidence,

---

¹ The scene is outside Barabas's house.   ² Succeed.

That being importuned by this Barnardine
To be a Christian, I shut him out,
And there he sat : now I, to keep my word,
And give my goods and substance to your house,
Was up thus early; with intent to go
Unto your friary, because you stayed.

 Itha. Fie upon 'em, master; will you turn Christian
when holy friars turn devils and murder one another?

 Bar. No, for this example I'll remain a Jew :
Heaven bless me ! what, a friar a murderer?
When shall you see a Jew commit the like ?

 Itha. Why, a Turk could ha' done no more.

 Bar. To-morrow is the sessions ; you shall to it.
Come, Ithamore, let's help to take him hence.

 F. Jac. Villains, I am a sacred person ; touch me not.

 Bar. The law shall touch you, we'll but lead you, we:
'Las, I could weep at your calamity!
Take in the staff too, for that must be shown :
Law wills that each particular be known. [*Exeunt.*

SCENE IV.

Enter BELLAMIRA *and* PILIA-BORSA.[1]

 Bell. Pilia-Borsa, did'st thou meet with Ithamore ?

 Pilia. I did. ·

 Bell. And did'st thou deliver my letter ?

 Pilia. I did.

 Bell. And what think'st thou? will he come ?

 Pilia. I think so, but yet I cannot tell ; for at the reading of the letter he looked like a man of another world.

  [1] The scene is a veranda of Bellamira's house.

Bell. Why so?

Pilia. That such a base slave as he should be saluted by such a tall [1] man as I am, from such a beautiful dame as you.

Bell. And what said he?

Pilia. Not a wise word, only gave me a nod, as who should say, "Is it even so?" and so I left him, being driven to a non-plus at the critical aspect of my terrible countenance.

Bell. And where didst meet him?

Pilia. Upon mine own freehold, within forty feet of the gallows, conning his neck-verse,[2] I take it, looking of [3] a friar's execution, whom I saluted with an old hempen proverb, *Hodie tibi, cras mihi,* and so I left him to the mercy of the hangman : but the exercise [4] being done, see where he comes.

Enter ITHAMORE.

Itha. I never knew a man take his death so patiently as this friar; he was ready to leap off ere the halter was about his neck; and when the hangman had put on his hempen tippet, he made such haste to his prayers, as if he had had another cure to serve. Well, go whither he will, I'll be none of his followers in haste : and, now I think on't, going to the execution, a fellow met me with a muschatoes [5] like a raven's wing, and a dagger with a hilt like a warming-pan, and he gave me a letter from one Madam Bellamira, saluting me in such sort as if he had meant to make clean my boots with his lips; the effect was, that I should come to her house. I wonder what the reason is; it may be she sees more in me than

---

[1] Brave.

[2] The verse which criminals had to read to entitle them to "benefit of clergy," and which was usually the first verse of the 51st Psalm.

[3] *i.e.* Looking *on*.   [4] Sermon.   [5] Mustachios.

I can find in myself: for she writes further, that she
loves me ever since she saw me, and who would not
requite such love? Here's her house, and here she
comes, and now would I were gone; I am not worthy
to look upon her.

Pilia. This is the gentleman you writ to.

Itha. Gentleman! he flouts me; what gentry can be
in a poor Turk of tenpence?[1] I'll be gone.   [*Aside.*

Bell. Is't not a sweet-faced youth, Pilia?

Itha. Again, "sweet youth!" [*Aside.*]—Did not you,
sir, bring the sweet youth a letter?

Pilia. I did, sir, and from this gentlewoman, who, as
myself, and the rest of the family, stand or fall at your
service.

Bell. Though woman's modesty should hale me back,
I can withhold no longer; welcome, sweet love.

Itha. Now am I clean, or rather foully out of the way.
     [*Aside.*

Bell. Whither so soon?

Itha. I'll go steal some money from my master to
make me handsome [*Aside*].—Pray pardon me, I must
go and see a ship discharged.

Bell. Canst thou be so unkind to leave me thus?

Pilia. An ye did but know how she loves you, sir!

Itha. Nay, I care not how much she loves me—
Sweet Bellamira, would I had my master's wealth for
     thy sake!

Pilia. And you can have it, sir, an if you please.

Itha. If 'twere above ground, I could and would have
it; but he hides and buries it up, as partridges do their
eggs, under the earth.

Pilia. And is't not possible to find it out?

Itha. By no means possible.

---

[1] A derogatory expression often found in writers of this period.

Bell. What shall we do with this base viliain then?

> [*Aside to* PILIA-BORSA.

Pilia. Let me alone ; do you but speak him fair.—

> [*Aside to her.*

But sir you know some secrets of the Jew,
Which, if they were revealed, would do him harm.

Itha. Ay, and such as—Go to, no more ! I'll make
him send me half he has, and glad he 'scapes so too.
I'll write unto him : we'll have money straight.

Pilia. Send for a hundred crowns at least.

Itha. Ten hundred thousand crowns. [*Writing.*]
" Master Barabas."

Pilia. Write not so submissively, but threatening him.

Itha. [*writing*] " Sirrah, Barabas, send me a hundred
crowns."

Pilia. Put in two hundred at least.

Itha. [*writing*] "I charge thee send me three hundred
by this bearer, and this shall be your warrant : if you do
not— no more, but so."

Pilia. Tell him you will confess.

Itha. [*writing*] " Otherwise I'll confess all."—Vanish,
and return in a twinkle.

Pilia. Let me alone ; I'll use him in his kind.

> [*Exit* PILIA-BORSA *with the letter.*

Itha. Hang him, Jew !

Bell. Now, gentle Ithamore, lie in my lap.—
Where are my maids? provide a running[1] banquet ;
Send to the merchant, bid him bring me silks,
Shall Ithamore, my love, go in such rags ?

Itha. And bid the jeweller come hither too.

Bell. I have no husband, sweet ; I'll marry thee.

Itha. Content : but we will leave this paltry land,
And sail from hence to Greece, to lovely Greece.

---

[1] Hasty.

I'll be thy Jason, thou my golden fleece ;
Where painted carpets o'er the meads are hurled,
And Bacchus' vineyards overspread the world :
Where woods and forests go in goodly green,
I'll be Adonis, thou shalt be Love's Queen.
The meads, the orchards, and the primrose-lanes,
Instead of sedge and reed, bear sugar-canes :
Thou in those groves, by Dis above,
Shalt live with me and be my love.

    Bell. Whither will I not go with gentle Ithamore?

Re-enter PILIA-BORSA.

    Itha. How now! hast thou the gold?

    Pilia. Yes.

    Itha. But came it freely? did the cow give down her milk freely?

    Pilia. At reading of the letter, he stared and stamped and turned aside. I took him by the beard, and looked upon him thus : told him he were best to send it : then he hugged and embraced me.

    Itha. Rather for fear than love.

    Pilia. Then, like a Jew, he laughed and jeered, and told me he loved me for your sake, and said what a faithful servant you had been.

    Itha. The more villain he to keep me thus ; here's goodly 'parel, is there not?

    Pilia. To conclude, he gave me ten crowns.

                [*Gives the money to* ITHAMORE.

    Itha. But ten? I'll not leave him worth a grey groat. Give me a ream [1] of paper : we'll have a kingdom of gold for 't.

    Pilia. Write for five hundred crowns.

---

[1] A quibble upon "realm" and "kingdom;" realm, which was often written without the "l," being commonly pronounced ream.

Itha. [*writing.*] "Sirrah, Jew, as you love your life send me five hundred crowns, and give the bearer one hundred.——" Tell him I must have 't.

Pilia. I warrant your worship shall have 't.

Itha. And if he ask why I demand so much, tell him I scorn to write a line under a hundred crowns.

Pilia. You'd make a rich poet, sir. I am gone. [*Exit.*

Itha. Take thou the money; spend it for my sake.

Bell. 'Tis not thy money, but thyself I weigh;
Thus Bellamira esteems of gold.   [*Throws it aside.*
But thus of thee.   [*Kisses him.*

Itha. That kiss again! she runs division [1] of my lips. What an eye she casts on me! It twinkles like a star.

Bell. Come, my dear love, let's in and sleep together.

Itha. O, that ten thousand nights were put in one, that we might sleep seven years together afore we wake!

Bell. Come, amorous wag, first banquet, and then sleep.   [*Exeunt.*

SCENE V.

Enter BARABAS, *reading a letter.* [2]

Bar. " Barabas, send me three hundred crowns.——"
Plain Barabas! O, that wicked courtesan!
He was not wont to call me Barabas.
" Or else I will confess:" ay, there it goes:
But, if I get him, *coupe de gorge* for that.
He sent a shaggy tottered [3] staring slave,

---

[1] A musical term.

[2] Dyce suggests that the scene is a room in Barabas's house, but as Barabas presently enquires of Pilia-Borsa when he shall see him at his house, their meeting probably takes place in the street.

[3] Tattered.

That when he speaks draws out his grisly beard,
And winds it twice or thrice about his ear ;
Whose face has been a grindstone for men's swords ;
His hands are hacked, some fingers cut quite off ;
Who, when he speaks, grunts like a hog, and looks
Like one that is employed in catzerie[1]
And crossbiting,[2]—such a rogue
As is the husband to a hundred whores :
And I by him must send three hundred crowns !
Well, my hope is, he will not stay there still ;
And when he comes : O, that he were but here !

Enter PILIA-BORSA.

Pilia. Jew, I must have more gold.

Bar. Why, want'st thou any of thy tale ?[3]

Pilia. No ; but three hundred will not serve his turn.

Bar. Not serve his turn, sir ?

Pilia. No, sir ; and, therefore, I must have five hundred more.

Bar. I'll rather——

Pilia. O good words, sir, and send it you were best !
see, there's his letter.   [*Gives letter.*

Bar. Might he not as well come as send ? pray bid him
come and fetch it ; what he writes for you, ye shall have
straight.

Pilia. Ay, and the rest too, or else——

Bar. I must make this villain away.   [*Aside.*
Please you dine with me, sir ;—and you shall be most
heartily poisoned.   [*Aside.*

Pilia. No, God-a-mercy. Shall I have these crowns ?

Bar. I cannot do it, I have lost my keys.

Pilia. O, if that be all, I can pick ope your locks.

Knavery (from *cazzo*).   [2] Swindling.   [3] Reckoning.

Bar. Or climb up to my counting-house window : you know my meaning.

Pilia. I know enough, and therefore talk not to me of your counting-house. The gold ! or know, Jew, it is in my power to hang thee.

Bar. I am betrayed.—   [*Aside.*
'Tis not five hundred crowns that I esteem,
I am not moved at that : this angers me,
That he, who knows I love him as myself,
Should write in this imperious vein. Why, sir,
You know I have no child, and unto whom
Should I leave all but unto Ithamore ?

Pilia. Here's many words, but no crowns: the crowns !

Bar. Commend me to him, sir, most humbly,
And unto your good mistress, as unknown.

Pilia. Speak, shall I have 'em, sir ?

Bar. Sir, here they are.—   [*Gives money.*
O, that I should part with so much gold !   [*Aside.*
Here, take 'em, fellow, with as good a will——
As I would see thee hanged [*Aside*] ; O, love stops my breath :
Never man servant loved as I do Ithamore !

Pilia. I know it, sir.

Bar. Pray, when, sir, shall I see you at my house ?

Pilia. Soon enough, to your cost, sir. Fare you well.
          [*Exit.*

Bar. Nay, to thine own cost, villain, if thou com'st !
Was ever Jew tormented as I am ?
To have a shag-rag knave to come, force from me
Three hundred crowns,—and then five hundred crowns !
Well, I must seek a means to rid 'em all,
And presently ; for in his villainy
He will tell all he knows, and I shall die for't.

I have it :
I will in some disguise go see the slave,
And how the villain revels with my gold.   [*Exit.*

SCENE VI.

Enter BELLAMIRA, ITHAMORE, *and* PILIA-BORSA.[1]

Bell. I'll pledge thee, love, and therefore drink it off.

Itha. Say'st thou me so? have at it; and do you
hear?   [*Whispers.*

Bell. Go to, it shall be so.

Itha. Of[2] that condition I will drink it up.
Here's to thee !

Bell. Nay, I'll have all or none.

Itha. There, if thou lov'st me do not leave a drop.

Bell. Love thee ! fill me three glasses.

Itha. Three and fifty dozen, I'll pledge thee.

Pilia. Knavely spoke, and like a knight-at-arms.

Itha. Hey, *Rivo Castiliano !*[3] a man's a man !

Bell. Now to the Jew.

Itha. Ha ! to the Jew, and send me money he were
best.

Pilia. What would'st thou do if he should send thee
none ?

Itha. Do nothing; but I know what I know; he's a
murderer.

Bell. I had not thought he had been so brave a man.

Itha. You knew Mathias and the governor's son; he
and I killed 'em both, and yet never touched 'em.

Pilia. O, bravely done.

---

[1] The scene is a verandah or open porch of Bellamira's house.
[2] *i.e.* On.
[3] A familiar Bacchanalian exhortation of doubtful origin.

Itha. I carried the broth that poisoned the nuns; and he and I, snickle hand too fast,[1] strangled a friar.

Bell. You two alone?

Itha. We two; and 'twas never known, nor never shall be for me.

Pilia. This shall with me unto the governor.
                                        [*Aside to* BELLAMIRA.

Bell. And fit it should: but first let's ha' more gold,—
                                        [*Aside to* PILIA-BORSA.

Come, gentle Ithamore, lie in my lap.

Itha. Love me little, love me long; let music rumble, Whilst I in thy incony[2] lap do tumble.

Enter BARABAS, *disguised as a French musician, with a lute, and a nosegay in his hat.*

Bell. A French musician! come, let's hear your skill.

Bar. Must tuna my lute for sound, twang, twang, first.

Itha. Wilt drink, Frenchman? here's to thee with a ——Pox on this drunken hiccup!

Bar. Gramercy, monsieur.

Bell. Prythee, Pilia-Borsa, bid the fiddler give me the posy in his hat there.

Pilia. Sirrah, you must give my mistress your posy.

Bar. *A votre commandement, madame.*

Bell. How sweet, my Ithamore, the flowers smell!

Itha. Like thy breath, sweetheart; no violet like 'em.

Pilia. Foh! methinks they stink like a hollyhock.

Bar. So, now I am revenged upon 'em all. The scent thereof was death; I poisoned it.   [*Aside.*

---

[1] A corrupt passage. " Snickle " is a noose or slipknot, and the word is commonly applied to the hangman's halter, and to snares set for hares and rabbits. Cunningham proposed to read " Snickle *hard and fast.*"

[2] Dainty, sweet.

Itha. Play, fiddler, or I'll cut your cat's guts into chitterlings.

Bar. *Pardonnez moi*, be no in tune yet; so now, now all be in.

Itha. Give him a crown, and fill me out more wine.

Pilia. There's two crowns for thee; play.

Bar. How liberally the villain gives me mine own gold! [*Aside.* BARABAS *then plays.*

Pilia. Methinks he fingers very well.

Bar. So did you when you stole my gold. [*Aside.*

Pilia. How swift he runs!

Bar. You run swifter when you threw my gold out of my window. [*Aside.*

Bell. Musician, hast been in Malta long?

Bar. Two, three, four month, madame.

Itha. Dost not know a Jew, one Barabas?

Bar. Very mush; monsieur, you no be his man?

Pilia. His man?

Itha. I scorn the peasant; tell him so.

Bar. He knows it already. [*Aside.*

Itha. 'Tis a strange thing of that Jew, he lives upon pickled grasshoppers and sauced mushrooms.

Bar. What a slave's this? the governor feeds not as I do. [*Aside.*

Itha. He never put on clean shirt since he was circumcised.

Bar. O rascal! I change myself twice a day. [*Aside.*

Itha. The hat he wears, Judas left under the elder [1] when he hanged himself.

Bar. 'Twas sent me for a present from the great Cham. [*Aside.*

Pilia. A musty slave he is;—Whither now, fiddler?

Bar. *Pardonnez moi, monsieur*, me be no well.

---

[1] Judas is said to have hanged himself on an elder-tree.

Pilia.   Farewell, fiddler! [*Exit* BARABAS] one letter more to the Jew.

Bell.   Prythee, sweet love, one more, and write it sharp.

Itha.   No, I'll send by word of mouth now—Bid him deliver thee a thousand crowns, by the same token, that the nuns loved rice, that Friar Barnardine slept in his own clothes ; any of 'em will do it.

Pilia.   Let me alone to urge it, now I know the meaning.

Itha.   The meaning has a meaning.   Come let's in :
To undo a Jew is charity, and not sin.   [*Exeunt.*

SCENE I.

Enter FERNEZE, Knights, MARTIN DEL BOSCO, *and*
Officers.[1]

FERN. Now, gentlemen, betake you to
your arms,
And see that Malta be well fortified ;
And it behoves you to be resolute ;
For Calymath, having hovered here so
long,
Will win the town, or die before the walls.
  1st Knight. And die he shall, for we will never yield.

Enter BELLAMIRA *and* PILIA-BORSA.

  Bell. O, bring us to the governor.
  Fern. Away with her ! she is a courtesan.
  Bell. Whate'er I am, yet, governor, hear me speak ;
I bring thee news by whom thy son was slain :
Mathias did it not ; it was the Jew.
  Pilia. Who, besides the slaughter of these gentlemen,
Poisoned his own daughter and the nuns,
Strangled a friar and I know not what
Mischief besides.
  Fern. Had we but proof of this——

---

[1] The scene is inside the council-house.

Mar.   X

Bell. Strong proof, my lord; his man's now at my
    lodging,
That was his agent; he'll confess it all.

Fern. Go fetch him straight [*Exeunt* Officers]. I
    always feared that Jew.

Enter Officers *with* BARABAS *and* ITHAMORE.

Bar. I'll go alone; dogs! do not hale me thus.

Itha. Nor me neither, I cannot outrun you, constable :—
O my belly!

Bar. One dram of powder more had made all sure;
What a damned slave was I!   [*Aside.*

Fern. Make fires, heat irons, let the rack be fetched.

1st Knight. Nay, stay, my lord; 't may be he will
    confess.

Bar. Confess! what mean you, lords? who should
    confess?

Fern. Thou and thy Turk; 'twas you that slew my
    son.

Itha. Guilty, my lord, I confess. Your son and Mathias
were both contracted unto Abigail; he forged a counterfeit challenge.

Bar. Who carried that challenge?

Itha. I carried it, I confess; but who writ it? Marry,
even he that strangled Barnardine, poisoned the nuns
and his own daughter.

Fern. Away with him! his sight is death to me.

Bar. For what, you men of Malta? hear me speak:
She is a courtesan, and he a thief,
And he my bondman. Let me have law,
For none of this can prejudice my life.

Fern. Once more, away with him; you shall have law.

Bar. Devils, do your worst! I'll live in spite of you.
                                        [*Aside.*

As these have spoke, so be it to their souls!—
I hope the poisoned flowers will work anon.   [*Aside.*
                [*Exeunt* Officers *with* BARABAS *and* ITHAMORE,
                    BELLAMIRA *and* PILIA-BORSA.

Enter KATHERINE.

Kath. Was my Mathias murdered by the Jew?
Ferneze, 'twas thy son that murdered him.
    Fern. Be patient, gentle madam, it was he ;
He forged the daring challenge made them fight.
    Kath. Where is the Jew? where is that murderer?
    Fern. In prison till the law has passed on him

Re-enter First Officer.

    1st Off. My lord, the courtesan and her man are
        dead :
So is the Turk and Barabas the Jew.
    Fern. Dead !
    1st Off. Dead, my lord, and here they bring his body
    Bosco. This sudden death of his is very strange.

Re-enter Officers *carrying* BARABAS *as dead.*

    Fern. Wonder not at it, sir, the Heavens are just :
Their deaths were like their lives, then think not of 'em.
Since they are dead, let them be buried ;
For the Jew's body, throw that o'er the walls,
To be a prey for vultures and wild beasts. —
So now away, and fortify the town.
                    [*Exeunt all leaving* BARABAS *on the floor.*

SCENE II.

BARABAS *discovered rising.*[1]

Bar. What, all alone? well fare, sleepy drink.
I'll be revenged on this accursèd town ;
For by my means Calymath shall enter in.
I'll help to slay their children and their wives,
To fire the churches, pull their houses down,
Take my goods too, and seize upon my lands.
I hope to see the governor a slave,
And, rowing in a galley, whipt to death.

Enter CALYMATH, Bassoes, *and* Turks.

Caly. Whom have we here, a spy?
Bar. Yes, my good lord, one that can spy a place
Where you may enter, and surprise the town :
My name is Barabas : I am a Jew.
Caly. Art thou that Jew whose goods we heard were
        sold
For tribute-money?
Bar. The very same, my lord :
And since that time they have hired a slave, my
        man,
To accuse me of a thousand villanies :
I was imprisonèd, but 'scaped their hands.
Caly. Did'st break prison?
Bar. No, no ;
I drank of poppy and cold mandrake juice :
And being asleep, belike they thought me dead,
And threw me o'er the walls : so, or how else,
The Jew is here, and rests at your command.

---

[1] The scene is outside the city walls, over which Barabas has
been thrown in accordance with Ferneze's orders.

Caly. 'Twas bravely done : but tell me, Barabas,
Canst thou, as thou report'st, make Malta ours?

Bar. Fear not, my lord, for here against the sluice,[1]
The rock is hollow, and of purpose digged.
To make a passage for the running streams
And common channels of the city.
Now, whilst you give assault unto the walls,
I'll lead five hundred soldiers through the vault,
And rise with them i' the middle of the town,
Open the gates for you to enter in ;
And by this means the city is your own.

Caly. If this be true, I'll make thee governor.

Bar. And if it be not true, then let me die.

Caly. Thou'st doomed thyself.   Assault it presently.

[*Exeunt.*

SCENE III.

Alarums within.   Enter CALYMATH, Bassoes, Turks, *and*
BARABAS, *with* FERNEZE *and* Knights *prisoners.*[2]

Caly. Now vail[3] your pride, you captive Christians,
And kneel for mercy to your conquering foe :
Now where's the hope you had of haughty Spain ?
Ferneze, speak, had it not been much better
T'have kept thy promise than be thus surprised ?

Fern. What should I say ?   We are captives and must
yield.

Caly. Ay, villains, you must yield, and under Turkish
yokes
Shall groaning bear the burden of our ire ;

---

[1] Old edition—"truce."   Dyce printed "trench."
[2] The scene is an open place in the city.   [3] Lower.

And, Barabas, as erst we promised thee,
For thy desert we make thee governor ;
Use them at thy discretion.

   Bar. Thanks, my lord.

   Fern. O fatal day, to fall into the hands
Of such a traitor and unhallowed Jew !
What greater misery could Heaven inflict ?

   Caly. 'Tis our command : and, Barabas, we give
To guard thy person these our Janizaries :
Entreat them well, as we have used thee.
And now, brave bassoes, come, we'll walk about
The ruined town, and see the wreck we made :—
Farewell, brave Jew ; farewell, great Barabas !

   Bar. May all good fortune follow Calymath !

              [Exeunt CALYMATH *and* Bassoes.

And now, as entrance to our safety,
To prison with the governor and these
Captains, his consorts and confederates.

   Fern. O villain ! Heaven will be revenged on thee.

          [Exeunt Turks, *with* FERNEZE *and* Knights.

   Bar. Away ! no more ; let him not trouble me.[2]
Thus hast thou gotten, by thy policy,
No simple place, no small authority,
I now am governor of Malta ; true, —
But Malta hates me, and, in hating me,
My life's in danger, and what boots it thee,
Poor Barabas, to be the governor,
Whenas thy life shall be at their command ?
No, Barabas, this must be looked into ;
And since by wrong thou got'st authority,
Maintain it bravely by firm policy,

---

   [1] *i.e.* Treat.
   [2] The scene is here supposed to shift to the governor's residence inside the citadel.

At least unprofitably lose it not:
For he that liveth in authority,
And neither gets him friends, nor fills his bags,
Lives like the ass, that Æsop speaketh of,
That labours with a load of bread and wine,
And leaves it off to snap on thistle-tops:
But Barabas will be more circumspect.
Begin betimes; occasion's bald behind:
Slip not thine opportunity, for fear too late
Thou seek'st for much, but canst not compass it.—
Within here!

    Enter FERNEZE, *with a* Guard.

 Fern. My lord?
 Bar. Ay, "lord;" thus slaves will learn.
Now, governor;—stand by there, wait within.
          [*Exeunt* Guard.
This is the reason that I sent for thee;
Thou seest thy life and Malta's happiness
Are at my arbitrement; and Barabas
At his discretion may dispose of both;
Now tell me, governor, and plainly too,
What think'st thou shall become of it and thee?
 Fern. This, Barabas; since things are in thy power,
I see no reason but of Malta's wreck,
Nor hope of thee but extreme cruelty;
Nor fear I death, nor will I flatter thee.
 Bar. Governor, good words; be not so furious.
'Tis not thy life which can avail me aught;
Yet you do live, and live for me you shall:
And, as for Malta's ruin, think you not
'Twere slender policy for Barabas
To dispossess himself of such a place?
For sith, as once you said, 'tis in this isle,

In Malta here, that I have got my goods,
And in this city still have had success,
And now at length am grown your governor,
Yourselves shall see it shall not be forgot :
For, as a friend not known but in distress,
I'll rear up Malta, now remediless.

    Fern. Will Barabas recover Malta's loss ?
Will Barabas be good to Christians ?

    Bar. What wilt thou give me, governor, to procure
A dissolution of the slavish bands
Wherein the Turk hath yoked your land and you ?
What will you give me if I render you
The life of Calymath, surprise his men
And in an outhouse of the city shut
His soldiers, till I have consumed 'em all with fire ?
What will you give him that procureth this ?

    Fern. Do but bring this to pass which thou pretendest,
Deal truly with us as thou intimatest,
And I will send amongst the citizens,
And by my letters privately procure
Great sums of money for thy recompense :
Nay more, do this, and live thou governor still.

    Bar. Nay, do thou this, Ferneze, and be free ;
Governor, I enlarge thee ; live with me,
Go walk about the city, see thy friends :
Tush, send not letters to 'em, go thyself,
And let me see what money thou canst make ;
Here is my hand that I'll set Malta free :
And thus we cast it : to a solemn feast
I will invite young Selim Calymath,
Where be thou present only to perform
One stratagem that I'll impart to thee,
Wherein no danger shall betide thy life,
And I will warrant Malta free for ever.

Fern. Here is my hand ; believe me, Barabas,
I will be there, and do as thou desirest.
When is the time ?

Bar. Governor, presently :
For Calymath, when he hath viewed the town,
Will take his leave and sail towards Ottoman.

Fern. Then will I, Barabas, about this coin,
And bring it with me to thee in the evening.

Bar. Do so, but fail not ; now farewell, Ferneze !—

[Exit FERNEZE.

And thus far roundly goes the business :
Thus loving neither, will I live with both,
Making a profit of my policy ;
And he from whom my most advantage comes
Shall be my friend.
This is the life we Jews are used to lead ;
And reason too, for Christians do the like.
Well, now about effecting this device ;
First to surprise great Selim's soldiers,
And then to make provision for the feast,
That at one instant all things may be done :
My policy detests prevention :
To what event my secret purpose drives,
I know ; and they shall witness with their lives.   *[Exit.*

SCENE IV.

Enter CALYMATH *and* Bassoes.[1]

Caly. Thus have we viewed the city, seen the sack,
And caused the ruins to be new-repaired,

---

[1] The scene is outside the city walls.

Which with our bombards[1] shot and basilisks
We rent in sunder at our entry :
And now I see the situation,
And how secure this conquered island stands
Environed with the Mediterranean Sea,
Strong-countermined with other petty isles ;
And, toward Calabria, backed by Sicily,
(Where Syracusian Dionysius reigned,)
Two lofty turrets that command the town ;
I wonder how it could be conquered thus.

Enter a Messenger.

   Mess. From Barabas, Malta's governor, I bring
A message unto mighty Calymath ;
Hearing his sovereign was bound for sea,
To sail to Turkey, to great Ottoman,
He humbly would entreat your majesty
To come and see his homely citadel,
And banquet with him ere thou leav'st the isle.

   Caly. To banquet with him in his citadel ?
I fear me, messenger, to feast my train
Within a town of war so lately pillaged,
Will be too costly and too troublesome :
Yet would I gladly visit Barabas,
For well has Barabas deserved of us.

   Mess. Selim, for that, thus saith the governor,
That he hath in his store a pearl so big,
So precious, and withal so orient,
As, be it valued but indifferently,
The price thereof will serve to entertain
Selim and all his soldiers for a month ;
Therefore he humbly would entreat your highness
Not to depart till he has feasted you.

---

[1] Cannons.

Caly. I cannot feast my men in Malta-walls,
Except he place his tables in the streets.

Mess. Know, Selim, that there is a monastery
Which standeth as an outhouse to the town :
There will he banquet them ; but thee at home,
With all thy bassoes and brave followers.

Caly. Well, tell the governor we grant his suit,
We'll in this summer evening feast with him.

Mess. I shall, my lord.   [*Exit.*

Caly. And now, bold bassoes, let us to our tents,
And meditate how we may grace us best
To solemnize our governor's great feast.   [*Exeunt.*

SCENE V.

Enter FERNEZE, Knights, *and* MARTIN DEL BOSCO.[1]

Fern. In this, my countrymen, be ruled by me,
Have special care that no man sally forth
Till you shall hear a culverin discharged
By him that bears the linstock,[2] kindled thus :
Then issue out and come to rescue me,
For happily I shall be in distress,
Or you released of this servitude.

1st Knight. Rather than thus to live as Turkish thralls,[3]
What will we not adventure ?

Fern. On then, begone.

Knights. Farewell, grave governor !

            [*Exeunt on one side* Knights *and* MARTIN DEL
                  BOSCO ; *on the other* FERNEZE.

---

[1] The scene is a street in Malta.
[2] The stick which held the match used by gunners.   [3] Slaves.

SCENE VI.

Enter, above, BARABAS, *with a hammer, very busy ;
and* Carpenters.[1]

Bar. How stand the cords? How hang these hinges?
  fast?
Are all the cranes and pulleys sure?
  1st Carp. All fast.
Bar. Leave nothing loose, all levelled to my mind.
Why now I see that you have art indeed.
There, carpenters, divide that gold amongst you :
                                   [*Gives money.*
Go swill in bowls of sack and muscadine!
Down to the cellar, taste of all my wines.
  1st Carp. We shall, my lord, and thank you.
                              [*Exeunt* Carpenters.
Bar. And, if you like them, drink your fill and die :
For so I live, perish may all the world !
Now Selim Calymath return me word
That thou wilt come, and I am satisfied.

Enter Messenger.

Now, sirrah, what, will he come?
  Mess. He will ; and has commanded all his men
To come ashore, and march through Malta streets,
That thou mayest feast them in thy citadel.
  Bar. Then now are all things as my wish would have
  'em,
There wanteth nothing but the governor's pelf,
And see, he brings it.

Enter FERNEZE.

Now, governor, the sum.

---

[1] The scene is a hall in the citadel, with a gallery at the end.

Fern. With free consent, a hundred thousand pounds.

Bar. Pounds say'st thou, governor? well, since it is
    no more,
I'll satisfy myself with that ; nay, keep it still,
For if I keep not promise, trust not me.
And, governor, now partake my policy :
First, for his army ; they are sent before,
Entered the monastery, and underneath
In several places are field-pieces pitched,
Bombards, whole barrels full of gunpowder
That on the sudden shall dissever it,
And batter all the stones about their ears,
Whence none can possibly escape alive.
Now as for Calymath and his consorts,
Here have I made a dainty gallery,
The floor whereof, this cable being cut,
Doth fall asunder ; so that it doth sink
Into a deep pit past recovery.
Here, hold that knife [*Throws down a knife*], and when
    thou seest he comes,
And with his bassoes shall be blithely set,
A warning-piece shall be shot off from the tower,
To give thee knowledge when to cut the cord
And fire the house ; say, will not this be brave ?

Fern. O excellent ! here, hold thee, Barabas,
I trust thy word, take what I promised thee.

Bar. No, governor, I'll satisfy thee first,
Thou shalt not live in doubt of anything.
Stand close. for here they come [FERNEZE *retires*]. Why,
    is not this
A kingly kind of trade to purchase towns
By treachery and sell 'em by deceit ?
Now tell me, worldlings, underneath the sun
If greater falsehood ever has been done ?

Enter CALYMATH *and* Bassoes.

Caly. Come, my companion bassoes ; see, I pray,
How busy Barabas is there above
To entertain us in his gallery ;
Let us salute him.   Save thee, Barabas !
    Bar. Welcome, great Calymath !
    Fern. How the slave jeers at him.   [*Aside.*
    Bar. Will 't please thee, mighty Selim Calymath,
To ascend our homely stairs ?
    Caly. Ay, Barabas ;—
Come, bassoes, ascend.
    Fern. [*coming forward*]. Stay, Calymath !
For I will show thee greater courtesy
Than Barabas would have afforded thee.
    Knight [*within.*] Sound a charge there !
              [*A charge sounded within.* FERNEZE *cuts the
                cord : the floor of the gallery gives way, and*
                BARABAS *falls into a caldron.*

Enter MARTIN DEL BOSCO *and* Knights.

    Caly. How now ! what means this ?
    Bar. Help, help me ! Christians, help !
    Fern. See, Calymath, this was devised for thee !
    Caly. Treason ! treason ! bassoes, fly !
    Fern. No, Selim, do not fly ;
See his end first, and fly then if thou canst.
    Bar. O help me, Selim ! help me, Christians !
Governor, why stand you all so pitiless ?
    Fern. Should I in pity of thy plaints or thee,
Accursèd Barabas, base Jew, relent?
No, thus I'll see thy treachery repaid,
But wish thou hadst behaved thee otherwise.
    Bar. You will not help me, then ?

Fern. No, villain, no.

Bar. And, villains, know you cannot help me now.—
Then, Barabas, breathe forth thy latest hate,
And in the fury of thy torments strive
To end thy life with resolution.
Know, governor, 'twas I that slew thy son ;
I framed the challenge that did make them meet :
Know, Calymath, I aimed thy overthrow.
And had I but escaped this stratagem,
I would have brought confusion on you all,
Damned Christian dogs ! and Turkish infidels !
But now begins the extremity of heat
To pinch me with intolerable pangs :
Die, life ! fly, soul ! tongue, curse thy fill, and die ! [*Dies.*

Caly. Tell me, you Christians, what doth this portend ?

Fern. This train he laid to have entrapped thy life .
Now, Selim, note the unhallowed deeds of Jews :
Thus he determined to have handled thee,
But I have rather chose to save thy life.

Caly. Was this the banquet he prepared for us ?
Let's hence, lest further mischief be pretended.[1]

Fern. Nay, Selim, stay ; for since we have thee here,
We will not let thee part so suddenly :
Besides, if we should let thee go, all's one,
For with thy galleys could'st thou not get hence,
Without fresh men to rig and furnish them.

Caly. Tush, governor, take thou no care for that,
My men are all aboard,
And do attend my coming there by this.

Fern. Why heard'st thou not the trumpet sound a
charge ?

Caly. Yes, what of that ?

---

[1] *i.e.* Intended.

Fern. Why then the house was fired,
Blown up, and all thy soldiers massacred.

Caly. O monstrous treason!

Fern. A Jew's courtesy:
For he that did by treason work our fall,
By treason hath delivered thee to us:
Know, therefore, till thy father hath made good
The ruins done to Malta and to us,
Thou canst not part; for Malta shall be freed,
Or Selim ne'er return to Ottoman.

Caly. Nay, rather, Christians, let me go to Turkey,
In person there to meditate your peace;
To keep me here will not advantage you.

Fern. Content thee, Calymath, here thou must stay,
And live in Malta prisoner: for come all the world
To rescue thee, so will we guard us now,
As sooner shall they drink the ocean dry
Than conquer Malta, or endanger us.
So march away, and let due praise be given
Neither to Fate nor Fortune, but to Heaven. [*Exeunt.*

EDWARD THE SECOND.

THE tragedy of *Edward II.* was entered in the Stationers' Books in 1593. The earliest edition of it is dated 1594, and was discovered in 1876 in the library at Cassel. The modern text is founded on the subsequent editions of 1598, 1612, and 1622. They differ very slightly, and are fairly free from corruptions. Marlowe used the narratives of Stowe and Holinshed, and was also slightly indebted to Fabyan's *Chronicle.*

DRAMATIS PERSONÆ.

KING EDWARD THE SECOND.

PRINCE EDWARD, his Son, afterwards King Edward
the Third.

EARL of KENT, Brother of King Edward the Second

GAVESTON.

WARWICK.

LANCASTER.

PEMBROKE.

ARUNDEL.

LEICESTER.

BERKELEY.

MORTIMER, the elder.

MORTIMER, the younger, his Nephew.

SPENSER, the elder.

SPENSER, the younger, his Son.

ARCHBISHOP of CANTERBURY.

BISHOP of COVENTRY.

BISHOP of WINCHESTER.

BALDOCK.

BEAUMONT.

TRUSSEL.

GURNEY.

MATREVIS.

LIGHTBORN.

SIR JOHN of HAINAULT.

LEVUNE.

RICE AP HOWEL.

Abbot, Monks, Herald, Lords, Poor Men, James, Mower,
Champion, Messengers, Soldiers, and Attendants.

QUEEN ISABELLA, Wife of King Edward the Second.

Niece to King Edward the Second, daughter of the
Duke of Gloucester.

Ladies.

EDWARD THE SECOND.

ACT THE FIRST.

SCENE I.

Enter GAVESTON, *reading a letter.*[1]

AV. "My father is deceased! Come, Gaveston,
And share the kingdom with thy dearest friend."
Ah! words that make me surfeit with delight!
What greater bliss can hap to Gaveston
Than live and be the favourite of a king!
Sweet prince. I come; these, these thy amorous lines
Might have enforced me to have swum from France,
And, like Leander, gasped upon the sand,
So thou would'st smile, and take me in thine arms.
The sight of London to my exiled eyes
Is as Elysium to a new-come soul;
Not that I love the city, or the men,

---

[1] The scene is a street in London

But that it harbours him I hold so dear.—
The king, upon whose bosom let me lie,
And with the world be still at enmity.
What need the arctic people love starlight,
To whom the sun shines both by day and night?
Farewell base stooping to the lordly peers!
My knee shall bow to none but to the king.
As for the multitude, that are but sparks,
Raked up in embers of their poverty;—
Tanti; I'll fawn first on the wind
That glanceth at my lips, and flieth away.
But how now, what are these?

Enter three Poor Men.

Men. Such as desire your worship's service.

Gav. What canst thou do?

1st P. Man. I can ride.

Gav. But I have no horse.   What art thou?

2nd P. Man. A traveller.

Gav. Let me see—thou would'st do well
To wait at my trencher and tell me lies at dinner-
        time;
And as I like your discoursing, I'll have you.
And what art thou?

3rd P. Man. A soldier, that hath served against the
        Scot.

Gav. Why, there are hospitals for such as you;
I have no war, and therefore, sir, begone.

3rd P. Man. Farewell, and perish by a soldier's
        hand,
That would'st reward them with an hospital.

Gav. Ay, ay, these words of his move me as much
As if a goose would play the porcupine,
And dart her plumes, thinking to pierce my breast.

But yet it is no pain to speak men fair :
I'll flatter these, and make them live in hope.   [*Aside.*
You know that I came lately out of France.
And yet I have not viewed my lord the king ;
If I speed well, I'll entertain you all.
  All. We thank your worship.
  Gav. I have some business.   Leave me to myself.
  All. We will wait here about the court.   [*Exeunt.*
  Gav. Do ; these are not men for me :
I must have wanton poets, pleasant wits,
Musicians, that with touching of a string
May draw the pliant king which way I please.
Music and poetry is his delight :
Therefore I'll have Italian masks by night,
Sweet speeches, comedies, and pleasing shows ;
And in the day, when he shall walk abroad,
Like sylvan nymphs my pages shall be clad ;
My men, like satyrs grazing on the lawns,
Shall with their goat-feet dance the antic hay.[1]
Sometime a lovely boy in Dian's shape,
With hair that gilds the water as it glides,
Crownets of pearl about his naked arms,
And in his sportful hands an olive-tree,
To hide those parts which men delight to see,
Shall bathe him in a spring ; and there hard by,
One like Actæon peeping through the grove,
Shall by the angry goddess be transformed,
And running in the likeness of an hart
By yelping hounds pulled down, shall seem to die ;—
Such things as these best please his majesty.
Here comes my lord the king, and the nobles
From the parliament.   I'll stand aside.   [*Retires.*

---

[1] Or heydeguy, a rural dance.

Enter KING EDWARD, LANCASTER, *the* Elder MORTIMER,
    Young MORTIMER, KENT, WARWICK, PEMBROKE,
    and Attendants.

K. Edw. Lancaster !

Lan. My lord.

Gav. That Earl of Lancaster do I abhor.   [*Aside.*

K. Edw. Will you not grant me this ? In spite of them
I'll have my will ; and these two Mortimers,
That cross me thus, shall know I am displeased. [*Aside.*

E. Mor. If you love us, my lord, hate Gaveston.

Gav. That villain Mortimer ! I'll be his death. [*Aside.*

Y. Mor. Mine uncle here, this earl, and I myself,
Were sworn to your father at his death,
That he should ne'er return into the realm :
And know, my lord, ere I will break my oath,
This sword of mine, that should offend your foes,
Shall sleep within the scabbard at thy need,
And underneath thy banners march who will,
For Mortimer will hang his armour up.

Gav. Mort Dieu !   [*Aside.*

K. Edw. Well, Mortimer, I'll make thee rue these words.
Beseems it thee to contradict thy king ?
Frown'st thou thereat, aspiring Lancaster?
The sword shall plane the furrows of thy brows,
And hew these knees that now are grown so stiff.
I will have Gaveston ; and you shall know
What danger 'tis to stand against your king.

Gav. Well done, Ned !   [*Aside.*

Lan. My lord, why do you thus incense your peers,
That naturally would love and honour you
But for that base and obscure Gaveston ?
Four earldoms have I, besides Lancaster—
Derby, Salisbury, Lincoln, Leicester,—

These will I sell, to give my soldiers pay,
Ere Gaveston shall stay within the realm ;
Therefore, if he be come, expel him straight.

 Kent.[1] Barons and earls, your pride hath made me mute ;
But now I'll speak, and to the proof, I hope.
I do remember, in my father's days,
Lord Percy of the north, being highly moved,
Braved Moubery in presence of the king ;
For which, had not his highness loved him well,
He should have lost his head ; but with his look
The undaunted spirit of Percy was appeased,
And Moubery and he were reconciled :
Yet dare you brave the king unto his face.—
Brother, revenge it, and let these their heads
Preach upon poles, for trespass of their tongues.

 War. O, our heads !

 K. Edw. Ay, yours ; and therefore I would wish you
  grant—

 War. Bridle thy anger, gentle Mortimer.

 Y. Mor. I cannot, nor I will not ; I must speak.—
Cousin, our hands I hope shall fence our heads,
And strike off his that makes you threaten us.
Come, uncle, let us leave the brain-sick king,
And henceforth parley with our naked swords.

 E. Mor. Wiltshire hath men enough to save our heads.

 War. All Warwickshire will love him for my sake.

 Lan. And northward Gaveston hath many friends.—
Adieu, my lord ; and either change your mind,
Or look to see the throne, where you should sit,
To float in blood ; and at thy wanton head,
The glozing head of thy base minion thrown.

   [*Exeunt all except* KING EDWARD, KENT, GAVE-
   STON *and* Attendants.

---

[1] Cunningham and Bullen have inaccurately given this speech to
King Edward.

K. Edw. I cannot brook these haughty menaces ;
Am I a king, and must be overruled ? —
Brother, display my ensigns in the field ;
I'll bandy[1] with the barons and the earls,
And either die or live with Gaveston.

    Gav. I can no longer keep me from my lord.

                              [Comes forward.

    K. Edw. What, Gaveston ! welcome !—Kiss not my
        hand—
Embrace me, Gaveston as I do thee.
Why should'st thou kneel ? know'st thou not who I am ?
Thy friend, thyself, another Gaveston !
Not Hylas was more mourned of Hercules,
Than thou hast been of me since thy exile.

    Gav. And since I went from hence, no soul in hell
Hath felt more torment than poor Gaveston.

    K. Edw. I know it.—Brother, welcome home my friend.
Now let the treacherous Mortimers conspire,
And that high-minded Earl of Lancaster :
I have my wish, in that I joy thy sight ;
And sooner shall the sea o'erwhelm my land,
Than bear the ship that shall transport thee hence.
I here create thee Lord High Chamberlain,
Chief Secretary to the state and me,
Earl of Cornwall, King and Lord of Man.

    Gav. My lord, these titles far exceed my worth.

    Kent. Brother, the least of these may well suffice
For one of greater birth than Gaveston.

    K. Edw. Cease, brother : for I cannot brook these
        words.
Thy worth, sweet friend, is far above my gifts,
Therefore, to equal it, receive my heart ;

---

[1] Contend.   The expression is no doubt borrowed from he old
game of bandy-ball, which was similar to golf.

If for these dignities thou be envied,
I'll give thee more ; for, but to honour thee.
Is Edward pleased with kingly regiment.[1]
Fear'st thou thy person ? thou shalt have a guard :
Wantest thou gold? go to my treasury:
Wouldst thou be loved and feared? receive my seal;
Save or condemn, and in our name command
Whatso thy mind affects, or fancy likes.

Gav. It shall suffice me to enjoy your love.
Which whiles I have, I think myself as great
As Cæsar riding in the Roman street,
With captive kings at his triumphant car.

Enter the BISHOP *of* COVENTRY.

K. Edw. Whither goes my lord of Coventry so fast?

B. of Cov. To celebrate your father's exequies.
But is that wicked Gaveston returned?

K. Edw. Ay, priest, and lives to be revenged on thee,
That wert the only cause of his exile.

Gav. 'Tis true : and but for reverence of these robes,
Thou should'st not plod one foot beyond this place.

B. of Cov. I did no more than I was bound to do ;
And, Gaveston, unless thou be reclaimed,
As then I did incense the parliament,
So will I now, and thou shalt back to France.

Gav. Saving your reverence, you must pardon me.

K. Edw. Throw off his golden mitre, rend his stole,
And in the channel[2] christen him anew.

Kent. Ah, brother, lay not violent hands on him !
For he'll complain unto the see of Rome.

Gav. Let him complain unto the see of hell;
I'll be revenged on him for my exile.

K. Edw. No, spare his life, but seize upon his goods:

---

[1] Rule.   [2] Gutter.

Be thou lord bishop and receive his rents,
And make him serve thee as thy chaplain:
I give him thee—here, use him as thou wilt.

 Gav. He shall to prison, and there die in bolts.

 K. Edw. Ay, to the Tower, the Fleet, or where thou wilt.

 B. of Cov. For this offence, be thou accurst of God!

 K. Edw. Who's there? Convey this priest to the Tower.

 B. of Cov. True, true.

 K. Edw. But in the meantime, Gaveston, away,
And take possession of his house and goods.
Come, follow me, and thou shalt have my guard
To see it done, and bring thee safe again.

 Gav. What should a priest do with so fair a house?
A prison may best beseem his holiness.   [*Exeunt.*

SCENE II.

Enter on one side the two MORTIMERS; *on the other,*
WARWICK *and* LANCASTER.[1]

 War. 'Tis true, the bishop is in the Tower,
And goods and body given to Gaveston.

 Lan. What! will they tyrannise upon the church?
Ah, wicked king! accursèd Gaveston!
This ground, which is corrupted with their steps,
Shall be their timeless[2] sepulchre or mine.

 Y. Mor. Well, let that peevish Frenchman guard him
   sure;
Unless his breast be sword-proof he shall die.

 E. Mor. How now! why droops the Earl of Lancaster?

 Y. Mor. Wherefore is Guy of Warwick discontent?

 Lan. That villain Gaveston is made an earl.

---

 [1] The scene is at Westminster.   [2] Untimely.

E. Mor. An earl!

War. Ay, and besides Lord Chamberlain of the realm.
And Secretary too, and Lord of Man.

E. Mor. We may not, nor we will not suffer this.

Y. Mor. Why post we not from hence to levy men?

Lan. "My Lord of Cornwall," now at every word!
And happy is the man whom he vouchsafes,
For vailing of his bonnet,[1] one good look.
Thus, arm in arm, the king and he doth march:
Nay more, the guard upon his lordship waits;
And all the court begins to flatter him.

War. Thus leaning on the shoulder of the king,
He nods and scorns and smiles at those that pass.

E. Mor. Doth no man take exceptions at the slave?

Lan. All stomach[2] him, but none dare speak a word.

Y. Mor. Ah, that bewrays their baseness, Lancaster!
Were all the earls and barons of my mind,
We'd hale him from the bosom of the king,
And at the court-gate hang the peasant up,
Who, swoln with venom of ambitious pride,
Will be the ruin of the realm and us.

War. Here comes my lord of Canterbury's grace.

Lan. His countenance bewrays he is displeased.

Enter the ARCHBISHOP *of* CANTERBURY *and an*
Attendant.

A. of Cant. First were his sacred garments rent and torn,
Then laid they violent hands upon him; next
Himself imprisoned, and his goods asseized:
This certify the Pope;—away, take horse. [*Exit* Attend.

Lan. My lord, will you take arms against the king?

A. of Cant. What need I? God himself is up in arms,
When violence is offered to the church.

---

[1] Removing it as a mark of respect.   [2] *i.e.* Feel resentment.

Y. Mor. Then will you join with us, that be his peers,
To banish or behead that Gaveston?

A. of Cant. What else, my lords? for it concerns me
        near;—
The bishopric of Coventry is his.

Enter QUEEN ISABELLA.

Y. Mor. Madam, whither walks your majesty so fast?

Q. Isab. Unto the forest, gentle Mortimer,
To live in grief and baleful discontent:
For now, my lord, the king regards me not,
But doats upon the love of Gaveston.
He claps his cheeks, and hangs about his neck,
Smiles in his face, and whispers in his ears;
And when I come he frowns, as who should say,
" Go whither thou wilt, seeing I have Gaveston."

E. Mor. Is it not strange that he is thus bewitched?

Y. Mor. Madam, return unto the court again:
That sly inveigling Frenchman we'll exile,
Or lose our lives; and yet, ere that day come,
The king shall lose his crown; for we have power,
And courage too, to be revenged at full.

A. of Cant. But yet lift not your swords against the king.

Lan. No; but we will lift Gaveston from hence.

War. And war must be the means, or he'll stay still.

Q. Isab. Then let him stay; for rather than my lord
Shall be oppressed with civil mutinies,
I will endure a melancholy life,
And let him frolic with his minion.

A. of Cant. My lords, to ease all this, but hear me
        speak :—
We and the rest, that are his counsellors,
Will meet, and with a general consent
Confirm his banishment with our hands and seals.

Lan. What we confirm the king will frustrate.

1. Mor. Then may we lawfully revolt from him.

War. But say, my lord, where shall this meeting be?

A. of Cant. At the New Temple.

Y. Mor. Content.

A. of Cant. And, in the meantime, I'll entreat you all
To cross to Lambeth, and there stay with me.

Lan. Come then, let's away.

Y. Mor. Madam, farewell!

Q. Isab. Farewell, sweet Mortimer; and, for my sake,
Forbear to levy arms against the king.

Y. Mor. Ay, if words will serve; if not, I must.

[*Exeunt.*

SCENE III.

Enter GAVESTON *and* KENT.

Gav. Edmund, the mighty Prince of Lancaster,
That hath more earldoms than an ass can bear,
And both the Mortimers, two goodly men,
With Guy of Warwick, that redoubted knight,
Are gone toward Lambeth—there let them remain.

[*Exeunt.*

SCENE IV.

Enter LANCASTER, WARWICK, PEMBROKE, *the* Elder
MORTIMER, Young MORTIMER, *the* ARCHBISHOP *of*
CANTERBURY *and* Attendants.[1]

Lan. Here is the form of Gaveston's exile:
May it please your lordship to subscribe your name.

---

[1] The scene is more probably the king's palace at Westminster
than the New Temple, as proposed by the archbishop.

A. of Cant. Give me the paper.

> [*He subscribes, as do the others after him.*

Lan. Quick, quick, my lord: I long to write my name.

War. But I long more to see him banished hence.

Y. Mor. The name of Mortimer shall fright the king,
Unless he be declined from that base peasant.

Enter KING EDWARD, GAVESTON, *and* KENT.

K. Edw. What, are you moved that Gaveston sits
    here?
It is our pleasure : we will have it so.

Lan. Your grace doth well to place him by your side,
For nowhere else the new earl is so safe.

E. Mor. What man of noble birth can brook this sight?
Quam male conveniunt!
See what a scornful look the peasant casts !

Pem. Can kingly lions fawn on creeping ants?

War. Ignoble vassal, that like Phaeton
Aspir'st unto the guidance of the sun !

Y. Mor. Their downfall is at hand, their forces down:
We will not thus be faced and over-peered.

K. Edw. Lay hands on that traitor Mortimer!

E. Mor. Lay hands on that traitor Gaveston!

Kent. Is this the duty that you owe your king?

War. We know our duties—let him know his peers.

K. Edw. Whither will you bear him? Stay, or ye shall
    die.

E. Mor. We are no traitors ; therefore threaten not.

Gav. No, threaten not, my lord, but pay them home!
Were I a king——

Y. Mor. Thou villain, wherefore talk'st thou of a king,
That hardly art a gentleman by birth?

K. Edw. Were he a peasant, being my minion,
I'll make the proudest of you stoop to him.

Lan. My lord, you may not thus disparage us.—
Away, I say, with hateful Gaveston !

E. Mor. And with the Earl of Kent that favours him.

[*Attendants* remove KENT *and* GAVESTON.

K. Edw. Nay, then, lay violent hands upon your king,
Here, Mortimer, sit thou in Edward's throne :
Warwick and Lancaster, wear you my crown :
Was ever king thus over-ruled as I ?

Lan. Learn then to rule us better, and the realm.

Y. Mor. What we have done, our heart-blood shall
    maintain.

War. Think you that we can brook this upstart's pride ?

K. Edw. Anger and wrathful fury stops my speech.

A. of Cant. Why are you moved ? be patient, my lord
And see what we your counsellors have done.

Y. Mor. My lords, now let us all be resolute,
And either have our wills, or lose our lives.

K. Edw. Meet you for this, proud overbearing peers ?
Ere my sweet Gaveston shall part from me,
This isle shall fleet[1] upon the ocean,
And wander to the unfrequented Inde.

A. of Cant. You know that I am legate to the Pope ;
On your allegiance to the see of Rome,
Subscribe, as we have done, to his exile.

Y. Mor. Curse him, if he refuse ; and then may we
Depose him and elect another king.

K. Edw. Ay, there it goes ! but yet I will not yield :
Curse me, depose me, do the worst you can.

Lan. Then linger not, my lord, but do it straight.

A. of Cant. Remember how the bishop was abused !
Either banish him that was the cause thereof,
Or I will presently discharge these lords
Of duty and allegiance due to thee.

[1] *i.e.* Float.

K. Edw. It boots me not to threat—I must speak fair :
The legate of the Pope will be obeyed.   [*Aside.*
My lord, you shall be Chancellor of the realm ;
Thou, Lancaster, High Admiral of our fleet ;
Young Mortimer and his uncle shall be earls ;
And you, Lord Warwick, President of the North ;
And thou of Wales.   If this content you not,
Make several kingdoms of this monarchy,
And share it equally amongst you all,
So I may have some nook or corner left,
To frolic with my dearest Gaveston.

 A. of Cant. Nothing shall alter us—we are resolved.

 Lan. Come, come, subscribe.

 Y. Mor. Why should you love him whom the world
  hates so?

 K. Edw. Because he loves me more than all the world.
Ah, none but rude and savage-minded men
Would seek the ruin of my Gaveston ;
You that be noble-born should pity him.

 War. You that are princely-born should shake him off :
For shame subscribe, and let the lown depart.

 E. Mor. Urge him, my lord.

 A. of Cant. Are you content to banish him the realm ?

 K. Edw. I see I must, and therefore am content :
Instead of ink I'll write it with my tears.   [*Subscribes.*

 Y. Mor. The king is love-sick for his minion.

 K. Edw. 'Tis done—and now, accursèd hand, fall off !

 Lan. Give it me—I'll have it published in the streets.

 Y. Mor. I'll see him presently despatched away.

 A. of Cant. Now is my heart at ease.

 War. And so is mine.

 Pem. This will be good news to the common sort.

 E. Mor. Be it or no, he shall not linger here.
        [*Exeunt all except* KING EDWARD.

K. Edw. How fast they run to banish him I love !
They would not stir, were it to do me good.
Why should a king be subject to a priest ?
Proud Rome ! that hatchest such imperial grooms,
For these thy superstitious taper-lights,
Wherewith thy antichristian churches blaze,
I'll fire thy crazed buildings, and enforce
The papal towers to kiss the lowly ground !
With slaughtered priests make Tiber's channel swell,
And banks raised higher with their sepulchres !
As for the peers, that back the clergy thus,
If I be king, not one of them shall live.

Re-enter GAVESTON.

Gav. My lord, I hear it whispered everywhere,
That I am banished, and must fly the land.

K. Edw. 'Tis true, sweet Gaveston--O ! were it false !
The legate of the Pope will have it so,
And thou must hence, or I shall be deposed.
But I will reign to be revenged of them ;
And therefore, sweet friend, take it patiently.
Live where thou wilt, I'll send thee gold enough ;
And long thou shalt not stay, or if thou dost,
I'll come to thee ; my love shall ne'er decline.

Gav. Is all my hope turned to this hell of grief?

K. Edw. Rend not my heart with thy too-piercing
   words :
Thou from this land, I from myself am banished.

Gav. To go from hence grieves not poor Gaveston ;
But to forsake you, in whose gracious looks
The blessedness of Gaveston remains :
For nowhere else seeks he felicity.

K. Edw. And only this torments my wretched soul
That, whether I will or no, thou must depart.

Be governor of Ireland in my stead,
And there abide till fortune call thee home.
Here take my picture, and let me wear thine;

                            [*They exchange pictures.*

O, might I keep thee here as I do this,
Happy were I! but now most miserable!

    Gav. 'Tis something to be pitied of a king.

    K. Edw. Thou shalt not hence—I'll hide thee,
        Gaveston.

    Gav. I shall be found, and then 'twill grieve me more.

    K. Edw. Kind words and mutual talk makes our grief
        greater:

Therefore, with dumb embracement, let us part—
Stay, Gaveston, I cannot leave thee thus.

    Gav. For every look, my love [1] drops down a tear:
Seeing I must go, do not renew my sorrow.

    K. Edw. The time is little that thou hast to stay,
And, therefore, give me leave to look my fill:
But come, sweet friend, I'll bear thee on thy way.

    Gav. The peers will frown.

    K. Edw. I pass [2] not for their anger—Come, let's go;
O that we might as well return as go.

              Enter QUEEN ISABELLA.

    Q. Isab. Whither goes my lord?

    K. Edw. Fawn not on me, French strumpet! get thee
        gone!

    Q. Isab. On whom but on my husband should I fawn?

    Gav. On Mortimer! with whom, ungentle queen—
I say no more—judge you the rest, my lord.

    Q. Isab. In saying this, thou wrong'st me, Gaveston;
Is't not enough that thou corrupt'st my lord,

----

    [1] " Lord " in the old editions; altered by Dyce to " love."
    [2] Care.

And art a bawd to his affections,
But thou must call mine honour thus in question?

Gav. I mean not so ; your grace must pardon me.

K. Edw. Thou art too familiar with that Mortimer,
And by thy means is Gaveston exiled :
But I would wish thee reconcile the lords,
Or thou shalt ne'er be reconciled to me.

Q. Isab. Your highness knows it lies not in my power.

K. Edw. Away then ! touch me not—Come, Gaveston.

Q. Isab. Villain ! 'tis thou that robb'st me of my lord.

Gav. Madam, 'tis you that rob me of my lord.

K. Edw. Speak not unto her ; let her droop and
pine.

Q. Isab. Wherein, my lord, have I deserved these
words ?
Witness the tears that Isabella sheds,
Witness this heart, that sighing for thee, breaks,
How dear my lord is to poor Isabel.

K. Edw. And witness Heaven how dear thou art to
me :
There weep : for till my Gaveston be repealed,
Assure thyself thou com'st not in my sight.

> [*Exeunt* EDWARD *and* GAVESTON.

Q. Isab. O miserable and distressèd queen !
Would, when I left sweet France and was embarked,
That charming Circe walking on the waves,
Had changed my shape, or at the marriage-day
The cup of Hymen had been full of poison,
Or with those arms that twined about my neck
I had been stifled, and not lived to see
The king my lord thus to abandon me !
Like frantic Juno will I fill the earth
With ghastly murmur of my sighs and cries ;
For never doated Jove on Ganymede

So much as he on cursèd Gaveston :
But that will more exasperate his wrath ;
I must entreat him, I must speak him fair ;
And be a means to call home Gaveston :
And yet he'll ever doat on Gaveston :
And so am I for ever miserable.

Re-enter LANCASTER, WARWICK, PEMBROKE, *the* Elder
MORTIMER, *and* Young MORTIMER.

Lan. Look where the sister of the King of France
Sits wringing of her hands, and beats her breast !
War. The king, I fear, hath ill-entreated her.
Pem. Hard is the heart that injuries [1] such a saint.
Y. Mor. I know 'tis 'long of Gaveston she weeps.
E. Mor. Why, he is gone.
Y. Mor. Madam, how fares your grace ?
Q. Isab. Ah, Mortimer ! now breaks the king's hate
    forth,
And he confesseth that he loves me not.
    Y. Mor. Cry quittance, madam, then : and love not
    him.
    Q. Isab. No, rather will I die a thousand deaths :
And yet I love in vain ;—he'll ne'er love me.
    Lan. Fear ye not, madam ; now his minion's gone,
His wanton humour will be quickly left.
    Q. Isab. O never, Lancaster ! I am enjoined
To sue upon you all for his repeal ;
This wills my lord, and this must I perform,
Or else be banished from his highness' presence.
    Lan. For his repeal, madam ! he comes not back,
Unless the sea cast up his shipwrecked body.
    War. And to behold so sweet a sight as that,
There's none here but would run his horse to death.

---

[1] " Injury," as before pointed out, was formerly used as a verb.

Y. Mor. But, madam, would you have us call him
    home ?

Q. Isab. Ay, Mortimer, for till he be restored,
The angry king hath banished me the court ;
And, therefore, as thou lov'st and tender'st me,
Be thou my advocate unto these peers.

    Y. Mor. What ! would you have me plead for Gave-
    ston ?

E. Mor. Plead for him that will, I am resolved.

Lan. And so am I, my lord : dissuade the queen.

Q. Isab. O Lancaster ! let him dissuade the king,
For 'tis against my will he should return.

War. Then speak not for him, let the peasant go.

Q. Isab. 'Tis for myself I speak, and not for him.

Pem. No speaking will prevail, and therefore cease.

Y. Mor. Fair queen, forbear to angle for the fish
Which, being caught, strikes him that takes it dead ;
I mean that vile torpedo, Gaveston,
That now, I hope, floats on the Irish seas.

Q. Isab. Sweet Mortimer, sit down by me awhile,
And I will tell thee reasons of such weight
As thou wilt soon subscribe to his repeal.

Y. Mor. It is impossible ; but speak your mind.

Q. Isab. Then thus, but none shall hear it but ourselves.
                        [*Talks to* Y. MORTIMER *apart.*

Lan. My lords, albeit the queen win Mortimer,
Will you be resolute, and hold with me ?

E. Mor. Not I, against my nephew.

Pem. Fear not, the queen's words cannot alter him.

War. No ? do but mark how earnestly she pleads !

Lan. And see how coldly his looks make denial !

War. She smiles ; now for my life his mind is changed !

Lan. I'll rather lose his friendship, I, than grant.

Y. Mor. Well, of necessity it must be so.

My lords, that I abhor base Gaveston,
I hope your honours make no question,
And therefore, though I plead for his repeal,
'Tis not for his sake, but for our avail :
Nay for the realm's behoof, and for the king's.

   Lan. Fie, Mortimer, dishonour not thyself !
Can this be true, 'twas good to banish him ?
And is this true, to call him home again ?
Such reasons make white black, and dark night day.

   Y. Mor. My lord of Lancaster, mark the respect.[1]

   Lan. In no respect can contraries be true.

   Q. Isab. Yet, good my lord, hear what he can allege.

   War. All that he speaks is nothing ; we are resolved.

   Y. Mor. Do you not wish that Gaveston were dead ?

   Pem. I would he were !

   Y. Mor. Why then, my lord, give me but leave to speak.

   E. Mor. But, nephew, do not play the sophister.

   Y. Mor. This which I urge is of a burning zeal
To mend the king. and do our country good.
Know you not Gaveston hath store of gold,
Which may in Ireland purchase him such friends
As he will front the mightiest of us all ?
And whereas he shall live and be beloved,
'Tis hard for us to work his overthrow.

   War. Mark you but that, my lord of Lancaster.

   Y. Mor. But were he here, detested as he is,
How easily might some base slave be suborned
To greet his lordship with a poniard,
And none so much as blame the murderer,
But rather praise him for that brave attempt,
And in the chronicle enrol his name
For purging of the realm of such a plague !

   Pem. He saith true.

---

[1] Consideration.

Lan. Ay, but how chance this was not done before?

Y. Mor. Because, my lords, it was not thought upon.
Nay, more, when he shall know it lies in us
To banish him, and then to call him home,
'Twill make him vail [1] the top-flag of his pride,
And fear to offend the meanest nobleman.

E. Mor. But how if he do not, nephew?

Y. Mor. Then may we with some colour rise in arms;
For howsoever we have borne it out,
'Tis treason to be up against the king;
So we shall have the people of our side,
Which for his father's sake lean to the king,
But cannot brook a night-grown mushroom,
Such a one as my lord of Cornwall is,
Should bear us down of the nobility.
And when the commons and the nobles join,
'Tis not the king can buckler Gaveston;
We'll pull him from the strongest hold he hath.
My lords, if to perform this I be slack,
Think me as base a groom as Gaveston.

Lan. On that condition, Lancaster will grant

War. And so will Pembroke and I.

E. Mor. And I.

Y. Mor. In this I count me highly gratified,
And Mortimer will rest at your command.

Q. Isab. And when this favour Isabel forgets,
Then let her live abandoned and forlorn.--
But see, in happy time, my lord the king,
Having brought the Earl of Cornwall on his way,
Is new returned; this news will glad him much;
Yet not so much as me; I love him more
Than he can Gaveston; would he love me
But half so much, then were I treble-blessed!

---

[1] Lower.

Re-enter KING EDWARD, *mourning.*

K. Edw. He's gone, and for his absence thus I mourn.
Did never sorrow go so near my heart
As doth the want of my sweet Gaveston ;
And could my crown's revenue bring him back,
I would freely give it to his enemies,
And think I gained, having bought so dear a friend.

Q. Isab. Hark ! how he harps upon his minion.

K. Edw. My heart is as an anvil unto sorrow,
Which beats upon it like the Cyclops' hammers,
And with the noise turns up my giddy brain,
And makes me frantic for my Gaveston.
Ah ! had some bloodless Fury rose from hell,
And with my kingly sceptre struck me dead,
When I was forced to leave my Gaveston !

Lan. Diablo ! What passions call you these ?

Q. Isab. My gracious lord, I come to bring you news.

K. Edw. That you have parleyed with your Mortimer!

Q. Isab. That Gaveston, my lord, shall be repealed.

K. Edw. Repealed ! the news is too sweet to be
true ?

Q. Isab. But will you love me, if you find it so ?

K. Edw. If it be so, what will not Edward do ?

Q. Isab. For Gaveston, but not for Isabel.

K. Edw. For thee, fair queen, if thou lov'st Gaveston ;
I'll hang a golden tongue about thy neck,
Seeing thou hast pleaded with so good success.

Q. Isab. No other jewels hang about my neck
Than these, my lord ; nor let me have more wealth
Than I may fetch from this rich treasury—
O how a kiss revives poor Isabel !

K. Edw. Once more receive my hand ; and let this be
A second marriage 'twixt thyself and me.

Q. Isab. And may it prove more happy than the first !
My gentle lord, bespeak these nobles fair,
That wait attendance for a gracious look,
And on their knees salute your majesty.

K. Edw. Courageous Lancaster, embrace thy king !
And, as gross vapours perish by the sun,
Even so let hatred with thy sovereign's smile.
Live thou with me as my companion.

Lan. This salutation overjoys my heart.

K. Edw. Warwick shall be my chiefest counsellor :
These silver hairs will more adorn my court
Than gaudy silks, or rich embroidery.
Chide me, sweet Warwick, if I go astray.

War. Slay me, my lord, when I offend your grace.

K. Edw. In solemn triumphs, and in public shows,
Pembroke shall bear the sword before the king.

Pem. And with this sword Pembroke will fight for
    you.

K. Edw. But wherefore walks young Mortimer aside ?
Be thou commander of our royal fleet ;
Or, if that lofty office like thee not,
I make thee here Lord Marshal of the realm.

Y. Mor. My lord, I'll marshal so your enemies,
As England shall be quiet, and you safe.

K. Edw. And as for you, Lord Mortimer of Chirke,
Whose great achievements in our foreign war
Deserves no common place, nor mean reward ;
Be you the general of the levied troops,
That now are ready to assail the Scots.

E. Mor. In this your grace hath highly honoured me,
For with my nature war doth best agree.

Q. Isab. Now is the King of England rich and strong,
Having the love of his renownèd peers.

K. Edw. Ay, Isabel, ne'er was my heart so light.

Clerk of the crown, direct our warrant forth
For Gaveston to Ireland :

Enter BEAUMONT *with warrant.*

Beaumont, fly
As fast as Iris or Jove's Mercury.

Bea. It shall be done, my gracious lord.　　　[*Exit.*

K. Edw. Lord Mortimer, we leave you to your charge.
Now let us in, and feast it royally.
Against our friend the Earl of Cornwall comes,
We'll have a general tilt and tournament ;
And then his marriage shall be solemnised.
For wot you not that I have made him sure [1]
Unto our cousin, the Earl of Gloucester's heir ?

Lan. Such news we hear, my lord.

K. Edw. That day, if not for him, yet for my sake,
Who in the triumph will be challenger,
Spare for no cost ; we will requit your love.

War. In this, or aught your highness shall command us.

K. Edw. Thanks, gentle Warwick : come, let's in and
　　　revel.　　　[*Exeunt all except the* MORTIMERS.

E. Mor. Nephew, I must to Scotland ; thou stayest
　　　here.
Leave now t'oppose thyself against the king.
Thou seest by nature he is mild and calm,
And, seeing his mind so doats on Gaveston,
Let him without controulment have his will.
The mightiest kings have had their minions :
Great Alexander loved Hephestion ;
The conquering Hercules for Hylas wept ;
And for Patroclus stern Achilles drooped.
And not kings only, but the wisest men :
The Roman Tully loved Octavius ;

----

[1] *i.e.* Affianced him

Grave Socrates wild Alcibiades.
Then let his grace, whose youth is flexible,
And promiseth as much as we can wish,
Freely enjoy that vain, light-headed earl;
For riper years will wean him from such toys.

Y. Mor. Uncle, his wanton humour grieves not me;
But this I scorn, that one so basely born
Should by his sovereign's favour grow so pert,
And riot it with the treasure of the realm.
While soldiers mutiny for want of pay,
He wears a lord's revenue on his back,
And Midas-like, he jets[1] it in the court,
With base outlandish cullions[2] at his heels,
Whose proud fantastic liveries make such show,
As if that Proteus, god of shapes, appeared.
I have not seen a dapper Jack so brisk;
He wears a short Italian hooded cloak,
Larded with pearl, and, in his Tuscan cap,
A jewel of more value than the crown.
While others walk below, the king and he
From out a window laugh at such as we,
And flout our train, and jest at our attire.
Uncle, 'tis this makes me impatient.

E. Mor. But, nephew, now you see the king is changed.

Y. Mor. Then so am I, and live to do him service:
But whiles I have a sword, a hand, a heart,
I will not yield to any such upstart.
You know my mind; come, uncle, let's away. [*Exeunt.*

---

[1] Struts, Fr., *jetter*.   [2] Scoundrels.

ACT THE SECOND.

SCENE I.

Enter Young SPENCER *and* BALDOCK.[1]

ALD. Spencer,
  Seeing that our lord the Earl of Glou-
    cester's dead,
  Which of the nobles dost thou mean
    to serve?   [his side ;
  Y. Spen. Not Mortimer, nor any of
Because the king and he are enemies.
Baldock, learn this of me, a factious lord
Shall hardly do himself good, much less us ;
But he that hath the favour of a king,
May with one word advance us while we live :
The liberal Earl of Cornwall is the man
On whose good fortune Spencer's hopes depends.
  Bald. What, mean you then to be his follower?
  Y. Spen. No, his companion : for he loves me well,
And would have once preferred me to the king.
  Bald. But he is banished ; there's small hope of
    him.
  Y. Spen. Ay, for a while ; but, Baldock, mark the
    end.
A friend of mine told me in secrecy

---

[1] Dyce supposes the scene to be a hall in Gloucester house.

That he's repealed, and sent for back again ;
And even now a post came from the court
With letters to our lady from the king ;
And as she read she smiled, which makes me think
It is about her lover Gaveston.

Bald. 'Tis like enough ; for since he was exiled
She neither walks abroad, nor comes in sight.
But I had thought the match had been broke off,
And that his banishment had changed her mind.

Y. Spen. Our lady's first love is not wavering ;
My life for thine she will have Gaveston.

Bald. Then hope I by her means to be preferred,
Having read unto her since she was a child.

Y. Spen. Then, Baldock, you must cast the scholar off,
And learn to court it like a gentleman.
'Tis not a black coat and a little band,
A velvet-caped coat, faced before with serge,
And smelling to a nosegay all the day,
Or holding of a napkin in your hand,
Or saying a long grace at a table's end,
Or making low legs to a nobleman,
Or looking downward with your eyelids close,
And saying, " Truly, an't may please your honour,"
Can get you any favour with great men ;
You must be proud, bold, pleasant, resolute,
And now and then stab, as occasion serves.

Bald. Spencer, thou know'st I hate such formal toys,
And use them but of mere hypocrisy.
Mine old lord whiles he lived was so precise,
That he would take exceptions at my buttons,
And being like pin's heads, blame me for the bigness ;
Which made me curate-like in mine attire,
Though inwardly licentious enough,
And apt for any kind of villany.

I am none of these common pedants, I,
That cannot speak without *propterea quod.*

  Y. Spen. But one of those that saith, *quandoquidem,*
And hath a special gift to form a verb.

  Bald. Leave off this jesting, here my lady comes.

Enter KING EDWARD'S Niece.

  Niece. The grief for his exile was not so much,
As is the joy of his returning home.
This letter came from my sweet Gaveston:
What need'st thou, love, thus to excuse thyself?
I know thou could'st not come and visit me:
[*Reads.*] "I will not long be from thee, though I die."
This argues the entire love of my lord;
[*Reads.*] "When I forsake thee, death seize on my heart:"
But stay thee here where Gaveston shall sleep.
                    [*Puts the letter into her bosom.*
Now to the letter of my lord the king.—
He wills me to repair unto the court,
And meet my Gaveston? why do I stay,
Seeing that he talks thus of my marriage-day?
Who's there? Baldock!
See that my coach be ready, I must hence.

  Bald. It shall be done, madam.

  Niece. And meet me at the park-pale presently.
                    [*Exit* BALDOCK.

Spencer, stay you and bear me company,
For I have joyful news to tell thee of;
My lord of Cornwall is a-coming over,
And will be at the court as soon as we.

  Y. Spen. I knew the king would have him home again.

  Niece. If all things sort[1] out, as I hope they will,
Thy service, Spencer, shall be thought upon.

---

[1] Turn.

Y. Spen. I humbly thank your ladyship.

Nicc. Come, lead the way; I long till I am there.

[*Exeunt.*

SCENE II.

Enter KING EDWARD, QUEEN ISABELLA, KENT, LAN-
CASTER, Young MORTIMER. WARWICK, PEMBROKE,
and Attendants.

K. Edw. The wind is good. I wonder why he stays:
I fear me he is wrecked upon the sea.

Q. Isab. Look, Lancaster, how passionate[1] he is,
And still his mind runs on his minion!

Lan. My lord,—

K. Edw. How now! what news? is Gaveston arrived?

Y. Mor. Nothing but Gaveston! what means your grace?
You have matters of more weight to think upon;
The King of France sets foot in Normandy.

K. Edw. A trifle! we'll expel him when we please.
But tell me, Mortimer, what's thy device
Against the stately triumph we decreed?

Y. Mor. A homely one, my lord, not worth the telling.

K. Edw. Pray thee let me know it.

Y. Mor. But, seeing you are so desirous, thus it is:
A lofty cedar-tree, fair flourishing,
On whose top-branches kingly eagles perch,
And by the bark a canker creeps me up,
And gets into the highest bough of all:
The motto, *Æque tandem.*

K. Edw. And what is yours, my lord of Lancaster?

Lan. My lord, mine's more obscure than Mortimer's.

Sorrowful.

Mar.   A A

Pliny reports there is a flying fish
Which all the other fishes deadly hate,
And therefore, being pursued, it takes the air :
No sooner is it up, but there's a fowl
That seizeth it; this fish, my lord, I bear,
The motto this : *Undique mors est.*

   Kent. Proud Mortimer ! ungentle Lancaster !
Is this the love you bear your sovereign ?
Is this the fruit your reconcilement bears ?
Can you in words make show of amity,
And in your shields display your rancorous minds !
What call you this but private libelling
Against the Earl of Cornwall and my brother ?

   Q. Isab. Sweet husband, be content, they all love you.

   K. Edw. They love me not that hate my Gaveston.
I am that cedar, shake me not too much ;
And you the eagles ; soar ye ne'er so high,
I have the jesses[1] that will pull you down ;
And *Æque tandem* shall that canker cry
Unto the proudest peer of Britainy.
Though thou compar'st him to a flying fish,
And threatenest death whether he rise or fall,
'Tis not the hugest monster of the sea,
Nor foulest harpy that shall swallow him.

   Y. Mor. If in his absence thus he favours him,
What will he do whenas he shall be present ?

   Lan. That shall we see ; look where his lordship comes.

Enter GAVESTON.

   K. Edw. My Gaveston !
Welcome to Tynemouth ! welcome to thy friend !
Thy absence made me droop and pine away ;

---

[1] The straps round a hawk's legs, with rings attached, to which
the falconer's leash was fastened.

For, as the lovers of fair Danae,
When she was locked up in a brazen tower,
Desired her more, and waxed outrageous,
So did it fare with me : and now thy sight
Is sweeter far than was thy parting hence
Bitter and irksome to my sobbing heart.

   Gav. Sweet lord and king, your speech preventeth [1]
      mine,
Yet have I words left to express my joy :
The shepherd nipt with biting winter's rage
Frolics not more to see the painted spring,
Than I do to behold your majesty.

   K. Edw. Will none of you salute my Gaveston ?
   Lan. Salute him ? yes ; welcome, Lord Chamberlain !
   Y. Mor. Welcome is the good Earl of Cornwall !
   War. Welcome, Lord Governor of the Isle of Man !
   Pem. Welcome, Master Secretary !
   Kent. Brother, do you hear them ?
   K. Edw. Still will these earls and barons use me thus.
   Gav. My lord, I cannot brook these injuries.
   Q. Isab. Ay me, poor soul, when these begin to jar.
                              [*Aside.*
   K. Edw. Return it to their throats, I'll be thy warrant.
   Gav. Base, leaden earls, that glory in your birth,
Go sit at home and eat your tenant's beef ;
And come not here to scoff at Gaveston,
Whose mounting thoughts did never creep so low
As to bestow a look on such as you.

   Lan. Yet I disdain not to do this for you.
      [*Draws his sword and offers to stab* GAVESTON.
   K. Edw. Treason ! treason ! where's the traitor ?
   Pem. Here ! here !
   K. Edw. Convey hence Gaveston ; they'll murder him.

---

[1] *i.e.* Anticipateth.

Gav. The life of thee shall salve this foul disgrace.

Y. Mor. Villain ! thy life, unless I miss mine aim.

[*Wounds* GAVESTON.

Q. Isab. Ah ! furious Mortimer, what hast thou done?

Y. Mor. No more than I would answer, were he slain.

[*Exit* GAVESTON *with* Attendants.

K. Edw. Yes, more than thou canst answer, though

he live ;

Dear shall you both abide this riotous deed.

Out of my presence ! come not near the court.

Y. Mor. I'll not be barred the court for Gaveston.

Lan. We'll hale him by the ears unto the block.

K. Edw. Look to your own heads ; his is sure enough.

War. Look to your own crown, if you back him thus.

Kent. Warwick, these words do ill beseem thy years.

K. Edw. Nay, all of them conspire to cross me thus :

But if I live, I'll tread upon their heads

That think with high looks thus to tread me down.

Come, Edmund, let's away and levy men,

'Tis war that must abate these barons' pride.

[*Exeunt* KING EDWARD, QUEEN ISABELLA,
and KENT.

War. Let's to our castles, for the king is moved.

Y. Mor. Moved may he be, and perish in his wrath !

Lan. Cousin, it is no dealing with him now,

He means to make us stoop by force of arms ;

And therefore let us jointly here protest,

To persecute that Gaveston to the death.

Y. Mor. By heaven, the abject villain shall not live !

War. I'll have his blood, or die in seeking it.

Pem. The like oath Pembroke takes.

Lan. And so doth Lancaster.

Now send our heralds to defy the king ;

And make the people swear to put him down.

Enter a Messenger.

Y. Mor. Letters! from whence?

Mess. From Scotland, my lord.

[*Giving letters to* MORTIMER.

Lan. Why, how now, cousin, how fares all our friends?

Y. Mor. My uncle's taken prisoner by the Scots.

Lan. We'll have him ransomed, man; be of good cheer.

Y. Mor. They rate his ransom at five thousand pound.
Who should defray the money but the king,
Seeing he is taken prisoner in his wars?
I'll to the king.

Lan. Do, cousin, and I'll bear thee company.

War. Meantime, my lord of Pembroke and myself
Will to Newcastle here, and gather head.

Y. Mor. About it then, and we will follow you.

Lan. Be resolute and full of secrecy.

War. I warrant you. [*Exit with* PEMBROKE.

Y. Mor. Cousin, and if he will not ransom him,
I'll thunder such a peal into his ears,
As never subject did unto his king.

Lan. Content, I'll bear my part—Holla! who's there?

Enter Guard.

Y. Mor. Ay, marry, such a guard as this doth well.

Lan. Lead on the way.

Guard. Whither will your lordships?

Y. Mor. Whither else but to the king.

Guard. His highness is disposed to be alone.

Lan. Why, so he may, but we will speak to him.

Guard. You may not in, my lord.

Y. Mor. May we not?

Enter KING EDWARD *and* KENT.

K. Edw. How now!
What noise is this? who have we there, is't you? [*Going.*

Y. Mor. Nay, stay, my lord, I come to bring you news;
Mine uncle's taken prisoner by the Scots.

K. Edw. Then ransom him.

Lan. 'Twas in your wars; you should ransom him.

Y. Mor. And you shall ransom him, or else——

Kent. What! Mortimer, you will not threaten him?

K. Edw. Quiet yourself, you shall have the broad seal,
To gather for him throughout the realm.

Lan. Your minion Gaveston hath taught you this.

Y. Mor. My lord, the family of the Mortimers
Are not so poor, but, would they sell their land,
'Twould levy men enough to anger you.
We never beg, but use such prayers as these.

K. Edw. Shall I still be haunted thus?

Y. Mor. Nay, now you're here alone, I'll speak my mind.

Lan. And so will I, and then, my lord, farewell.

Y. Mor. The idle triumphs, masks, lascivious shows,
And prodigal gifts bestowed on Gaveston,
Have drawn thy treasury dry, and made thee weak;
The murmuring commons, overstretchèd, break.

Lan. Look for rebellion, look to be deposed;
Thy garrisons are beaten out of France,
And, lame and poor, lie groaning at the gates.
The wild Oneyl, with swarms of Irish kerns,[1]
Lives uncontrolled within the English pale.
Unto the walls of York the Scots make road,[2]
And unresisted drive away rich spoils.

Y. Mor. The haughty Dane commands the narrow seas,
While in the harbour ride thy ships unrigged.

Lan. What foreign prince sends thee ambassadors?

Y. Mor. Who loves thee, but a sort of flatterers?

Lan. Thy gentle queen, sole sister to Valois,
Complains that thou hast left her all forlorn.

---

[1] Foot soldiers.   [2] *i.e.* Inroad.

Y. Mor. Thy court is naked, being bereft of those
That make a king seem glorious to the world :
I mean the peers, whom thou should'st dearly love :
Libels are cast again thee in the street :
Ballads and rhymes made of thy overthrow.

Lan. The Northern borderers seeing their houses burnt,
Their wives and children slain, run up and down,
Cursing the name of thee and Gaveston.

Y. Mor. When wert thou in the field with banner spread,
But once ? and then thy soldiers marched like players,
With garish robes, not armour ; and thyself,
Bedaubed with gold, rode laughing at the rest,
Nodding and shaking of thy spangled crest,
Where women's favours hung like labels down.

Lan. And therefore came it, that the fleering[1] Scots,
To England's high disgrace, have made this jig[2] ;

> " Maids of England, sore may you mourn,—
>> For your lemans[3] you have lost at Bannocks-
>>> bourn,—
>> With a heave and a ho !
>> What weeneth the King of England,
>> So soon to have won Scotland ?—
>>> With a rombelow ! "

Y. Mor. Wigmore shall fly,[4] to set my uncle free.

Lan. And when 'tis gone, our swords shall purchase
    more.
If ye be moved, revenge it as you can ;
Look next to see us with our ensigns spread.

> [*Exit with* Young MORTIMER.

K. Edw. My swelling heart for very anger breaks !

---

[1] Jeering.
[2] This jig or ballad is taken, with slight variations, from Fabyan's
Chronicle. At the time the scene refers to, the battle of Bannock-
burn had not been fought.   [3] Lovers.
[4] Wigmore was the name of young Mortimer's estate.

How oft have I been baited by these peers,
And dare not be revenged, for their power is great!
Yet, shall the crowing of these cockerels
Affright a lion?   Edward, unfold thy paws,
And let their lives' blood slake thy fury's hunger.
If I be cruel and grow tyrannous,
Now let them thank themselves, and rue too late.

Kent. My lord, I see your love to Gaveston
Will be the ruin of the realm and you,
For now the wrathful nobles threaten wars,
And therefore, brother, banish him for ever.

K. Edw. Art thou an enemy to my Gaveston?

Kent. Ay, and it grieves me that I favoured him.

K. Edw. Traitor, begone! whine thou with Mortimer.

Kent. So will I, rather than with Gaveston.

K. Edw. Out of my sight, and trouble me no more!

Kent. No marvel though thou scorn thy noble peers,
When I thy brother am rejected thus.

K. Edw. Away!   [*Exit* KENT.
Poor Gaveston, that has no friend but me,
Do what they can, we'll live in Tynemouth here,
And, so I walk with him about the walls,
What care I though the earls begirt us round?—
Here cometh she that's cause of all these jars.

Enter QUEEN ISABELLA *with* KING EDWARD'S Niece, *two*
Ladies, GAVESTON, BALDOCK *and* Young SPENCER.

Q. Isab. My lord, 'tis thought the earls are up in arms.

K. Edw. Ay, and 'tis likewise thought you favour 'em.

Q. Isab. Thus do you still suspect me without cause?

Niece. Sweet uncle! speak more kindly to the queen.

Gav. My lord, dissemble with her, speak her fair.

K. Edw. Pardon me, sweet, I had forgot myself.

Q. Isab. Your pardon is quickly got of Isabel.

K. Edw. The younger Mortimer is grown so brave,
That to my face he threatens civil wars.

Gav. Why do you not commit him to the Tower?

K. Edw. I dare not, for the people love him well.

Gav. Why, then we'll have him privily made away.

K. Edw. Would Lancaster and he had both caroused
A bowl of poison to each other's health!
But let them go, and tell me what are these.

Niece. Two of my father's servants whilst he liv'd,—
May't please your grace to entertain them now.

K. Edw. Tell me, where wast thou born? what is thine
arms?

Bald. My name is Baldock, and my gentry
I fetch from Oxford, not from heraldry.

K. Edw. The fitter art thou, Baldock, for my turn.
Wait on me, and I'll see thou shall not want.

Bald. I humbly thank your majesty.

K. Edw. Knowest thou him, Gaveston?

Gav. Ay, my lord;
His name is Spencer, he is well allied;
For my sake, let him wait upon your grace:
Scarce shall you find a man of more desert.

K. Edw. Then, Spencer, wait upon me; for his sake
I'll grace thee with a higher style ere long.

Y. Spen. No greater titles happen unto me,
Than to be favoured of your majesty!

K. Edw. Cousin, this day shall be your marriage-feast.
And, Gaveston, think that I love thee well,
To wed thee to our niece, the only heir
Unto the Earl of Gloucester late deceased.

Gav. I know, my lord, many will stomach me,
But I respect neither their love nor hate.

K. Edw. The headstrong barons shall not limit me;
He that I list to favour shall be great.

Come, let's away ; and when the marriage ends,
Have at the rebels, and their 'complices !　　[*Exeunt.*

SCENE III.

Enter KENT, LANCASTER, Young MORTIMER, WARWICK,
PEMBROKE, *and others.*[1]

Kent. My lords, of love to this our native land
I come to join with you and leave the king ;
And in your quarrel and the realm's behoof
Will be the first that shall adventure life.

Lan. I fear me, you are sent of policy,
To undermine us with a show of love.

War. He is your brother, therefore have we cause
To cast[2] the worst, and doubt of your revolt.

Kent. Mine honour shall be hostage of my truth :
If that will not suffice, farewell, my lords.

Y. Mor. Stay, Edmund ; never was Plantagenet
False of his word, and therefore trust we thee.

Pem. But what's the reason you should leave him now ?

Kent. I have informed the Earl of Lancaster.

Lan. And it sufficeth.　Now, my lords, know this,
That Gaveston is secretly arrived,
And here in Tynemouth frolics with the king.
Let us with these our followers scale the walls.
And suddenly surprise them unawares

Y. Mor. I'll give the onset.

War. And I'll follow thee.

Y. Mor. This tottered[3] ensign of my ancestors,
Which swept the desert shore of that dead[4] sea

---

[1] The scene is in the neighbourhood of Tynemouth Castle.
[2] Conjecture.　　　　　　　　[3] Tattered.
[4] In all Latin deeds the Mortimers are called " de Mortuo mari."
—*Cunningham.*

Whereof we got the name of Mortimer,
Will I advance upon this castle's walls.
Drums, strike alarum, raise them from their sport,
And ring aloud the knell of Gaveston!

Lan. None be so hardy as to touch the king:
But neither spare you Gaveston nor his friends. [*Exeunt.*

SCENE IV.

Enter severally KING EDWARD *and* Young SPENCER.

K. Edw. O tell me, Spencer, where is Gaveston?
Spen. I fear me he is slain, my gracious lord.
K. Edw. No, here he comes; now let them spoil and
  kill.

Enter QUEEN ISABELLA, KING EDWARD'S Niece,
GAVESTON, *and* Nobles.

Fly, fly, my lords, the earls have got the hold;
Take shipping and away to Scarborough;
Spencer and I will post away by land.

Gav. O stay, my lord, they will not injure you.
K. Edw. I will not trust them; Gaveston, away!
Gav. Farewell, my lord.
K. Edw. Lady, farewell.
Niece. Farewell, sweet uncle, till we meet again.
K. Edw. Farewell, sweet Gaveston: and farewell, niece.
Q. Isab. No farewell to poor Isabel thy queen?
K. Edw. Yes, yes, for Mortimer, your lover's sake.
Q. Isab. Heaven can witness I love none but you:
            [*Exeunt all but* QUEEN ISABELLA.
From my embracements thus he breaks away.
O that mine arms could close this isle about,

---

[1] The scene is inside Tynemouth castle.

That I might pull him to me where I would !
Or that these tears, that drizzle from mine eyes,
Had power to mollify his stony heart,
That when I had him we might never part.

> *Enter* LANCASTER, WARWICK, Young MORTIMER,
> *and others.   Alarums within.*

Lan. I wonder how he 'scaped !

Y. Mor. Who's this ? the queen !

Q. Isab. Ay, Mortimer, the miserable queen,
Whose pining heart her inward sighs have blasted,
And body with continual mourning wasted :
These hands are tired with haling of my lord
From Gaveston, from wicked Gaveston,
And all in vain ; for, when I speak him fair,
He turns away, and smiles upon his minion.

 Y. Mor. Cease to lament, and tell us where's the king ?

 Q. Isab. What would you with the king ? is't him you
  seek ?

Lan. No, madam, but that cursèd Gaveston.
Far be it from the thought of Lancaster
To offer violence to his sovereign.
We would but rid the realm of Gaveston :
Tell us where he remains, and he shall die.

 Q. Isab. He's gone by water unto Scarborough ;
Pursue him quickly, and he cannot 'scape ;
The king hath left him, and his train is small.

 War. Foreslow [1] no time, sweet Lancaster ; let's march.

 Y. Mor. How comes it that the king and he is parted ?

 Q. Isab. That thus your army, going several ways,
Might be of lesser force : and with the power
That he intendeth presently to raise,
Be easily suppressed ; therefore be gone.

----

[1] Delay.

Y. Mor. Here in the river rides a Flemish hoy ;
Let's all aboard, and follow him amain.

Lan. The wind that bears him hence will fill our sails :
Come, come aboard, 'tis but an hour's sailing.

Y. Mor. Madam, stay you within this castle here.

Q. Isab. No, Mortimer, I'll to my lord the king.

Y. Mor. Nay, rather sail with us to Scarborough.

Q. Isab. You know the king is so suspicious,
As if he hear I have but talked with you,
Mine honour will be called in question ;
And therefore, gentle Mortimer, be gone.

Y. Mor. Madam, I cannot stay to answer you,
But think of Mortimer as he deserves.

[*Exeunt all except* QUEEN ISABELLA.

Q. Isab. So well hast thou deserved, sweet Mortimer,
As Isabel could live with thee for ever.
In vain I look for love at Edward's hand,
Whose eyes are fixed on none but Gaveston.
Yet once more I'll importune him with prayer :
If he be strange and not regard my words,
My son and I will over into France,
And to the king my brother there complain,
How Gaveston hath robbed me of his love :
But yet I hope my sorrows will have end,
And Gaveston this blessèd day be slain. · [*Exit.*

SCENE V.

Enter GAVESTON, *pursued.*[1]

Gav. Yet, lusty lords, I have escaped your hands,
Your threats, your larums, and your hot pursuits ;

Scene : the open country.

And though divorcèd from King Edward's eyes,
Yet liveth Pierce of Gaveston unsurprised,
Breathing, in hope (malgrado[1] all your beards,
That muster rebels thus against your king),
To see his royal sovereign once again.

Enter WARWICK, LANCASTER, PEMBROKE, Young MOR-
   TIMER, Soldiers, JAMES, *and other* Attendants of PEM-
   BROKE.

   War. Upon him, soldiers, take away his weapons.
   Y. Mor. Thou proud disturber of thy country's peace,
Corrupter of thy king ; cause of these broils,
Base flatterer, yield ! and were it not for shame,
Shame and dishonour to a soldier's name,
Upon my weapon's point here should'st thou fall,
And welter in thy gore.
   Lan. Monster of men !
That, like the Greekish strumpet,[2] trained to arms
And bloody wars so many valiant knights ;
Look for no other fortune, wretch, than death !
King Edward is not here to buckler thee.
   War. Lancaster, why talk'st thou to the slave ?
Go, soldiers, take him hence, for, by my sword,
His head shall off : Gaveston, short warning
Shall serve thy turn : it is our country's cause,
That here severely we will execute
Upon thy person.   Hang him at a bough.
   Gav. My lord !—
   War. Soldiers, have him away ;—
But for thou wert the favourite of a king,
Thou shalt have so much honour at our hands[3]—

---

[1] Ital., meaning "in spite of."   [2] Helen of Troy.
[3] Dyce suggests that a line following this, in which Warwick says
that Gaveston shall be *beheaded*, has dropped out.

Gav. I thank you all, my lords : then I perceive,
That heading is one, and hanging is the other,
And death is all.

Enter ARUNDEL.

Lan. How now, my lord of Arundel?

Arun. My lords, King Edward greets you all by me.

War. Arundel, say your message.

Arun. His majesty,
Hearing that you had taken Gaveston,
Entreateth you by me, yet but he may
See him before he dies ; for why, he says,
And sends you word, he knows that die he shall ;
And if you gratify his grace so far,
He will be mindful of the courtesy.

War. How now?

Gav. Renownèd Edward, how thy name
Revives poor Gaveston !

War. No, it needeth not :
Arundel, we will gratify the king
In other matters : he must pardon us in this.
Soldiers, away with him !

Gav. Why, my lord of Warwick,
Will not these delays beget my hopes?
I know it, lords, it is this life you aim at,
Yet grant King Edward this.

Y. Mor. Shalt thou appoint
What we shall grant? Soldiers, away with him :
Thus we'll gratify the king,
We'll send his head by thee ; let him bestow
His tears on that, for that is all he gets
Of Gaveston, or else his senseless trunk.

Lan. Not so, my lords, lest he bestow more cost
In burying him than he hath ever earned.

Arun. My lords, it is his majesty's request,
And in the honour of a king he swears,
He will but talk with him, and send him back.

War. When? can you tell?   Arundel, no; we wot,
He that the care of his realm remits,
And drives his nobles to these exigents
For Gaveston, will, if he sees [1] him once,
Violate any promise to possess him.

Arun. Then if you will not trust his grace in keep,
My lords, I will be pledge for his return.

Y. Mor. 'Tis honourable in thee to offer this;
But for we know thou art a noble gentleman,
We will not wrong thee so, to make away
A true man for a thief.

Gav. How mean'st thou, Mortimer? that is over-base.

Y. Mor. Away, base groom, robber of king's renown!
Question with thy companions and mates.

Pem. My Lord Mortimer, and you, my lords, each one,
To gratify the king's request therein.
Touching the sending of this Gaveston,
Because his majesty so earnestly
Desires to see the man before his death,
I will upon mine honour undertake
To carry him, and bring him back again;
Provided this, that you my lord of Arundel
Will join with me.

War. Pembroke, what wilt thou do?
Cause yet more bloodshed? is it not enough
That we have taken him, but must we now
Leave him on "had I wist," [2] and let him go?

Pem. My lords, I will not over-woo your honours,

---

[1] "Seize" in the old editions.   Cunningham made this alteration.
[2] An exclamation implying repentance of a rash deed —*Dyce.*

But if you dare trust Pembroke with the prisoner,
Upon mine oath, I will return him back.

Arun. My lord of Lancaster, what say you in this?

Lan. Why, I say, let him go on Pembroke's word.

Pem. And you, Lord Mortimer?

Y. Mor. How say you, my lord of Warwick?

War. Nay, do your pleasures, I know how 'twill prove.

Pem. Then give him me.

Gav. Sweet sovereign, yet I come
To see thee ere I die.

War. Yet not perhaps,
If Warwick's wit and policy prevail.   [*Aside.*

Y. Mor. My lord of Pembroke, we deliver him you:
Return him on your honour.   Sound, away!

> [*Exeunt all except* PEMBROKE, ARUNDEL, GAVE-
> STON, JAMES, *and other* Attendants *of*
> PEMBROKE.

Pem. My lord of Arundel, you shall go with me.
My house is not far hence : out of the way
A little, but our men shall go along.
We that have pretty wenches to our wives,
Sir, must not come so near to baulk their lips.

Arun. 'Tis very kindly spoke, my lord of Pembroke ;
Your honour hath an adamant of power
To draw a prince.

Pem. So, my lord.   Come hither, James :
I do commit this Gaveston to thee,
Be thou this night his keeper ; in the morning
We will discharge thee of thy charge : be gone.

Gav. Unhappy Gaveston, whither goest thou now?

> [*Exit with* JAMES *and the other* Attendants.

Horse-boy. My lord, we'll quickly be at Cobham.

> [*Exeunt.*

ACT THE THIRD.

SCENE I.

Enter GAVESTON *mourning.* JAMES, *and other* Attendants *of* PEMBROKE.[1]

Gav. O treacherous Warwick! thus to
    wrong thy friend.
James. I see it is your life these arms
    pursue.
Gav. Weaponless must I fall, and die
    in bands?
O! must this day be period of my life?
Centre of all my bliss! An ye be men,
Speed to the king.

Enter WARWICK *and* Soldiers.

  War. My lord of Pembroke's men,
Strive you no longer—I will have that Gaveston.
  James. Your lordship does dishonour to yourself,
And wrong our lord, your honourable friend.
  War. No, James, it is my country's cause I follow.
Go, take the villain; soldiers, come away.
We'll make quick work. Commend me to your master,
My friend, and tell him that I watched it well.
Come, let thy shadow[2] parley with King Edward.

---

[1] The scene changes to another part of the country.   [2] Ghost.

Gav. Treacherous earl, shall I not see the king?

War. The king of Heaven perhaps, no other king.
Away! [*Exeunt* WARWICK *and* Soldiers *with* GAVESTON.

James. Come, fellows, it booted not for us to strive,
We will in haste go certify our lord. [*Exeunt.*

SCENE II.

Enter KING EDWARD *and* Young SPENCER, BALDOCK,
and Nobles of the KING'S *side, and* Soldiers *with
drums and fifes.*[1]

K. Edw. I long to hear an answer from the barons
Touching my friend, my dearest Gaveston.
Ah! Spencer, not the riches of my realm
Can ransom him! ah, he is marked to die!
I know the malice of the younger Mortimer,
Warwick I know is rough, and Lancaster
Inexorable, and I shall never see
My lovely Pierce of Gaveston again!
The barons overbear me with their pride.

Y. Spen. Were I King Edward, England's sovereign,
Son to the lovely Eleanor of Spain,
Great Edward Longshanks' issue, would I bear
These braves, this rage, and suffer uncontrolled
These barons thus to beard me in my land,
In mine own realm? My lord, pardon my speech:
Did you retain your father's magnanimity,
Did you regard the honour of your name,
You would not suffer thus your majesty
Be counterbuft of your nobility.
Strike off their heads, and let them preach on poles!

---

[1] The scene is near Boroughbridge, in Yorkshire.

No doubt, such lessons they will teach the rest,
As by their preachments they will profit much,
And learn obedience to their lawful king.

 K. Edw. Yea, gentle Spencer, we have been too mild,
Too kind to them ; but now have drawn our sword,
And if they send me not my Gaveston,
We'll steel it on their crest, and poll their tops.

 Bald. This haught resolve becomes your majesty
Not to be tied to their affection,
As though your highness were a schoolboy still,
And must be awed and governed like a child.

Enter the Elder Spencer, *with his truncheon and* Soldiers.

 E. Spen. Long live my sovereign, the noble Edward—
In peace triumphant, fortunate in wars !

 K. Edw. Welcome, old man. com'st thou in Edward's
  aid ?
Then tell thy prince of whence, and what thou art.

 E. Spen. Lo, with a band of bowmen and of pikes,
Brown bills and targeteers, four hundred strong,
Sworn to defend King Edward's royal right,
I come in person to your majesty,
Spencer, the father of Hugh Spencer there,
Bound to your highness everlastingly,
For favour done, in him, unto us all.

 K. Edw. Thy father, Spencer ?

 Y. Spen. True, an it like your grace,
That pours, in lieu of all your goodness shown,
His life, my lord, before your princely feet.

 K. Edw. Welcome ten thousand times, old man, again.
Spencer, this love, this kindness to thy king,
Argues thy noble mind and disposition.
Spencer, I here create thee Earl of Wiltshire,
And daily will enrich thee with our favour,

That, as the sunshine, shall reflect o'er thee.
Beside, the more to manifest our love,
Because we hear Lord Bruce doth sell his land.
And that the Mortimers are in hand withal,
Thou shalt have crowns of us t' outbid the barons :
And, Spencer, spare them not, lay it on.
Soldiers, a largess, and thrice welcome all !

Y. Spen. My lord, here comes the queen.

Enter QUEEN ISABELLA, PRINCE EDWARD, *and* LEVUNE.

K. Edw. Madam, what news ?

Q. Isab. News of dishonour, lord, and discontent.
Our friend Levune, faithful and full of trust,
Informeth us, by letters and by words.
That Lord Valois our brother, King of France,
Because your highness hath been slack in homage,
Hath seizèd Normandy into his hands.
These be the letters, this the messenger.

K. Edw. Welcome, Levune.   Tush, Sib, if this be all
Valois and I will soon be friends again.—
But to my Gaveston ; shall I never see,
Never behold thee now ?—Madam, in this matter,
We will employ you and your little son ;
You shall go parley with the King of France.—
Boy, see you bear you bravely to the king,
And do your message with a majesty.

P. Edw. Commit not to my youth things of more weight
Than fits a prince so young as I to bear,
And fear not, lord and father, Heaven's great beams
On Atlas' shoulder shall not lie more safe,
Than shall your charge committed to my trust.

Q. Isab. Ah, boy ! this towardness makes thy mother
    fear
Thou art not marked to many days on earth.

K. Edw. Madam, we will that you with speed be shipped,
And this our son ; Levune shall follow you
With all the haste we can despatch him hence.
Choose of our lords to bear you company ;
And go in peace, leave us in wars at home.

   Q. Isab. Unnatural wars, where subjects brave their
       king ;
God end them once ! My lord, I take my leave,
To make my preparation for France.

                   [Exit with PRINCE EDWARD.

           Enter ARUNDEL.

   K. Edw. What, Lord Arundel, dost thou come alone ?
   Arun. Yea, my good lord, for Gaveston is dead.
   K. Edw. Ah, traitors ! have they put my friend to death ?
Tell me, Arundel, died he ere thou cam'st,
Or didst thou see my friend to take his death ?

   Arun. Neither, my lord ; for as he was surprised,
Begirt with weapons and with enemies round,
I did your highness' message to them all ;
Demanding him of them, entreating rather,
And said, upon the honour of my name,
That I would undertake to carry him
Unto your highness, and to bring him back.

   K. Edw. And tell me, would the rebels deny me that ?
   Y. Spen. Proud recreants !
   K. Edw. Yea, Spencer, traitors all.
   Arun. I found them at the first inexorable ;
The Earl of Warwick would not bide the hearing,
Mortimer hardly ; Pembroke and Lancaster
Spake least : and when they flatly had denied,
Refusing to receive me pledge for him,
The Earl of Pembroke mildly thus bespake ;
" My lords, because our sovereign sends for him,

And promiseth he shall be safe returned,
I will this undertake, to have him hence,
And see him re-delivered to your hands."

   K. Edw. Well, and how fortunes it that he came not?

   Y. Spen. Some treason, or some villany, was the cause.

   Arun. The Earl of Warwick seized him on his way;
For being delivered unto Pembroke's men,
Their lord rode home thinking his prisoner safe;
But ere he came, Warwick in ambush lay,
And bare him to his death; and in a trench
Strake off his head, and marched unto the camp.

   Y. Spen. A bloody part, flatly 'gainst law of arms!

   K. Edw. O shall I speak, or shall I sigh and die!

   Y. Spen. My lord, refer your vengeance to the sword
Upon these barons; hearten up your men;
Let them not unrevenged murder your friends!
Advance your standard, Edward, in the field,
And march to fire them from their starting holes.

   K. Edw. [*kneeling*]. By earth, the common mother of
      us all,
By Heaven, and all the moving orbs thereof,
By this right hand, and by my father's sword,
And all the honours 'longing to my crown,
I will have heads, and lives for him, as many
As I have manors, castles, towns, and towers!—   [*Rises.*
Treacherous Warwick! traitorous Mortimer!
If I be England's king, in lakes of gore
Your headless trunks, your bodies will I trail,
That you may drink your fill, and quaff in blood,
And stain my royal standard with the same,
That so my bloody colours may suggest
Remembrance of revenge immortally
On your accursèd traitorous progeny,
You villains, that have slain my Gaveston!

And in this place of honour and of trust,
Spencer, sweet Spencer, I adopt thee here:
And merely of our love we do create thee
Earl of Gloucester, and Lord Chamberlain.
Despite of times, despite of enemies.

Y. Spen. My lord, here's a messenger from the barons
Desires access unto your majesty.

K. Edw. Admit him near.

       Enter the Herald, *with his coat of arms.*

Her. Long live King Edward, England's lawful lord!

K. Edw. So wish not they, I wis, that sent thee hither.
Thou com'st from Mortimer and his 'complices,
A ranker rout of rebels never was.
Well, say thy message.

Her. The barons up in arms, by me salute
Your highness with long life and happiness;
And bid me say, as plainer to your grace,
That if without effusion of blood
You will this grief have ease and remedy,
That from your princely person you remove
This Spencer, as a putrifying branch,
That deads the royal vine, whose golden leaves
Empale your princely head, your diadem,
Whose brightness such pernicious upstarts dim,
Say they; and lovingly advise your grace,
To cherish virtue and nobility,
And have old servitors in high esteem,
And shake off smooth dissembling flatterers:
This granted, they, their honours, and their lives,
Are to your highness vowed and consecrate.

Y. Spen. Ah, traitors! will they still display their pride?

K. Edw. Away, tarry no answer, but be gone!
Rebels, will they appoint their sovereign

His sports, his pleasures, and his company?
Yet, ere thou go, see how I do divorce

                              [Embraces SPENCER.

Spencer from me.—Now get thee to thy lords,
And tell them I will come to chastise them
For murdering Gaveston; hie thee, get thee gone!
Edward with fire and sword follows at thy heels.

                                [Exit Herald.

My lords, perceive you how these rebels swell?
Soldiers, good hearts, defend your sovereign's right,
For now, even now, we march to make them stoop.
Away!   *[Exeunt. Alarums, excursions, a great fight,*
                  and a retreat sounded, within.

   Re-enter KING EDWARD, *the* Elder SPENCER, Young
      SPENCER, *and* Noblemen *of the* KING'S *side.*

  K. Edw. Why do we sound retreat? upon them, lords!
This day I shall pour vengeance with my sword
On those proud rebels that are up in arms,
And do confront and countermand their king.

  Y. Spen. I doubt it not, my lord, right will prevail.

  E. Spen. 'Tis not amiss, my liege, for either part
To breathe awhile; our men, with sweat and dust
All choked well near, begin to faint for heat;
And this retire refresheth horse and man.

  Y. Spen. Here come the rebels.

    Enter Young MORTIMER, LANCASTER, WARWICK,
          PEMBROKE, *and others.*

  Y. Mor. Look, Lancaster, yonder is Edward
Among his flatterers.

  Lan. And there let him be
Till he pay dearly for their company.

  War. And shall, or Warwick's sword shall smite in vain.

K. Edw. What, rebels, do you shrink and sound
    retreat ?

Y. Mor. No, Edward, no, thy flatterers faint and fly.

Lan. They'd best betimes forsake thee, and their trains,[1]
For they'll betray thee, traitors as they are.

Y. Spen. Traitor on thy face, rebellious Lancaster !

Pem. Away, base upstart, bravest thou nobles thus ?

E. Spen. A noble attempt, and honourable deed,
Is it not, trow ye, to assemble aid,
And levy arms against your lawful king !

K. Edw. For which ere long their heads shall satisfy,
To appease the wrath of their offended king.

Y. Mor. Then, Edward, thou wilt fight it to the last,
And rather bathe thy sword in subjects' blood,
Than banish that pernicious company ?

K. Edw. Ay, traitors all, rather than thus be braved,
Make England's civil towns huge heaps of stones,
And ploughs to go about our palace-gates.

War. A desperate and unnatural resolution !
Alarum !—to the fight !
St. George for England, and the barons' right.

K. Edw. Saint George for England, and King
    Edward's right.

        [*Alarums.   Exeunt the two parties severally.*

SCENE III.

Enter KING EDWARD *and his followers, with the*
Barons *and* KENT, *captives.*[2]

K. Edw. Now, lusty lords, now, not by chance of war,
But justice of the quarrel and the cause,

---

[1] Stratagems.   [2] The scene is another part of the battle-field.

Vailed [1] is your pride ; methinks you hang the heads,
But we'll advance them, traitors ; now 'tis time
To be avenged on you for all your braves,
And for the murder of my dearest friend,
To whom right well you knew our soul was knit,
Good Pierce of Gaveston, my sweet favourite. .
Ah, rebels ! recreants ! you made him away.

    Kent. Brother, in regard of thee, and of thy land,
Did they remove that flatterer from thy throne.

    K. Edw. So, sir, you have spoke; away, avoid our
       presence !   [*Exit* KENT.
Accursèd wretches, was't in regard of us,
When we had sent our messenger to request
He might be spared to come to speak with us,
And Pembroke undertook for his return,
That thou, proud Warwick, watched the prisoner,
Poor Pierce, and headed him 'gainst law of arms?
For which thy head shall overlook the rest,
As much as thou in rage outwent'st the rest.

    War. Tyrant, I scorn thy threats and menaces :
It is but temporal that thou canst inflict.

    Lan. The worst is death, and better die to live
Than live in infamy under such a king.

    K. Edw. Away with them, my lord of Winchester !
These lusty leaders, Warwick and Lancaster,
I charge you roundly—off with both their heads !
Away !

    War. Farewell, vain world !

    Lan. Sweet Mortimer, farewell.

    Y. Mor. England, unkind to thy nobility,
Groan for this grief, behold how thou art maimed !

    K. Edw. Go, take that haughty Mortimer to the Tower,
There see him safe bestowed ; and for the rest,

              [1] Humbled.

Do speedy execution on them all.
Begone !

Y. Mor. What, Mortimer ! can ragged stony walls
Immure thy virtue that aspires to Heaven ?
No, Edward, England's scourge, it may not be ;
Mortimer's hope surmounts his fortune far.

> [*The captive Barons are led off.*

K. Edw. Sound drums and trumpets ! March with me,
          my friends,
Edward this day hath crowned him king anew.

> [*Exeunt all except* Young SPENCER, LEVUNE,
>   *and* BALDOCK.

Y. Spen. Levune, the trust that we repose in thee,
Begets the quiet of King Edward's land.
Therefore begone in haste, and with advice
Bestow that treasure on the lords of France,
That, therewith all enchanted, like the guard
That suffered Jove to pass in showers of gold
To Danae, all aid may be denied
To Isabel, the queen, that now in France
Makes friends, to cross the seas with her young son,
And step into his father's regiment.[1]

Levune. That's it these barons and the subtle queen
Long levelled at.

Bal. Yea, but, Levune, thou seest
These barons lay their heads on blocks together ;
What they intend, the hangman frustrates clean.

Levune. Have you no doubt, my lords, I'll clap so close
Among the lords of France with England's gold,
That Isabel shall make her plaints in vain,
And France shall be obdurate with her tears.

Y. Spen. Then make for France, amain—Levune, away !
Proclaim King Edward's wars and victories.   [*Exeunt.*

---

[1] Rule.

ACT THE FOURTH.

SCENE I.

Enter KENT.[1]

KENT. Fair blows the wind for France ;
blow gentle gale,
Till Edmund be arrived for England's
good !
Nature, yield to my country's cause
in this.
A brother ? no, a butcher of thy friends !
Proud Edward, dost thou banish me thy presence ?
But I'll to France, and cheer the wrongèd queen,
And certify what Edward's looseness is.
Unnatural king ! to slaughter noblemen
And cherish flatterers ! Mortimer. I stay
Thy sweet escape : stand gracious, gloomy night,
To his device.

Enter Young MORTIMER, *disguised.*

Y. Mor. Holla ! who walketh there ?
Is't you, my lord ?
Kent. Mortimer, 'tis I ;
But hath thy potion wrought so happily ?
Y. Mor. It hath, my lord ; the warders all asleep,

[1] The scene is in the neighbourhood of the Tower of London.

I thank them, gave me leave to pass in peace.
But hath your grace got shipping unto France?

   Kent. Fear it not.   *[Exeunt.*

SCENE II.

Enter QUEEN ISABELLA *and* PRINCE EDWARD.[1]

   Q. Isab. Ah, boy ! our friends do fail us all in France :
The lords are cruel, and the king unkind ;
What shall we do?

   P. Edw. Madam, return to England,
And please my father well, and then a fig
For all my uncle's friendship here in France.
I warrant you, I'll win his highness quickly ;
'A loves me better than a thousand Spencers.

   Q. Isab. Ah, boy, thou art deceived, at least in this,
To think that we can yet be tuned together ;
No, no, we jar too far. Unkind Valois !
Unhappy Isabel ! when France rejects,
Whither, oh ! whither dost thou bend thy steps ?

Enter SIR JOHN *of* HAINAULT.

   Sir J. Madam, what cheer?

   Q. Isab. Ah ! good Sir John of Hainault.
Never so cheerless, nor so far distrest.

   Sir J. I hear, sweet lady, of the king's unkindness ;
But droop not, madam ; noble minds contemn
Despair : will your grace with me to Hainault,
And there stay time's advantage with your son ?
How say you, my lord, will you go with your friends,
And shake off all our fortunes equally ?

   P. Edw. So pleaseth the queen, my mother, me it likes :

---

[1] The scene is in Paris.

The King of England, nor the court of France.
Shall have me from my gracious mother's side,
Till I be strong enough to break a staff;
And then have at the proudest Spencer's head.

 Sir J. Well said, my lord.

 Q. Isab. O, my sweet heart, how do I moan thy wrongs,
Yet triumph in the hope of thee, my joy!
Ah, sweet Sir John! even to the utmost verge
Of Europe, or the shore of Tanais,
We will with thee to Hainault—so we will:—
The marquis is a noble gentleman:
His grace, I dare presume, will welcome me.
But who are these?

   Enter KENT *and* YOUNG MORTIMER.

 Kent. Madam, long may you live,
Much happier than your friends in England do!

 Q. Isab. Lord Edmund and Lord Mortimer alive!
Welcome to France! the news was here, my lord,
That you were dead, or very near your death.

 Y. Mor. Lady, the last was truest of the twain:
But Mortimer, reserved for better hap,
Hath shaken off the thraldom of the Tower,
And lives t' advance your standard, good my lord.

 P. Edw. How mean you? and the king, my father, lives!
No, my Lord Mortimer, not I, I trow.

 Q. Isab. Not, son! why not? I would it were no worse.
But, gentle lords, friendless we are in France.

 Y. Mor. Monsieur le Grand, a noble friend of yours,
Told us, at our arrival, all the news—
How hard the nobles, how unkind the king
Hath showed himself; but, madam, right makes room
Where weapons want; and, though a many friends
Are made away, as Warwick, Lancaster,

And others of our party and faction ;
Yet have we friends, assure your grace, in England
Would cast up caps, and clap their hands for joy,
To see us there, appointed[1] for our foes.

Kent. Would all were well, and Edward well reclaimed,
For England's honour, peace, and quietness.

Y. Mor. But by the sword, my lord, 't must be deserved;[2]
The king will ne'er forsake his flatterers.

Sir J. My lords of England, sith th' ungentle king
Of France refuseth to give aid of arms
To this distressèd queen his sister here,
Go you with her to Hainault ; doubt ye not,
We will find comfort, money, men and friends
Ere long, to bid the English king a base.[3]
How say'st, young prince ? what think you of the match ?

P. Edw. I think King Edward will outrun us all.

Q. Isab. Nay, son, not so ; and you must not discourage
Your friends, that are so forward in your aid.

Kent. Sir John of Hainault, pardon us, I pray ;
These comforts that you give our woful queen
Bind us in kindness all at your command.

Q. Isab. Yea, gentle brother ; and the God of heaven
Prosper your happy motion, good Sir John.

Y. Mor. This noble gentleman, forward in arms,
Was born, I see, to be our anchor-hold.
Sir John of Hainault, be it thy renown,
That England's queen, and nobles in distress,
Have been by thee restored and comforted.

Sir J. Madam, along, and you my lords, with me,
That England's peers may Hainault's welcome see.

[*Exeunt.*

---

[1] Ready equipped.   .   [2] *i.e.* Earned.
[3] *i.e.* Challenge an encounter. The phrase refers to the old game
of prison bars or prisoner's base, where a player runs out of bounds
and challenges an opponent to pursue him.

SCENE III.

Enter KING EDWARD, ARUNDEL, *the* Elder *and*
Younger SPENCER, *and others.*[1]

K. Edw. Thus after many threats of wrathful war,
Triumpheth England's Edward with his friends ;
And triumph, Edward, with his friends uncontrolled '
My lord of Gloucester, do you hear the news ?

Y. Spen. What news, my lord ?

K. Edw. Why, man, they say there is great execution
Done through the realm ; my lord of Arundel,
You have the note, have you not ?

Arun. From the Lieutenant of the Tower, my lord. ·

K. Edw. I pray let us see it. [*Takes the note.*] What
have we there ?

Read it, Spencer.   [*Hands the note to* Young SPENCER,
who reads the names.

Why, so : they barked apace a month ago :
Now, on my life, they'll neither bark nor bite.
Now, sirs, the news from France ? Gloucester, I trow
The lords of France love England's gold so well
As Isabella gets no aid from thence.
What now remains ? have you proclaimed, my lord,
Reward for them can bring in Mortimer ?

Y. Spen. My lord, we have ; and if he be in England,
'A will be had ere long, I doubt it not.

K. Edw. If, dost thou say ? Spencer, as true as death,
He is in England's ground ; our portmasters
Are not so careless of their king's command.

Enter a Messenger.

How now, what news with thee ? from whence come these ?

---

[1] The scene is an apartment in the king's palace at Westminster.

Mess. Letters, my lord, and tidings forth of France :—
To you, my lord of Gloucester, from Levune.

          [*Gives letters to* Young SPENCER.

    K. Edw. Read.

    Y. Spen. [*reads*].

"My duty to your honour premised, &c., I have,
according to instructions in that behalf, dealt with the
King of France his lords, and effected, that the queen,
all discontented and discomforted, is gone : whither, if
you ask, with Sir John of Hainault, brother to the
marquis, into Flanders. With them are gone Lord
Edmund, and the Lord Mortimer, having in their company divers of your nation, and others ; and, as constant
report goeth, they intend to give King Edward battle in
England, sooner than he can look for them. This is all
the news of import.

        Your honour's in all service, LEVUNE."

    K. Edw. Ah, villains ! hath that Mortimer escaped ?
With him is Edmund gone associate ?
And will Sir John of Hainault lead the round ?
Welcome, a God's name, madam, and your son ;
England shall welcome you and all your rout.
Gallop apace, bright Phœbus, through the sky,
And dusky night, in rusty iron car,
Between you both shorten the time, I pray,
That I may see that most desirèd day,
When we may meet these traitors in the field.
Ah, nothing grieves me, but my little boy
Is thus misled to countenance their ills.
Come, friends, to Bristow,[1] there to make us strong ;
And, winds, as equal be to bring them in,
As you injurious were to bear them forth !   [*Exeunt.*

---

[1] Bristol.

SCENE IV.

Enter QUEEN ISABELLA, PRINCE EDWARD, KENT, Young
MORTIMER, *and* SIR JOHN *of* HAINAULT.[1]

Q. Isab. Now, lords, our loving friends and countrymen,
Welcome to England all, with prosperous winds !
Our kindest friends in Belgia have we left,
To cope with friends at home : a heavy case
When force to force is knit, and sword and glaive
In civil broils make kin and countrymen
Slaughter themselves in others, and their sides
With their own weapons gore !　But what's the help ?
Misgoverned kings are cause of all this wreck ;
And, Edward, thou art one among them all,
Whose looseness hath betrayed thy land to spoil,
Who made the channel overflow with blood
Of thine own people : patron shouldst thou be.
But thou——

Y. Mor. Nay, madam, if you be a warrior,
You must not grow so passionate in speeches.
Lords,
Sith that we are by sufferance of Heaven
Arrived, and armèd in this prince's right,
Here for our country's cause swear we to him
All homage, fealty, and forwardness ;
And for the open wrongs and injuries
Edward hath done to us, his queen and land,
We come in arms to wreak it with the sword ;
That England's queen in peace may repossess
Her dignities and honours : and withal
We may remove these flatterers from the king,
That havoc England's wealth and treasury.

---

[1] The scene is in the neighbourhood of Harwich.

Sir J. Sound trumpets, my lord, and forward let us
    march.
Edward will think we come to flatter him.

Kent. I would he never had been flattered more!

                            [*Exeunt.*

SCENE V.

Enter KING EDWARD, BALDOCK, *and* YOUNG SPENCER.[1]

Y. Spen. Fly, fly, my lord! the queen is over-strong:
Her friends do multiply, and yours do fail.
Shape we our course to Ireland, there to breathe.

K. Edw. What! was I born to fly and run away,
And leave the Mortimers conquerors behind?
Give me my horse, and let's reinforce our troops:
And in this bed of honour die with fame.

Bald. O no, my lord, this princely resolution
Fits not the time; away! we are pursued.   [*Exeunt.*

Enter KENT, *with sword and target.*

Kent. This way he fled, but I am come too late.
Edward, alas! my heart relents for thee.
Proud traitor, Mortimer, why dost thou chase
Thy lawful king, thy sovereign, with thy sword?
Vile wretch! and why hast thou, of all unkind,
Borne arms against thy brother and thy king?
Rain showers of vengeance on my cursèd head,
Thou God, to whom in justice it belongs
To punish this unnatural revolt!
Edward, this Mortimer aims at thy life!
O fly him, then! But, Edmund, calm this rage,
Dissemble, or thou diest; for Mortimer

---

[1] The scene is in the neighbourhood of Bristol.

And Isabel do kiss, while they conspire :
And yet she bears a face of love forsooth.
Fie on that love that hatcheth death and hate !
Edmund, away !   Bristow to Longshanks' blood
Is false : be not found single for suspect :
Proud Mortimer pries near unto thy walks.

Enter QUEEN ISABELLA, PRINCE EDWARD, Young
        MORTIMER, *and* SIR JOHN *of* HAINAULT.

Q. Isab. Successful battle gives the God of kings
To them that fight in right and fear his wrath.
Since then successfully we have prevailed.
Thankèd be Heaven's great architect, and you.
Ere farther we proceed, my noble lords,
We here create our well-belovèd son,
Of love and care unto his royal person,
Lord Warden of the realm, and sith the fates
Have made his father so infortunate,
Deal you, my lords, in this, my loving lords,
As to your wisdoms fittest seems in all.

Kent. Madam, without offence, if I may ask,
How will you deal with Edward in his fall ?

P. Edw. Tell me, good uncle, what Edward do you
        mean ?

Kent. Nephew, your father : I dare not call him king.

Y. Mor. My lord of Kent, what needs these questions?
'Tis not in her controlment, nor in ours,
But as the realm and parliament shall please,
So shall your brother be disposèd of.—
I like not this relenting mood in Edmund.
Madam, 'tis good to look to him betimes.
                        [*Aside to the* QUEEN.

Q. Isab. My lord, the Mayor of Bristow knows our
        mind.

Y. Mor. Yea, madam, and they 'scape not easily
That fled the field.

Q. Isab. Baldock is with the king.
A goodly chancellor, is he not, my lord?

Sir J. So are the Spencers, the father and the son.

Kent. This Edward is the ruin of the realm.

Enter RICE AP HOWELL, *with the* Elder SPENCER
prisoner, and Attendants.

Rice. God save Queen Isabel, and her princely son!
Madam, the mayor and citizens of Bristow,
In sign of love and duty to this presence,
Present by me this traitor to the state,
Spencer, the father to that wanton Spencer,
That, like the lawless Catiline of Rome,
Revelled in England's wealth and treasury.

Q. Isab. We thank you all.

Y. Mor. Your loving care in this
Deserveth princely favours and rewards.
But where's the king and the other Spencer fled?

Rice. Spencer the son, created Earl of Gloucester,
Is with that smooth-tongued scholar Baldock gone,
And shipped but late for Ireland with the king.

Y. Mor. Some whirlwind fetch them back or sink them
    all!—   [*Aside.*
They shall be started thence, I doubt it not.

P. Edw. Shall I not see the king my father yet?

Kent. Unhappy Edward, chased from England's
    bounds.   [*Aside.*

Sir J. Madam, what resteth, why stand you in a muse?

Q. Isab. I rue my lord's ill-fortune; but alas!
Care of my country called me to this war.

Y. Mor. Madam, have done with care and sad com-
    plaint;

Your king hath wronged your country and himself,
And we must seek to right it as we may.
Meanwhile, have hence this rebel to the block.

   E. Spen. Rebel is he that fights against the prince ;
So fought not they that fought in Edward's right.

   Y. Mor. Take him away, he prates :

            [*Exeunt* Attendants *with the* Elder SPENCER.

                        You, Rice ap Howell,
Shall do good service to her majesty,
Being of countenance in your country here,
To follow these rebellious runagates.
We in meanwhile, madam, must take advice,
How Baldock, Spencer, and their complices,
May in their fall be followed to their end.   [*Exeunt.*

SCENE VI.

Enter the Abbot, Monks, KING EDWARD, Young SPENCER,
   and BALDOCK (*the three latter disguised*).[1]

   Abbot. Have you no doubt, my lord ; have you no
      fear ;
As silent and as careful we will be,
To keep your royal person safe with us,
Free from suspect, and fell invasion
Of such as have your majesty in chase,
Yourself, and those your chosen company,
As danger of this stormy time requires.

   K. Edw. Father, thy face should harbour no deceit.
O ! hadst thou ever been a king, thy heart,
Pierced deeply with a sense of my distress,
Could not but take compassion of my state.

---

    [1] The scene is in the abbey of Neath.

Stately and proud, in riches and in train,
Whilom I was, powerful, and full of pomp:
But what is he whom rule and empery
Have not in life or death made miserable?
Come, Spencer; come, Baldock, come, sit down by me;
Make trial now of that philosophy,
That in our famous nurseries of arts
Thou suck'dst from Plato and from Aristotle.
Father, this life contemplative is Heaven.
O that I might this life in quiet lead!
But we, alas! are chased; and you, my friends,
Your lives and my dishonour they pursue.
Yet, gentle monks, for treasure, gold nor fee,
Do you betray us and our company.

  Monk. Your grace may sit secure, if none but we
Do wot of your abode.

  Y. Spen. Not one alive, but shrewdly I suspect
A gloomy fellow in a mead below.
'A gave a long look after us, my lord;
And all the land I know is up in arms,
Arms that pursue our lives with deadly hate.

  Bald. We were embarked for Ireland, wretched we!
With awkward winds and sore tempests driven
To fall on shore, and here to pine in fear
Of Mortimer and his confederates.

  K. Edw. Mortimer! who talks of Mortimer?
Who wounds me with the name of Mortimer,
That bloody man? Good father, on thy lap
Lay I this head, laden with mickle care.
O might I never open these eyes again!
Never again lift up this drooping head!
O never more lift up this dying heart!

  Y. Spen. Look up, my lord.—Baldock, this drowsiness
Betides no good; here even we are betrayed.

Enter, with Welsh hooks, RICE AP HOWELL, *a* Mower,
and LEICESTER.

Mow. Upon my life, these be the men ye seek.

Rice. Fellow, enough.—My lord, I pray be short,
A fair commission warrants what we do.

Leices. The queen's commission, urged by Mortimer;
What cannot gallant Mortimer with the queen?
Alas! see where he sits, and hopes unseen
To escape their hands that seek to reave his life.
Too true it is, *Quem dies vidit veniens superbum,
Hunc dies vidit fugiens jacentem.*[1]
But, Leicester, leave to grow so passionate.
Spencer and Baldock, by no other names.
I do arrest you of high treason here.
Stand not on titles, but obey the arrest;
'Tis in the name of Isabel the queen.
My lord, why droop you thus?

K. Edw. O day the last of all my bliss on earth
Centre of all misfortune! O my stars,
Why do you lour unkindly on a king?
Comes Leicester, then, in Isabella's name
To take my life, my company from me?
Here, man, rip up this panting breast of mine,
And take my heart in rescue of my friends!

Rice. Away with them!

Y. Spen. It may become thee yet
To let us take our farewell of his grace.

Abbot. My heart with pity earns[2] to see this sight,
A king to bear these words and proud commands.

[*Aside.*

K. Edw. Spencer, ah, sweet Spencer, thus then must
    we part?

---

[1] Seneca, *Thyestes*, 613.   [2] *i.e.* Yearns.

Y. Spen. We must, my lord, so will the angry Heavens.

K. Edw. Nay, so will hell and cruel Mortimer;
The gentle Heavens have not to do in this.

Bald. My lord, it is in vain to grieve or storm.
Here humbly of your grace we take our leaves;
Our lots are cast; I fear me, so is thine.

K. Edw. In Heaven we may, in earth ne'er shall we
    meet:
And, Leicester, say, what shall become of us?

Leice. Your majesty must go to Killingworth.[1]

K. Edw. Must! it is somewhat hard, when kings must
    go.

Leice. Here is a litter ready for your grace,
That waits your pleasure, and the day grows old.

Rice. As good be gone, as stay and be benighted.

K. Edw. A litter hast thou? lay me in a hearse,
And to the gates of hell convey me hence;
Let Pluto's bells ring out my fatal knell,
And hags howl for my death at Charon's shore,
For friends hath Edward none but these,
And these must die under a tyrant's sword.

Rice. My lord, be going; care not for these,
For we shall see them shorter by the heads.

K. Edw. Well, that shall be, shall be: part we must!
Sweet Spencer, gentle Baldock, part we must!
Hence feignèd weeds! unfeignèd are my woes;
               [Throws off his disguise.
Father, farewell! Leicester, thou stay'st for me,
And go I must. Life, farewell, with my friends.
          [Exeunt KING EDWARD *and* LEICESTER.

Y. Spen. O! is he gone? is noble Edward gone?
Parted from hence? never to see us more?
Rend, sphere of Heaven! and, fire, forsake thy orb!

---

[1] Kenilworth.

Earth, melt to air! gone is my sovereign.
Gone, gone, alas! never to make return.

    Bald. Spencer, I see our souls are fleeting hence ;
We are deprived the sunshine of our life :
Make for a new life, man ; throw up thy eyes,
And heart and hands to Heaven's immortal throne ;
Pay nature's debt with cheerful countenance :
Reduce we all our lessons unto this,
To die, sweet Spencer, therefore live we all :
Spencer, all live to die, and rise to fall.

    Rice. Come, come, keep these preachments till you
come to the place appointed. You, and such as you are,
have made wise work in England ; will your lordships
away ?

    Mow. Your lordship, I trust, will remember me ?

    Rice. Remember thee, fellow ! what else ? Follow me
to the town.   [*Exeunt.*

ACT THE FIFTH.

SCENE I.

Enter KING EDWARD, LEICESTER, *the* BISHOP *of*
WINCHESTER, *and* TRUSSEL.[1]

LEICES. Be patient, good my lord, cease
to lament,
Imagine Killingworth Castle were your
court,   [space,
And that you lay for pleasure here a
Not of compulsion or necessity.

K. Edw. Leicester, if gentle words might comfort me,
Thy speeches long ago had eased my sorrows;
For kind and loving hast thou always been.
The griefs of private men are soon allayed,
But not of kings.   The forest deer, being struck,
Runs to an herb[2] that closeth up the wounds;
But, when the imperial lion's flesh is gored,
He rends and tears it with his wrathful paw,
And highly scorning that the lowly earth
Should drink his blood, mounts up to the air.
And so it fares with me, whose dauntless mind
The ambitious Mortimer would seek to curb,

[1] The scene is an apartment in Kenilworth Castle.
[2] Dittany, a species of *Origanum*.   Elizabethan poets often allude
to the supposed virtues of this herb.

And that unnatural queen, false Isabel,
That thus hath pent and mewed me in a prison :
For such outrageous passions cloy my soul,
As with the wings of rancour and disdain,
Full often am I soaring up to Heaven,
To plain me to the gods against them both.
But when I call to mind I am a king,
Methinks I should revenge me of my wrongs,
That Mortimer and Isabel have done.
But what are kings, when regiment [1] is gone,
But perfect shadows in a sunshine day ?
My nobles rule, I bear the name of king :
I wear the crown, but am controlled by them,
By Mortimer, and my unconstant queen,
Who spots my nuptial bed with infamy ;
Whilst I am lodged within this cave of care,
Where sorrow at my elbow still attends,
To company my heart with sad laments,
That bleeds within me for this strange exchange.
But tell me, must I now resign my crown,
To make usurping Mortimer a king ?

 B. of Win. Your grace mistakes ; it is for England's
  good,
And princely Edward's right we crave the crown.

 K. Edw. No, 'tis for Mortimer, not Edward's head ;
For he's a lamb, encompassèd by wolves,
Which in a moment will abridge his life.
But if proud Mortimer do wear this crown,
Heavens turn it to a blaze of quenchless fire !
Or like the snaky wreath of Tisiphon,
Engirt the temples of his hateful head ;
So shall not England's vine be perishèd,
But Edward's name survives, though Edward dies.

    [1] Rule.

Leices. My lord, why waste you thus the time away?
They stay your answer; will you yield your crown?

K. Edw. Ah, Leicester, weigh how hardly I can brook
To lose my crown and kingdom without cause;
To give ambitious Mortimer my right,
That like a mountain overwhelms my bliss,
In which extreme my mind here murdered is.
But what the heavens appoint, I must obey!
Here, take my crown; the life of Edward too;

　　　　　　　　　　　[Taking off the crown.

Two kings in England cannot reign at once.
But stay awhile, let me be king till night,
That I may gaze upon this glittering crown;
So shall my eyes receive their last content,
My head, the latest honour due to it,
And jointly both yield up their wishèd right.
Continue ever thou celestial sun;
Let never silent night possess this clime:
Stand still you watches of the element;
All times and seasons, rest you at a stay,
That Edward may be still fair England's king!
But day's bright beam doth vanish fast away,
And needs I must resign my wishèd crown.
Inhuman creatures! nursed with tiger's milk!
Why gape you for your sovereign's overthrow!
My diadem I mean, and guiltless life.
See, monsters, see, I'll wear my crown again!

　　　　　　　　　　　[He puts on the crown.

What, fear you not the fury of your king?
But, hapless Edward, thou art fondly[1] led;
They pass not[2] for thy frowns as late they did,
But seek to make a new-elected king;
Which fills my mind with strange despairing thoughts,

---

[1] Foolishly.　　　　　　[2] *i.e.* Care not.

Which thoughts are martyred with endless torments.
And in this torment comfort find I none,
But that I feel the crown upon my head :
And therefore let me wear it yet awhile.

Trus. My lord, the parliament must have present news,
And therefore say, will you resign or no ?

        [*The* KING *rageth.*

K. Edw. I'll not resign, but whilst I live be king.
Traitors, be gone ! and join you with Mortimer !
Elect, conspire, install, do what you will : —
Their blood and yours shall seal these treacheries !

B. of Win. This answer we'll return, and so farewell.

        [*Going with* TRUSSEL.

Leices. Call them again, my lord, and speak them fair ;
For if they go, the prince shall lose his right.

K. Edw. Call thou them back, I have no power to speak.

Leices. My lord, the king is willing to resign.

B. of Win. If he be not, let him choose.

K. Edw. O would I might ! but heavens and earth
  conspire
To make me miserable ! Here receive my crown ;
Receive it ? no, these innocent hands of mine
Shall not be guilty of so foul a crime.
He of you all that most desires my blood,
And will be called the murderer of a king,
Take it. What, are you moved ? pity you me ?
Then send for unrelenting Mortimer,
And Isabel, whose eyes, being turned to steel,
Will sooner sparkle fire than shed a tear.
Yet stay, for rather than I'll look on them,
Here, here !   [*Gives the crown.*
    Now, sweet God of Heaven,
Make me despise this transitory pomp,
And sit for aye enthronizèd in Heaven !

Come, death, and with thy fingers close my eyes,
Or if I live, let me forget myself.

   B. of Win. My lord—

   K. Edw. Call me not lord; away—out of my sight:
Ah, pardon me: grief makes me lunatic!
Let not that Mortimer protect my son;
More safety there is in a tiger's jaws,
Than his embracements.   Bear this to the queen,
Wet with my tears, and dried again with sighs:

                  [Gives a handkerchief.

If with the sight thereof she be not moved,
Return it back and dip it in my blood.
Commend me to my son, and bid him rule
Better than I.   Yet how have I transgressed,
Unless it be with too much clemency?

   Trus. And thus most humbly do we take our leave.

   K. Edw. Farewell;

      [Exeunt the BISHOP *of* WINCHESTER *and* TRUSSEL.

         I know the next news that they bring
Will be my death; and welcome shall it be:
To wretched men, death is felicity.

   Enter BERKELEY, *who gives a paper to* LEICESTER.

   Leices. Another post! what news brings he

   K. Edw. Such news as I expect—come, Berkeley, come,
And tell thy message to my naked breast.

   Berk. My lord, think not a thought so villainous
Can harbour in a man of noble birth.
To do your highness service and devoir,
And save you from your foes, Berkeley would die.

   Leices. My lord, the council of the queen commands
That I resign my charge.

   K. Edw. And who must keep me now?   Must you,
   my lord?

Berk. Ay, my most gracious lord—so 'tis decreed.

K. Edw. [*taking the paper.*] By Mortimer, whose name
    is written here !

Well may I rend his name that rends my heart !

[*Tears it.*

This poor revenge has something eased my mind.

So may his limbs be torn, as is this paper !

Hear me, immortal Jove, and grant it too !

Berk. Your grace must hence with me to Berkeley
    straight.

K. Edw. Whither you will ; all places are alike,

And every earth is fit for burial.

Leices. Favour him, my lord, as much as lieth in you.

Berk. Even so betide my soul as I use him.

K. Edw. Mine enemy hath pitied my estate,

And that's the cause that I am now removed.

Berk. And thinks your grace that Berkeley will be
    cruel ?

K. Edw. I know not : but of this am I assured,

That death ends all, and I can die but once.

Leicester, farewell !

Leices. Not yet, my lord : I'll bear you on your way.

[*Exeunt.*

SCENE II.

Enter QUEEN ISABELLA *and* YOUNG MORTIMER.

Y. Mor. Fair Isabel, now have we our desire ;

The proud corrupters of the light-brained king

Have done their homage to the lofty gallows,

And he himself lies in captivity.

Be ruled by me, and we will rule the realm.

[1] The scene is an apartment in the royal palace.

Mar.   D D

In any case take heed of childish fear,
For now we hold an old wolf by the ears,
That, if he slip, will seize upon us both,
And gripe the sorer, being griped himself.
Think therefore, madam, that imports us much
To erect your son with all the speed we may,
And that I be protector over him ;
For our behoof will bear the greater sway
Whenas a king's name shall be under writ.

Q. Isab. Sweet Mortimer, the life of Isabel,
Be thou persuaded that I love thee well,
And therefore, so the prince my son be safe,
Whom I esteem as dear as these mine eyes,
Conclude against his father what thou wilt,
And I myself will willingly subscribe.

Y. Mor. First would I hear news he were deposed,
And then let me alone to handle him.

Enter Messenger.

Letters ! from whence ?
  Mess. From Killingworth, my lord.
  Q. Isab. How fares my lord the king ?
  Mess. In health, madam, but full of pensiveness.
  Q. Isab. Alas, poor soul, would I could ease his grief !

Enter the Bishop *of* Winchester *with the crown.*

Thanks, gentle Winchester. [*To the* Messenger.] Sirrah,
    be gone.   [*Exit* Messenger.
  B. of Win. The king hath willingly resigned his crown.
  Q. Isab. O happy news ! send for the prince, my son.
  B. of Win. Further, or this letter was sealed, Lord
    Berkeley came,
So that he now is gone from Killingworth ;
And we have heard that Edmund laid a plot

To set his brother free ; no more but so.
The lord of Berkeley is as pitiful
As Leicester that had charge of him before.

   Q. Isab. Then let some other be his guardian.

   Y. Mor. Let me alone, here is the privy seal.

               [*Exit the* BISHOP *of* WINCHESTER.

Who's there ?—Call hither Gurney and Matrevis.

               [*To* Attendants *within.*

To dash the heavy-headed Edmund's drift,
Berkeley shall be discharged, the king removed,
And none but we shall know where he lieth.

   Q. Isab. But, Mortimer, as long as he survives,
What safety rests for us, or for my son ?

   Y. Mor. Speak, shall he presently be despatched and
      die ?

   Q. Isab. I would he were, so 'twere not by my means.

       Enter MATREVIS [1] *and* GURNEY.

   Y. Mor. Enough.
Matrevis, write a letter presently
Unto the lord of Berkeley from ourself
That he resign the king to thee and Gurney ;
And when 'tis done, we will subscribe our name.

   Mat. It shall be done, my lord.   [*Writes.*

   Y. Mor. Gurney.

   Gur. My lord.

   Y. Mor. As thou intend'st to rise by Mortimer,
Who now makes Fortune's wheel turn as he please,
Seek all the means thou canst to make him droop,
And neither give him kind word nor good look.

   Gur. I warrant you, my lord.

   Y. Mor. And this above the rest : because we hear
That Edmund casts [2] to work his liberty,

     [1] *i.e.* Sir John Maltravers.   [2] Plots.

Remove him still from place to place by night,
Till at the last he come to Killingworth,
And then from thence to Berkeley back again ;
And by the way, to make him fret the more.
Speak curstly to him : and in any case
Let no man comfort him if he chance to weep,
But amplify his grief with bitter words.

Mat. Fear not, my lord, we'll do as you command.

Y. Mor. So now away ; post thitherwards amain.

Q. Isab. Whither goes this letter ? to my lord the king ?
Commend me humbly to his majesty,
And tell him that I labour all in vain
To ease his grief, and work his liberty :
And bear him this as witness of my love.　[*Gives a ring.*

Mat. I will, madam.　　　　　　　[*Exit with* GURNEY.

Y. Mor. Finely dissembled.　Do so still, sweet queen.
Here comes the young prince with the Earl of Kent.

Q. Isab. Something he whispers in his childish ears.

Y. Mor. If he have such access unto the prince,
Our plots and stratagems will soon be dashed.

Q. Isab. Use Edmund friendly as if all were well.

Enter PRINCE EDWARD, *and* KENT *talking with him.*

Y. Mor. How fares my honourable lord of Kent ?

Kent. In health, sweet Mortimer : how fares your
　　grace ?

Q. Isab. Well, if my lord your brother were enlarged.

Kent. I hear of late he hath deposed himself.

Q. Isab. The more my grief.

Y. Mor. And mine.

Kent. Ah, they do dissemble !　　　　　　　[*Aside.*

Q. Isab. Sweet son, come hither, I must talk with thee.

Y. Mor. You being his uncle, and the next of blood,
Do look to be protector o'er the prince.

Kent. Not I, my lord ; who should protect the son,
But she that gave him life ?   I mean the queen.

P. Edw. Mother, persuade me not to wear the crown :
Let him be king—I am too young to reign.

Q. Isab. But be content, seeing 'tis his highness'
pleasure.

P. Edw. Let me but see him first, and then I will.

Kent. Ay, do, sweet nephew.

Q. Isab. Brother, you know it is impossible.

P. Edw. Why, is he dead ?

Q. Isab. No, God forbid.

Kent. I would those words proceeded from your heart.

Y. Mor. Inconstant Edmund, dost thou favour him,
That wast a cause of his imprisonment ?

Kent. The more cause have I now to make amends.

Y. Mor. [*Aside to* Q. ISAB.] I tell thee, 'tis not meet
that one so false
Should come about the person of a prince.
My lord, he hath betrayed the king his brother,
And therefore trust him not.

P. Edw. But he repents, and sorrows for it now.

Q. Isab. Come, son, and go with this gentle lord and
me.

P. Edw. With you I will, but not with Mortimer.

Y. Mor. Why, youngling, 'sdain'st thou so of Mortimer ?
Then I will carry thee by force away.

P. Edw. Help, uncle Kent ! Mortimer will wrong me.

Q. Isab. Brother Edmund, strive not : we are his
friends ;
Isabel is nearer than the Earl of Kent.

Kent. Sister, Edward is my charge, redeem him.

Q. Isab. Edward is my son, and I will keep him.

Kent. Mortimer shall know that he hath wrongèd me !—

Hence will I haste to Killingworth Castle,
And rescue aged Edward from his foes,
To be revenged on Mortimer and thee.

> [*Aside. Exeunt on one side* QUEEN ISABELLA,
> PRINCE EDWARD, *and* YOUNG MORTIMER ;
> *on the other* KENT.

SCENE III.

Enter MATREVIS *and* GURNEY *and* Soldiers, *with* KING
EDWARD.[1]

Mat. My lord, be not pensive, we are your friends ;
Men are ordained to live in misery,
Therefore come,—dalliance dangereth our lives.

K. Edw. Friends, whither must unhappy Edward go ?
Will hateful Mortimer appoint no rest ?
Must I be vexèd like the nightly bird,
Whose sight is loathsome to all wingèd fowls ?
When will the fury of his mind assuage ?
When will his heart be satisfied with blood ?
If mine will serve, unbowel straight this breast,
And give my heart to Isabel and him ;
It is the chiefest mark they level at.

Gur. Not so, my liege, the queen hath given this charge
To keep your grace in safety ;
Your passions make your dolours to increase.

K. Edw. This usage makes my misery to increase.
But can my air of life continue long
When all my senses are annoyed with stench ?
Within a dungeon England's king is kept,
Where I am starved for want of sustenance.

---

[1] The scene is within Kenilworth castle.

My daily diet is heart-breaking sobs,
That almost rent the closet of my heart ;
Thus lives old [1] Edward not relieved by any,
And so must die, though pitièd by many.
O, water, gentle friends, to cool my thirst,
And clear my body from foul excrements !

    Mat. Here's channel [2] water, as your charge is given ;
Sit down, for we'll be barbers to your grace.

    K. Edw. Traitors, away ! what, will you murder me,
Or choke your sovereign with puddle water ?

    Gur. No ; but wash your face, and shave away your
        beard,
Lest you be known and so be rescuèd.

    Mat. Why strive you thus ? your labour is in vain !

    K. Edw. The wren may strive against the lion's strength,
But all in vain : so vainly do I strive
To seek for mercy at a tyrant's hand.

          [*They wash him with puddle water, and shave
             off his beard.*

Immortal powers ! that knows the painful cares
That wait upon my poor distressèd soul,
O level all your looks upon these daring men,
That wrongs their liege and sovereign, England's king !
O Gaveston, 'tis for thee that I am wronged,
For me, both thou and both the Spencers died !
And for your sakes a thousand wrongs I'll take.
The Spencers' ghosts, wherever they remain,
Wish well to mine ; then tush, for them I'll die.

    Mat. 'Twixt theirs and yours shall be no enmity.
Come, come away ; now put the torches out,
We'll enter in by darkness to Killingworth.

---

[1] Stow often speaks of Edward II. as the " old king," although
he was only forty-three at the time of his murder.
  [2] Kennel, gutter.

Gur. How now, who comes there?

Mat. Guard the king sure : it is the Earl of Kent.

K. Edw. O gentle brother, help to rescue me !

Mat. Keep them asunder ; thrust in the king.

Kent. Soldiers, let me but talk to him one word.

Gur. Lay hands upon the earl for his assault.

Kent. Lay down your weapons, traitors ! yield the king !

Mat. Edmund, yield thou thyself, or thou shalt die.

Kent. Base villains, wherefore do you gripe me thus ?

Gur. Bind him and so convey him to the court.

Kent. Where is the court but here ? here is the king ;
And I will visit him ; why stay you me ?

Mat. The court is where Lord Mortimer remains ;
Thither shall your honour go ; and so farewell.

> [*Exeunt* MATREVIS *and* GURNEY, *with* KING
> EDWARD.

Kent. O miserable is that commonweal,
Where lords keep courts, and kings are locked in prison !

Sol. Wherefore stay we ? on, sirs, to the court !

Kent. Ay, lead me whither you will, even to my death,
Seeing that my brother cannot be released.   [*Exeunt.*

SCENE IV.

Enter Young MORTIMER.[1]

Y. Mor. The king must die, or Mortimer goes down ;
The commons now begin to pity him :
Yet he that is the cause of Edward's death,
Is sure to pay for it when his son's of age ;
And therefore will I do it cunningly.

---

[1] The scene is an apartment in the royal palace.

This letter, written by a friend of ours,
Contains his death, yet bids them save his life. [*Reads.*
" *Edwardum occidere nolite timere, bonum est*
Fear not to kill the king, 'tis good he die."
But read it thus, and that's another sense :
" *Edwardum occidere nolite, timere bonum est*
Kill not the king, 'tis good to fear the worst."
Unpointed as it is, thus shall it go,
That, being dead, if it chance to be found,
Matrevis and the rest may bear the blame,
And we be quit that caused it to be done.
Within this room is locked the messenger
That shall convey it, and perform the rest :
And by a secret token that he bears,
Shall he be murdered when the deed is done.—
Lightborn, come forth !

Enter LIGHTBORN.

Art thou so resolute as thou wast ?
    Light. What else, my lord ? and far more resolute.
    Y. Mor. And hast thou cast [1] how to accomplish it ?
    Light. Ay, ay, and none shall know which way he
        died.
    Y. Mor. But at his looks, Lightborn, thou wilt relent.
    Light. Relent ! ha, ha ! I use much to relent.
    Y. Mor. Well, do it bravely, and be secret.
    Light. You shall not need to give instructions ;
'Tis not the first time I have killed a man.
I learned in Naples how to poison flowers ;
To strangle with a lawn thrust down the throat ;
To pierce the windpipe with a needle's point ;
Or whilst one is asleep, to take a quill
And blow a little powder in his ears :

-----

[1] Contrived.

Or open his mouth and pour quicksilver down.
And yet I have a braver way than these.

   Y. Mor. What's that?

   Light. Nay, you shall pardon me ; none shall know
     my tricks.

   Y. Mor. I care not how it is, so it be not spied.
Deliver this to Gurney and Matrevis.   [*Gives letter.*
At every ten mile end thou hast a horse.
Take this ; [*Gives money*] away ! and never see me more.

   Light. No !

   Y. Mor. No ;
Unless thou bring me news of Edward's death.

   Light. That will I quickly do.   Farewell, my lord.
                             [*Exit.*

   Y. Mor. The prince I rule, the queen do I command,
And with a lowly congé to the ground,
The proudest lords salute me as I pass ;
I seal, I cancel, I do what I will.
Feared am I more than loved ;—let me be feared,
And when I frown, make all the court look pale.
I view the prince with Aristarchus' eyes,
Whose looks were as a breeching to a boy.
They thrust upon me the protectorship,
And sue to me for that that I desire.
While at the council-table, grave enough,
And not unlike a bashful puritan,
First I complain of imbecility,
Saying it is *onus quam gravissimum :*
Till being interrupted by my friends,
Suscepi that *provinciam* as they term it ;
And to conclude, I am Protector now.
Now is all sure : the queen and Mortimer
Shall rule the realm, the king ; and none rules us.
Mine enemies will I plague, my friends advance ;

And what I list command who dare control?
Major sum quam cui possit fortuna nocere.[1]
And that this be the coronation-day,
It pleaseth me, and Isabel the queen. [*Trumpets within.*
The trumpets sound. I must go take my place.

Enter KING EDWARD THE THIRD, QUEEN ISABELLA,
　　the ARCHBISHOP *of* CANTERBURY, Champion *and*
　　Nobles.[2]

　　A. of Cant. Long live King Edward, by the grace of
　　　　God,
King of England and Lord of Ireland !
　　Cham. If any Christian, Heathen, Turk, or Jew,
Dare but affirm that Edward's not true king,
And will avouch his saying with the sword,
I am the champion that will combat him.
　　Y. Mor. None comes, sound trumpets.
　　　　　　　　　　　　　　　　[*Trumpets sound.*
　　K. Edw. Third. Champion, here's to thee.
　　　　　　　　　　　　　　　　[*Gives a purse.*
　　Q. Isab. Lord Mortimer, now take him to your charge.

　　　　Enter Soldiers, *with* KENT *prisoner.*

　　Y. Mor. What traitor have we there with blades and
　　　　bills?
　　Sol. Edmund, the Earl of Kent.
　　K. Edw. Third. What hath he done?
　　Sol. 'A would have taken the king away perforce,
As we were bringing him to Killingworth.
　　Y. Mor. Did you attempt his rescue, Edmund? speak.
　　Kent. Mortimer, I did ; he is our king,
And thou compell'st this prince to wear the crown.
　　Y. Mor. Strike off his head ! he shall have martial law.

───────────────

[1] Ovid, *Metam.* vi. 195.　　[2] The scene is now at Westminster.

Kent. Strike off my head ! base traitor, I defy thee !

K. Edw. Third. My lord, he is my uncle, and shall live.

Y. Mor. My lord, he is your enemy, and shall die.

Kent. Stay, villains !

K. Edw. Third. Sweet mother, if I cannot pardon him,
Entreat my Lord Protector for his life.

Q. Isab. Son, be content ; I dare not speak a word.

K. Edw. Third. Nor I, and yet methinks I should
    command :
But, seeing I cannot. I'll entreat for him—
My lord, if you will let my uncle live.
I will requite it when I come to age.

Y. Mor. 'Tis for your highness' good, and for the
    realm's.—
How often shall I bid you bear him hence?

Kent. Art thou king ? must I die at thy command ?

Y. Mor. At our command.—Once more away with
    him.

Kent. Let me but stay and speak ; I will not go.
Either my brother or his son is king,
And none of both them thirst for Edmund's blood :
And therefore, soldiers. whither will you hale me ?

             [*Soldiers hale* KENT *away, to be beheaded.*

K. Edw. Third. What safety may I look for at his hands,
If that my uncle shall be murdered thus ?

Q. Isab. Fear not, sweet boy, I'll guard thee from thy
    foes ;
Had Edmund lived, he would have sought thy death.
Come, son, we'll ride a-hunting in the park.

K. Edw. Third. And shall my uncle Edmund ride
    with us ?

Q. Isab. He is a traitor ; think not on him ; come.
                                   [*Exeunt.*

SCENE V.[1]

Enter MATREVIS *and* GURNEY.[2]

Mat. Gurney, I wonder the king dies not.
Being in a vault up to the knees in water,
To which the channels of the castle run,
From whence a damp continually ariseth,
That were enough to poison any man,
Much more a king brought up so tenderly.

Gur. And so do I, Matrevis: yesternight
I opened but the door to throw him meat,
And I was almost stifled with the savour.

Mat. He hath a body able to endure
More than we can inflict: and therefore now
Let us assail his mind another while.

Gur. Send for him out thence, and I will anger him.

Mat. But stay, who's this?

Enter LIGHTBORN.

Light. My Lord Protector greets you. [*Gives letter.*

Gur. What's here? I know not how to construe it.

Mat. Gurney, it was left unpointed for the nonce:
"*Edwardum occidere nolite timere.*"
That's his meaning.

Light. Know ye this token? I must have the king.
[*Gives token.*

Mat. Ay, stay awhile, thou shalt have answer straight.
This villain's sent to make away the king. [*Aside.*

Gur. I thought as much. [*Aside.*

Mat. And when the murder's done,

---

[1] "The death-scene of Marlowe's King," said Charles Lamb,
"moves pity and terror beyond any scene, ancient or modern, with
which I am acquainted."

[2] The scene is within Berkeley castle.

See how he must be handled for his labour.
Pereat iste! Let him have the king.   [*Aside.*
What else? here is the key, this is the lock,[1]
Do as you are commanded by my lord.

  Light. I know what I must do. Get you away.
Yet be not far off, I shall need your help ;
See that in the next room I have a fire,
And get me a spit, and let it be red-hot.

  Mat. Very well.

  Gur. Need you anything besides?

  Light. What else? A table and a feather-bed.

  Gur. That's all?

  Light. Ay, ay; so, when I call you, bring it in.

  Mat. Fear not thou that.

  Gur. Here's a light, to go into the dungeon.

          [*Gives a light, and then exit with* MATREVIS.[2]

  Light. So now
Must I about this gear :[3] ne'er was there any
So finely handled as this king shall be.
Foh, here's a place indeed, with all my heart !

    K. Edw. Who's there? what light is that? wherefore
        com'st thou?

  Light. To comfort you, and bring you joyful news.

    K. Edw. Small comfort finds poor Edward in thy
        looks.
Villain, I know thou com'st to murder me.

  Light. To murder you, my most gracious lord !
Far is it from my heart to do you harm.
The queen sent me to see how you were used,
For she relents at this your misery :

---

[1] "Lake" in the old editions, Mr. Bullen suggested "lock."
[2] The scene now discloses the interior of the dungeon in which
King Edward is confined.   [3] Business.

And what eyes can refrain from shedding tears,
To see a king in this most piteous state?

K. Edw. Weep'st thou already? list awhile to me.
And then thy heart, were it as Gurney's is,
Or as Matrevis', hewn from the Caucasus,
Yet will it melt, ere I have done my tale.
This dungeon where they keep me is the sink
Wherein the filth of all the castle falls.

Light. O villains!

K. Edw. And there in mire and puddle have I stood
This ten days' space; and, lest that I should sleep,
One plays continually upon a drum.
They give me bread and water, being a king:
So that, for want of sleep and sustenance,
My mind's distempered, and my body's numbed,
And whether I have limbs or no I know not.
O, would my blood dropped out from every vein,
As doth this water from my tattered robes.
Tell Isabel, the queen, I looked not thus,
When for her sake I ran at tilt in France,
And there unhorsed the Duke of Cleremont.

Light. O speak no more, my lord! this breaks my
        heart.
Lie on this bed,[1] and rest yourself awhile.

K. Edw. These looks of thine can harbour nought but
        death:
I see my tragedy written in thy brows.
Yet stay; awhile forbear thy bloody hand,
And let me see the stroke before it comes,
That even then when I shall lose my life,
My mind may be more steadfast on my God.

Light. What means your highness to mistrust me thus?

---

[1] *i.e.* The feather-bed provided by Gurney and Matrevis.

K. Edw. What mean'st thou to dissemble with me thus?

Light. These hands were never stained with innocent
   blood,

Nor shall they now be tainted with a king's.

K. Edw. Forgive my thought [1] for having such a
   thought.

One jewel have I left; receive thou this.   [*Giving jewel.*

Still fear I, and I know not what's the cause,

But every joint shakes as I give it thee.

O, if thou harbourest murder in thy heart,

Let this gift change thy mind, and save thy soul

Know that I am a king: O, at that name

I feel a hell of grief! where is my crown?

Gone, gone! and do I still remain alive?

Light. You're overwatched, my lord; lie down and
   rest.

K. Edw. But that grief keeps me waking, I should
   sleep;

For not these ten days have these eye-lids closed.

Now as I speak they fall, and yet with fear

Open again.   O wherefore sitt'st thou here?

Light. If you mistrust me, I'll begone, my lord.

K. Edw. No, no, for if thou mean'st to murder me,

Thou wilt return again, and therefore stay.   [*Sleeps.*

Light. He sleeps.

K. Edw. [*waking*].   O let me not die yet!   O stay a
   while!

Light. How now, my lord?

K. Edw. Something still buzzeth in mine ears,

And tells me if I sleep I never wake:

This fear is that which makes me tremble thus.

And therefore tell me, wherefore art thou come?

Light. To rid thee of thy life.—Matrevis, come!

---

[1] Mr. Fleay proposes to read "fault."

Enter MATREVIS *and* GURNEY.

K. Edw. I am too weak and feeble to resist :—
Assist me, sweet God, and receive my soul !

Light. Run for the table.

K. Edw. O spare me, or despatch me in a trice.

[MATREVIS *brings in a table.*

Light. So, lay the table down, and stamp on it,
But not too hard, lest that you bruise his body.

[KING EDWARD *is murdered.*

Mat. I fear me that this cry will raise the town,
And therefore, let us take horse and away.

Light. Tell me, sirs, was it not bravely done ?

Gur. Excellent well : take this for thy reward.

[GURNEY *stabs* LIGHTBORN. *who dies.*

Come, let us cast the body in the moat,
And bear the king's to Mortimer our lord :
Away !   [*Exeunt with the bodies.*

SCENE VI.

Enter YOUNG MORTIMER *and* MATREVIS.[1]

Y. Mor. Is't done, Matrevis, and the murderer dead ?

Mat. Ay, my good lord ; I would it were undone !

Y. Mor. Matrevis, if thou now growest penitent
I'll be thy ghostly father ; therefore choose,
Whether thou wilt be secret in this,
Or else die by the hand of Mortimer.

Mat. Gurney, my lord, is fled, and will, I fear
Betray us both, therefore let me fly.

Y. Mor. Fly to the savages !

Mat. I humbly thank your honour.   [*Exit.*

[1] The scene is an apartment in the royal palace.

Mar.   E E

Y. Mor. As for myself, I stand as Jove's huge tree,
And others are but shrubs compared to me.
All tremble at my name, and I fear none ;
Let's see who dare impeach me for his death !

Enter QUEEN ISABELLA.

Q. Isab. Ah, Mortimer, the king my son hath news
His father's dead, and we have murdered him !

Y. Mor. What if he have ? the king is yet a child.

Q. Isab. Ay, but he tears his hair, and wrings his hands,
And vows to be revenged upon us both.
Into the council-chamber he is gone,
To crave the aid and succour of his peers.
Ay me ! see where he comes, and they with him ;
Now, Mortimer, begins our tragedy.

Enter KING EDWARD THE THIRD, Lords, *and* Attendants.

1st Lord. Fear not, my lord, know that you are a king.

K. Edw. Third. Villain !—

Y. Mor. Ho, now, my lord !

K. Edw. Third. Think not that I am frighted with thy
      words !
My father's murdered through thy treachery ;
And thou shalt die, and on his mournful hearse
Thy hateful and accursèd head shall lie,
To witness to the world, that by thy means
His kingly body was too soon interred.

Q. Isab. Weep not, sweet son !

K. Edw. Third. Forbid me not to weep ; he was my
      father :
And, had you loved him half so well as I,
You could not bear his death thus patiently.
But you, I fear, conspired with Mortimer.

1st Lord. Why speak you not unto my lord the king ?

Y. Mor. Because I think it scorn to be accused.
Who is the man dares say I murdered him?

K. Edw. Third. Traitor! in me my loving father speaks,
And plainly saith, 'twas thou that murder'dst him.

Y. Mor. But has your grace no other proof than this?

K. Edw. Third. Yes, if this be the hand of Mortimer.
                                         [*Shewing letter.*

Y. Mor. False Gurney hath betrayed me and himself.
                                         [*Aside.*

Q. Isab. I feared as much; murder cannot be hid.
                                         [*Aside.*

Y. Mor. It is my hand; what gather you by this?

K. Edw. Third. That thither thou didst send a murderer.

Y. Mor. What murderer? Bring forth the man I
     sent.

K. Edw. Third. Ah, Mortimer, thou knowest that he is
     slain;
And so shalt thou be too—Why stays he here
Bring him unto a hurdle, drag him forth;
Hang him, I say, and set his quarters up;
But bring his head back presently to me.

Q. Isab. For my sake, sweet son, pity Mortimer

Y. Mor. Madam, entreat not. I will rather die,
Than sue for life unto a paltry boy.

K. Edw. Third. Hence with the traitor! with the mur-
     derer!

Y. Mor. Base Fortune, now I see, that in thy wheel
There is a point, to which when men aspire,
They tumble headlong down: that point I touched,
And, seeing there was no place to mount up higher,
Why should I grieve at my declining fall?—
Farewell, fair queen; weep not for Mortimer,
That scorns the world, and, as a traveller,
Goes to discover countries yet unknown.

K. Edw. Third. What! suffer you the traitor to delay?

> [*Young* MORTIMER *is taken away by* 1st Lord *and* Attendants.

Q. Isab. As thou receivedst thy life from me,
Spill not the blood of gentle Mortimer!

K. Edw. Third. This argues that you spilt my father's
blood,
Else would you not entreat for Mortimer.

Q. Isab. I spill his blood? no.

K. Edw. Third. Ay, madam, you; for so the rumour
runs.

Q. Isab. That rumour is untrue; for loving thee,
Is this report raised on poor Isabel.

K. Edw. Third. I do not think her so unnatural.

2nd Lord. My lord, I fear me it will prove too true.

K. Edw. Third. Mother, you are suspected for his death
And therefore we commit you to the Tower
Till farther trial may be made thereof:
If you be guilty, though I be your son,
Think not to find me slack or pitiful.

Q. Isab. Nay, to my death, for too long have I lived,
Whenas my son thinks to abridge my days.

K. Edw. Third. Away with her, her words enforce these
tears,
And I shall pity her if she speak again.

Q. Isab. Shall I not mourn for my beloved lord,
And with the rest accompany him to his grave?

2nd Lord. Thus, madam, 'tis the king's will you shall
hence.

Q. Isab. He hath forgotten me; stay, I am his mother.

2nd Lord. That boots not; therefore, gentle madam,
go.

Q. Isab. Then come, sweet death, and rid me of this
grief.   [*Exit.*

Reenter 1st Lord, *with the head of* Young MORTIMER.

1st Lord. My lord, here is the head of Mortimer.

K. Edw. Third. Go fetch my father's hearse, where it
shall lie ;

And bring my funeral robes. [*Exeunt* Attendants.

Accursèd head,

Could I have ruled thee then, as I do now,

Thou had'st not hatched this monstrous treachery !—

Here comes the hearse : help me to mourn, my lords.

Reenter Attendants *with the hearse and funeral robes.*

Sweet father, here unto thy murdered ghost

I offer up this wicked traitor's head :

And let these tears, distilling from mine eyes,

Be witness of my grief and innocency. [*Exeunt.*

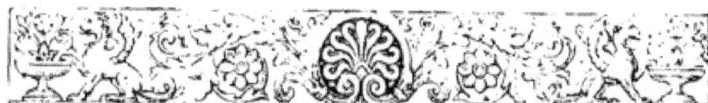

APPENDIX.

— · · ⟩ ⁙ ⟨ · · —

EDWARD ALLEYN.

EDWARD ALLEYN (often spelt Allen), famous both as an actor and as the founder of Dulwich College, was born in 1566 in London, according to Fuller, near Devonshire House. He was the younger son of a porter to the Queen, who acquired some property. His name first appears in a list of the Earl of Worcester's players in 1586. This was about the time of the appearance of *Tamburlaine*, and Alleyn came into popularity on the same wave as Marlowe. In *Tamburlaine*, *The Jew of Malta*, etc., as Thomas Heywood the dramatist writes in 1633, in a prologue to the latter play, Alleyn

" was
The attribute of peerless, being a man
Whom we may rank with (doing no one wrong)
Proteus for shapes, and Roscius for a tongue,
So could he speak, so vary."

Alleyn also took the part of *Faustus*, for in the inventory of his theatrical apparel we find "Faustus Jerkin, his cloke," and Samuel Rowlands writes,

" The gull gets on a surplice,
With a cross upon his breast,
Like Allen playing Faustus,
In that manner was he drest."

Years previously Alleyn had been extolled by Nash in his *Pierce Pennilesse*, wherein we read:—" Not Roscius nor

Esope, those tragedians admired before Christ was born, could ever perform more in action than famous Ned Allen." This was written in 1592, when Alleyn was only twenty-six years of age. In the same year he married Joan Woodward, daughter by a former marriage of the then wife of Philip Henslowe.

During the plague of 1593, the year of Marlowe's death, we find Alleyn on a provincial tour through Bristol, Shrewsbury, Chester, and York. In the year following he was back in London, and acquired an interest in the baiting-house at Paris Garden in Southwark, to which frequent allusion is made by contemporary dramatists. Four years afterwards he tried with Henslowe to obtain the post of Master of the royal game of bears, bulls, and mastiffs. This office was not secured, however, till 1604, the year of Alleyn's last recorded appearance on the stage, and appears to have been held by Alleyn till his death. On special occasions he took part in the sports himself, and Stow describes how he baited a lion before the King. Alleyn and Henslowe had built the Fortune Theatre in Golden Lane, Cripplegate, during the year 1600, but the Paris Garden was doubtless the chief source of Alleyn's wealth.

In 1605 the manor of Dulwich was purchased by Alleyn at a total cost of £10,000 ; he did not however obtain the whole estate till 1614, although before this date he had removed to Dulwich, and in 1613 had begun the construction of the College. In 1619 the opening ceremonies took place, when Alleyn entertained the company, including Lord Chancellor Bacon, at a banquet. Greatly to the advantage of the new foundation, Alleyn managed the affairs of the College personally. At this time he appears as the patron of Dekker, Taylor the water-poet, and other writers ; although he had now become a person of consequence, the friend of bishops and nobles, he still kept up his connection with his old profession and his old friends. In 1623 he married (for the second time) a daughter of Dr. Donne, the Dean of St. Paul's, and died in 1626, leaving so far as is known no children.

Alleyn was evidently a man of great shrewdness and business capacity, and seems to have possessed at the same time a very fine and lovable nature. There can be no question concerning his high rank as an actor. Ben Jonson, in an epigram addressed to "Edward Allen," refers to

> " Skilful Roscius and grave Æsope,
> Who both these graces in thyself hast more
> Out-stript, than they did all that went before :
> And present worth in all dost so contract,
> As others speak, but only thou dost act."

Fuller records the general opinion concerning Alleyn in these words :— " He was the Roscius of our age, so acting to the life that he made any part (especially a majestic one) to become him." He appears to have had no relations with Shakespeare, and we do not find him acting in any of Shakespeare's plays. The full-length portrait at Dulwich, reproduced as a frontispiece to this volume, indicates the majestic presence, to which Fuller alludes, of the impersonator of *Tamburlaine*.

BALLAD OF FAUSTUS.

THE JUDGMENT OF GOD SHOWED UPON ONE JOHN FAUSTUS, DOCTOR IN DIVINITY.

FROM THE ROXBURGHE COLLECTION, VOL. II. 235. *Brit. Mus.*

Tune of Fortune my Foe.

All Christian men, give ear a while to me,
How I am plung'd in pain, but cannot die :
I liv'd a life the like did none before,
Forsaking Christ, and I am damn'd therefore.

At Wittenburge, a town in Germany,
There was I born and bred of good degree ;

Of honest stock, which afterwards I sham'd ;
Accurst therefore, for Faustus was I nam'd.

In learning, loe, my uncle brought up me,
And made me Doctor in Divinity ;
And, when he dy'd, he left me all his wealth,
Whose cursed gold did hinder my soul's health.

Then did I shun the holy Bible-book,
Nor on Gods word would ever after look ;
But studied accursed conjuration,
Which was the cause of my utter damnation.

The devil in fryars weeds appear'd to me,
And streight to my request he did agree,
That I might have all things at my desire :
I gave him soul and body for his hire.

Twice did I make my tender flesh to bleed,
Twice with my blood I wrote the devils deed,
Twice wretchedly I soul and body sold,
To live in peace and do what things I would.

For four and twenty years this bond was made,
And at the length my soul was truly paid !
Time ran away, and yet I never thought
How dear my soul our Saviour Christ had bought.

Would I at first been made a beast by kind !
Then had not I so vainly set my mind :
Or would, when reason first began to bloom,
Some darksome den had been my deadly tomb !

Woe to the day of my nativity !
Woe to the time that once did foster me !
And woe unto the hand that seal'd the bill !
Woe to myself, the cause of all my ill !

The time I passed away, with much delight,
'Mongst princes, peers, and many a worthy knight :
I wrought such wonders by my magick skill,
That all the world may talk of Faustus still.

The devil he carried me up into the sky,
Where I did see how all the world did lie ;
I went about the world in eight daies space,
And then return'd unto my native place.

What pleasure I did wish to please my mind
He did perform, as bond and seal did bind :
The secrets of the stars and planets told,
Of earth and sea, with wonders manifold.

When four and twenty years was almost run,
I thought of all things that was past and done ;
How that the devil would soon claim his right,
And carry me to everlasting night.

Then all too late I curst my wicked deed,
The dread whereof doth make my heart to bleed
All daies and hours I mourned wondrous sore,
Repenting me of all things done before.

I then did wish both sun and moon to stay,
All times and seasons never to decay ;
Then had my time nere come to dated end,
Nor soul and body down to hell descend.

At last, when I had but one hour to come,
I turn'd my glass, for my last hour to run,
And call'd in learned men to comfort me :
But faith was gone, and none could comfort me.

By twelve a clock my glass was almost out :
My grieved conscience then began to doubt ;
I wisht the students stay in chamber by ;
But, as they staid, they heard a dreadful cry.

Then presently they came into the hall,
Whereas my brains was cast against the wall ;
Both arms and legs in pieces torn they see,
My bowels gone : this was an end of me.

You conjurers and damned witches all,
Example take by my unhappy fall :

Give not your soul's and bodies unto hell,
See that the smallest hair you do not sell.

But hope that Christ his kingdom you may gain,
Where you shall never fear such mortal pain ;
Forsake the devil and all his crafty ways,
Embrace true faith that never more decays.

A NOTE

CONTAYNINGE THE OPINION OF ONE CHRISTOFER MAR-
LYE, CONCERNYNGE HIS DAMNABLE OPINIONS AND
JUDGMENT OF RELYGION AND SCORNE OF GODS
WORDE.[1]

FROM MS. HARL. 6853, FOL. 320.

THAT the Indians and many Authors of Antiquitei have assuredly written of aboue 16 thowsande yeers agone, wher Adam is proved to have leyved within 6 thowsande yeers.

He affirmeth[2] That Moyses was but a Juggler, and that one Heriots can do more then hee.

That Moyses made the Jewes to travell fortie yeers in the wildernes (which iorny might have ben don in lesse then one yeer) er they came to the promised lande, to the intente that those who were privei to most of his subtileteis might perish, and so an everlastinge supersticion remayne in the hartes of the people.

That the firste beginnynge of Religion was only to keep men in awe.

That it was an easye matter for Moyses, beinge brought

---

[1] The original title has been partly scored through with a pen, and altered as follows :—*A Note delivered on Whitson eve last of the most horreble blasphemes utteryd by Christofer Marly who within iii dayes after came to a soden and fearfull end of his life.*

[2] The words printed in italics have been scored through in the MS.

up in all the artes of the Egiptians, to abvse the Jewes, being a rvde and grosse people.

That Christ was a Bastard, and his mother dishonest.

That he was the sonne of a carpenter, and that, yf the Jewes amonge whome he was borne did crvcifye him, thei best knew him and whence he came.

That Christ deserved better to dye than Barrabas, and that the Jewes made a good choyce, though Barrabas were both a theife and a murtherer.

That yf ther be any God or good Religion, then it is in the Papistes, becavse the service of God is performed with more ceremonyes, as elevacion of the masse, organs, singinge men, *shaven crownes,* &c. That all protestantes ar hipocriticall Asses.

That, yf he wer put to write a new religion, he wolde vndertake both a more excellent and more admirable methode, and that all the new testament is filthely written.

That the Women of Samaria wer whores, and that Christ knew them dishonestlye.

That St. John the Evangelist was bedfellow to Christe, that he leaned alwayes in his bosom, that he vsed him as the synners of Sodome.

That all thei that love not tobacco and boyes are fooles.

That all the Appostelis wer fishermen and base fellowes, neither of witt nor worth, that Pawle only had witt, that he was a timerous fellow in biddinge men to be subiect to magistrates against his conscience.

That he had as good right to coyne as the Queen of Englande, and that he was acquainted with one Poole, a prisoner in newgate, whoe hath great skill in mixture of metalls, and havinge learned such thinges of him, he ment, through help of a connynge stampe-maker, to coyne french crownes, pistolettes, and englishe shillinges.

That, yf Christ had instituted the Sacramentes with more cerymonyall reverence, it would have ben had in more admiracion, that it wolde have ben much better beinge administred in a Tobacco pype.

That the Angell Gabriell was Bawde to the holy Ghoste, because he brought the salutation to Marie.

That one Richard Cholmelei [1] hath confessed that he was perswaded by Marloes reason to become an Athieste.

Theis thinges, with many other, shall by good and honest men be proved to be his opinions and common speeches, and that this Marloe doth not only holde them himself, but almost in every company he commeth, perswadeth men to Athiesme willinge them not to be afrayed of bugbeares and hobgoblins and vtterly scornynge both God and his ministers, as I Richard Bome [sic] will justify bothe by my othe and the testimony of many honest men, and almost all men with whome he hath conversed any tyme will testify the same : and, as I thincke, all men in christianitei ought to endevor that the mouth of so dangerous a member may be stopped.

He sayeth moreover that he hath coated a number of contrarieties out of the scriptures, which he hath geeven to some great men, who in convenient tyme shalbe named. When theis thinges shalbe called in question, the witnesses shalbe produced.

RYCHARD BAME.

[I see no reason to question the substantial truth of these accusations. We may set aside the charge of coining, which, with the words about the sacrament in a tobacco pipe, and the Holy Ghost as a bawd, were clearly mere jests ; and also the bravado about " boys and tobacco," and again, that about the Jews knowing best what Christ deserved. All the other propositions which Marlowe is here stated to affirm have, without exception, been substantially held, more or less widely, by students of science and of the Bible in our own days. No one has developed the humorous possibilities of the Pentateuch to the same extent as Bishop Colenso, although recent critics regard Moses as a more

---

[1] In the margin are the words "he is layd for," meaning that steps have been taken to discover him.

mythical hero than Marlowe could; but the antiquity of Indian literature, the awe-inspiring functions of religion at certain stages of civilization, the religious superiority of Catholicism to Protestantism, the feeble style of the New Testament and the character of the Apostles, the circumstances surrounding the birth of Jesus, the nature of his intimacy with Mary Magdalene, etc., the connection between the relationship of Jesus and John and those relationships which were common among the noblest of the Greeks, Epaminondas or Socrates—all these are matters concerning which many authorities seem now to side with Marlowe. Such acute and audacious utterances—in part traceable, it may be, to the influence of Francis Kett—are of great assistance in enabling us to realise Marlowe's personality.]

THE END.

BRADBURY, AGNEW, & CO., PRINTERS, WHITEFRIARS.